Society and Politics in Snorri Sturluson's *Heimskringla*

Society and Politics in Snorri Sturluson's *Heimskringla*

Sverre Bagge

University of California Press

Berkeley / Los Angeles / Oxford

University of California Press
Berkeley and Los Angeles, California

University of California Press
Oxford, England

Copyright © 1991 by The Regents of the
University of California

Library of Congress Cataloging-in-Publication
Data

Bagge, Sverre, 1942–
    Society and politics in Snorri Sturluson's
Heimskringla / Sverre Bagge.
        p.   cm.
    Includes bibliographical references and index.
    ISBN 0-520-06887-4 (alk. paper)
    1. Snorri Sturluson, 1179?–1241. Ólafs saga
helga. 2. Iceland—Politics and government.
3. Iceland—Social conditions. 4. Politics in
literature. 5. Literature and society—iceland.
I. Title.
PT7278.B34   1991
839′61—dc20   91-2038
                                              CIP

Printed in the United States of America

1 2 3 4 5 6 7 8 9

The paper used in this publication meets the
minimum requirements
of American National Standard for Information
Sciences—Permanence
of Paper for Printed Library Materials, ANSI
Z39.48-1984 ⊚

Contents

Preface

This book is an attempt to use medieval historiography as a source for attitudes to man, politics, and society. Preparing it, I have trespassed on many unfamiliar fields and received help and inspiration from a number of people, in readings and personal conversations. I have been able to discuss parts of the book at a number of seminars at the University of Bergen and then at the Department of Scandinavian Studies in London in 1988 and at a conference on Medieval historiography in Paris, arranged by the European Science Foundation in 1989. In the final stage, Knut Helle, Magnús Stéfansson, Christian Meyer, Bjarne Fidjestøl, and Jón Viðar Sigurðson read the whole manuscript and made valuable comments. I give them all my best thanks. I also want to thank Christian Meyer for drawing the map of Norway and Jón Viðar Sigurðsson for guiding me in the mysteries of word processing during the final stage of the preparation of the manuscript. Finally, I thank the Norwegian Research Council (NAVF) for a grant that enabled me to devote myself fully to research on *Heimskringla* in 1986–87 and to study its background in European historiography during a stay in Cambridge.

Introduction

The Problem

This book deals with *Heimskringla,* the most famous of the Old Norse collections of kings' sagas, written by the Icelander Snorri Sturluson in the first half of the thirteenth century, probably around 1230. My intention is to examine the work's picture of man, society, and politics as well as Snorri's approach to his subject matter against a European background. The purpose of this examination is partly to characterize Snorri as a historian, partly to analyze ideas about society and politics in early thirteenth-century Norway and Iceland, and to some extent even to contribute to our knowledge of Snorri's society as it actually was.

Since the last century, in connection with the national movement after the separation from Denmark in 1814, *Heimskringla* has held a special place in Norwegian culture. It was for a long time one of the most widely read books in Norway and is still regarded as a kind of national symbol. Until recently, the teaching of Norwegian medieval history in the schools was very much based on the stories of the kings in *Heimskringla,* and many Norwegians have a vivid impression of the people and scenes of the period from the drawings by famous artists, which were first prepared for the 1899 translation and which have been included in almost all later translations.

Despite its assured reputation as a classic, there has been relatively little research on *Heimskringla.* Scholarly interest has mainly been concentrated on its textual relationship to earlier sagas or on its trustworthiness as a historical source, in accordance with the tradition of *Quel-*

lenkunde, inherited from the nineteenth century. Then there have been some literary analyses of style and composition (Nordal, 1973 [orig. 1920]: 132 ff.; Lie, 1937). The question of Snorri's general interpretation of history and his picture of Norwegian society and social change was first placed on the agenda by Halvdan Koht in 1913 (Koht, 1921: 76 ff.). Koht regarded Snorri very much like a modern historian with an overall interpretation of the past and explained this interpretation from his experience of thirteenth century society and politics. Koht's approach was followed up among others by Schreiner (1926) and Sandvik (1955). Compared to the discussion caused by Koht's synthesis of Norwegian history in the Middle Ages (chap. 2 below), his interpretation of Snorri seems to have been fairly uncontroversial among historians, though some philologists and historians of literature have voiced their opposition.

Since the 1960s considerable changes have taken place in the study of Old Norse literature. The field has become more international, both in the sense that new milieus have taken part in it and in the sense that there has been increasing interest in analyzing this literature against a European background and studying it with the theories and methods current in other fields. In practice, this had led to widely different approaches: literary analyses according to structuralist or other principles, attempts to reconstruct the social milieu or the mentality of the sagas through theories derived from social anthropology or related subjects, and, not the least, attempts to trace Christian attitudes and European learning in the sagas, in clear opposition to traditional Scandinavian scholarship (cf. Clover, 1985: 239 ff.). However, these approaches have been mainly applied to the Icelandic family sagas and only in a very limited degree to the kings' sagas in general and *Heimskringla* in particular. The attempts that have been made to interpret Snorri both through theories of primitive mentality (Gurevich, 1969, 1971), Christian philosophy and theology (Weber, 1987, and to some extent Lönnroth, e.g., 1969), or a combination of modern literary and social analysis (Lönnroth, 1973), are mainly sketches. The celebration of the seven-hundredth anniversary of Snorri's birth in 1979 resulted in some new publications (Ciklamini, 1978, and the collection of articles in *Snorri: Átta alda minning*) but hardly in new interpretations of *Heimskringla* as a whole.

On the following pages, I shall try to place Snorri in an international context, in accordance, I hope, with modern scholarship. As a historian, however, my main interest lies in *Heimskringla* as a description of society and as evidence of social and political attitudes, not in literary or aesthetic aspects. Generally, though recognizing the importance of an author's intellectual milieu and the influence from others, I am inclined to pay more attention to society. This at least seems a natural approach in Snorri's case, as he was a prominent politician, and *Heimskringla* immediately gives the impression of dealing with secular politics. Thus, I shall follow in the line of Koht, whose approach I find extremely fruitful and stimulating, though his actual results are evidently in need of revision in the light of recent research over the more than seventy years that have passed since he first presented them.

Heimskringla seems to be little known outside the Nordic countries, despite the fact that it has been translated into the main European languages and that, from a modern point of view—as I intend to demonstrate in the following—it compares favorably with most contemporary works of history both as a narrative and an analysis of history. Thus, it is barely mentioned in the more recent surveys of medieval historiography, such as Smalley (1974), Hay (1977), Guenée (1980), and Schmale (1985). An important exception is Gurevich, who frequently uses it to illustrate medieval mentality and who has also dealt with it separately (Gurevich, 1983; cf. 1969 and 1971).

An examination of *Heimskringla* according to the principles stated above thus appears like a promising project, the more so as there has been considerable interest in medieval historiography in recent years. As in Europe, in the Nordic countries, the study of historiography was for a long time almost to be identified with *Quellenkunde.* An important early example of the study of historiography as part of intellectual history, with special emphasis on the basic patterns of thought governing historical narrative, is the work of Bernheim and his school.[1] But the great breakthrough for this approach came after World War II with scholars like Spörl (1965: 278 ff., 298 ff.), Lammers (1961), Koch (1965: 321 ff.) and Beumann (e.g., 1965: 135 ff.; 1969). In the Anglo-Saxon world, important contributions were made at a somewhat later date by Brandt (1966), Southern (1970–1973), Green (1972), Smalley (1974), and others.[2] The French Annales school, with its strong emphasis on *mentalité* in the last two or three decades, has not been particularly concerned with historiography, apart from some important works by Duby, who has used various historiographical works to reconstruct aristocratic ideology (e.g., 1973; 1977: 134 ff., 149 ff.; 1986). The general approach of this school, in emphasizing collective mentality and common patterns of thought and in linking intellectual history to actual social conditions, offers valuable insight. By contrast, the German tradition, often giving excellent analysis of texts, has a tendency to overemphasize philosophical principles and to isolate the intellectual world from society as a whole.

Notwithstanding my concentration on one particular work by an author who was certainly not representative of medieval man in general, the ultimate aim of my examination is to use historiography to explore mentality and the connection between culture and society. Medieval historiography contains extensive descriptions of society and politics which are paralleled in no other category of sources and which it must be possible to use, despite the obvious difficulties involved. More specifically, my problem may be outlined as follows.

One aspect of the "civilizing process," which, according to Norbert Elias (1977) and others, Europe underwent from the Middle Ages to the modern period, was the development of "political man" (homo politicus), a parallel to the *homo oeconomicus* of early capitalism. According to Elias, the warrior of the Middle Ages, who acted spontaneously and according to his impulses and expressed his feelings directly, was substituted by the cold, calculating politician and courtier of the absolutist age, who was used to suppressing his feelings, hiding his opinions, and sacrificing immediate gain for long-term advantage. In a similar way, Max Weber regards "rationalization" as one of the essential features in the evolution of modern society, though in the political sphere he is more concerned with emancipation from religious assumptions than with control of immediate impulses (1964, II: 923 ff., 1034 ff.). To both Elias and Weber these changes have to do with changes in society itself, above all the development of the modern state. Similar general ideas are reflected in much of the *histoire de mentalité* of the French Annales school, though other aspects of human life than political behavior have been more prominent here. By contrast, the social anthropologist F. G. Bailey (1980) describes the game of politics as being essentially the same in societies as different as the New York mafia, modern Britain, and the Pathans of Pakistan, for example. Despite the strong emphasis on politics in traditional historiography, however, very few historians have been concerned with the general problem of political behavior in the Middle Ages.

For an examination of this problem, the narrative sources are essential. They contain an overwhelming amount of material concerning political behavior. But they do not allow us to observe it directly. They tell us how political behavior was described in the Middle Ages, not necessarily how medieval politicians behaved. There are in principle two ways of dealing with this problem. Traditional political historiography has to a large extent been founded on the implicit assumption that medieval politicians acted more or less as modern ones, and that contemporary descriptions of it, in terms of honor, chivalry, personal friendship or hatred, or religious or moral considerations are the results of deliberate distortions or lack of understanding for what was going on. By contrast, historians of *mentalité* have been more ready, perhaps too ready, to assume that what is described in the sources corresponds to how medieval politicians actually behaved.[3]

The step from descriptions of political behavior in the medieval sources to actual behavior at the time is thus a difficult one. Moreover, it is impossible to derive very much information on this subject in general from one single narrative source. Nevertheless, it seems important to me to have this problem in mind when analyzing historiographical works, even if the immediate purpose of the present analysis is the more modest one of analyzing descriptions of political behavior.

My book is thus neither an examination of a particular historical problem based on one or more sources, nor a full literary and ideological analysis of one particular text, but something in between. As for *Heimskringla* as a source, I am not interested in the traditional question of the truth of individual statements, such as the time or place of the battle of Svǫlð, why St. Óláfr was actually deposed, and so forth. When mentioning such questions, I refer to Snorri's opinion of them, unless otherwise stated. My purpose in analyzing Snorri on these and other points is to reconstruct his general ideas of society and political behavior. For this purpose, I shall read *Heimskringla* as if it were a description of an actual society. My next problem will then be to find out what this society actually corresponds to: Snorri's imagination, norms and ideas in his milieu, or society as it actually was in contemporary Norway or Iceland or some kind of combination of these alternatives. This approach raises considerable problems.

First, there is the problem of the individual author. How can one distinguish between Snorri's personal ideas and those that were common in his milieu? Would it not be more rewarding to take Old Norse literature as a whole or a part of it selected not by author but by subject matter or some other principle and use it as a source for political behavior and ideas of society, without caring about literary form, the author's personal view, or the influence of one text upon another? My answer to this is that Snorri seems to be such an original author and *Heimskringla* so much of a unity that a fairly detailed analysis of Snorri's authorship is necessary in order to reach definite conclusions on the kind of political game and society presented there. To this, one might object further that if an individual author is to be chosen, a less intelligent one than Snorri would be preferable, because he would be more representative of common attitudes. This is no doubt true, but such authors tend to take so much for granted that it is very difficult for a modern observer to find out what the scattered events they present are really about. An author of Snorri's intelligence and ability to observe, who in addition was an active politician, offers exceptional opportunities of analyzing political behavior and the rules governing it in a medieval society. Admittedly, Snorri may not be representative of contemporary thought and it may often be difficult to distinguish between his personal attitudes and opinions and those that were common in his milieu. I have no standard method of solving this problem, but I shall try to distinguish between explicit comments in the text and what can be read between the lines, and I will compare him to other, contemporary authors (see chap. 1 below).

Second, there is the problem of using a historiographical work dealing with a period long before the author's own time as a source for contemporary ideas of society and politics: apart from the short section dealing with the very distant past, the narrative of *Heimskringla* covers the period from the late ninth century till 1177, two years before Snorri was born. Though Snorri probably did not share the modern historicist assumption that the past is qualitatively different from the present (see chap. 5), he may well have imagined people then to have behaved differently from what his contemporaries would do, such as, more heroically or with greater cruelty, or he may have assumed that magic or supernatural intervention was more frequent then.[4] Generally, medieval works of history and not least the sagas, were also works of literature, and this may have determined their presentation of people's behavior. Once more, it is difficult to state a definite method. However, such a long text as *Heimskringla* offers some opportunities of distinguishing between normal behavior as appears in episodes throughout the work and particularly romantic or heroic stories. A comparison with other saga writers may be helpful in this case as well.

As for combining the examination of *Heimskringla* as a source for ideas of society and political behavior with analyzing the text in itself, this is perhaps less of a problem than it may seem in the first place. After all, political behavior—in a broad sense—is not one of several themes, it is what *Heimskringla* is mainly about. An examination of this problem should therefore be able to uncover central aspects of Snorri's historical authorship. This does not mean that it can explain everything in it, nor do I intend to treat every aspect of the work. Philologists in particular may miss one aspect, the analysis of Snorri's sources and his relationship to his predecessors. This is the aspect of *Heimskringla* and the saga literature that has been treated most extensively—almost exclusively—hitherto, and though far from all problems have been solved, I am not interested in this context in making further contributions to this field and have tried to confine the discussion of such matters to a minimum. As I am equally interested in Snorri's implicit assumptions or "mentality" as in his explicit opinions, I do not always find it important to trace whether he has invented or constructed a particular passage or has taken it from his predecessors. Moreover, it turns out that Snorri is a sufficiently independent mind not to have copied slavishly from his predecessors but usually to have his reasons for omitting or including particular passages. Evidently this does not mean that a comparison between Snorri and his predecessors is irrelevant. Quite the contrary, it is often of great importance for solving the general problems I have outlined on the preceding pages. I have therefore included comparisons between Snorri and his predecessors throughout the text, whenever I have found it necessary. A summary of these passages and a general conclusion on his way of writing history and analyzing politics as compared to that of his predecessors are to be found in chapter 6.

My intention is thus not to solve the problem of medieval political behavior as outlined above, but to use it as a clue to analyzing Snorri. I hope, however, that such an analysis may make it easier to discuss political behavior in other narrative sources and ultimately in society as it actually was. Though I may be accused of not keeping strictly to the narrow path in choosing my themes, I hope that my readers will find that the material on the following pages is not only there because it suits my interests, but also has some internal unity.

My reason for choosing a work from the outskirts of Europe instead of one of the well-known European historians of the Middle Ages is not to give a representative picture of medieval historiography. Apart from such trivial reasons as *Heimskringla* being more familiar to me than most European works and a wish to make it more known among modern historians, this choice is made exactly because *Heimskringla* seems to differ from what is usual in the period and even to differ in the "modern" direction, to some extent anticipating the secular, political historiography of the Renaissance. On the following pages I intend to show this difference and explain the reasons for it.

The book is arranged in the following way. The main problem, political behavior and its relation to society, is treated in chapters 2 to 4, first the conflicts (chap. 2), then Snorri's descriptions of society, human nature, and morality (chaps. 3 to 4). In chapters 1 and 5, on Snorri as an author and a historian, I shall analyze more directly Snorri's own contribution, as opposed to general attitudes in his milieu. Chapter 1 mainly deals with composition, chronology, and Snorri's concept of authorship. The reason for dividing this from chapter 5 and placing it in the beginning of the book is that it is also intended as a general presentation of the contents of *Heimskringla,* placing the various stories, which are treated more in detail in the following, in their appropriate context. In chapter 5, I shall then try to show how Snorri's ideas of the game of politics determine his general interpretation of history, which differs on important points from the main trend in contemporary European historiography. Finally, in chapter 6, I shall compare Snorri with the historiographical tradition in Norway and Iceland and in Europe in general and try to explain his particular approach in terms of social and cultural conditions in Norway and Iceland. The rest of this introduction contains a general presentation of the work and its author and sketches of Norwegian medieval history and the evolution of Old Norse historiography. This is primarily intended for readers who are not familiar with Old Norse studies.

The General Background: Snorri and Norwegian History

Heimskringla deals with the history of the Norwegian kings, mainly from the late ninth till the late twelfth century. It thus covers the period of the formation and early development of the Norwegian monarchy. The "story" of this, as told by modern scholars, runs approximately as follows.[5] Norway was united under one king for the first time by Haraldr hárfagri (c. 890/900–945), who conquered most of the country. The decisive battle, celebrated by scalds and saga writers, took place in Hafrsfjord, near what is now Stavanger, probably shortly before 900. After Haraldr's death, various pretenders sought to take over his position but no one succeeded completely. The country remained divided in several lordships, though fewer and larger than before Haraldr. There were frequent internal struggles, in which the Swedish and particularly the Danish king often intervened. For long periods, the Danish king even controlled parts of the country. The external and internal struggles of this period were intimately connected with the Viking expeditions, most of the pretenders having enriched themselves in this way or having served under foreign kings.

One of these warlords, King Óláfr Haraldsson (1015–1030), later known as St. Óláfr, managed to unite the country once more and made Christianity the official religion. Óláfr was later defeated and killed in the battle of Stiklestad (1030) by his internal opponents in alliance with King Cnut the Great, who ruled both Denmark and England. Nevertheless, in a long-term perspective his reign made a turning point. During the following century, Norway remained a united monarchy, though for some periods ruled by several kings as co-rulers. Its independence was maintained, and sometimes its kings even conducted aggressive wars against Denmark or the British Isles. Christianity became firmly established and the ecclesiastical organization was built up, until an independent Church-province, led by the archbishop of Nidaros, was established in 1152/1153. This organization also served to give the king a firmer hold on the country. Further, the lay magnates now became more closely attached to the king, thus furthering the process of centralization.

This development was apparently broken off in the 1130s, when a disputed succession inaugurated a series of civil wars which went on intermittently until 1240. Actually, this period was an important phase in the centralization of the country, and the wars themselves to some extent contributed to this. They seem to have started as struggles between individual rulers and their friends and clients and then gradually developed into prolonged wars between permanent parties, which controlled different parts of the country. In the 1160s Erlingr Ormsson, nicknamed skakki (crooked-neck), assembled the leading churchmen and the majority of the aristocracy around the kingdom of his son Magnús. His opponents increasingly had to seek support from marginal groups or at least the less prominent members of society. One of these opponents, however, Sverrir Sigurðsson (1177–1202), managed, largely through his own political and strategic ability, to fight his way to the throne and defeat the party of Erlingr, though he had to fight various rebellions until his death. Under Sverrir and his successors, a new aristocracy emerged, to a considerable extent recruited from below and more closely attached to the king. Sverrir and his adherents had considerable problems with the Church, to some extent also with the old aristocracy. They developed a "party ideology," which was anticlerical, "democratic"—in the sense that it encouraged recruitment from below to political positions—and strongly monarchical. This remained the official ideology of the dynasty for a long time, though in a somewhat diluted form. The dynasty of Sverrir remained on the throne, though they had to strike a compromise with the leaders of the opposite party. In the years following Sverrir's death the old and the new aristocracy, to some extent also the Church, increasingly became united under a strong monarchy. Norway then entered its "age of greatness" (1240–1319). This was a period of strong monarchy, administrative centralization, internal peace, cultural achievement, and a relatively strong external position.

Snorri's *Heimskringla* was written toward the end of the period of civil wars, when the dynasty of Sverrir was fairly firmly established on the throne. According to some scholars, Snorri's general interpretation of history was influenced by contemporary or recent Norwegian conditions, notably the conflict between monarchy and aristocracy. He thus tells largely the same story as that of modern historiography, though in the guise of dramatic events. As I shall develop later, I do not share this opinion.

Snorri begins his history with the pagan God Óðinn, the mythical founder of the dynasty. In contrast to Saxo Grammaticus in Denmark, who devotes a major part of his work to the "prehistory," Snorri dismisses the early period rather briefly. The kings from Óðinn, according to Snorri a contemporary of the Roman conquerors (*Yngl.* chap. 5), until the mid-ninth century, are grouped together in the *Ynglinga saga,* which is little more than an extended genealogy. The reason for this may have been lack of information, to some extent also doubts of the reliability of the sources that were available. The real narrative of the Norwegian kings start with Hálvdan svarti, the father of the great conqueror Haraldr hárfagri. *Heimskringla* ends early in 1177, when King Magnús Erlingsson won what seemed the final victory over the last rebel faction, the Birchlegs, in the battle of Ré. This was immediately before the rise of Sverrir, who became the leader of the remains of the defeated army shortly afterward. Snorri's reason for ending his story here was probably that the following events had already been treated in detail in *Sverris saga*. From a modern point of view it seems curious that he does not in any way anticipate Sverrir's rise to power. If we did not know better, we would have thought that the battle of Ré marked the final victory for the dynasty contemporary to Snorri.

During most of the nineteenth century, Snorri was considered the most important source for the early history of Norway. In 1911 the Swedish historian Lauritz Weibull published a series of "critical examinations" on early Nordic history in which he rejected most of the information given by Snorri and other Icelandic historians on Nordic history of the tenth and eleventh centuries, demanding that all conclusions should be based on contemporary evidence or on later evidence only if it could be controlled.[6] This meant that most of what one believed to know about this period was thrown away in a single stroke. Weibull's book created violent disputes, but his ideas gradually established themselves as the orthodox opinion, at least in Denmark and Sweden, to some extent also in Norway. In 1931 the Norwegian historian Edvard Bull declared:

> We . . . have to give up all illusions that Snorri's mighty epic bears any deeper resemblance to what actually happened in the period between the battle of Hafrsfjord and the battle of Ré. (Bull, 1931: 9)

Bull was more skeptical than most, but his statement is nevertheless an indication of a general trend. Historians are reluctant to use Snorri as a source, at least for events before the twelfth century, though they have not been very explicit concerning what to trust and what not. The problem is that there is little else to use. There is some archeological evidence. As for written materials, the earlier sagas that are extant are not much older than *Heimskringla* and were mostly also Snorri's sources. From around 1150 there is some documentary evidence, above all papal letters and other ecclesiastical sources. Foreign sources, such as the *Anglo-Saxon Chronicle* (Earle and Plummer, 1892–1899) and Adam of Bremen's *Gesta Hammaburgensis ecclesiae pontificum* (c. 1070) contain some information on the tenth and eleventh centuries. Apart from this, the main source of information is the scaldic poems, mostly laudatory addresses to kings, which are quoted extensively by Snorri and other historians. Because of their complicated metrical form these poems are believed to have been preserved orally over the centuries, though the possibility evidently exists that some of them may be later inventions. They contain some basic information on the names of kings, battles, and so forth, but no real narrative. Finally, we know that Snorri used written sources from the early twelfth century which are now lost and from which he probably derived some basic information concerning main events, deaths of kings, and so forth.[7]

Bull's statement concerning Snorri has to do with trustworthiness but also with relevance. Like most early historians, Snorri describes numerous battles and dramatic events, in which modern historians take little interest, while omitting what they find most interesting, such as government, administration, social and economic conditions, and the material necessary to trace the main lines in the development of society. Even when dealing with political events, he is often vague concerning the exact contents of treaties, the claims of the parties in a conflict, and so forth. In short, both because of increased skepticism concerning the trustworthiness of Snorri and other saga writers and because of the development of modern Norwegian historiography away from history of events to history of social structure, *Heimskringla* has largely lost its dominant position in Norwegian historiography. At the same time, this historiographical development has opened new possibilities for using Snorri as evidence for thirteenth-century attitudes to man, society, and history.

Snorri's Life and Authorship

Heimskringla is named after its opening words *Kringla heimsins* (the circle of the world). The text has been preserved in several medieval manuscripts and fragments, most of which are Icelandic. What is considered the most important manuscript, *Kringla,* written c. 1250–1280, was destroyed in the fire in Copenhagen in 1728, except for one leaf, which had been brought to Stockholm and is still there. Its text, however, is known from seventeenth-century transcripts (Lie, 1961: 302; Louis-Jensen, 1976: 16 ff.). No extant manuscript of *Heimskringla* names Snorri as its author before the translations by the Norwegian antiquarians Laurents Hanssøn (1550) and Peder Claussøn Friis (1599). However, there seems to be good reasons to believe, as most scholars do, that this attribution stems from medieval manuscripts that are now lost.[8] This hypothesis is supported by casual references in other sagas to information derived from Snorri, which is actually to be found in *Heimskringla.* It thus appears that we may fairly safely consider Snorri the author of *Heimskringla.* In contrast to most other works of the Old Norse literature, with *Heimskringla* we then find ourselves fortunate in not only being able to name the author, but also being faced with an author about whom very much is known. Snorri was one of the mightiest chieftains of thirteenth-century Iceland, and the contemporary *Íslendinga saga,* written by his nephew Sturla Þórðarson (in the collection *Sturlunga saga*), contains much information on his life and political activities.

Snorri was born at Hvammur in Western Iceland in 1179.[9] He had prominent ancestors on both sides, but it was his father, Sturla Þórðarson the Elder, who brought the family into the foremost rank of the Icelandic aristocracy. Snorri, however, was not immediately able to take over his father's position. He was the third son and only four years old at his father's death in 1183. By the time he had grown up, his mother had wasted most of his fortune. But Snorri had a great advantage in being fostered by Jón Loptsson of the Oddaverja family. This family, at the time the mightiest of the country, ruled a large part of Southern Iceland. The time Snorri spend at Oddi, until Jón's death in 1197, was also important from another point of view. Oddi was a center of learning and historical studies,[10] and Jón was a learned man; he was related to the Norwegian royal family—his mother was the daughter of King Magnús berfoetr—and had personal memories of Norwegian history from the years he had spent there. Snorri may thus have received general education and inspiration for his future historical studies at Oddi, besides direct information on past events from Jón.

Thanks to his connection with the Oddaverjar, Snorri was able to contract a very rich marriage in 1199, which laid the foundation for his future prominence. In the following years he increased his power by collecting *goðorð* (chieftainties) and *staðir* (churches),[11] particularly in the region around Borgarfjörður, thus furthering the process of power concentration which during the first half of the thirteenth century divided the country into a few large territories (ríki), governed by mighty chieftains. In the years 1215–1218 and once more 1222–1231 he was *lǫgsǫgumaðr,* the official judicial spokesman at the *Alþingi.* This was not a position that gave much power, but it was very prestigious and thus an indication of rank and importance. During Snorri's first period as a *lǫgsǫgumaðr* his relations with the Oddaverjar became more strained, and in the following period Snorri and his kindred, the Sturlungar, surpassed the Oddaverjar in power and influence. In 1218–1220 Snorri went to Norway for the first time. He was well received and became a close friend of Earl Skúli Barðarson, the real ruler of the country during King Hákon Hákonarson's minority. He became a member of the Norwegian *hirð* (the organization of royal retainers), first with the rank of *skutilsveinn* (the second highest), then as a *lendr maðr* (the highest), and promised Skúli to promote the unification of Iceland with Norway. In practice, however, his Norwegian connections mainly served to further his own interests as an Icelandic chieftain. The last period of his life, after his first return from Norway, coincided with one of the most dramatic periods of internal strife in the history of the Icelandic free state, and Snorri played a prominent part in these struggles. In 1237 Snorri temporarily withdrew from the internal strife in Iceland to spend two years with his friend Skúli in Norway, but this involved him in another struggle, the one between Skúli and King Hákon, which led to Skúli's rebellion late in 1239. King Hákon now considered Snorri his enemy, and their relations deteriorated further when Snorri left Norway against the king's express orders in 1239. The king now ordered his chief representative in Iceland, Gizurr Þorvaldsson, to take Snorri captive and return him to Norway, or kill him. Gizurr had been married to Snorri's daughter, but the marriage had been dissolved. Gizurr allied himself with another former son-in-law of Snorri, Kolbeinn ungi, opened a lawsuit against Snorri, and used arms to further his claims. In September 1241 he attacked Snorri at his farm Reykjaholt and had him killed.

Snorri's political career thus ended in failure and death. As a politician he has generally not been regarded highly by modern historians. According to common opinion, he was intelligent, ambitious, probably not very courageous in war, and behaved with a curious mixture of hardness and weakness, which seems to cover a fundamental uncertainty. No one, however, has disputed his ability to analyze politics. There may be some connection here: the politician's determination and ability to reach sudden decisions and the historian's reflection are not easily combined. However, much remains to be done before we have a complete picture of the internal strife in Iceland during these years and the basic conditions of politics in the last phase of the Icelandic free state, and this makes it difficult to form a definite opinion on Snorri's ability as a politician. For the present purpose, I shall confine myself to pointing out that Snorri both had considerable political experience and good connections to Norway and the Norwegian court. The relevance of this for his work remains to be examined.

Apart from *Heimskringla,* Snorri is also, according to a manuscript dated around 1300, the author of the *Younger Edda,* a handbook on scaldic poetry, which is an important source for Old Norse mythology and for contemporary theory of language (see most recently Clunies Ross, 1987; von See, 1988). He is also the author of the *Separate Saga of St. Óláfr.* The former is probably a comparatively early work, for the most part written before Snorri's first journey to Norway, though it cannot have been finished until after 1223. The *Separate Saga* is largely identical with the Óláfr's saga of *Heimskringla* and is usually considered to have been written earlier. Further, most scholars attribute one of the most famous of the Icelandic family sagas to Snorri, *Egils saga Skalla-grímssonar.* This has usually been considered an early work, though Jónas Kristjánsson has suggested a date after *Heimskringla* (1977: 470 ff.). There appears to be universal agreement that both the *Separate Saga of St. Óláfr* and *Heimskringla* were written after Snorri's first journey to Norway. Though Snorri may have received much of his historical information in Iceland, the geographical accuracy of both works strongly indicates an author who had visited large parts of the country. This also applies to *Egils saga.* The conventional dates are c. 1220–1225 for the *Separate Saga* and c. 1230 for the *Heimskringla.* The latter date is suggested by a casual reference in *Sturlunga saga* to a visit to Reykjaholt by Snorri's nephew Sturla Sigvatsson, during which he made transcripts of saga books that his uncle had composed. The period c. 1230 was also a peaceful interlude in Snorri's struggles with his rivals, which may have offered an opportunity for literary activities. The exact date of these works, however, is of slight importance for our evaluation of Snorri as a historian. We know fairly well that both were composed when he was a mature man, with long experience as an Icelandic politician of the first rank and with good knowledge of Norwegian conditions and connection with the Norwegian court. As his works deal with the fairly distant past, it is doubtful whether we can expect them to be influenced by particular events in his own life, though we cannot quite rule out the possibility that varying attitudes to the Norwegian monarchy may be reflected in them.

Snorri's Background and Sources

Heimskringla represents the climax of Old Norse historiography in a double sense: it comes at the end of about half a century of extensive saga writing and includes material contained in most earlier works dealing with the Norwegian kings. It is also generally considered the best and most mature example of a kings' saga, both from a literary and a historiographical point of view. Its sources have been dealt with extensively by a number of scholars. There has also been considerable discussion on the origin of the saga literature.

The two historiographical traditions of contemporary Europe, the clerical and the aristocratic (see Brandt, 1966), have their parallels in Old Norse historiography. It is customary among students of language and literature to distinguish between the "learned" and the "popular" style (Halvorsen, 1962: 119 ff.), the former being influenced by Latin and usually the medium of clerics, whereas the latter corresponds to local traditions and is the medium of the laity and the classical saga literature. In historiography the learned works usually but not always reflect religious and clerical points of view and generally bear close resemblance to European clerical historiography. The other tradition shows some similarity to European aristocratic historiography, but is more original. As its specifically aristocratic features are less prominent the term "secular" is more suitable than "aristocratic."

There is a solid tradition in scholarship for this distinction and for stressing the unique achievement of Icelandic saga writing in contrast to the learned and clerical culture of contemporary Europe, particularly within the so-called Germanistic school. In the last decades, however, there has been a tendency in the opposite direction, stressing the basic unity of medieval culture and attempting to interpret the sagas in terms of European, Christian philosophy and theology (e.g., Lönnroth, 1964, 1965, 1969; Pálsson, 1971, 1984, and 1986; Harris, 1986; Weber, 1987; see also Clover, 1985: 264 ff.). To some extent, this has been a healthy reaction against much obscure Germanic romanticism of the last century and has also been stimulating in attempting to link the North to the common European culture. Generally, however, I think this reaction has gone too far, not the least because it tends to minimize the difference that existed between the two cultures in Europe as a whole (cf. also von See, 1988: 13 ff. and *passim*). I shall touch upon this problem repeatedly in the following pages and confine myself to a few remarks regarding Snorri's predecessors in this context.

The first historical works dealing with the Norwegian kings by the Icelanders Sæmundr and Ari, which date from the early twelfth century and are now lost, cannot be easily fitted in with either category. They were apparently short, dry summaries of events, their authors exerting themselves in establishing an exact absolute and relative chronology. This is the impression we get from Ari's *Íslendingabók,* which is now extant. His *Konunga ævi* (kings' lives) was most probably an appendix to *Íslendingabók,* which was removed later, though some scholars have maintained that it was a separate work (see Ellehøj, 1964: 43 ff. with ref.). These works lacked both the vivid narrative of the secular saga and the religious interpretation of the clerical one. The fact that both these authors were priests is of less relevance in this context, as Sæmundr certainly and Ari probably combined his priesthood with the position as a chieftain. This combination was quite usual in eleventh- and early twelfth-century Iceland. Sæmundr apparently wrote in Latin, whereas Ari wrote in the vernacular. Both must have influenced a number of later historians, but the extent of this influence is difficult to detect and hotly disputed.[12]

The so-called Norwegian synoptics represent the next stage in the development, as far as extant works are concerned. The three works that can be classified under this heading, Theodoricus Monachus's *Histo-*

ria de antiquitate regum norwagiensium (c. 1180, in Latin), the anonymous *Historia Norvegiae* (before 1178, c. 1220, also in Latin), and *Ágrip
af Nóregs konunga sǫgum* (c. 1190, anonymous, in Old Norse) are written from a distinctly clerical point of view. The milieu of *Historia
Norvegiae* is unknown, whereas the two others show connection with the
archiepiscopal see of Nidaros. The oldest history of St. Óláfr, *Passio
Olavi,* written by Archbishop Eysteinn Erlendsson (1161–1188), also
belongs to this milieu, but is better classified as a saint's legend than as
historiography in the real sense. The clerical point of view of these three
works is expressed both in their ideology, classifying the kings according
to the Augustinian schema of the *rex iustus* and *rex iniquus,* their frequent appeals to God's intervention, and their concern with the moral
aspect of human acts. As in many contemporary European clerical
chronicles and in contrast to the classical saga, their narrative is mostly
dry. Many of the dramatic episodes that occur in the later sagas are
omitted, and those included are told in a short and undramatic way.[13]
Ágrip bears some resemblance to the classical sagas in that its author
remains in the background and that it contains some vivid stories, told
very much in the classical saga style. In the two Latin works, however,
the author comes forward explicitly, commenting on the events. The
chief interest of these authors is clearly in interpretation, not in narrative. They want to uncover the moral and religious significance of the
events (Bagge, 1989a). Characteristically, they reserve rhetorical embroidery to expository and interpretative passages.

The birth of secular historiography, the classical saga, must be
roughly contemporary with "the Norwegian synoptics." The secular saga
was once believed to have developed gradually from clerical historiography. The "intermediate forms," represented by works like the *Oldest
Saga* of St. Óláfr, which is preserved only in fragments, and the *Saga
Óláfs Tryggvasonar* by Oddr Snorrason munkr, were considered evidence of this. Recent research having both questioned the connection
between the *Oldest Saga* and hagiography and the early date of the
work, no direct evidence remains that the "intermediate forms" represent an early stage in the development.[14] Nor does this seem very likely
on a priori grounds. The two forms are so different that it hardly seems a
likely explanation that the latter should have developed from the former
over a period of about twenty years.

It is very difficult to detect early forms of secular saga writing. Most
works are difficult to date, and those that can be shown to be early with
reasonable certainty, like the second and larger part of *Sverris saga* and
Orkneyinga saga, both probably written shortly after 1200, represent
saga art in its full development: the characteristic short, terse "saga
style," the vivid narrative, the pre-dominance of relative as opposed to

absolute chronology, the secular attitude, and the use of speeches and dialogue for purposes of analysis and interpretation, while the author remains in the background. Concerning this latter point, however, some development may be detected, both in the various versions of Oddr munkr's *Saga Óláfs Tryggvasonar* and in the difference between the first part of *Sverris saga* (*Grýla*), which was probably written already in the 1180s, and the rest (Holm-Olsen, 1977: 58 ff.; 1987: 79 ff.). In the discussion of sources of the extant sagas, a number of earlier sagas, mostly separate sagas of individual kings, are thought to have existed before the extant ones. If this is the case, the origin of the secular saga is to be found some time back in the twelfth century. This is not very helpful, however, since nothing is known of the contents and style of most of these works. As a matter of fact, with a few exceptions, their very existence remains doubtful.

The most important exception to this is *Hryggjarstykki,* the existence of which is attested both by *Morkinskinna* and *Heimskringla.* This work was written by the Icelander Eiríkr Oddsson, probably in the 1160s, and covered either the whole or parts of the period 1130–1161. If the former hypothesis is correct and the detailed and very similar treatment of the wars between Haraldr gilli's descendants 1155–1161 in *Morkinskinna, Fagrskinna,* and *Heimskringla* stem from *Hryggjarstykki,* then we have evidence of the fully developed secular saga as early as the mid-twelfth century. The most recent scholar who has treated the matter, Bjarni Guðnason, denies this, however, and maintains that the work was a biography of the pretender Sigurðr slembir and only covered the years of his struggle for the throne, 1136–1139 (Guðnason, 1978). If this is correct, there may be some evidence for its dependence on a hagiographic tradition and thus for the idea of the secular saga developing from clerical historiography. Sigurðr was tortured to death by his enemies and bore his pains with the utmost tranquillity of mind, chanting psalms all the time. The description of this clearly resembles a story of a martyr. To what extent the story of Sigurðr can also be understood as a description of a secular hero, remains to be considered (see later discussion). It may be mentioned in the same context that Ludvig Holm-Olsen suggests a similar model for another saga, the earlier part of *Sverris saga* (1953: 91 ff.). However, Guðnason also points to other influences behind the work, notably oral storytelling, as is described in the *Sturlunga saga* in connection with the wedding at Reykjahólar in Iceland in 1119 (*Sturl.* I: 18 ff.; see, e.g., Jónsson, 1923: 198 ff.).

Even if we accept the idea of influence from hagiography on the description of Sigurðr's death, it is difficult to see that this explains very much of the distinctive features of the classical saga. First, we cannot exclude the possibility that descriptions of men like Sigurðr and Sverrir may equally well have been derived from stories of secular heroes. Second—and most important—most of the distinctive traits of the classical saga are conspicuously absent from saints' lives, namely the characteristic saga style, the retreat of the author, the speeches and dialogues used as interpretation and comment, and the description of the heroes. For instance, the *vitae* of the saints almost never describe their heroes' appearances, whereas the sagas usually do. The descriptions of character are also very different, both in style and content. The "hagiographic explanation" thus seems to be no explanation at all. It may possibly explain some features of individual works and even to some extent—though this is more doubtful—why they were written, but it is unable to account for the characteristic features of the classical saga. And this is after all the whole problem.

Thus, the question of the origin of the saga still lies in the dark. The problem is difficult, perhaps impossible to solve. But it must be pointed out that the sort of research that has been practiced hitherto is not very likely to lead to its solution. In accordance with the bookprose theory, which for a long time has been the prevailing orthodoxy in saga studies (see Clover, 1985: 241 f.), scholars have mainly been interested in tracing the origin of extant texts back to other, earlier texts, extant or not. This approach must sooner or later lead to a dead end. How can the earliest text be explained? In general, it is hardly possible to explain new developments in literature simply by comparing texts. Social and intellectual milieus must be taken into account, and this has not been done very much in scholarly research on saga origins.

Though it is outside the scope of the present work to discuss the question of saga origins and the milieus behind the first sagas in general, something must be said on the relative importance of the Norwegian royal court and the aristocratic milieus of Iceland. Most of the sagas of this early period seem to have been written by Icelanders. In contrast to the Icelandic family sagas, which are mostly later, they deal with matters outside Iceland, but by no means exclusively confined to Norway. There are sagas of the Orkney earls, of the chieftains of the Faroe Islands, the Danish kings, and the *jómsvíkingar* (the Vikings of Jóm, i.e., the island of Wollin in the Baltic), and there are indications that there were also sagas of the earls of Lade and their kinsman Hákon Ívarsson. Thus, the kings' sagas were not necessarily the result of Norwegian royal patronage. There seems to have been a general interest in such stories within the Icelandic aristocracy, which in some cases, though by no means always, may have to do with kinship ties with the persons or families described in the sagas.

The sagas of Norwegian kings that belong to this period are Oddr Snorrason's and Gunnlaugr Leifsson's sagas of Óláfr Tryggvason, the

Oldest Saga and the *Legendary Saga* of St. Óláfr, and the earlier part of *Sverris saga,* the so-called *Grýla.* This latter work was written under the king's supervision by the Icelandic abbot Karl Jónsson, and is thus clearly an example of royal patronage.[15] Whether the original initiative was Karl's own or Sverrir's is a debated question, as is the question of the initiative and milieu behind the latter—and larger—part of the saga, which was written after Sverrir's death in 1202.[16] The two sagas of Óláfr Tryggvason are both composed by Icelanders but originally written in Latin. Oddr's is preserved in translation, whereas Gunnlaugr's is lost but can partly be reconstructed from *Óláfs saga Tryggvasonar hin mesta,* a compilation from around 1300. These works seem to represent an intermediate form between clerical and secular historiography, combining a distinctly clerical outlook with vivid narrative. Their particular interest in King Óláfr Tryggvason has been explained as an expression of the wish to emphasize the king who brought Christianity to Iceland against his more important namesake St. Óláfr (Lönnroth, 1963: 54 ff.). There may thus have been a specifically Icelandic reason for writing about this particular Norwegian king. By contrast, Norwegian interests are likely to have been more prominent in the case of the two sagas of St. Óláfr. St. Óláfr was prominent in the propaganda of both parties in the ideological warfare between King Sverrir on the one side and King Magnús Erlingsson and his descendants on the other, the latter for a long time receiving support from the Church. Though the works in question can hardly be regarded as direct propaganda for either party in this conflict, it is not unreasonable to see a connection between Óláfr's political importance at the time and historical interest in his life.[17] Whether this also applies to the slighty later saga of St. Óláfr by the Icelander Styrmir Kárason, which is only preserved in fragments,[18] or whether this is a product of an Icelandic milieu, is more difficult to tell.

The following period, approximately 1220–1235 is the period of the great compendia on the Norwegian kings and in general a period in which Norwegian matters dominate saga writing. These works are, in addition to Snorri's *Separate Saga of St. Óláfr* and *Heimskringla,* the anonymous *Morkinskinna* (c. 1220) and *Fagrskinna* (c. 1225). Of these sagas, *Fagrskinna* is clearly written in close connection with the Norwegian court, possibly also by a Norwegian,[19] whereas the rest are commonly considered to have been written by Icelanders. Their connection with Norway and the Norwegian court remains doubtful. Are they a continuation of the Icelandic interest in heroes and chieftains of other countries in the North of the preceding period, or is some kind of Norwegian patronage behind them? Arguments in favor of the latter point of view are the undoubted interest in history and intellectual work in general at the contemporary Norwegian court as well as the fact that the political links between the Norwegian king and the Icelandic chieftains became closer as the result of the attempts by the Norwegian king to bring Iceland under his dominion. As we have discussed, Snorri had close connections with the leading circles of Norway and became involved in these attempts. Norwegian influence behind the conception and execution of the work cannot therefore be excluded, but the matter must ultimately be decided by internal evidence. The question is more difficult to decide in the case of *Morkinskinna*, as we know nothing of its author, and there has been little research on the work. But we may note that it contains many more stories of Icelanders than the two other works.

Morkinskinna deals with the period from the death of St. Óláfr till the death of King Eysteinn Haraldsson, that is, 1030–1157, but may possibly have extended till 1177 (the battle of Ré). It is more loosely structured than the two other works, often consisting of rather disconnected stories, and there are clear indications that it has been reworked and interpolated. *Fagrskinna* covers the period from Hálfdan svarti in the middle of the ninth century till the battle of Ré (1177). It is the shortest of the three and also the least saga-like. Despite its secular attitude, it resembles the clerical works in its short and often dry narrative and in omitting many dramatic stories, above all those dealing with internal strife, to some extent also in its *rex iustus*-ideology (see later discussion). Together with *Heimskringla* these two works represent the kings' saga writing in its full maturity. On most points, however, it is difficult to trace a development compared to the earlier works, though it can be done concerning scaldic poetry. The more frequent and conscious use of this clearly has to do with the fact that these works dealt with a remote period, from which few sources were available.[20] Generally, *Heimskringla* clearly represents progress compared to its two immediate predecessors. This has been frequently pointed out by scholars and will be demonstrated in the following.

The relationship between these sagas mutually and with the earlier saga tradition has been the subject of considerable learned discussion, which need not detain us here. From our point of view the sources of *Heimskringla* are the most important aspect of the question. Snorri mentions some of his sources explicitly, such as Ari and Eiríkr Oddsson, but most of them must be reconstructed by comparison with other sources. There is general agreement that he used *Morkinskinna*, and most scholars also think that he used *Fagrskinna* for *Heimskringla*, though not for the *Separate Saga*. As for earlier sagas he has evidently used Oddr Snorrason's *Óláfs saga Tryggvasonar*. The question of the sources for his biography of St. Óláfr is more complex, but he used most of the stories contained in the *Legendary Saga,* however it is unknown whether he knew this work directly or found the same material in a source which is now lost, such as Styrmir's history. Coming at the end of an extensive, if not particularly long tradition, Snorri thus seems to have borrowed from most of his predecessors.

1

The Author

Introduction

A full analysis of Snorri as an author involves almost every aspect of *Heimskringla*. This will not be attempted here. But it is difficult to use *Heimskringla* as a source for ideas of politics, man, and society without having some ideas on its author and his literary purpose and achievement. In this chapter, I shall therefore discuss three topics: Snorri's principles of source criticism and historical truth; his composition, which in a historical work is largely identical with chronological principles; and finally the concepts of authorship stated explicitly or implicitly by Snorri and his contemporaries, compared to the authorial practice that appears in *Heimskringla*. Is *Heimskringla* written by an author who regards himself as such and follows a deliberate plan, or is it a compilation?

The Meaning of Authorship in Snorri

Although there is sufficient evidence that Snorri in one way or another was responsible for writing or editing the collection of kings' sagas known as *Heimskringla,* and thus can be regarded as its author, the exact meaning of this latter term seems more doubtful. Most scholars, since the mid-nineteenth century (e.g., Munch, 1857: 1032, 1040 ff.; Petersen, 1866: 235 ff.; and Storm, 1873: 1 ff., 77 ff., etc.), have regarded him as an author in more or less the modern sense. Halvdan Koht in 1913 went further in this direction, not only regarding Snorri as an independent writer and a critical examiner of his sources, but as a historian with an overall interpretation of the period he was describing (1921: 76 ff., see also chap. 2). Both Koht's critics among the philologists and the relatively few scholars who examined Snorri's scholarship and literary style in the following period have believed in Snorri as an author in the real sense and given additional arguments for this (Nordal, 1973: 132 ff.; Lie, 1937). There are, however, different opinions. In the nineteenth century P. E. Müller (1823) and Konrad Maurer (1867: 119 ff.) regarded *Heimskringla* as mainly a compilation of earlier, written works, and this view has been revived by Lars Lönnroth, who points partly to the rather vague references to Snorri's authorship in the sources and partly to the considerable differences between the individual sagas of *Heimskringla* (Lönnroth, 1964: 83 ff.; see also Olsen, 1965: 68).

A similar but more radical hypothesis has been brought forward by M. I. Steblin-Kamensky: the concept of authorship did not exist in the medieval North. There was no word for "author" as distinct from "scribe" and no "authorial view" in the works (1973: 51 ff.). Nor was there any distinction between fiction and historical literature. Authors were simply transmitting "syncretic truth," neither deliberately creating a story like modern authors of fiction, nor reconstructing the past like modern historians (1973: 21 ff.). Consequently, one searches in vain for a consistent view of history in a work like Snorri's *Heimskringla* (1973: 61 f.).[1] In one sense, Steblin-Kamensky's ideas are a return to the older view of Snorri as a compiler, and more generally they are related to the romantic idea of the sagas and other older literature as the expression of a collective "Volksgeist." But they are better regarded as a part of a new tendency to examine the specific character or "mentality" of cultures of the past, which is also expressed in recent studies of oral cultures (see Ong, 1982 with ref.). No study of *Heimskringla* from this point of view has appeared, but there has been an increasing interest during the last two decades in the oral background to the Icelandic sagas, which has led to some revision of the bookprose theory, though no new synthesis has emerged (Scholes and Kellogg, 1966: 43 ff.; Clover, 1985: 273 ff.).

In one sense, it is a perfectly legitimate task to analyze the ideas of politics, man, and society in *Heimskringla,* even if Steblin-Kamensky is right, as we will then have the opportunity to examine the *mentalité collective* of which Snorri was a part without the complication of an individual author whose ideas might be different from those of his milieu. But it is of crucial importance both for the analysis itself and for the use of its results to know to what extent we are dealing with a real author, a compiler, or the expression of collective mentality. A full examination of this question, however, would amount to a complete literary analysis of *Heimskringla.* This will not be attempted here. I shall mostly confine myself to drawing conclusions from Snorri's treatment of the various topics dealt with below. Some problems, however, need especial examination, the first of which is Snorri's own concept of historical authorship, including his attitude to the use of sources for reconstructing the past.

Snorri's Prologue: Critical Principles and Authorship

The question of historical authorship is intimately linked to that of sources and critical principles. If the historian regards himself simply as a man who writes down what others have told him or collects or transcribes earlier authors, we can hardly talk of authorship in the real sense. In Snorri's case, we are able to study his own reflections on his sources and thus on his role as an author.

Two prologues by Snorri have been preserved. In the extant manuscripts, the one serves as the prologue to *Heimskringla,* whereas the other belongs to the *Separate Saga of St. Óláfr.* This must be a later arrangement, however. Originally, they are two versions of the same prologue. The chronological relationship between them is uncertain and has been the subject of some debate.[2] They are not very different. Both give short summaries of the earliest history of the Norwegian kings, while at the same time presenting Snorri's sources, which fall into three groups: (1) poetic genealogies or other poetry dealing with ancient times; (2) scaldic poetry, contemporary with the kings they deal with; and (3) Ari fróði. The *Heimskringla* prologue (= *Prol. Hkr.*) gives the three groups in the order indicated above, the other prologue (= *Prol. OH*) starts with Ari. The latter is also a little more detailed on the subject of scaldic poetry.

Modern scholars have been enthusiastic about Snorri's critical principles and have considered him almost a modern historian (e.g., Storm, 1873: 89 ff.; Indrebø, 1917: 139 f.; Nordal, 1973: 133 ff.). There is some justice in this enthusiasm. Admittedly, medieval authors clearly understood the value of eyewitnesses, frequently referred to their own and other trustworthy men's experience, and often divided their works chronologically according to the kind of sources they had at their disposal. They might for instance distinguish between the recent past, the last fifty to a hundred years when there were still men living who had themselves experienced the events or had heard the testimony of eyewitnesses, and the more distant past, which had to be reconstructed from written sources (Guenée, 1980: 80 ff.). But authority played a major role in medieval evaluation of sources and often precluded independent judgment (ibid.: 77 ff., 131 ff.). Further, medieval historians did not take what we consider the logical step from attributing higher value to the testimony of eyewitnesses to developing a general theory of the relative trustworthiness of sources. According to Guenée, the first discussion of this question in European historiography dates from 1498. Even explicit choices between conflicting testimony are very rare and unknown before the twelfth century (ibid.: 130).

Still, Snorri is a medieval and not a modern historian, and his achievement should not be exaggerated. Though both the fact that he classifies his sources and his method of classification appear very modern, it is by no means certain that he anticipates modern principles of source criticism. He deals with his groups of sources one by one, treating them as evidence for events taking place at different times. The point is thus not to make a choice between them. But some differences in trustworthiness are also involved. Though Snorri does not reject the information contained in the first group of sources, but refers to the fact that old and wise men have believed in it, he clearly regards the part of his work which is based on this information, the *Ynglinga saga,* as less trustworthy than the rest.

Ari and his sources receive the most detailed treatment. Ari was born one winter after the death of King Haraldr harðráði, that is, probably in 1068,[3] and knew directly or indirectly several persons who were born in the tenth century and could remember events that took place during the reigns of Óláfr Tryggvason, St. Óláfr, or even earlier.[4] They were old, wise, and had good memory and lived so near after the events that they had access to first- or secondhand evidence. This is stated in quite general terms, without a more exact account of their will and ability to tell the truth about each particular event. This view of historical evidence is in principle the same as the contemporary view of legal evidence. That is, the question of trustworthiness is not decided on through an examination of each particular point in the testimonies of the witnesses or material evidence, as in modern law, but on the basis of the general trustworthiness of the witnesses, which was in its turn largely dependent on reputation, social status, and in some cases formal rules specifying their proximity to the event in question. Snorri's method of reckoning back from Ari, via the old persons he knew, to the events themselves may be compared to the contemporary procedure in cases of *óðalsréttr* (hereditary right to property).[5]

In the case of scaldic poetry, Snorri refers to internal evaluation of evidence. This is quite natural in one sense. Scalds are evidently not there to tell the truth; no one would dream of suing them as legal evidence. Consequently, reasons must be given for their trustworthiness. Snorri chooses to accept everything the scalds serving a king tell in his own presence or before his sons about his journeys and battles ("ferðir eða orrostur") because they would not attribute to him what every one present knew he had not done; that would have been blame and not praise.[6] Though modern historians are inclined to be more skeptical on this point, Snorri here approaches the modern distinction between the "hard facts" contained in a source and its author's bias or embellishment. Further, he states the two important modern principles of preferring contemporary evidence and evidence that could be controlled. Finally, in *Prol. OH* he points to the *form* of the scaldic poems, which protects them against changes when they are transmitted from generation to generation, whereas ordinary stories are not always remembered correctly.[7] This principle, together with that of tracing the evidence back to its original source, serves as a criterion of evaluation of the first group of evidence. Poems composed after the events, which are not subject to control and whose evidence cannot be traced back to known and reliable witnesses, must clearly be considered the least trustworthy of Snorri's groups of evidence. Theoretically, this principle also allows Snorri to prefer scaldic poems to the evidence of Ari and his sources.[8]

The sources that Snorri presents in his prologue are only a small part of what he has used. He gives a few references to other sources later in his work, but he has evidently used a large number of written sources, some of which are now extant, which he does not mention at all. Why just this selection? Storm thinks that Snorri is here giving his critical principles, rather than enumerating his sources (1873: 92). However, both his discussion of his groups of sources one by one and his chronological arrangement make this less likely. Further, he confines himself entirely to the oldest period. The fact that he only mentions Ari among his written sources means that he is only concerned with events before his death (1148). In practice, he refers to no event after the death of Haraldr harðráði (1066) in the prologue. His summary of events stops with Haraldr hárfagri, and in accounting for Ari's sources, he is only concerned with persons who had information on events that took place in the early eleventh century or earlier. The most likely explanation must therefore be that the relatively recent past, for which he drew a large part of his materials from sources that are now extant, presented no particular problem from the point of view of source criticism.[9] His written sources may have been well known, and there were still men alive who had second- or even firsthand information on events that took place after the mid-twelfth century.

Further, Snorri has hardly derived very much of his information on the earliest period from Ari, though his detailed reference to his sources seems to suggest this. Ari's history of the Norwegian kings must have been very short, according to most scholars mainly consisting of chronological information. In any case, it cannot have contained more than a small percentage of *Heimskringla*'s material from the period before 1148 (Ellehøj, 1965: 43 ff.). For most of this period, works that are now extant must have been far more important as sources, such as Oddr munkr's *Saga Óláfs Tryggvasonar* and the early sagas of St. Óláfr. Both these kings, particularly the latter, were well known to Snorri's audience, who most probably also knew the written sagas. Even events that took place as far back as the late tenth century thus seem to have presented no particular problem to Snorri, when there was evidence available in the form of written sagas. Consequently, his critical principles apply mainly to the period before the accession of Óláfr Tryggvason, that is, 995.

Admittedly, Snorri does occasionally refer to sources for later periods as well. But the reason for these references is usually some special problem or event. There had evidently been different opinions on the length of St. Óláfr's reign (see later discussion), and Snorri appeals to well-known authorities as Ari and Sigvatr to confirm his own interpretation. He mentions witnesses who had seen a particular gift from King Haraldr harðráði to Steigar-Þórir (*HHarð.* chap. 24), probably not so much as evidence as to give additional information on its continued existence. He refers to eyewitnesses to some events concerning the battle of Holmengrå (1139) where the pretender Sigurðr slembir was defeated and captured, such as the fate of some of Sigurðr's adherents and the torture of Sigurðr (*Ingi* chaps. 10–12). These eyewitnesses had told their stories to Eiríkr Oddsson, who had written them down in his *Hryggjarstykki.*[10] In the story of the fate of Ívarr skrauthanki, later bishop of Nidaros, and his close friend Ívarr dynta, both adherents of Sigurðr and Magnús, of whom the former was saved and the latter killed, the reference to the sources serves to add a personal touch: Guðríðr Birgisdóttir, who told this story to Eiríkr Oddsson, had heard Ívarr skrauthanki say that it was the worst that had ever happened to him when Ívarr dynta was led away to be killed and bade his friends farewell. And Sigurðr slembir behaved with such extreme dignity and self-control when he was tortured, that it might seem incredible, if it were not attested to by a trustworthy witness. This is an example of the normal way of using eyewitnesses in the Middle Ages, which is above all to be found in miracle stories: the more extraordinary the event, the greater the need of a trustworthy witness. By contrast, ordinary events from the relatively recent past are normally believed if there are no particular reasons against believing it (see Schoebe, 1965: 647 f.; Guenée, 1980: 131).

The reference to Hallfrøðr vandræðaskáld as a source for events during the reign of Óláfr Tryggvason (OT chap. 83: 407) seems to amount to a general account of sources. Storm even gives examples of

Snorri revising Oddr munkr's account through information derived from Hallfrøðr's verses (1873: 136 f.; see also discussion below). But he does not do this consistently and evidently trusts Oddr to a great extent. The reference to Hallfrøðr should perhaps be better understood as information on the particular importance of this man than as a statement on Snorri's use of his sources. There is a similar reference to scalds as eyewitnesses in the account of the battle of Stiklestad. Snorri names three scalds whom Óláfr places in a shield castle, ordering them to compose verses on what goes on in the battle (OH ch. 206). But the scalds were killed during the battle and none of them is therefore quoted in Snorri's actual report of it, which is based on the verses of Sigvatr, who was not present (e.g., chaps. 206, 212, 213, 224 ff.), and on other sources. Thus, the story is probably intended more as a description of Óláfr and his relationship to his scalds than as an account of Snorri's sources.

Finally, Snorri has the following comment in his characterization of Haraldr harðráði:

> Yet many more of his famous deeds have not been set down, both because of our lack of information and because we do not wish to put down in writing stories not sufficiently witnessed. Even though we have heard mentioned, or touched upon, a number of things, it seems better that they be added later, rather than that they need to be omitted then. Much about King Harald is incorporated in poems delivered by Icelanders before him or his sons. For that reason he was a great friend of theirs.[11]

This passage is not Snorri's original creation; it occurs in exactly the same form in *Fagrskinna* (*Fsk.* chap. 47: 202 f.) and thus need not express Snorri's critical principles at all. Given Snorri's independence and critical ability, however, we cannot exclude the possibility that he has done some research concerning Haraldr's deeds and copied the passage because it suited his own purpose. Even so, it is difficult to regard it as evidence of a consistent application of the critical principles stated in the prologue. Though Snorri mentions scalds, his intention is certainly not to use them to examine critically the works of his predecessors, *Morkinskinna* and *Fagrskinna*. The reference to Haraldr's interests in scalds is probably equally important as the reference to them as sources. Admittedly, Snorri does use the scalds extensively in his account of Haraldr's career in Byzantium. But so do the authors of *Morkinskinna* and *Fagrskinna*. Snorri must have used both the two latter, and, as usually, steered a middle way between them, including some but not all of *Morkinskinna*'s stories (Storm, 1873: 179 f.; Indrebø, 1917: 201 ff.). The reference to information that is not included in *Fagrskinna* and *Heimskringla* may possibly be to *Morkinskinna,* in addition to oral information ("heyrt roeður"). Snorri's reason for discussing sources in this connection may be that the events took place in a distant part of the world and accordingly were difficult to verify, in the same way as events from a distant past. Moreover, the function of this passage is more to emphasize Haraldr's greatness than to evaluate the sources critically: the passage clearly states that Haraldr performed more deeds than those that are included in *Heimskringla.* In mentioning the number of deeds that are not included, the author is able to convince his readers both of the absolute trustworthiness of those that are and of the likelihood that Haraldr was an even greater hero than he appears in the pages of *Heimskringla.*

Snorri's attitude to source criticism in practice can only be known through a detailed examination of his use of his sources throughout *Heimskringla,* which I shall not attempt here. From his explicit references to such matters in the prologue and other places, however, it seems that source criticism to Snorri, in contrast to modern historians, is not there to be exercised all the time, but only on particular occasions, regarding events that seem hard to believe or happening in distant times or places.[12] This means that Snorri is closer to medieval ideas of source criticism than it might appear at first sight, and accordingly there is a wide gap between his concept of historical scholarship and that of modern historians, which also has consequences for his notion of himself as an author.

First, Snorri is mainly concerned with testimony of witnesses, not with evidence. His statement in the prologue is an example of what Collingwood calls "scissors and paste history" (1966: 257 ff.). The historian is not an independent author who recreates the past according to his own imagination and critical evaluation of the evidence. He is simply a "writer" who copies or writes down the written or oral narratives of other men after some initial examination of their trustworthiness. Characteristically, there are several examples of Snorri directly copying passages from his predecessors, and there would certainly be more, if all his sources had been preserved. Like other saga writers he tries to harmonize different versions of the same event, often including both in his narrative. He is only much more clever in this art than his contemporaries, so that his steps are more difficult to trace (Nordal, 1973: 151 f.). Thus, he avoids as far as possible to use the principles stated in the prologue to choose between his sources. In this respect, he more resembles an editor than an author in the modern sense. Steblin-Kamensky's observations on terminology (mentioned earlier) also seem highly relevant here. In addition, we may point to the word *saga,* which is used both for the oral or written story of an individual event and for the continuous narrative in literary form. This is further evidence of the concept of "author" as a person who put together histories that already existed: the real history was the event itself, which could be told by various people and finally written down (Weber, 1972: 197 f.). The vague definition of a historical work is also expressed in the fact that the "sagas," that is, the works as we understand them, were freely extended, abbreviated, or mingled with one another in the process of transcription. It is also significant, as Steblin-Kamensky points out (1973: 52 ff.), that most saga authors are anonymous. Admittedly, we know Snorri's name, but only indirectly: Snorri has apparently not found it worthwhile to give his name in the prologue. This is in clear contrast to the custom in scaldic poetry. Most scalds are known by name. Snorri himself may once more serve as an example: he was duly recorded as the author of a laudatory poem to Earl Skúli during his first trip to Norway. The reason for this difference seems to be that it was considered an art to compose a scaldic poem. The art in this case did not consist in telling a story, but in the particular, highly developed verbal embroidery, which needed a real craftsman. A story was not created in the same sense, it was simply ancient memory written down.

Second, there is not a single word in the prologue on the choice of material for Snorri's work. The main theme is defined as the stories (frásagnir) of "the princes who have held kingdom in the Northern countries and who have spoken Danish tongue [i.e., the language of the Nordic countries]." As most of Snorri's work deals with Norway, this is inaccurate. The main point, however, is that "history" is something given, in practice contained in the written and oral testimony from the past. There is no question of choosing between more or less relevant information, of explaining or in other ways relating events to each other or of creating a coherent story out of scattered materials. So far, Steblin-Kamensky seems to be right.

However, this is not all there is to say. Though there is hardly reason to be very optimistic regarding Snorri's trustworthiness as a source for older Norwegian history, his account of his sources and methods show him as more than simply a copyist. He has criteria that enable him to distinguish between more and less trustworthy information and even to some extent to choose between conflicting evidence. Though he is not a modern, critical historian, his reflections on these matters in the prologue are truly remarkable by medieval standards. This means that he must also be more than a compiler. Though not necessarily an author in the modern sense, he seems to have examined his materials closely and reflected on what to include or not. This impression is further confirmed by his actual use of his sources. Though Storm probably goes too far in treating him like a modern historian, his comparison of Snorri and his predecessors gives an impressive picture of an independent and orderly mind, who clears up inconsistencies and creates a coherent account (Storm, 1873: 104 ff.), frequently rejecting material that is contained in his sources, though probably more out of regard for relevance than for trustworthiness. Though I do not intend to examine Snorri from point of view of source criticism, my own research in the following will confirm Storm's general impression. Further, Snorri's prologue is not necessarily evidence of a specifically medieval attitude. Statements similar to Snorri's can be found in numerous historians from the recent past; after all, Collingwood applied his term to a considerable part of nineteenth-century historiography and not only to that of Antiquity and the Middle Ages (1966: 258 ff.).[13]

Snorri's Chronology

The chronology of Snorri and other saga writers has received considerable attention from modern historians. This has mostly had a practical reason. As chronology is fundamental to any examination of historical development and that of early Norwegian history raises considerable problems, much research has been directed at sorting out these problems. In this context, I am not interested in the chronological order in which the events told by Snorri took place—if they took place at all—nor in Snorri's correctness in this respect. I am interested, first, in chronology as a clue to Snorri's arrangement of his material and second, in his attitude to time.

Composition and chronology are closely interrelated in historical works and present a problem that is familiar even to modern historians: chronological or thematic arrangement? On the one hand, as history deals with time, an exact chronology is fundamental to explanation. On the other hand, the story should have inner coherence. Then, how should one present two chains of events that happen at the same time in different places? And how should minor events, unrelated to the main stories but nevertheless of some importance, and structural observations be integrated? Modern historians, who are not simply telling stories but analyze societies and social change, have of course various methods of solving such problems which were not available to their medieval predecessors. In the Middle Ages we can in principle distinguish between two solutions, the annalistic presentation, according to which each separate event is told in strict chronological sequence, and storytelling, in which the author tries to tell a coherent story. In practice we normally find intermediate forms. In the North, Ari's *Íslendingabók* is in most respects an example of the former arrangement. His narrative is mostly short and dry, whereas he exerts himself in placing persons and events on a fixed time-scale. His chrononological framework is the succession of Icelandic *lǫgsǫgumenn* but at strategic points, he links this time-reckoning to the "absolute" Christian chronology (Einarsdóttir, 1964: 42 ff.). The secular historiography of the medieval North, the genuine sagas, clearly belongs to the second category, in giving priority to narrative. Nevertheless, the kings' sagas in general and *Heimskringla* in particular pay considerable attention to exact chronology. Snorri tries—largely successfully—to combine the two principles. In this respect he differs from his Danish counterparts Svend Aggesen and Saxo, who have no chronological framework and do not indicate the length of time between the events (Einarsdóttir, 1964: 240). The Icelandic family sagas are also generally less precise than Snorri in this respect (ibid.: 243 ff.).

Snorri's normal chronological arrangement is the following. He gives the king's age at his accession and the length of the reign. Within this framework he places the stories that usually fill most of the reign. Each story has normally its own, "inner" chronology, like in the Icelandic sagas, often quite exact. They are often but not always linked to the main chronology of the reign through a starting point or an end. Snorri thus does not normally follow the annalistic principle of linking each separate event directly to the "absolute" chronology of the reign, though he is very often able to give the same chronological information. In the last part of *Heimskringla,* dealing with the civil wars 1130–1177, the whole story of the conflicts is dated fairly exactly, whereas the "empty" time, the peaceful periods in between, is measured. All major events can thus be placed within a fixed time sequence. This was a period where the sources were fairly good. It was also a period full of dramatic events. Consequently, most of the saga is concerned with the protagonists in the wars. The point of view varies. The story of the pretender Sigurðr slembir (1136–1139) is to a large extent told from his point of view, whereas in the period from 1155 on, the story is mainly told from the point of view of the Ingi-party. But like in *Sverris saga* and other parts of *Heimskringla,* sudden shifts in point of view are used for dramatic effect.

The beginning of the period is the death of King Sigurðr jórsalafari the day after the feast of the Annunciation at the age of forty, when he had ruled twenty-seven years, (26 March 1130, *Msyn.* chap. 33). This marks the first winter of the co-reign between his son Magnús and his brother Haraldr gilli. In their fourth winter, (1133–1134), they start to quarrel, and war breaks out. The day before the feast of St. Lawrence (9 August 1134) they fight the battle of Fyrileif (MB.HG chaps. 1–3). Haraldr is defeated and flees to Denmark, but returns the same autumn, establishes himself in Viken, assembles a fleet, and goes westward to attack Magnús in Bergen (MB.HG chaps. 3–4). Snorri gives no date for these events, until Haraldr turns up in Bergen on Christmas

Eve. The battle in Bergen then takes place after the Christmas celebrations, on *affaradagr jolinna* (twelfth night, 7 January 1135, MB.HG chaps. 6–7). Haraldr wins, and Magnús is taken captive, blinded, castrated, and put in a monastery.

The saga continues in largely the same way. In wartime the movements of the parties are normally dated approximately by time of the year.[14] It is usually indicated where they spent winter (e.g., ME chaps. 4, 9 and the examples in n. 14). Occasionally, the exact day on which the event took place is indicated.[15] This is usually the case with larger battles, although, curiously enough, the battle ending the work, that of Ré, is left undated.[16] Exact dates are also used for dramatic effect, as in the story of the battle of Sekken in 1162 and Erlingr skakki's sudden attack on Nidaros in 1165.[17] The peaceful periods are "empty time," but they are measured so as to make it possible to place the events within a fixed chronology. Scattered miracles of St. Óláfr, other isolated events, and "structural passages" (characterizations of persons, etc.) are left undated, but are placed on natural interludes between major events.[18] Compared to other sagas of *Heimskringla* there are few such passages in this part of the work. The chronological order is strictly preserved, except for short biographical notes when people are introduced into the main action.

This part of *Heimskringla* shows Snorri at work on the most well-documented period he was covering. He had at his disposal a fairly fixed chronology, of which he only made relatively minor modifications. Further, there was generally one story to tell, the war between the pretenders. The few events that did not belong to this story, such as the attacks of the Wends, the visit of Cardinal Nicholas, and some miracles of St. Óláfr, could easily be fitted in at interludes in the main story. The earlier parts of *Heimskringla* present greater difficulties. But there is no direct correspondence between the exactness of Snorri's chronology and the amount of chronological information at his disposal. The clearest example of this is the saga of St. Óláfr.

The Composition of *Óláfs saga*

The saga of St. Óláfr is by far the longest in *Heimskringla,* comprising about one-third of the work or over five hundred pages in Finnur Jónsson's edition. It is also commonly regarded as Snorri's masterpiece, full of dramatic stories, great "scenes," and vivid descriptions of character. At the same time, its chronology is as exact as that of the sagas of the period of the civil wars, and Snorri largely succeeds in making a coherent whole of the mass of separate events that took place during the great king's reign. How has he managed this?

Though we do not know all of Snorri's sources, it seems unlikely that any of them has contained a very exact chronology of the reign of St. Óláfr. A large number of the events Snorri relates are also found in earlier sagas, notably the *Legendary Saga,* but most of them are not dated, neither relatively nor absolutely. Such stories (þættir) normally have only inner, relative chronology. A fixed chronology of the reign must therefore have been worked out at a fairly late date, and given Snorri's power of construction and ability as a historian, he is much more likely to have done it than some predecessor of whom little is known, as for instance Styrmir Kárason. This is common opinion among scholars (Storm, 1873: 156 f.; Koht, 1921: 127 ff.; Aðalbjarnarson, 1945: lxxxviii ff.; Einarsdóttir, 1964: 234 ff.).

Only rarely did Snorri have exact chronological information at his disposal. He discusses the length of Óláfr's reign in some detail, referring to earlier sources: Óláfr had ruled the country for fifteen years when he went into exile, including the first winter, when Earl Sveinn was also the ruler of the country. He spent one winter in exile, which makes his whole reign sixteen winters (OH chap. 179: 416 f.). The battle of Stiklestad, in which Óláfr was killed, took place on 29 July, which Snorri dates according to the Roman calendar.[19] Snorri does not give the year according to Christian reckoning, but his relative chronology indicates 1030, which is the one that is generally accepted by scholars. Óláfr must then have arrived in Norway in the autumn 1014 and defeated his adversaries in the battle of Nesjar the next spring. Modern historians date these events one year later, thus giving Óláfr a reign that is one year shorter.[20] Further, Snorri could derive some chronological information on Óláfr's life as a Viking and the rule of the earls Eiríkr and Sveinn from his predecessors, which can also to some extent be controlled by other sources (Johnsen, 1916a; Koht, 1921: 124 ff.). Within his reign, however, there are few "fixed points."[21] The problem of chronology then turns into a problem of composition. Which are the principles governing Snorri's chronological arrangement?

The saga can conveniently be divided into four parts:

1. Óláfr's career until he becomes king of Norway (chaps. 1–56). Apart from short glimpses from his childhood, Snorri begins his story of Óláfr when he went on his first Viking expedition at the age of twelve. He then tells fairly briefly of his various raids, battles, and exploits in the Baltic and England (chaps. 1–20, 27–28), gives a sketch of the conditions in Norway, where the earls Eiríkr and Sveinn ruled in alliance with the great magnates, and then turns to Óláfr's return to his country and describes in great detail his way to the throne, ending with the battle of Nesjar.

2. Óláfr as king (chaps. 57–180). This is by far the longest part of the

saga, about 320 out of 530 pages in Finnur Jónsson's edition. It deals with the events following the battle of Nesjar until the alliance between King Cnut and the Norwegian magnates, which leads to Óláfr's deposition and his exile from the country, that is, the years 1015–1029 according to Snorri's chronology, 1016–1029 according to that of modern historians.

3. Óláfr's martyrdom. Here Snorri describes his journey through Norway and Sweden to Russia, his miracles and religious experiences during his exile, his decision to return, his journey back, which increasingly suggests his coming martyrdom, and then finally the battle of Stiklestad, in which he is killed (chaps. 181–229).

4. Óláfr as a saint and national symbol. This includes the miracles after his death, the growing belief in his sainthood and disappointment with the Danish rule, and finally the decision to make his son Magnús king (chaps. 230–251).

Parts one and three present no particular problems. They mostly contain straightforward narrative; Óláfr is the hero, and his actions are mainly told in the order they must have occurred, according to the logic of the story. In part four there are several themes and the scene shifts between them: Óláfr's burial and miracles, stories of some of his men after the battle, and the growing opposition against the Danish rulers. This part of the saga comes closest to the annalistic chronicle, although its central theme is the change in the people's attitude to Óláfr, partly because of his miracles, partly because of the harshness of the Danish rulers. The shifts of "scenes" are more frequent in this part than in one and three, but compared to two, the problems of composition are relatively small.

Part two, then, presents major problems of composition, as it contains a number of different stories, which to a considerable extent go on at the same time. Most of these events can be grouped under the following headings:

1. The conflict with the king of Sweden. This starts shortly after Óláfr's accession to the throne, in late winter 1015–1016, according to Snorri's chronology, and drags on until early 1018. It concerns both the king of Sweden's claim of supremacy over Norway after his victory over Óláfr's predecessor, Óláfr Tryggvason, in 1000, and a dispute over the borderline between Sweden and Eastern Norway. Having maintained his independence, Óláfr asks for peace and requests to marry the king of Sweden's daughter. There are long and delicate negotiations, the king of Sweden stubbornly resists Óláfr's offers, but is finally forced to submit by his own people (see discussion below).

2. The rest of Óláfr's "foreign policy." This concerns the Orkneys, the Faroe Islands, and Iceland, which he tries to submit under his rule, with more or less success.

3. Óláfr's conflicts with the Norwegian petty kings and magnates. This includes a number of stories, starting with the rebellion of the petty kings of Eastern Norway (the Oppland kings), who had originally supported him when he claimed the throne. The rebellion is put down, and Óláfr manages to capture all his five adversaries in one coup. Further, Óláfr's conflicts with the great magnates, Erlingr Skjálgsson, Einarr pambarskefir, and others, later in his reign belong here (see later discussion).

4. Óláfr's Christianization of Norway.

5. Comments on Óláfr as a ruler, his character and personal life.

6. Óláfr's conflict with King Cnut. This last topic is introduced in chapter 130, where Cnut sends an embassy to Norway to claim the throne, a claim that Óláfr scornfully rejects, and fills most of the remaining chapters of part two. Here Snorri describes Óláfr's raid against Denmark, together with the Swedish king Ǫnundr and their narrow escape from Cnut's army in the battle of Helgå. He goes on to tell of Cnut's expedition against Norway, in which he is accepted as king by the people, while Óláfr remains inactive in Eastern Norway. The conflict with Cnut gradually merges with the one with the magnates, who increasingly enter his service. The dramatic climax of both conflicts is Óláfr's expedition westward in winter, his battle against Erlingr Skjálgsson, who is taken captive after a heroic fight and killed against the kings order. The rebellion that follows makes Óláfr's exile inevitable.

In narrating these events, Snorri tries to combine the principles of strict chronology and internal coherence. Nearly all events are dated, and it is usually quite easy to follow Óláfr's movements and actions from time to time, often in considerable detail (see Einarsdóttir, 1964: 234 ff. and below, app.). Though there are some exceptions, Snorri normally breaks off longer stories in order to adhere to the chronological sequence. As this strict chronology is most probably Snorri's own invention, this seems very strange: why did he not choose the simplest way, treating the different stories in sequence and adapting his chronology to that? The reason must be some general principles governing the division of his material.

There are two such principles. The first is the main arrangement of the saga, which resembles a classical tragedy, describing the hero's initial success, then the turning point and his ultimate failure and death. In addition, Snorri's Óláfr saga has a final part, dealing with the hero's victory after death.[22] This perspective is underlined by Snorri himself both in his own comment on Óláfr's career after his exile (chap. 181), in Óláfr's own reflections on his past life, where he concludes that everything had gone well during the first ten years of his reign, whereas he had met with increasing difficulties the following five (chap. 187) and in Snorri's summary of Óláfr's reign so far in the summer after the tenth winter (1024). It is probably also significant that Snorri explicitly indicates that this was the tenth winter of Óláfr's reign, whereas in most cases the number has to be reconstructed from the context. As is evident both from Snorri's narrative and his summary, the story of Óláfr so far has been a series of successes. Afterward, it increasingly becomes a tragedy. This determines Snorri's main arrangement of the topics mentioned above.

Óláfr's most conspicuous successes, the peace with Sweden, the Christianization of Norway, and the victory over the Oppland kings naturally ought to take place in the beginning of the saga. The other events in Óláfr's foreign policy are to some extent divided according to their success or failure. His victory over the Orkney earls is placed early, his failure to gain control over Iceland and the Faroes comes toward the end of the saga. The central issue of Óláfr's internal policy, his conflicts with the magnates, mainly belongs to the later part of the saga, after Cnut's demand on Norway. Structural passages are placed in between, often on turning points. The presentation of Óláfr's normal life as a king comes immediately after his final conquest of the country, in connection with his first winter in Nidaros (chap. 57). After his exile, Snorri views his reign in retrospect, in order to explain why he was deposed by his people. In addition to his summary of Óláfr's successful years, Snorri gives a short summary of his achievements after the peace with Sweden.

This structure, however, is only able to explain Snorri's arrangement of his narrative in a very general way. To account for its detail, we have to turn to Snorri's second principle, which is Óláfr's itinerary. This evolves around his winter quarters, that is, three different places: Nidaros or Trøndelag, Opplandene, and Viken, usually Borg. In most cases Óláfr changes between these places according to a fixed pattern, the one indicated above. The exceptions to this are his three successive winters in Nidaros (1018–1021) and the stay in Borg instead of Opplandene in the fourteenth winter (1027–1028). It is notable that Óláfr never spends the winter in Western Norway and on the whole visits this part of the country sporadically. Snorri evidently regards this as a result of Erlingr Skjálgsson's strong position in the region. Most of Óláfr's visits here actually have to do with his conflict with Erlingr. A possible explanation to Snorri's belief in such a regular pattern is his reference to a rule forbidding the king to take *veitslur* in the same region more than every third year.[23] However, Snorri does not refer to this rule in connection with kings other than Óláfr.

This regular cycle of winter quarters enables Snorri to arrange most events in a logical fashion. The king's itinerary in summer is usually determined by his last winter quarter and that scheduled for the following winter. Events usually take place in the region where the king stays at the moment, whether or not the king directly takes part in them. Thus the negotiations with Sweden take place while Óláfr is in Viken, events in Trøndelag and Northern Norway while he is in Nidaros, and events concerning the Orkneys, the Faroes, and Iceland while he is in Trøndelag or Western Norway. This is the most likely explanation of Óláfr's prolonged stay in Trøndelag (1018–1021): he received important visits from emissaries from the Orkneys three successive years and thus had to stay in an appropriate place. Further, Snorri could conveniently place a number of Óláfr's successes in the north, including his visit to Northern Norway, within this period.

By combining the two principles, the contrast between Óláfr's successful and unsuccessful years and his itinerary, we can thus account for most of Snorri's chronological arrangement, including some episodes that may at first sight appear strange. The story of the negotiations with the Swedish king falls in three parts (chaps. 67–72, 77–80 and 87–94), each divided by some chronological distance, during which the story moves to other places and events. The first part ends late in 1017, when all attempts to move King Óláfr of Sweden seem to have been in vain. The next part starts in February the next year, with the meeting in Uppsala, and goes on until the messengers have returned to Óláfr with the news that the Swedish king has been forced to a settlement. Then the story logically turns back to Óláfr and his activities until he turns up at the border the following autumn, to wait in vain for the Swedish king to fulfill his promise of marrying his daughter to him. The rest of the story follows immediately upon this, namely Óláfr's marriage to Ástríðr and the rebellion in Sweden, which finally makes the Swedish king come to terms with Óláfr. This story is fairly long, covering about two years according to its internal chronology. It belongs logically to the early part of Óláfr's reign, and Snorri may even have been able to date it approximately through his knowledge of the succession of Swedish kings, as King Óláfr of Sweden died shortly after the peace with Norway (see n. 21). The story further demands Óláfr's presence in Eastern Norway, or at least makes it desirable, since the envoys return to him. Then logically some other events in Eastern Norway ought to take place at the same time. If not, Snorri had to keep Óláfr in Eastern Norway over a very long period, to be able to fit in the story of the Oppland kings. Moreover, this story actually plays a role in the story of the negotiations with Sweden, since the Swedish princess Ingigerðr refers to it when comparing her father's success in hunting with Óláfr's in capturing the five kings.

Snorri usually mentions Óláfr's activity in establishing or strengthening Christianity when arriving in new places. His main achievement in this respect concerns the inner regions of the country, his predecessor

Óláfr Tryggvason having converted the coast. The real narrative of
Óláfr's Christianization, however, is concentrated in two places, chapters 104 to 114, dealing with Northern Norway, Trøndelag, and the inner
regions of Eastern Norway, and chapter 121, dealing with the inner
regions of Western Norway, including Valdres. According to the chronology of the saga, the former takes place in 1019–1021 and the latter in
1023. As mentioned earlier, this topic naturally belongs to the successful
early part of the reign. But why just these years?

According to Snorri, Óláfr visits Northern Norway only once in his
reign, which is natural, considering the distance. The most convenient
time is between two winters in Nidaros, that is, either 1019 or 1020, of
which years Snorri chooses the former. The final establishment of Christianity in Trøndelag must evidently have taken place during one of the
king's visits there. This gives the following choices: 1015–1016, 1019–
1021, or 1026–1027. The years 1019–1021 are ideal, both because of the
length of the king's stay there and the general lack of dramatic events
between his conflict with Sweden early in his reign and with Denmark
toward its end. Although the winter 1015–1016 would have been a possible alternative, 1026–1027—after the turning point—is clearly too late,
as the coup against Ǫlvi was also one of Óláfr's political successes, which
allowed him to establish one of his most faithful men in this important
region. Further, in choosing the last of Óláfr's successive winters in
Nidaros, Snorri is able to devote a longer sequence solely to Óláfr's
efforts for Christianity: having killed Ǫlvi at Egge and suppressed pagan
cultism in Inner Trøndelag, Óláfr travels southward through the inner
regions and wins them for Christianity, an activity that reaches its dramatic climax in the victory over Dala-Guðbrandr.[24] This activity then
brings the king to his scheduled winter quarter, Opplandene. To his
evident satisfaction, Snorri is thus able to concentrate a large part of
Óláfr's work for Christianity in a continuous narrative. The inner region
of Western Norway, however, does not fit in with this itinerary and is
accordingly postponed until a more suitable occasion. This turns up two
years later in connection with another story, which brings Óláfr to Western Norway, the story of Ásbjǫrn selsbani.

This story has a crucial function in the saga. It brings Óláfr into
conflict with two of the mightiest men in the country, Erlingr Skjálgsson
at Sola and Þórir hundr at Bjarkøy, thereby introducing the central
theme of the second half of the saga: Óláfr's fall. It also shows one of the
reasons for the magnates' rebellion against Óláfr, his refusal to accept a
compromise and his insistence on punishing all violations of the royal
dignity. In the saga it is the first of a series of such stories. According to
Snorri, Ásbjǫrn's first expedition to Southern Norway to buy grain takes
place in the autumn of 1022 and his return and killing of Selþórir the

next spring. This latter event involves the king and must accordingly be fitted in with his itinerary. The best time for a journey to Western Norway is a year when the king has spent the winter in Viken and will spend the next in Nidaros. This makes it natural for him to sail along the coast, thus avoiding taking *veitslur* at Opplandene, where, according to normal schedule, he had spent the previous winter. The fact that the story takes place at Easter-time is a further argument for this. Though it is clearly not impossible to go from any of the other winter quarters to Karmøy at this time of the year—after all, Ásbjǫrn came the whole way from Northern Norway—the best starting point for such a journey is evidently Viken. Óláfr's early visit to Karmøy is also a good opportunity to continue the story of his Christianization by including the inner regions of Western Norway. Having finished his work in Valdres, the king continues his journey over land to his winter quarter in Nidaros.

In order to fit in all of this, Snorri had to choose between the following years: 1019, 1023, or 1026. The year 1019 is too early, as Óláfr spends most of the year in Eastern Norway in order to arrive at a settlement with the king of Sweden and only goes to Nidaros late in the year. And because of the events taking place in the aftermath of the story, 1026 is too late.[25] The year 1023, however, is ideal from still another point of view: it is immediately before the turning point, to which the story of Ásbjǫrn actually contributes. It thus introduces one of the central themes of the latter half of the saga, the conflict between Óláfr and the magnates, which, in connection with King Cnut's attack, leads to Óláfr's exile.

In his summaries of Óláfr's reign, Snorri distinguishes between his first ten years, which were successful, and his last five, which were increasingly difficult. From a strictly chronological point of view, the turning point ought to take place in 1024. The summary of Óláfr's reign that summer comes shortly after Ásbjǫrn's death. Óláfr suffered a setback when Erlingr Skjálgsson forced him to accept indemnity for Ásbjǫrn's offense the year before and further when Ásbjǫrn broke his promise of replacing Selþórir as *ármaðr*. With Ásbjǫrn killed, Óláfr had had his revenge, and the conflict had turned out well so far. On the other hand, the strong pressure on Þórir hundr from his sister-in-law, Asbjǫrn's mother, to take revenge was an ill omen for the future, thus indicating a turning point in Óláfr's reign. The events occurring immediately after Snorri's summary, the beginning of the stories of Óláfr's attempts to gain control over Iceland and the Faroes, are not very dramatic. Both attempts turn out to be failures, however, and are therefore appropriately placed just here.

The real turning point comes the next year, when Cnut sends an embassy to demand submission. In this context, Snorri not only points to the danger from the external enemy but also to the internal opposition, which Cnut seeks to mobilize against Óláfr. The reference to Erlingr Skjálgsson's sons who enter Cnut's service in England serves as an example of this. He has already anticipated this theme both with the story of Ásbjǫrn selsbani and with his information on Einarr þambarskelfir's meeting with Cnut in England in 1023. The conflict with Cnut and the growing opposition from the magnates then become the main themes of the second half of Óláfr's reign.

In this part of the saga much of the action takes place in the border regions and Eastern Norway. Snorri does not, however, depart from his normal rhythm, and allows Óláfr a last stay in Nidaros, in 1026–1027. A series of conflicts with magnates in Trøndelag and the north is clustered around this stay. Furthermore, the last events concerning Óláfr's foreign policy are presented here, the failure of his attempts to include Iceland and the Faroes under his dominion. Since journeys to and from these islands normally started and ended in Trøndelag or Western Norway, it was convenient to have the king here at the time. Accordingly, these events take place around the year 1026, despite the fact that Óláfr must have been rather busy at the time defending his kingdom against Cnut.

Thus, Snorri's chronology is clearly a construction, based on a few principles. It gives a certain unity and coherence to the apparently chaotic mass of events of Óláfr's reign and serves to emphasize the dramatic contrast between his successful first ten years and the increasing failure of the last five. Further, the regular winter quarters enable Snorri to give a clear and logical account of his movements and to have the king in the right place when messengers turn up from abroad. His construction is thus evidence of his interest in chronology, his orderly mind, and not least his main purpose in writing the saga.

From a literary point of view, Snorri's arrangement of his material is an example of interlacing or stranding, which is a well-known technique in medieval literature, including the Old Norse sagas (Vinaver, 1971: 68 ff.; Clover, 1982: 68 ff.). Both Snorri and other saga writers use it for literary effect, for instance when preparing a battle or a dramatic encounter by describing alternately the movements of the two parties.[26] In the story of Ásbjǫrn selsbani, Snorri very effectfully shifts the "scene" to create dramatic effect, from the king's court where Þórarinn Nefjólfsson is using all his cunning to postpone Ásbjǫrn's execution, to Skjálgr Erlingsson's meeting with his father and their mobilization to save Asbjǫrn.[27] The cuts in the longer stories, such as that of the negotiations between Norway and Sweden, are generally quite effective.

Thus, Snorri clearly belongs to a literary milieu that admired such shifts of scene in narrative. This may have made his compromise between coherent narrative and strict chronology easier to achieve, though the main reason for this arrangement is to be found in the principles referred to above, rather than in aesthetic considerations. It is not strictly speaking a compromise between chronology and internal coherence. Rather, by sacrificing the internal coherence of each particular story, Snorri achieves the greater coherence of Óláfr's reign as a whole.

The Composition of the Other Sagas of *Heimskringla*

The sagas we have considered hitherto are the most structured of the whole of *Heimskringla*. The relatively recent civil wars offered Snorri exceptional opportunities for composing a detailed and coherent story with a strict chronology, whereas the wealth of material and the unusual importance of St. Óláfr's reign inspired him to a great and bold construction. The rest of the sagas are more loosely structured, but according to the same basic ideas.

The short saga of Hálfdan svarti, of whom probably little was known, falls into two main parts: first, Hálfdan's battles and conquests (chaps. 1–4) and second, his marriage, the birth of his son Haraldr, and the dreams about him and Hálfdan's death (chaps. 5–8). This latter part of the saga is actually a preparation for the next one, that of Haraldr hárfagri. Hálfdan is even subordinated to Haraldr through the fact that the story of his death is introduced through a Finn with occult powers telling Haraldr of it. Thus, Hálfdan's death is told in retrospect, which is a clear sign of subordinate importance. A "structural" passage, the characterization of Hálfdan and his reign, is placed within this part, between Ragnhildr's and Hálfdan's dreams and the birth of King Haraldr, thus ending the part in which Hálfdan himself is the protagonist to introduce his much greater son (chap. 7). Snorri gives the length of Hálfdan's reign and dates his accession to the kingdom of Agder to his eighteenth year (chaps 1, 9) but has no exact chronology apart from that. However, he often gives relative chronology within the various campaigns (e.g., chaps. 3–4).

Haraldr hárfagri's conquest of Norway forms an almost continuous story, which fills most of the first half of his saga (chaps. 1–23). The saga starts with Haraldr's problems immediately after his succession, when he is attacked by the neighboring kings. Having repelled these attacks, he gets the idea of conquering Norway from Gyða, who refuses to become his mistress unless he rules the whole of Norway, and he promises not to cut his hair until he has done so. Snorri is apparently the first to create a coherent story out of this conquest,[28] that is, if he is also the author of *Egils saga,* which is usually believed to be earlier than *Heimskringla*. According to both these sagas, Haraldr starts his conquest by going north, through Opplandene, conquers Trøndelag, allying himself with

Earl Hákon at Lade, and then finally moves south along the coast of
Western Norway, until he has conquered Sogn (*HHárf.* chaps. 3–12;
Egils saga chap. 3). This part of the conquest, which lasts for four years,
has a quite exact internal chronology, but is not dated by years of
Haraldr's reign. The story in *Heimskringla* is broken off through one
structural passage on Haraldr's government and administration (chap.
6). After Haraldr's conquest of Sogn, the story is broken off in a curious
way, Haraldr setting off to Eastern Norway, where he is attacked by the
king of Sweden (chaps. 13–17). After Haraldr's victory here and a short
reference to the first sons born to him, Snorri turns to the battle of
Hafrsfjord, though without really linking it to what has happened before, neither chronologically nor causally (chap. 18; see below). The
final stage in the conquest is the expedition to the Orkneys (chap. 22),
after which Snorri comments that Haraldr had conquered the whole of
Norway in ten years and could now cut his hair. However, Snorri does
not quite seem to have made up his mind whether the conquest was
finished at this point or if it had been already completed after the battle
of Hafrsfjord, when he lets Haraldr marry Gyða (chap. 20).

In any case, the end of the conquest offers Snorri the opportunity to
comment on various matters of more subordinate interest to the main
story, such as the emigration of various magnates to Iceland and other
islands in the West and Haraldr's children and their descendants (chaps.
19, 21). The second half of the saga (chaps. 23–43) is more loosely
structured, containing various stories of Haraldr and above all his sons.
It is arranged in a quasi-annalistic way, dating the events by decades in
Haraldr's life. It ends with his death, a short characterization of him,
and an interpretation of his mother's dream, which also summarizes his
life and achievements (chap. 42). Then there is a short chapter on Eiríkr
blóðøx, his eldest son and successor as supreme king.

The next saga, of Haraldr's youngest son Hákon, who expelled his
elder brother and ruled the country for twenty-six years according to
Snorri's chronology, has three main stories, the events relating to Hákon's accession to the throne (chaps. 1–8), Hákon's attempt to Christianize Norway and his conflict with the people of Trøndelag because of this
(chaps. 13–18), and the Eiríkssons' (Eiríkr blóðøx's sons) repeated attacks against Norway until Hákon's death in the battle of Fitjar (chaps.
19–32). Between the first and the second stories, Snorri collects some
background information concerning the Eiríkssons and their stay in Denmark, on Tryggvi Óláfsson—Óláfr Tryggvason's father—on the early
history of Jämtland, which now accepted Hákon as king, and gives a
characterization of Hákon as a ruler. By contrast, the third story follows
immediately upon the second. This link is not only chronological but
causal. Snorri ends his story of Hákon's attempt at Christianization by

telling that he was assembling an army and that there were rumors that he intended to use it against the pagan population of Trøndelag. Then he learned that the Eiríkssons were attacking Viken and had to use his army against them instead (chap. 20). After this, there is no question of Christianization. Snorri's explanation is not quite convincing, as there are long periods of peace between the Eiríkssons' attack. The first of these is not dated, but it clearly took place long before the second, which Snorri dates to Hákon's twentieth year. The third attack then came six years after this one. If Hákon really had intended to use force against the people of Trøndelag, he would have had ample time to do so between the attacks from Denmark. A piece of information concerning Hákon as a ruler is attached to the story of the Eiríkssons, namely the introduction of the *leiðangr*, the people's defense organization (chap. 20). Compared to the preceding saga, that of Hákon thus appears very well structured. A considerable part of this structure, however, was established already before Snorri in *Ágrip* and *Fagrskinna*.[29]

The next saga deals with Hákon's successors, the Eiríkssons, who are introduced already in Hákon's saga, in connection with their attacks on him. The main theme of this saga is the war between the kings and the earls of Lade, the rulers of Trøndelag, first Sigurðr, who is killed by treachery, then his son Hákon, who fights to revenge his father and maintain his position as the ruler of Trøndelag. This war is divided into two parts (chaps. 3–6 and 9–13) by a peace settlement lasting for three years. The Eiríkssons' fight against the earls of Lade is part of their general policy of exterminating their rivals, which also makes them attack the petty kings of Eastern Norway. The link between these two stories is formed by their belief—correct or not—in an alliance between Earl Hákon and the latter and the renewal of the war between the kings and Hákon as a consequence of their killing the petty kings Tryggvi and Guðrøðr. The saga thus has a strong unity. Some structural passages, characterizations of the kings and their rule and episodes not related to the main story, are placed at the beginning or end of the saga and during the peace interval (chaps. 1–2, 7–8, 14–16). The death of two of the brothers are told toward the end of the saga, but the reign of the rest continues into the next saga, that of Óláfr Tryggvason. Though the facts told here are found in the earlier sagas as well, Snorri seems to be the first to link them together to a coherent story.[30]

The story of the Eiríkssons and Hákon continues in the next saga, of Óláfr Tryggvason, alternating with Óláfr's early life (chaps. 1–50; see below). This arrangement is found in only one of Snorri's predecessors, Oddr munkr (see below). All the others tell the story of Óláfr after the death of Earl Hákon. On the other hand, Snorri resembles his predecessors in making Earl Hákon the central person, and the events in which he takes part are mostly told from his point of view. The reign of Hákon forms more or less a separate saga in most of Snorri's predecessors. It consists of three main stories. The first is Hákon's intrigues in Denmark to destroy the friendship between King Haraldr Gormsson of Denmark and the Eiríkssons so as to conquer Norway (OT chaps. 9–18; see below). The second is Hákon's breach with him over the question of religion and the subsequent invasion of the *jómsvíkingar* and the battle of Hjǫrungavágr (OT chaps. 26–28, 33–42). The last is the story of Hákon's fall, in which the link with the parallel story of Óláfr's early life is established (OT chaps. 45–50). Between the main stories, there are shorter episodes, on Hákon's marriage and children and the early life of his son Eiríkr (chaps. 19–20), and the death of King Haraldr grenski and the birth of his son Óláfr, the future St. Óláfr (chaps. 43–44). As the stories of the two previous reigns, this is a logical and coherent story, but in contrast to them, the general arrangement is also found in Snorri's predecessors.[31]

The saga of Óláfr Tryggvason is the second longest in *Heimskringla* (about two hundred pages in Finnur Jónsson's edition). If we omit the fifty-eight pages dealing with Earl Hákon, Óláfr Tryggvason is still one of the kings that receives most attention. Only Haraldr harðráði (150 pages) and St. Óláfr (530 pages) can rival him. In the Norwegian and particularly the Icelandic tradition, including Snorri, Óláfr is the great missionary king—almost the equal of St. Óláfr—and at the same time the great warrior hero. Óláfr's saga contains three stories, his early life and accession to the throne (until chap. 50), his missionary activity in Norway and Iceland (chaps. 53–59, 65–84, 95–96), and his last battle at Svǫlð, where he is attacked by an overmighty fleet, led by the kings of Denmark and Sweden and the Norwegian Earl Eiríkr of Lade, and is defeated and probably killed after a heroic fight (chaps. 89–94, 97–113). As usual, structural passages and smaller episodes are spread between these stories. In this case, however, the main story is more often broken off, like in the saga of St. Óláfr, and for the same reason, namely, Snorri's wish to present a very exact chronology. The saga of Óláfr Tryggvason follows a sort of annalistic principle, according to which nearly all events are dated by years in Óláfr's reign. To achieve this, it is necessary to break off continuous stories, such as the Christianization of Norway, which could hardly have taken place during only one year, and the story of Óláfr's journey to Wendland, which eventually led to his fall at Svǫlð, in the year 1000, the same year that Iceland, according to commonly accepted tradition, was converted to Christianity. This arrangement is to a very large extent Snorri's achievement. Before him there are fairly detailed stories of Óláfr's early life, Earl Hákon's attempt to entice him to Norway to kill him, and the battle of Svǫlð, but these sagas give only the briefest summaries of his missionary activity (*Ágr.* chaps. 16–20; Theod. chaps. 7–14; HN: 111 ff.; *Fsk.* chaps. 21–22). The source for this, as for the rest of the stories Snorri tells of Óláfr, is Oddr munkr. Oddr is often a good storyteller, and many of his stories have been borrowed directly by Snorri. Oddr's work also contains some chronological information that Snorri could use. Generally, however, it is muddled and disorganized, and it is a considerable achievement to make the life and reign of Óláfr into the sort of coherent story that is found in *Heimskringla* (see Storm, 1873: 142 f.; Andersson, 1977).

After the reign of St. Óláfr, there follow the two eventful reigns of his son Magnús góði (the Good) and his half-brother Haraldr harðráði.[32] Both concern approximately the same kind of events: war against Denmark and the relationship to the Norwegian magnates. The saga of Magnús contains three stories, his accession to the throne—a continuation of the end of the saga of St. Óláfr—the expulsion of the Danish rulers and his peace with the Danish King Harthacnut (chaps. 1–6), his harsh rule and attempts to revenge his father and his "conversion" through Sigvatr's *Bersǫglisvísur* (chaps. 13–16), and his accession to the Danish throne and fight against the Wends and the Danish pretender Sveinn Úlfsson (chaps. 17–35). The saga ends with Magnús's attempt to gain England, from which he abstains through a letter from the English king (chaps. 36–37)—a deliberate contrast to the end of Haraldr's reign? Various minor episodes are then placed between the first and the second stories (chaps. 7–12).

Snorri then turns to the saga of Haraldr harðráði, which contains five stories: (1) Haraldr's early life as a mercenary in the service of the Greek emperor (chaps. 1–17); (2) his return to Norway, alliance with Sveinn Úlfsson against Magnús, Magnús's acceptance of him as his co-ruler, and their reign together until Magnús's death (chaps. 18–28); (3) Haraldr's war against Denmark (chaps. 29–35, 58–67, 71); (4) Haraldr's conflicts with various Norwegian magnates (chaps. 39–53, 69–70, 72–74); (5) Haraldr's expedition against England and his defeat and death in the battle of Stamford Bridge (chaps. 75–97). Structural passages, minor events, and miracles of St. Óláfr are placed at various points between these major events (chaps. 36–38, 54–57, 98–101). The chronology of this saga is far less strict than those of the two Óláfrs and the reason for the frequent changes between the war against Denmark and the internal conflicts with the Norwegian magnates is not chronological. The two conflicts are linked, above all through the person of Hákon Ívarsson, who leaves for Denmark because of his conflict with Haraldr. Having been reconciled with Haraldr, he saves the life of King Sveinn in the battle of Nissá, which leads to renewed conflict between him and Haraldr (chap. 68).

For the part of *Heimskringla* dealing with events after the battle of Stiklestad, Snorri relies more heavily on written sources, which are now to be found in *Fagrskinna* and *Morkinskinna*. *Morkinskinna* contains a number of stories about Magnús and the co-reign between him and Haraldr, from which Snorri has selected a few. *Fagrskinna* is usually shorter than *Heimskringla*. All sagas, however, basically deal with the same subjects, though Snorri is original in giving the story of Haraldr's negotiations with Hákon Ívarsson after killing Einarr þambarskelfir, and Hákon's subsequent defection to Denmark. This also means that the connection between the war with Denmark and the conflicts with the Norwegian magnates is more explicit in Snorri than in his predecessors.

The period between Haraldr's fall in the battle of Stamford Bridge (1066) and the death of King Sigurðr jórsalafari in 1130 is quite uneventful and accordingly treated briefly. The peaceful reign of Óláfr kyrri (1066–1093) has no story, and his saga is consequently the shortest in *Heimskringla,* containing only scattered comments and episodes. The reign of the Magnússons (1103–1030) is also fairly short and loosely structured. Apart from Sigurðr's journey to Jerusalem, there is no long, continuous story to tell. However, the competition between the kings (mannjafnaðr) gives Snorri the opportunity of describing a dramatic contrast (chap. 21; see below). Toward the end of the saga, Haraldr gilli turns up, presenting himself as Sigurðr's brother and being accepted at the court. This part then serves as a preparation for the coming conflict between him and his nephew Magnús. The saga between these two, of Magnús berfoetr (1093–1103), is more eventful and consequently arranged in the usual way. The major events are Magnús's accession to the throne and the rebellion against him (chaps. 1–7), his first and second expedition to the West (chaps. 8–11 and 23–25) and his conflict with Sweden (chaps. 12–15). Minor events and miracles of St. Óláfr are placed between the conflict with Sweden and the second expedition to the West (chaps. 16–22), whereas the characterization of the king comes at the end (chap. 26). Snorri's composition is here very similar to that of his sources, *Morkinskinna* and *Fagrskinna*. The main difference between these two is that *Fagrskinna* is shorter, keeping strictly to the main events of the kings' reigns, whereas *Morkinskinna* in addition contains a number of single stories in which the kings take part. The author of *Fagrskinna* has apparently found these stories less relevant to his main theme, and Snorri seems mostly to have been of the same opinion, though he includes some of them and is generally more detailed than the author of *Fagrskinna*.

As in the history of the civil wars and Óláfr's saga, Snorri tries to combine a strict chronology and coherent storytelling. How far he succeeds in this to some extent depends on what actually took place in the reign and the chronological information at his disposal. Normally, how-ever, each saga is constructed around a few great conflicts, which form its dominant theme, whereas events of minor importance, which are usually left undated, are placed in between the main stories. In this respect, Snorri adheres to the pattern established by his predecessors, notably the parts of *Fagrskinna* and *Morkinskinna* dealing with the pe-riod after the late eleventh century. For the older periods, however, this composition and above all the more strict chronology is in all likelihood Snorri's own achievement. The model must have been there before him, but he is the only historian to apply it to periods for which there was no chronological information available. He is also unique in another way: he is much more particular in telling the events in a strict chronological order.

The Concept of Time Implicit in Snorri's Chronology

Snorri's chronology can be considered a compromise between two principles, the "absolute" Christian chronology and the "relative" chro-nology of the traditional saga.[33] Though Snorri, in contrast to some other Norwegian and Icelandic historians, never links his chronology to the years after the birth of Christ, he has a consistent chronological framework for all the kings' reigns from Hálfdan svarti until the battle of Ré. Given one fixed point, which is easily supplied from other histori-ans, the whole series can be converted to the usual A.D. reckoning, which is frequently done in modern editions and translations.

However, these chronological systems are more than simply two meth-ods of reckoning; they have been considered evidence of two fundamen-tally different concepts of time (Steblin-Kamensky, 1973: 123 ff.; Gure-vich, 1983: 96 ff.). The saga chronology represents primitive time, which is immanent in the actions and events themselves and cannot be ab-stracted from them, whereas the learned chronology is just such an abstract scheme, which makes it possible to place any event on a fixed, linear time-scale. In the Icelandic family sagas time is only rarely to be separated from events. Occasionally, it is told that a winter, a year, and so forth passed between two events or that nothing happened over a certain period of time. But most often, the empty time between the events is not indicated; time passes only "within" the events. In a similar way, time is inseparably linked to the rhythm of nature and activity within agriculture, and so forth, in the time reckoning of everyday life, as is indicated in the laws and similar sources (see Hastrup, 1985: 17 ff.). I shall leave open the question of the exact difference between this idea of time and ours, whether it is impossible in primitive thought to imagine "empty time" or one is simply not interested in measuring time when nothing happens, although I am personally inclined to favor the latter opinion.[34]

Turning to the kings' sagas and *Heimskringla* in particular, we find that Snorri is clearly interested in measuring "empty time" and thus in fixing events on a time-scale. One may therefore conclude, as most modern historians seem to have done, that Snorri basically represents modern chronological principles in the garb of a somewhat different form of reckoning. If we compare Snorri to some of his predecessors, as for instance Oddr munkr, the author of the *Saga Ólafs Tryggvasonar,* we can easily see that he has taken a great step in the direction of modern chronology, ordering Oddr's chaotic mass of events into a fairly logical sequence, which allows us for the most part to follow the king's activity year by year. The same applies to the saga of St. Óláfr. If we had all Snorri's sources before us, we would no doubt have been able to trace his rearrangement and organization of his whole material. Concerning the last third of the work, the sagas from Haraldr harðráði on, we know most of Snorri's sources and can see that most of this work had already been done. If we compare Snorri with the earlier *Sverris saga,* which admittedly deals with recent events, we can also see that he is no pioneer in this respect, as this saga has also a clear and consistent chronology.

Why have the authors of the kings' sagas chosen this compromise? Since "empty time" is handled as well in the sagas as it is in the learned chronology, it is probably not a question of retaining as much as possible of "popular" chronology. The sagas are very different from annals, not primarily in being less exact in their chronology, for they may occasionally be very exact, but in their choice of materials. They contain relatively more "stories" in the real sense and less scattered information, and they are more directly concentrated on the kings' reigns. They are royal biographies or dynastic history, not general history. Consequently, the kings' life or reign becomes the most natural chronological unit. It therefore seems likely that the chronological arrangement is more than simply a way of measuring time but is used deliberately to structure the whole story.

As to modern historians, chronology was to Snorri and at least many of his contemporaries an ordering principle. To us, however, it is only that. The unit of measurement does not matter at all, whether it is the birth of Christ, the Muslim *hegira,* or the beginning of the French republic. To Snorri and his contemporaries it did matter. Time was still personal and could not as easily be abstracted from events. To use a particular way of reckoning time meant to place things in a particular context.

If we read through the whole of *Heimskringla,* we find considerable variations in the exactness of the chronology and the way events are dated. Evidently, the chronology becomes more exact in the more recent period than in the beginning of the saga, as Snorri became better informed. But this is by no means the whole explanation. The saga of St. Óláfr has the strictest chronology of all the sagas, although this was not based on very much exact information on Snorri's part. Moreover, throughout the work there are certain events that are normally dated, whereas others are not.

It is for instance curious that Snorri does not give the date of Cardinal Nicholas Brekespeare's visit to Norway in 1152/1153 to establish the archbishopric of Nidaros (*Ingi* chap. 23), nor do his two predecesors and probable sources, *Fagrskinna* (*Fsk*.: 351 f.) and *Morkinskinna* (*Msk*: 453 f.). The reason may have been that it was unknown to them, but this is an unlikely explanation, considering the numerous examples of obscure events from distant periods which are dated. An alternative explanation is that it was too well known to need mentioning. Given the distance, about eighty years, and the fact that Snorri gives the dates of events that must have been even better known, such as the day of the battle of Stiklestad, this is also unlikely. It is more reasonable to assume that the authors regarded it as outside the normal chain of events and thus less important to date. In a similar way, most miracles are undated, or at least, they are never dated according to the reigns of the kings.[35] Further, royal weddings and births are very rarely dated. This latter fact is particularly significant. As Snorri normally seems to know the kings' age at the time they succeeded, he could easily have dated their births, but was apparently not interested.[36] Finally, there are a lot of "single" episodes that took place over only a short period, which are not normally dated. Such episodes were apparently more difficult to date than longer conflicts, which were transmitted as whole stories with a fairly strict relative chronology. There are also "single" episodes that are dated, but without being brought into the normal chain of events. One such example is the attack on Konghelle by the Wends in 1135. This is told in great detail, according to contemporary eyewitnesses. It is dated exactly and placed in the right chronological order, between Haraldr's victory over Magnús in Bergen (January 1135) and Sigurðr slembir's arrival (summer/autumn 1136): the first warning came on the first Sunday after Easter (14 April 1135), whereas the attack took place on St. Lawrence's day (10 August) the same year. But the year is given as five years after the death of King Sigurðr, not the summer after Haraldr's victory, which is probably meant as an indication that it belonged to a different series of events.[37]

By contrast, the longer stories contain a fairly exact relative chronology, though this is not necessarily linked to the "absolute" chronology of the reign. From a modern point of view it seems rather pointless to inform the readers that Haraldr hárfagri spent a particular winter in Trøndelag and then the next spring went southward with a large fleet (*HHárf.* chaps. 10–11), when we are not informed which winter in his reign this was. To Snorri this internal chronology was apparently of primary interest, either for literary reasons—exact time may be a means to create excitement—or to stress the importance of the events in question.

This interest in relative chronology also serves to explain why Snorri never uses the Christian chronology. The events "belonging to" a particular king should be placed on his time-scale, not on anyone else's, nor according to "absolute time." He occasionally gives information on the length of the reigns of kings of other countries, but rarely relates it explicitly to the chronology of the Norwegian kings, though he must often have been able to do so.[38] However, events relating to persons who are not kings are often dated according to the kings' reigns and thus regarded as "belonging to" them. This is done consistently in the saga of St. Óláfr. The sagas proceed according to a fixed time-scale, "belonging to" the king to whom it is dedicated. Most events are told in the order they happened, so that series of events are normally broken off when something happens at the same time in a different place.

Occasionally, Snorri sacrifices strict chronology in the interest of coherent narrative. He recapitulates the background when introducing new persons into his story, such as Hárekr at Tjøtta (OH chap. 104), Erlingr Skjálgsson (OH chap. 21–23), and Erlingr skakki (*Ingi* chap. 17), or when the kings get involved in new regions, such as the Orkneys (OH chap. 96 ff.) and Jámtland (OH chap. 137). The coup against the Oppland kings and the captive King Hroerekr's attempt on Óláfr's life take place in spring 1017 but Snorri continues the story of Hroerekr until his death in 1020 before he returns to other events in 1017. Other stories told out of sequence are that of the scald Jǫkul (OH chap. 182) and that of Moera-Karl, who is sent by Óláfr to the Faroes in 1027 and killed the following year. Generally, shorter stories are more likely to be told in sequence than longer ones.

However, there are also some examples of the latter, such as the story of Ásbjǫrn selsbani and that of the Orkney earls. The latter is inserted at the point where Ásbjǫrn meets Óláfr, that is, at Easter 1023, which means that the first half of the story, of Ásbjǫrn's first expedition the year before, is told after events taking place early in 1023. In the story of the Orkney earls, Snorri gives a short summary of the history of the islands from the time of Haraldr hárfagri and then gradually becomes more detailed when approaching his main theme, how the islands were brought under King Óláfr. The story is inserted after Óláfr's fifth winter (1018–1019), which he spends in Nidaros. This means that the story of the Orkney earls starts at the first contact between them and King Óláfr, when Þorkell fóstri is sent by Earl Þorkell to Norway (chap. 98). This arrangement thus serves to link the story of the earls to Snorri's main story, that of St. Óláfr. Apart from length, it is hardly possible to give a general explanation of when Snorri prefers to tell a continuous story and when to divide it up in the interest of chronology, but it may possibly have to do with geographical distance and thus with thematic relevance. The Orkneys are fairly distant and events there usually of little relevance to Norway. Consequently, frequent changes of scene between Norway and the Orkneys might seem too abrupt. This explanation receives some support from other parts of *Heimskringla*.

The long story of Haraldr harðráði's adventures in the service of the Emperor of Constantinople, before he became king of Norway, is placed within the reign of Magnús góði, so that Haraldr is reintroduced in Norwegian history at the time he came to claim the throne (*HHarð.* chaps. 1–17). There is nothing in the way these stories are told that indicate that they are subordinate to the main line of events of the kings' sagas. They are told "in full," not as summaries. A comparison with two other early lives of kings, however, suggests that this is nevertheless the case.

The early lives of Óláfr Tryggvason and St. Óláfr are not treated in this way. The former is interlaced with the story of Earl Hákon, whereas the latter starts immediately after the death of Óláfr Tryggvason and covers most of the period until Óláfr's return fourteen years later; and the rule of the earls Eiríkr and Sveinn are mainly treated as a background for the following reign of St. Óláfr. The saga of St. Óláfr departs less from what is usual than that of Óláfr Tryggvason, as most of it deals with Óláfr's actions at an age when he is able to be a leader in war, and nothing much happens in Norway in the meantime. But the saga of Óláfr Tryggvason is truly exceptional. Snorri gives much attention to his mother's dramatic escape after his father's death, first while pregnant, then with Óláfr as a baby; further, Snorri treats his adventures in Russia and other faraway countries in great detail, in between the many dramatic events that took place during the reigns of the Eiríkssons and Earl Hákon.

Óláfr's father Tryggvi is killed by the Eiríkssons, apparently in the eighth year of their reign.[39] Then a few other events relating to the Eiríkssons are told, which must have taken place at approximately the same time. Snorri then returns to Tryggvi's widow Ástríðr, thus starting the saga of Óláfr. The story of her escape from Norway to Sweden covers approximately one year. Two years later, when Óláfr is three years old, they depart for Russia, but are captured by Vikings and are sold as slaves. Óláfr spends six years in Estonia until he is redeemed by his uncle and brought to Russia, at the age of nine. He then spends the next nine years there (OT chaps. 1–8).

Snorri now breaks off the story of Óláfr to return to the conflict between Earl Hákon and the Eiríkssons. He tells the story of Hákon and Gull-Haraldr (chaps. 9–14; see below) and of the death of Haraldr gráfeldr, which he places fifteen years after the death of King Hákon góði, that is, at approximately the time when Óláfr arrived in Russia. He continues by telling of Hákon's arrival in Norway, of his marriage, children, and so forth, and a few events from the beginning of his reign (chaps. 15–20), after which he returns to Óláfr, his departure from Russia, his first raids, and his marriage to Queen Geira of Wendland. He does not relate the two stories exactly to one another, only indicating that the events told previously took place when Óláfr was in Russia (chap. 21). In the following chapter, he frequently shifts between Hákon and Óláfr, telling of Óláfr's stay in Wendland with Geira and of the Emperor Otto's attack on Denmark, the Christianization of Denmark, and Haraldr Gormsson of Denmark's attempt to convert Hákon to Christianity and Hákon's rebellion against him because of this (chaps. 23–28). These events cover three years in Óláfr's life, but no other date is given. Óláfr spends the following four years as a Viking, then arrives in the Scilly Isles and settles in England (chaps. 29–32). Leaving Óláfr in England, Snorri now returns to Norway and Earl Hákon, concentrating on events there (chaps. 33–45) until the two stories are finally woven together with Hákon's message to Óláfr to entice him to Norway and Óláfr's arrival and Hákon's death (chaps. 46–50). This part of the saga contains the battle of Hjǫrungavágr, where Hákon defeated the *jómsvíkingar,* who tried to conquer Norway on behalf of the Danish king. This battle is described in great detail.

The story of Óláfr contains a fairly exact chronology, whereas no events are dated in the story of Earl Hákon. Because of this, we cannot trace exactly the chronological relationship between the two series of events, but it seems that Snorri has adhered as closely as possible to the chronological sequence. However, there are no examples of events concerning Hákon being told before those concerning Óláfr. Snorri seems consistently to tell of Óláfr first and Hákon next. According to his normal principles the events taking place in Norway or between Norway and Denmark clearly ought to be the more important. They include both the death of a king and the introduction of the new ruler, the subordination of the Norwegian ruler to the king of Denmark and then his independence, and finally, what was probably the greatest Norwegian victory over the Danes. The story of these events is also much longer than that of Óláfr (fifty-eight against twenty-three pages in Finnur Jónsson's edition). There could therefore be no question of subordinating it to the story of Óláfr by telling the whole of it in retrospect. But neither could the opposite be done: Óláfr Tryggvason was too important for that.

The lack of dates in the reign of Earl Hákon also seems curious. Snorri does not even give its length. The reason for this could hardly be that he did not know, as he evidently constructed dates from a much earlier period. And how could he reconstruct the chronology of such obscure events as the length of Óláfr's stay as a boy in Estonia or Russia when he did not know the date of the war between King Haraldr Gormsson and the Emperor Otto? He was also able to date the battle of Hjǫrungavágr. He tells that St. Óláfr's father, Haraldr grenski, was killed the year after this battle (chaps. 43–44). This happened the same summer as St. Óláfr was born. Snorri then tells that St. Óláfr was baptized by Óláfr Tryggvason when he was three years old, in King Óláfr's third year (chap. 60). As King Óláfr ruled for five years and St. Óláfr was thirty-three years old when he died in the battle of Stiklestad in 1030, this must have happened in 998, and the battle of Hjǫrungavágr must have taken place in 994, the year before Óláfr became king.[40] The reason for the lack of dates in Earl Hákon's reign is therefore not that Snorri did not know, but the earl's status. He did not belong to the dynasty, and Snorri apparently did not consider him a rightful ruler in the same way as the kings, despite his respect for his ability as a ruler and warrior.

A possible alternative solution to this curious arrangement is that Snorri has simply copied it from his main source for the story of Óláfr Tryggvason, Oddr munkr. As the work of the latter is a biography of Óláfr, this composition is more natural there. Apart from the fact that Snorri's free use of his sources often makes this kind of explanation less satisfactory, his composition and selection of materials differ so much from that of Oddr that he would hardly have told the story in this way only because of his source. As we have seen, none of his other sources have this arrangement. They normally give the whole biography of a king in his particular saga, even if this means going backward in time.

Snorri's particular arrangement is thus not a conventional way of expressing status, but must also have to do with his own principles of composition. Both in this and other respects, he is more concerned with exact chronology and orderly arrangement than his predecessors: the various reigns must be brought together in one time sequence. This may seem like an expression of the principle of absolute chronology, but is more likely to be a chronology linked to the royal genealogy rather than to each individual king. In this way, Snorri is able to create a certain unity within the whole of *Heimskringla* and to express himself on the relative importance of the various reigns.

Chronology is thus an indication of status. This conclusion may be pushed one step further. As mentioned before, there is a clear difference between the exactness of chronology in the various sagas. To some extent, this can be explained from the number of events that took place during each particular reign and the information at Snorri's disposal. The exact chronology of the period 1130–1177 is evidently to be explained in this way. This is a chronology of events more than a chronology of reigns. Three reigns, however, stand out in this respect, those of Haraldr hárfagri and the two Óláfrs. Concerning these reigns Snorri adheres to some sort of annalistic principle, not confining himself to his normal procedure of linking the chain of events to the reign at a few points. In the case of the former, he proceeds by decades, in the case of the two latter by individual years. The reign of Haraldr hárfagri is not told in great detail, nor is its chronology very exact, obviously because of lack of information. When Snorri has nevertheless made an extra attempt at exactness, the reason must be King Haraldr's importance as the greatest conqueror of the dynasty and the man who made Norway into one kingdom. The importance of the two Óláfrs goes without saying. They were responsible for the Christianization of the country and were also great heroes and warriors.

Snorri's chronology is thus evidence of a concept of time which is quite different from ours, despite its deceptive similarity to modern chronological principles. Because *Heimskringla* is a collection of royal biographies, events are linked to the kings' reigns, and chronology is used to emphasize certain events and certain kings at the cost of others. This also means that the concept of time implicit in this arrangement shows considerable similarity to that of the Icelandic family sagas. The kings' sagas do not necessarily represent a more abstract concept of time; it is only that "empty time" is more relevant to them than to the family sagas, because they attempt to describe a person of such importance that even the uneventful periods of his life are historically relevant. This reasoning may even be pushed one step further: nor is dating by the birth of Christ necessarily more abstract. This dating relates events to the reign of the eternal king, who after his incarnation has become the governor of the whole world. All events and even "empty time" are therefore relevant to his reign, and exact chronology receives much greater importance than in the lives of ordinary human beings. The "obsession with chronology" in medieval clerical historiography (see Guenée, 1980: 147 f.) therefore has not only a practical purpose but is the expression of a need to impose a supernatural order on the apparently chaotic events of this world, similar to the one that is expressed in the typological thinking: the history of the world is arranged in a particular order, the seven ages. The length of the various ages can be calculated, and in the present age, the sixth, which started with the birth of Christ, all events receive order and meaning by being chronologically related to Christ, who is now the supreme ruler of the world.

The difference between the chronological systems of Snorri's time and our own should therefore not primarily be explained in terms of ability or not to attain modern principles of chronology but rather in terms of different interests. Snorri was perfectly able to give modern, "absolute" chronology. In some cases we can even show that he knew this better than appears directly from his work. His system could be used for reckoning time as exactly as ours and was clearly intended as such. Snorri belonged to a learned tradition of men who made considerable attempts to create an ordered chronology, which was also essential for analyzing and explaining the events. In addition, however, it had symbolic importance and served to distinguish the most important persons and events from the rest of the material of the saga. Whether an event was dated or not and the way it was dated had to do not only with the amount of available information but with its importance and relevance to the main theme of Snorri's story. Snorri is most interested in the longer conflicts, either over the Norwegian throne or between the king and individual magnates or between the Norwegian king and kings of other countries, and consequently most interested in the chronology of events related to such conflicts. In Snorri's chronology time is not general time; it belongs to each particular king.

Authorship and Historical Truth

The kind of authorship we find in Snorri is not easily classified according to modern categories, including those of Steblin-Kamensky. Confining ourselves to the two topics under examination so far, we can point out that the analysis of Snorri's prologue has largely confirmed Steblin-Kamensky's denial of "authorial consciousness" to the saga writers. Snorri apparently conceives of his task as telling the truth of the past according to the testimony of the best witnesses, has a vague idea of historical authorship, and copies freely from his predecessors. However, my analysis of Snorri's chronology and composition shows him as more than a transcriber or compiler and rather as an author with definite ideas as to what to include and what not, and both able and willing to make bold reconstructions and rearrangements in his sources in order to create a coherent history. He is thus both more and less independent in his attitude to his materials than a modern historian. Does this reconstruction then conform to Steblin-Kamensky's concept of "syncretic truth"?

I must confess that I have some problems in grasping the fundamental difference between Steblin-Kamensky's syncretic truth and that of modern historical scholarship. He attributes to the historian the task of recording the exact facts of the past, whereas the author of fiction is allowed to generalize to bring out the "deeper truth." These two activities are radically different and cannot occur in the same work (Steblin-Kamensky, 1973: 21 ff.). This distinction between fiction and history resembles that of Aristotle, according to whom fiction is a more scientific and serious activity, because it tells what might happen, thereby giving general truth, whereas history simply records the number of disconnected events happening in the real world (Aristotle, *Poetics* ix. 1–3, 1451 a–b; see also Amory, 1979: 74 n. 27). However, although Aristotle's ideas on literature, though clearly not generally accepted, are still taken seriously by modern students of aesthetics and literary theory, his ideas of history seem obsolete today. Historians and philosophers of history, whether belonging to the idealist and hermeneutic tradition, such as Collingwood (e.g., 1966: 205 ff.), or of a more materialist and sociological persuasion, such as the Marxists and the French Annales school, are agreed that historians should create a coherent story of a meaningful synthesis out of the events they assemble (see Iggers, 1975: 8 ff., 32 ff.). This difference corresponds to the more fundamental difference between ancient Greek thought, according to which knowledge was primarily a priori and history consequently could not be the subject of knowledge in the real sense, and modern thought, which regards knowledge primarily as empirical (see, e.g., Collingwood, 1966: 24 and below). In practice, the historian's reconstruction of the past resembles a work of fiction to a considerable degree. He or she does not simply record or find the facts of the past, but tries to give a general picture of a society or a milieu or to reconstruct a coherent story from more or less scattered pieces of evidence (see Hallberg, 1974: 104; Andersson, 1977: 91). How much of this is the "truth" about the past and how much is created by the historian's own imagination? The use of imagination does not create a qualitative difference between history and historical fiction, but evidently a difference of degree. A modern historian is not allowed to invent facts or compose speeches for his actors in order to illustrate his historical interpretation, and he is supposed to make clear to his readers the distinction between the evidence and his own interpretation of it. The exact way of doing this may vary—there are genres of historiography as well as of fiction. The historian may choose to present the evidence and then allow his readers to follow his reconstruction step by step or he may simply tell the story and refer to the evidence that supports it in the notes. This latter way of doing it does not differ radically from fiction—or from the sagas. Further evidence of the similarity between history and fiction is the fact that historiographical works can be subjected to literary analysis in a similar way as works of fiction (see White, 1974).

Consequently, Snorri's extensive reworking of his materials is in my opinion to be regarded more as attempts at historical reconstruction than as fiction or "syncretic truth." Snorri's composition, chronology, and selection of materials are determined first by an idea of his theme and what is relevant to it and second by an idea of historical causation. Compared to his predecessors, he creates a more logical sequence of events. This is above all evident in his reconstruction of the chronology of the reign of St. Óláfr. Snorri's description of Óláfr's career as a classical tragedy and his corresponding arrangement of its events largely confirms Steblin-Kamensky's thesis of the failure to distinguish between history and fiction in Old Norse literature. However, both this and other "fictional" elements in Snorri, such as the speeches, very much serve the same purpose as modern historical reconstruction. Snorri has made a considerable intellectual effort in removing inconsistencies and creating a chronological sequence that might serve the purpose of explaining the events. His demands of the evidence that is necessary to prove this reconstruction is radically different from ours. But the reconstruction itself belongs to the same category as a modern historical reconstruction. Snorri believes in an orderly world in which events generally happen for some reason that can be reconstructed by human intelligence, and he uses his intelligence in a way that makes him both an independent au-thor in a real sense and a historian.

Although Steblin-Kamensky is probably right in denying the consis-tent distinction between historiography and fiction in Old Norse and Icelandic literature, the difference between modern historiography and Snorri and his contemporaries in this respect should not be overrated. There is a difference in the degree of imagination allowed and there are different rules of representation. Snorri is not supposed to distinguish in detail between facts and interpretation and he is allowed greater free-dom in integrating the interpretation in his narrative than his modern counterparts, notably in inventing speeches and dialogues and even to some extent actions and circumstances. For the purpose of using the saga writers as sources for the events they describe, this technique, combined with their principles of source criticism, makes a very great difference compared to modern historiography and urges the historian to the utmost care. From a theoretical point of view, their attitude to truth seems less radically different from our own, and one may doubt whether the concept of "syncretic truth" is very helpful as a means to understanding medieval attitudes on the matter.

We can then conclude that Steblin-Kamensky is largely right in his insistence on the fundamental difference between the concept of author-ship in the saga writers' milieu and the modern one as far as the general framework is concerned. Both the terminology and general statements, such as Snorri's prologue, indicate that there was no consistent distinc-tion between author and scribe and between historiography and fiction and no demand to the author in the direction of creating an original work. However, there may be a considerable difference between such an intellectual framework and what people actually do. In the case of Snorri, and probably many other saga writers as well, there can be no doubt that he did try to reconstruct the past in a way that in principle largely resembles that of modern historians. There is nothing really astonishing in this. Theories are often developed to explain what is actually going on. Consequently, modern authorship in practice may well antedate the corresponding theory.[41]

More research is evidently necessary to arrive at definite conclusions concerning the question of authorship in practice,[42] But I think we may draw some inferences from the topics discussed so far. Though the individual sagas show some variation in chronology and composition, this variation can largely be explained in terms of different subject matter and special emphasis on particular kings. Further, Snorri's chronology and composition show consistent principles, despite the fact that he does not explicitly state his criteria for selection of materials. First, *Heimskringla* is the history of the Norwegian dynasty from its mythical ancestor Oðinn until King Magnús Erlingsson in the late twelfth century. Rulers who did not belong to it, such as the earls of Lade, clearly receive less attention. The kings are normally the protagonists during their reigns, and it is evident from comparison with other sagas that Snorri has omitted much material that he considered irrelevant to the story of the kings. The importance of the kings is further expressed in the chronology. Second, Snorri's interest in "political history" is evident both from the space he gives this theme and from his chronology: the external and internal conflicts in which the Norwegian kings take part are usually dated according to their reigns, whereas scattered references to ecclesiastical matters, miracles, administration, and building activity are not.

We can get a clearer picture of Snorri's authorship in practice by analyzing his sources, which to some extent have been identified. Though this field has received some attention, much remains to be done. Scholars have usually been more interested in identifying sources and reconstructing lost sagas than in examining how Snorri and other saga writers used this material. As my interest in this context lies in another direction, I shall not attempt a general analysis here, confining myself to comparing passages that are directly relevant to Snorri's view of politics and society. To anticipate briefly the result of this analysis: insofar as we know Snorri's sources, his treatment of them points to the same consistent arrangement and independent authorship as we have found so far. Thus, although we must always consider the possibility that Snorri's known or unknown sources may lead him in particular directions, it seems that we can start our examination of his ideas of society and politics with the working hypothesis that he is the author of *Heims-kringla* in a sense that is not radically different from the modern one.

The Practical Problem: How To Identify the Authorial Point of View?

From a practical point of view, the "objective" style of the sagas creates considerable problems of interpretation. The author remains in the background, very rarely commenting explicitly on what he tells. Further, the problem is not only—or not primarily—to identify Snorri's opinions as distinct from those of other authors, but to trace "the authorial point of view" in general, in the form of praise or condemnation of various acts, explanations, and so forth. The idea that there are interpretations and subjective points of view behind the apparently objective façade of the sagas was first stated by Koht, but was for a long time resisted by philologists and historians of literature. In these milieus the radical revision of the belief in the objectivity of the sagas came in the mid-1960s with the attempts to place the sagas in a European context and trace in them contemporary Christian or aristocratic ideas. In 1970 Lars Lönnroth stated the new principles in a general form and discussed the methods for analyzing the authorial point of view in the sagas (Lönnroth, 1970: 157 ff.). His views seem to have gained wide acceptance (see Clover, 1985: 265 ff.).

We can divide the material of the sagas into three categories: (1) "scenes" and narrative; (2) short summaries; and (3) speeches and dialogues.[43] The first category contains the fundamental units of the saga literature, which are often referred to as "sagas" (sǫgur). These stories are often told in much the same way by various authors and may ultimately be derived from oral sources. The difference between this category and the next one is not always clear. Snorri's narrative can be more or less detailed. Particularly in the early part of *Heimskringla,* important chains of events are told in a very summary way, such as Hálfdan svarti's wars or Haraldr hárfagri's conquest of Norway. But normally *Heimskringla* consists of a number of stories, often vividly told, which are tied together by short passages, summarizing events between them or describing things as they normally were. "Structural" passages, characterizations of the kings, and descriptions of their way of government, good or bad conditions in the country, and so forth belong to this category.

As for the last category, the speeches and to some extent the dialogue were probably composed by the saga writers themselves, as was the case both in ancient and medieval European historiography,[44] though some famous "words" may well have been transmitted orally or through scaldic poems, such as the dialogue between St. Óláfr and Erlingr Skjálgsson during their last battle. In Old Norse historiography speeches are characteristic of the secular tradition, whereas the most explicitly clerical works, *Historia Norvegiae* and Theodoricus's *Historia de antiquitate regum Norvagiensium,* lack them. Besides *Sverris saga, Heimskringla* is the work that contains most speeches, 25 percent of its text being direct speech as compared to 11 percent in *Fagrskinna* (Hallberg, 1978: 117 ff.; Knirk, 1981: 140). From a literary point of view, the speeches may both represent a dramatic climax and be a device of retardation (Knirk, 1981: 75 ff.). From the point of view of historical interpretation their most important function is as a substitution for the authorial comment, which may be the reason why they are so much more prominent in the secular tradition, where the author "hides" behind his narrative, than in the clerical, in which he comes forward explicitly. The speeches may thus serve to show the motives of the actors, to analyze situations or to specify issues involved in a conflict.

Obviously, the summaries and structural passages, above all the characterizations of persons (Lönnroth, 1970: 165 ff. and below), are more likely to contain value judgments and personal points of view than the ordinary narrative. Such passages can hardly have been fixed in the oral tradition because they would be more difficult to remember than real stories. Further, to summarize means to point out the essential, which is evidently a more subjective activity than to tell a story. In a similar way, the speeches often directly serve the purpose of analysis and commentary and are therefore a clue to the author's own opinion. However, these two categories are not sufficient to give the whole picture. The narrative cannot simply be regarded as neutral information, whereas the author's opinions are reconstructed from scattered comments.[45] First, though they are certainly subjective, personal comments may also have been borrowed from earlier sources, and being often superimposed on the narrative, they need not necessarily represent the author's real interests and opinions, at least not his only ones. Second, narrative that does not contain value judgments is not "objective" in the sense that it does not reflect the attitudes or ideas of an author or his milieu. The stories told in the sagas are a small selection of all that took place and have in addition been arranged and reworked by the author. The principles governing this process are evidently based not only on literary taste but also on political, moral, or religious values. Most probably, the reason for the "objective" description is not that actions were not evaluated but that the criteria of evaluation were well known and did not have to be set forth explicitly (Lönnroth, 1970: 163; see also below). There is no hard and fast method of reconstructing such values from the stories, but the saga writers clearly had a number of indirect ways of expressing their points of view, such as scenic arrangement, shifts in perspective to increase or decrease identification with a particular character, prophecies or warnings, and so forth (Lönnroth, 1970: 170 ff., 177 ff.). At least, the narrative may prove a test case for the conclusions based on speeches and scattered authorial comments.

An additional difficulty in the stories is to identify the point of view of the individual author. First, we have the problem that the stories are traditional and may have been derived from earlier sources in approximately the same form. The events told in them may even have happened. We thus have to deal with the opposite problem of the one facing traditional source criticism: we must abstract the "hard facts" to be able to discover the bias (see the remarks of Pickering, 1977: 1 ff.).

The most obvious way of distinguishing Snorri's own opinions is to compare him to his sources. As we have already seen, this can often be illuminating. But the problem is that far from all of his sources are known or extant. The comparative method must therefore largely consist in drawing analogies from the passages that are also found in earlier texts. In addition, conclusions may be drawn from Snorri's arrangement of his material. His composition, which is very elaborate and in which he shows considerable independence, must in one way or another be a clue to his historical interpretation. Thus, while not spurning close reading of strategic passages, I shall pay particular attention to *Heimskringla* as a whole as a clue to Snorri's interpretation of history. This approach is even more necessary when my purpose is not only to define Snorri's original contribution to Old Norse historiography but to analyze common opinions and attitudes in his milieu. I shall start by treating *Heimskringla* more or less as if it were documentary evidence and describe the society that emerges from its pages. In the last chapters of this book (5–6), I shall then distinguish more clearly between Snorri and his milieu and between his description and contemporary Norwegian and Icelandic society.

2

The Conflicts

Introduction

The clue to understanding Snorri's society, as well as his ideas of political behavior, is his conflicts. To Snorri, as to most medieval historians, history is history of events, and the events that are most relevant to history are conflicts. My analysis of the composition and chronology of *Heimskringla* has shown that the conflicts form the main theme of the work, whereas most other events have a subordinate position. In some way or another most of *Heimskringla* deals with conflicts. When there are none, as in the long reign of King Óláfr kyrri (the quiet/peaceful) (1066–1093), Snorri confines himself to a few pages.

What Are the Conflicts About?

Concerning the subject of the conflicts, the most influential modern theory so far has been the one brought forward by Halvdan Koht in 1913 (Koht, 1921: 76–92), that, as constructed by the saga writers, the main theme of *Heimskringla* is the struggle between monarchy and aristocracy. From this starting point, however, Koht's theory challenged the prevailing orthodoxy at the time in two ways. First, Koht maintained that the saga writers were not only conscious authors and critical examiners of the sources, but historians, who interpreted the past according to a general view of society and human nature. Second, however, Koht's purpose with this reinterpretation of the sagas was to reject the idea of a constant struggle between monarchy and aristocracy, in favor of a theory, inspired by Marxist thought, of a fundamental community of interest between the two, which was finally manifested in the strong state of the thirteenth century (see Dahl, 1959: 239 ff., 247 ff.; Helle, 1960–1961: 349 ff.). According to Koht, the struggle between monarchy and aristocracy which most historians before him had found in the sources was the product of Snorri's and other saga writers' interpretation of the past in the light of King Sverrir's conflict with the aristocracy in the late twelfth century.

Koht's and other Marxist historians' reinterpretations of Norwegian medieval history have been frequently discussed up until the present time (see Helle, 1960–61: 349 ff. and 1981: 163 ff.). His interpretation of Snorri and the saga writers has been accepted in its main outlines by most historians who have treated the subject, notably Johan Schreiner (1926: 82–126) and Gudmund Sandvik (1955: 45 ff., 98 ff.), while meeting considerable opposition from the philologists and historians of literature (Paasche, 1969: 56 ff.; Lie, 1937: 85 ff., 119 ff.; and 1960–1961: 26 ff.).

In regarding the saga writers as having been influenced in their historical interpretation by society as they knew it from their own experience, Koht has formulated principles that are essential for all later discussion of the sagas. However, in attributing to them the anachronism of modeling the past on their own society and historical interpretation, he may in turn have made himself guilty of another anachronism, that is, that of transferring modern ideas of historical development and political conflicts to the Middle Ages. I shall discuss the problem of historical development later. As for the conflict between monarchy and aristocracy which Koht regards as Snorri's *leitmotif,* it may be pointed out that modern historians almost instinctively think in classes and social groups, whereas there are good reasons to believe that political conflicts, at least in the earlier Middle Ages, were primarily conflicts between individuals or groups based on personal loyalty between their members (Heers, 1977a: 1 ff.; see also 1977b; Fourquin, 1978: 27 ff.; Bagge, 1986: 147 ff., 165 f., etc.). The idea of the aristocracy as a class fighting the monarchy as an institution may therefore very well turn out to be the result of Koht's and other modern historians' reading of Snorri.

Koht's main arguments from his interpretation of *Heimskringla* are derived from the saga of St. Ólafr. Two general passages here apparently point to a conflict between the king and the aristocracy. Early in the saga, before Ólafr's return to Norway, Snorri describes the great wealth and power of the *lendir menn* (landed men), concluding that the kings and earls who governed the country were completely dependent on them.[1] Toward the end, having described the growing opposition against Ólafr, which led him into exile, he sums up his rule as a king by stating that he was exiled from his country because he banned robbery and Viking expeditions and gave high and low the same punishment, thus offending the magnates, who rebelled against him (OH chap. 181: 422).

Koht's use of these passages is an example of his method in overcoming the apparent "objectivity" of the sagas. However, we cannot exclude the possibility that these generalizations are conventional phrases with scant importance for the work as a whole or that they have a different meaning from the one that seems most likely to a modern interpreter. In other words: the generalizations must be tested against the narrative, above all the story of St. Óláfr's fall.

The Fall of St. Óláfr

The problem of St. Óláfr's fall was not a new one at Snorri's time. It was apparently first posed and answered by the clerical authors of the second half of the twelfth century. To them, Óláfr's deposition and death was the same problem as the death of Charles the Good was to Galbert of Brugge: how could a good and saintly king be deposed and killed by his own people? The pattern established by numerous martyrologies made the answer ready: his adversaries were evil men, acting at the devil's instigation, either opposing Óláfr's Christianity or his strict justice, which gave every one the punishment he deserved, regardless of social rank. Unlike Galbert the clerical authors more than a hundred years later could rest assured that his death was in reality a victory: Óláfr entered the heavenly kingdom as a martyr and through his death he finally conquered Norway for Christianity and became its eternal king.

Already in the oldest tradition, Halvdan Koht meant to detect a difference between a religious and a secular interpretation of Óláfr's reign, the former emphasizing his fight for Christianity, the latter his strict justice (1921: 87 f.). The difference should not be exaggerated. The description of Óláfr's strict justice is, as Koht himself partly admits, derived from the picture of the *rex iustus* in the ecclesiastical tradition.[2] But Koht is right that there is a shift of emphasis in the following period, the early thirteenth century. In *Fagrskinna,* Óláfr is undoubtedly the traditional *rex iustus,* but his Christianity and martyrdom are clearly toned down. His fall is the result of the magnates reacting against his strict justice (*Fsk.*: 160 f., 166, 173 f., 177). In the *Oldest Saga* and the *Legendary Saga* the epic element is introduced, the aforementioned works being short and rather dry summaries of the main events of Óláfr's reign. The author of the *Legendary Saga* also attempts to connect the epic narrative to the explanation of Óláfr's rise and fall, notably the story of Ásbjǫrn selsbani. But the stories of this saga are for the most part an end in themselves, without much connection with this problem.

Snorri thus had before him two kinds of tradition, which to some extent resemble the clerical and the aristocratic traditions of European historiography: on the one hand an explanation in religious and moral terms, on the other a series of dramatic stories. Snorri's original achievement as a historian is to connect the two in an attempt to give an overall interpretation of Óláfr's reign.

As we have seen, Snorri's explicit explanation of Óláfr's fall is derived from that of the clerical historians: Óláfr is the *rex iustus,* who is killed by the magnates because they cannot tolerate his strict justice. In addition he points to King Cnut's gold, which tempted the majority of the magnates to join him. This is also a traditional explanation, to which Snorri attaches rather less importance than most of his predecessors.[3] According to Snorri, Cnut would not have succeeded if the magnates were not already hostile to Óláfr.[4]

Further, Snorri uses the speech of the Danish bishop Sigurðr before the battle of Stiklestad, where Óláfr was killed, to explain the reasons for his fall. Though Sigurðr is primarily the spokesman of King Cnut, his speech is addressed to the magnates and emphasizes their grievances. In his short summary of Óláfr's career, Sigurðr presents him as a robber and evil-doer from the beginning to the present time. He started out as a Viking, then usurped the kingdom of Norway, thus robbing its rightful rulers, King Cnut, King Óláfr of Sweden, and the earls, of their property. His further acts of aggression were directed against the Oppland kings—his own kinsmen—the magnates and the people, to such an extent that there is hardly a magnate present who has not suffered a major injury for which to seek revenge. And finally, he has come back with a pack of brigands and foreigners to make himself king once more (OH chap. 218). The speech is one of several examples of Snorri—like other saga writers—allowing the adversaries of their heroes to present their case. At the same time, it gives a fairly adequate summary of Óláfr's career as already told by Snorri, though he evidently intends the speech to present it from a distorted perspective. From a political point of view, it gives a third explanation of the conflict between Óláfr and the magnates, that of a power struggle over individual interests.

To some extent, all three explanations are compatible with the interpretation of Óláfr's reign as a constitutional struggle, the *rex iustus*-idea stressing its ideological aspects, Bishop Sigurðr's speech the aspect of power politics, and Cnut's gifts and military power serving to strengthen the opposition and make Óláfr's defeat inevitable. If we turn to the narrative, however, it becomes clear that the opposition against Óláfr is not the expression of a fundamental conflict of interest between monarchy and aristocracy, but the result of a series of conflicts between the man Óláfr and individual members of the aristocracy.

The *rex iustus*-explanation plays no significant part in the narrative.

There are no examples of Óláfr coming into conflict with magnates because of banning robbery or Viking expeditions. On the contrary, his adherents take part in Viking expeditions like anyone else.[5] And though Óláfr's strict justice may have aggravated some of his conflicts, these conflicts are not usually over legal or moral principles, but concern Óláfr's personal interests.

Óláfr's Conflicts with the Magnates

The conflicts leading to Óláfr's fall start with the episode of Ásbjǫrn selsbani, which according to Snorri's chronology took place in 1022–1023, immediately before the turning point of the saga (chaps. 117–120; see also above). Ásbjǫrn is a prominent man in Northern Norway who tries to increase his power and influence in the region through lavish hospitality. As this becomes difficult because of bad harvests in the North, he goes south to his maternal uncle Erlingr Skjálgsson to buy grain. That same year, however, the king has forbidden grain export from Western Norway because of his intention to go there on *veitsla*. Erlingr runs into a dilemma. On the one hand, he does not want to offend the king, on the other, he cannot afford to lose face by letting down a kinsman. He tries to solve the dilemma by allowing Ásbjǫrn to buy grain from his slaves, whom he has allowed to grow something on their own. But the king's *ármaðr* (local representative), Selþórir at Avaldsnes, does not accept this excuse, confiscates the grain, and sends Ásbjǫrn home empty-handed, to the scorn of his neighbors. The next year Ásbjǫrn revenges himself, killing Selþórir in the presence of the king, who is just then visiting Avaldsnes. Ásbjǫrn is taken captive and condemned to death, but Erlingr's son Skjálgr, who is then at Óláfr's *hirð*, hurries to his father for aid, while his friend Þórarinn Nefjólfsson through various pretexts manages to postpone the execution until after the Easter holidays. Erlingr then arrives with a large force just in time to save Ásbjǫrn, forcing the king to accept compensation for the death of his *ármaðr* in return for Ásbjǫrn's life. Though the king is very angry, they arrive at a settlement. Peace, however, turns out to be of short duration. New issues arise between them and lead to full enmity (chap. 121: 262). When Cnut turns against Norway, Erlingr joins him. Snorri tells of only one more meeting between him and Óláfr, in Erlingr's ship during the battle in which Erlingr is killed.

The Selsbani episode is the first of the conflicts that ultimately lead to Óláfr's fall and is at the same time the cause of some of the others. It apparently poisons the atmosphere between Óláfr and Erlingr in a way that leads to new conflicts. It also creates enmity between Óláfr and the mighty Þórir hundr at Bjarkøy, Ásbjǫrn's uncle. Ásbjǫrn is reconciled with Óláfr on the condition that he takes the place of the dead Selþórir as Óláfr's *ármaðr* at Karmøy. When returning home to arrange things before his final departure, he is persuaded by Þórir to break the settlement and remain at home, rather than becoming the king's "slave" (OH chap. 120: 260 f.). He is then killed by Óláfr's *hirðmaðr* (retainer) Ásmundr Grankelsson, when Ásmundr's friend Karli, also Óláfr's *hirðmaðr,* points out Ásbjǫrn to him and thus becomes his accomplice (OH chap. 123). As a revenge, Þórir kills Karli and becomes Óláfr's enemy (OH chap. 133). Like Erlingr, Þórir is reconciled with the king, though hardly in a way that is likely to lead to lasting friendship. Óláfr's man Finnr Árnason humiliates him and forces him to pay an enormous indemnity (OH chap. 139). Þórir then leaves the country before he has paid the full amount, enters King Cnut's service in England, and becomes one of the leaders of Óláfr's enemies in the battle of Stiklestad, even giving Óláfr one of his deadly wounds (OH chap. 139: 325 f., chaps. 219, 221, 228, etc.).

The other conflicts between Óláfr and individual magnates, three in number, all take place toward the end of Óláfr's reign, after Cnut has made his claim on Norway. Óláfr has made Ásmundr Grankelsson his *hirðmaðr* and representative in Ásmundr's home district of Northern Norway as a counterweight against Hárekr at Tjøtta. When Hárekr runs into conflict with Ásmundr and his father Grankell over a hunting and fishing ground and Óláfr supports the latter, Hárekr joins Óláfr's adversaries (OH chaps. 106, 123, 140, 169, 170). A little later, conflict is imminent between King Óláfr and the Árnasons, his closest friends among the *lendir menn,* because of Þorbergr Árnason protecting an Icelander who has killed the king's *ármaðr.* Þorbergr is in a conflict of loyalty, because of the services the Icelander has done to his wife in the past (OH chap. 138). Like Erlingr Skjálgsson earlier, Þorbergr and his brothers assemble an army and force the king to accept indemnity for his *ármaðr.* But this time the settlement lasts.

Snorri thus accentuates the political reasons for Óláfr's fall. The ecclesiastical sagas and *Fagrskinna* are mainly concerned with the ideological reasons for this, Óláfr's strict justice and his fight for Christianity. The stories that serve to build up Snorri's picture, are not his own, however. Most of them are found in the *Legendary Saga,* and the one which is not, that of Hárekr at Tjøtta, may have been borrowed from Styrmir's *Óláfs saga.* Both by his chronological arrangement and his way of linking these stories together, Snorri apparently uses them in a different way from his predecessors to create a picture of the political issues involved in the rebellion against Óláfr. By contrast, the *Legendary Saga* gives them less prominence and more directly than Snorri tries to subordinate them to the ideological picture of the conflict.[6]

Snorri's ideological explanation of Óláfr's fall thus turns out to be a conventional piece of *rex iustus*-ideology, borrowed from earlier, clerical authors, whereas his real explanation lies in a series of power struggles between Óláfr and individual magnates. The individuals in question are the very men who led the army against him at Stiklestad (OH chaps. 219–220). This seems to indicate that Snorri is more interested in individual conflicts than in the relationship between the king and the aristocracy in general. If the examples are to be generalized, the most likely hypothesis is that Snorri intends them as examples of the way in which even other magnates became Óláfr's enemies, as is indicated by Bishop Sigurðr's words that there was hardly a single man in the army who did not have cause for revenging himself on Óláfr. The alternative hypothesis, that Snorri intends them as an illustration of the general conflict of interest between the monarchy and the aristocracy receives little support from the rest of *Heimskringla*.

"Constitutional" Conflicts in General

Questions of "constitutional" relevance are also touched upon in other parts of Óláfr's saga. An important passage in this context is the discussion between the petty kings of Eastern Norway, shortly after Óláfr's arrival, of whether or not they should support his claim on the country (OH chap. 36). Both this discussion and the preceding one in which Óláfr presents his claims before his mother and stepfather are very detailed, and, as far as we know, created entirely by Snorri himself.[7] They therefore offer exceptionally good opportunities of analyzing his own view of the conflict between St. Óláfr and his rivals.

The leading spokesman for the opposition against Óláfr is King Hroerekr, whose speech expresses the wish of the magnates and petty kings to rule for themselves with as little interference as possible from their superior, the king of Norway. It appears both from Hroerekr's description of Óláfr and from the following events that his intentions are the very opposite of this. However, the constitutional significance of this speech and the discussion of the Oppland kings should not be exaggerated. At the meeting, Hroerekr's arguments against Óláfr are countered by his brother King Hringr. The two kings disagree on one fundamental point. Hringr accepts Óláfr's argument that a victory for one kinsman is a victory for the whole kin, whereas Hroerekr does not (see below). Apart from this, the ideological difference between the two kings is small. Their discussion is not a question of strong monarchy versus "constitutionalism," nor of "patriotism" versus collaboration with foreigners. Both kings are moved by self-interest, but differ as to what will serve it best.

Hroerekr is content with the prevailing situation, finds that the interests of the petty kings are often best served with foreign kings, because they are usually less interfering than indigenous ones and fears that Óláfr will become an interfering king in the same way as his ancestors. Hringr, on the other hand, does not deny this, but objects that Óláfr's *hamingja* (luck) will decide whether or not he will win. But if he wins, it will be a great advantage to have supported him from the beginning.

This discussion is therefore not evidence that Snorri regards the conflict between Óláfr and the petty kings in "constitutional" terms. First, both kings argue in terms of individual advantage, not in terms of group solidarity between the magnates and petty kings. Second, it is by no means evident how these interests are best served. On the one hand, as Hroerekr points out, a strong king may interfere with the independence of the petty kings. On the other hand, entering the service of such a king may bring great advantages, as Hringr points out, and Snorri demonstrates in other contexts. Further, if he had wanted, Snorri would have had the opportunity of letting Óláfr present the monarchical point of view in contrast to Hroerekr's "constitutionalism." He makes Óláfr address a long speech to his mother and stepfather before the meeting of the petty kings (OH chap. 35). Admittedly, this speech shows Óláfr as an ambitious and courageous young man, but there is nothing in it that could not have been said before the petty kings. Óláfr singles out the Danish king and Earl Sveinn as his enemies and expects the petty kings—as his relatives, in accordance with Hringr's way of reasoning— to support him, to avenge the shame of the kindred, and throw off the Danish yoke.

The conflicts between the king and the aristocracy during Óláfr's reign are best analyzed together with the reigns before and after, that is, from the late tenth century, when men like Einarr þambarskelfir, Erlingr Skjálgsson, and Hárekr at Tjøtta rose to prominence until Haraldr harðráði's struggles against the leading magnates of the previous reigns in the 1050s and 1060s. To a modern observer, the continuity of the political constellation in the reigns of St. Óláfr, Magnús góði, and Haraldr harðráði is striking: on the one side the king, on the other a group of powerful magnates. Any attempt on the part of the king to extend his power inevitably leads to conflict with one or more of these men. In the case of St. Óláfr, this conflict, in combination with King Cnut's attempts to include Norway in his North Sea Empire, leads to his fall. When the people and magnates react against the harsh Danish rule, two of Óláfr's leading adversaries, Einarr þambarskelfir and Kálfr Árnason, bring Óláfr's young son Magnús back to Norway, expel the Danish rulers, and make him king (MG chaps. 1–5). Magnús tries to continue his father's policy, but meets with stubborn resistance and abstains, largely leaving the magnates in the position they had obtained since the battle of Stiklestad (MG chaps. 13–16). Finally, Haraldr harðráði once more pursues his half-brother's aggressive policy and succeeds in killing or expelling some of his most formidable rivals (*HHarð.* chaps. 39–53, 69–70, 72–74).

This continuity has not completely escaped Snorri. He points out the basic similarity in character between Óláfr and Haraldr. To some extent he also brings out the consistent policy of some of the magnates. Kálfr Árnason and Einarr þambarskelfir maneuver for gain, appointing and deposing kings to suit their own interests, until they finally succumb to the machinations of Haraldr harðráði. Snorri even hints at a conflict of interest between the king and the magnates as a group. His description of the enormous power of the *lendir menn* at Óláfr's succession and the earls' concessions to them give the contrast to Óláfr's strictly monarchical regime. The earls were dependent on the magnates and bought the support of men like Erlingr Skjálgsson and Einarr þambarskelfir with large concessions. The description of the great power of the *lendir menn* also serves to characterize their regime in opposition to Óláfr's, although its main function is probably to describe the difficulties Óláfr faced when fighting for the kingdom. When Óláfr wins the power, one of the main reasons for his difficulties is that he denies these men the rights they have held under his predecessors. This is clearly part of a deliberate policy, which is also expressed in his attempts to raise "new men" to power, a policy that Hárekr at Tjøtta regards as an affront against the old, established kindreds. In some of the episodes, like Óláfr's conflict with Erlingr Skjálgsson and Haraldr's with Einarr þambarskelfir, general principles are clearly involved. Óláfr denies them the *veitslur* (royal revenues) they have held under his predecessors, stating that he will not make his own *óðal* (hereditary property) the property of the *lendir menn*.

In general, however, it is exactly the long-term perspective that makes the contrast between Snorri's description and that of a modern political or constitutional historian so striking. Snorri describes a series of conflicts between individual kings and individual magnates, which do not differ in principle from any other conflict in which mighty men are involved. Characteristically, the petty kings of Opplandene direct the same complaints against Óláfr for aggressive behavior as Óláfr himself against Erlingr Skjálgsson (OH chap. 74: 124 f.; see also chap. 116: 240). Only rarely do the magnates unite as a group against the king. When they do, it is most easily explained from the fact that magnates who risk to lose against a mightier adversary will naturally unite to fight him. In this respect, Stiklestad is highly exceptional. The normal way of things is better illustrated through the events following King Haraldr's murder of Einarr þambarskelfir.

The conflict between Haraldr and Einarr is introduced through a description of Haraldr's character: he was a domineering (ríklundaðr) man and more so the more he became settled in the country. Very few men had the courage to speak against him (*HHarð*. chap. 42). One who did so, however, was Einarr þambarskelfir, who was the mightiest man in Trøndelag. He was very rich, held *veitslur* from the king—from Magnús's time—and was the leader of the people, defending their interests and the laws at the popular assemblies (*HHarð*. chaps. 40, 43). Einarr was no friend of Haraldr. In contrast to his predecessors, who explain it from events during the co-reign between Haraldr and Magnús, Snorri gives no explicit explanation of this enmity. But it appears from the story itself and from the scaldic stanza by Haraldr, which Snorri quotes, that it is primarily a question of power: Haraldr tolerates no opposition, Einarr is frequently crossing his plans, and Haraldr is afraid of Einarr's great power. Einarr also distrusts Haraldr and is constantly surrounded by a large number of armed men. Matters are brought to a head when Einarr protects a thief who has been in his service, dragging him away from the assembly with armed force. Friends of both parties go between, and a meeting between them is arranged. Einarr and his son Eindriði enter the king's house and are both killed by the king's men (*HHarð*. chap. 44). Einarr's numerous adherents outside are helpless, as men usually are when they have lost their leader, and the king and his men are able to escape.

Haraldr is now in a desperate situation. The people of Trøndelag are against him, and he fears Hákon Ívarsson, the kinsman of Einarr's wife and one of the most brilliant young men at the time (*HHarð*. chap. 45: 138; see also chap. 39). Haraldr turns to Finnr Árnason, a close friend of the late King Óláfr and thus to himself and related to both by marriage, while at the same time a friend of Hákon Ívarsson. The plan is to make Finnr reach a settlement with Hákon. The outcome of this attempt shall not detain us here (see later discussion). The point is that the murder of Einarr does not provoke a general rebellion of the magnates. Only his own kinsmen and the people of Trøndelag, who had lost their leader, react. Further, Haraldr can use his friendship with another magnate to achieve a settlement. Haraldr's subsequent conflicts with magnates are also individual and for various personal reasons, like Magnús's before him. Magnús seeks revenge for the death of his father by aiding in the killing of Hárekr at Tjøtta and exiling Kálfr Árnason and others of his father's leading adversaries (MG chaps. 12–15). The conflict between Haraldr and Hákon Ívarsson is renewed when Haraldr learns that Hákon has saved the life of King Sveinn of Denmark in the battle of Nissá, in return for Sveinn's former favors toward him (*HHarð*. chap. 69; see also chaps. 49, 64). When Finnr Árnason leaves Haraldr to join King

Sveinn in Denmark, it is also for purely personal reasons, because he blames Haraldr for the death of his brother Kálfr (*HHarð*. chaps. 51–53). Finnr had been a close friend of St. Ólafr and fought with him at Stiklestad and is thus in no way a representative of an aristocratic opposition against the monarchy.

A general conflict between the king and the magnates is even more difficult to find in *Heimskringla* as a whole than in the sagas of Ólafr and his immediate successors (see Paasche, 1969: 68 ff.). Haraldr hárfagri's conquest is evidently to some extent at the cost of the petty kings and magnates. Some of them also emigrate to Iceland and other places to escape from Haraldr's tyranny (*HHárf*. chap. 19: 125). But Haraldr's unification of Norway also means new opportunities for the magnates. He has the resources to award his men generously. Thus the earls in Haraldr's service had larger incomes than the petty kings before. At the news of this, many great men entered Haraldr's service (*HHárf*. chap. 6). Examples of this are, among others, Earl Hákon of Lade and Earl Rǫgnvaldr of Møre (*HHárf*. chaps. 9–10, see also chap. 8). Haraldr's conquest thus serves as an illustration of King Hringr's reasoning concerning the advantages of supporting Ólafr's claims. We may note that in both cases we have to do with generalizations: Snorri explicitly points out both the advantages and disadvantages of a strong monarchy from the point of view of the magnates. From the king's point of view, this example points to another lesson, which is equally important, that is, that support is essential to be able to rule. A king cannot afford a conflict with all or most of the magnates at the same time. To what extent he succeeds in this and to what extent his reign is peaceful or the opposite, is largely a question of character.

Ólafr is a "great chieftain" and as such a strong and domineering person. This is frequently stressed in Snorri's characterizations of him and above all in the contrast between him and his peaceful and moderate stepfather, Sigurðr sýr (sow), with strong agricultural interests. Snorri makes the latter point out the personal aspect of the "constitutional" conflict in his words to Ólafr after his victory at Nesjar, advising him to attack once more and crush the enemy, for he will have difficulties in winning the loyalty of the great men with his own domineering temper and their habit of resisting their superiors (OH chap. 52). In a similar way, Haraldr's character serves as the main explanation of his frequent conflicts with the magnates. Being great kings, however, both Ólafr and Haraldr have qualities that make them attractive to other great men, such as courage, generosity, eloquence, and intelligence.

The kings' character is also most probably Snorri's explanation of the contrast between the period until the death of Haraldr harðráði in 1066, when the kings and the magnates struggled for power, and the following one, notably the civil wars from 1130, during which the magnates actually dominated the government, a contrast that Sandvik regards as the expression of a fundamental change in the political system (Sandvik, 1955: 94 f.). It appears from Snorri's description that the latter period was one of weak kings who allowed the magnates to dominate. Nor should the contrast between this period and the earlier one be exaggerated. Admittedly, Haraldr hárfagri's successor Eiríkr blóðøx and his sons are involved in violent conflicts with their rivals or the people and are finally deposed. But Hákon góði is the ideal king from the point of view both of the magnates and the people (HG chaps. 1, 32: 218) and meets no real opposition except in the question of religion (HG chaps. 13–18, see also below). Óláfr Tryggvason is harsh and ruthless against his enemies, particularly in connection with his campaign for Christianity. This policy affects some of the magnates, such as Járnskeggi and Þórir hjǫrtr.[8] Apart from such examples, however, there is little to suggest that his relations to the magnates were bad. On the contrary, he is the king who promotes men like Erlingr Skjálgsson, Einarr þambarskelfir, and Hárekr at Tjǫtta, who create such problems for his successor St. Óláfr. Earl Hákon, who grows tyrannical toward the end of his life, lusting for the wives and daughters of the men of Trøndelag and is deposed because of this, is a popular ruler during most of his reign (OT chaps. 45, 48–50). It is thus difficult to find a general conflict of interest between the king and the magnates during this period, the more so as the reasons for the conflicts that do occur, vary considerably.

Conclusion

We thus have to reject the theory brought forward by Koht and other historians of the conflict between monarchy and aristocracy as the main theme of the *Heimskringla*. Without excluding the possibility that Snorri may describe "constitutional" conflicts between the king and larger parts of the population or even show particular interest in such conflicts, we must conclude that the majority of his conflicts are conflicts between individuals, in which the king is involved in a similar way as any other mighty man. Rather than regarding them in "constitutional" terms or from the point of view of the *rex iustus*-ideology, these conflicts are better understood as "feuds," which in the Nordic countries are best known from the Icelandic sagas.

The Feud

The feud is known from numerous societies, both within medieval Europe (see Bloch, 1967 I: 125 ff.; Brunner, 1959: 1 ff.) and in other regions of the world (e.g., see Gluckmann, 1965: 111 ff., 136 ff.; Barth, 1981: 72 ff.). According to the common definition (see Pospisil, 1968: 389 ff. for the following), it is to be distinguished from peaceful solutions of conflicts by legal means on the one hand and war on the other. It differs from legal conflicts by involving violence, but in contrast to war, it takes places between groups within a society, which means that it often takes a more moderate form and is conducted according to stricter rules. Its purpose is to "secure revenge, reprisal, or glory for a particular individual or family within the group." It had a particular importance in Iceland during the free-state period (before 1262), owing to the complete lack of a central authority to enforce judicial decisions (Heusler, 1912: 19 ff., etc.; Byock, 1982: 24 ff. and 1984: 86 ff.). Basically, there were three ways of solving conflicts in medieval Iceland: (1) private settlement with the opposite party; (2) bringing the matter to the popular assembly; and (3) the feud. The narrative sources often give the impression that a feud was the normal result of a conflict, a picture that is further emphasized by agitation from secular and ecclesiastical authorities to replace it by public justice. Though some historians have accepted this picture, it is no doubt exaggerated (see Wallace-Hadrill, 1962: 121 ff.; Gluckman, 1965: 111 f.; Miller, 1983: 339 ff.; Wormald, 1980: 54 ff.): feuds are emphasized in the narrative sources because they contain interesting and dramatic events, whereas peaceful settlement is mentioned more rarely. However, the feud is the clue to the whole system, as war in Clausewitz's analysis of foreign policy: war is essential, not because it happens all the time, but because the possibility of war must be taken into account in all political decisions. The outcome of both private settlement and action at the popular assembly is determined by the power and resources of the parties in question, not by abstract principles of justice or legal rules. Consequently, one must always consider the likely result of a feud when negotiating a settlement.

Politically, there are two different ways of regarding the feud. It is a way for most people, magnates and ordinary people alike, of resolving conflicts or seeking compensation for loss in honor or material wealth. And it is a means for the magnates to gain power and influence. The power of the Icelandic magnates depended very much on their judicial and political function. Through the institution of advocacy they could exploit the conflicts of their inferiors: when a man had a complaint against someone more powerful than himself, the best thing to do was usually to go to another mighty man—normally his *goði* (chieftain)— and let him take over the case, in return for the profit that might arise from it. Though this meant giving up the material value involved in the case, he retained his honor and might even gain some protection against potential aggressors in the future (Byock, 1982: 37 ff.; 1988: 124 ff.).

Further, conflicts arising out of various incidents between the magnates themselves or their servants or clients could be used to launch an attack on a mighty rival and weaken his position.

These two ways of regarding the feud, as a reaction against an infringement on one's honor, property, and so forth, and as a means to further one's political interests, are both found in the sagas. Roughly, the former point of view is the dominant one in the family sagas, the latter in the *Sturlunga saga*. Ethically and psychologically, the difference is similar. In the Icelandic family sagas the feuds are often described as the results of a strict code of honor, which demanded men to risk their lives or kill their friends, often for rather trivial matters. The heroes of these sagas are often tragic figures, who sacrifice their own happiness for the sake of duty. By contrast, the feuds in the *Sturlunga saga* mainly seem to be moves in a game for individual advantage (Heusler, 1912: 29 f.; see also 1911: 48 ff.; Bandle, 1969: 12 ff.). The reason for this difference may be that *Sturlunga saga* more directly reflects the intense power struggle in early thirteenth-century Iceland, whereas the family sagas have a more literary character.[9] But the change in viewpoint may also have something to do with actual changes in Icelandic society, from a relatively stable society with a large number of magnates who maneuvered for gain and tried to protect their adherents while having a common interest in keeping the conflicts within certain limits, to the violent conflicts between a few great magnates, governing real principalities, who ruthlessly exploited any conflict that could gain them advantages at the cost of their rivals.

Formally, at least some of the conflicts we have considered above bear a striking resemblance to feuds as they are found in medieval Iceland and other societies. Thus, the conflict sparked off by Ásbjǫrn selsbani's fateful expedition escalates step by step, an action from one party leading to a response from the other, while an increasing number of men on both sides progressively become involved. Asbjǫrn belongs to a network of kinsmen, which corresponds fairly well to the kind of groups that are normally involved in feuds. The opposite party is a little more difficult to define. St. Óláfr is not simply a member of a faction or kindred group, he is the king of the whole country and in some sense the legitimate superior of his adversaries. In this particular conflict, however, and several others, he can most adequately be regarded as a faction leader, his faction consisting of clients, more than kinsmen. I shall discuss the composition of the factions later and confine myself here to pointing out that the conflicts that led to the deposition of St. Óláfr bear considerable resemblance to a series of feuds.

My next question is then whether Snorri considers these feuds solely as sparked off by accidental clashes that lead to an escalation, as most authors of Icelandic family sagas seem to do, or whether he describes them as deliberate power struggles, in which such clashes are used as pretexts for furthering the actors' own interests.

Accidental Clashes and Long-Term Interests

To some extent, Snorri's initial description of the immense power of the two *lendir menn* Erlingr Skjálgsson and Einarr þambarskelfir serves as a background for the story both of Óláfr and his immediate succesors, until Einarr's death at the hands of Haraldr harðráði. Erlingr is depicted as the real ruler of most of Western Norway, though without the name of king. Einarr has a similar position in Trøndelag, holding large *veitslur* during the reign of the earls, but is hardly as independent, given the latters' traditional power in the region. Einarr remains in the background during most of Óláfr's reign, to emerge as the foremost of the *lendir menn* under his successors.[10] Snorri gives no stories of direct clashes between him and Óláfr and does not state directly why he left Óláfr for Cnut. Indirectly one may infer that he had been disappointed by not being given the same status as under Óláfr's predecessors, Óláfr Tryggvason and the earls. Einarr is therefore an example of a magnate whose long-term interests run into conflict with Óláfr's. Óláfr wants a more direct power over the country than his predecessors, whereas Einarr fights to keep his traditional position and if possible improve it. The same applies even more to Erlingr Skjálgsson.

Erlingr had been promoted to his position in Western Norway by Óláfr Tryggvason, who had given him the same *veitslur* in the region as Haraldr hárfagri gave his sons (OT chap. 58; see also *HHárf.* chap. 33 and below). The earls who succeeded Óláfr had tried in vain to reduce his power and had finally made their peace with him through a marriage alliance (OH chaps. 21, 31). Erlingr had then stood on their side against Óláfr. This forms the background for their first meeting, which takes place after the battle of Nesjar and after Óláfr's first winter in Nidaros, that is, according to Snorri's chronology in spring 1016 (OH chap. 60). Ólafr comes southward with a large fleet and is acclaimed by the people along the coast. At his arrival in Karmsund, messengers go between him and Erlingr, and a meeting is arranged. According to Snorri's general picture of the situation, Óláfr ought now to be in a superior position: he is accepted king over the whole country, and his leading enemies are either dead or in exile, Earl Sveinn having died shortly before (OH chap. 55). This political aspect, however, is not prominent in Snorri's description of the "scene" between Óláfr and Erlingr. He is more interested in the personal aspect, the meeting between two proud and strong-willed men. Erlingr offers Óláfr his friendship on the condition that he is allowed to keep his *veitslur*. Óláfr refuses, referring to Erlingr's alliance with his enemies and stating the principle that the *lendir menn* should not be "entitled by birth" to his patrimony.[11] Erlingr has not the stamina to resist the king, but neither is he inclined to submit. After a temporary stalemate, Erlingr's friends go between and persuade him to submit to the king, pointing out that he will continue to be the mightiest *lendr maðr* even without the *veitslur*. Erlingr then leaves the decision to the king, and they are seemingly reconciled. Snorri does not state explicitly the terms of the reconciliation, but it is evident from the subsequent story that Óláfr has refused Erlingr to keep his *veitslur*. Snorri seems primarily to explain this result by Óláfr's personality: though Erlingr is one of the proudest, noblest, and most strong-willed magnates of Norwegian history, he must submit to the overwhelming force of Óláfr's personality. It appears, however, that Snorri also considers the political situation. In the story of Ásbjǫrn selsbani Erlingr refers to the fact that he twice earlier has been in an inferior position when meeting the king (OH chap. 120: 259).

In addition, Snorri's narrative seems to suggest another observation, that the result of the meeting between two such great and noble characters should have been that Óláfr, having stated the principle of his free disposition over royal property and received Erlingr's submission, out of generosity allowed Erlingr to retain his *veitslur*.[12] One might even infer that this in Snorri's opinion would have been the most prudent course of action for Óláfr. As it turned out, Óláfr was unable to keep Erlingr from the *veitslur*, but by trying to do so had him as his enemy instead of as his friend.

This conflict of interests is also in the foreground in the next "scene" between the two (OH chap. 116), which takes place immediately after Óláfr's settlement with Einarr þambarskelfir, when the king is in an even stronger position than before. His attempts to reduce Erlingr's power by using Áslákr fitjaskalli—Erlingr's kinsman—against him, however, have met with no success, and Óláfr arranges a new meeting to try to come to terms with Erlingr. In the following dialogue, Óláfr refers to complaints from many men who have been suppressed by Erlingr, including Áslákr, and hints that Erlingr's aggressive behavior is directed against Óláfr himself. In his answer, Erlingr shows his respect for the king and shows himself willing to submit to him but not to his low-born servants, and he defends his position as the leading man in Western Norway. Once more, friends of the two men go between and a settlement is reached. Snorri's account of its terms is rather vague, but it appears that Erlingr must have reasons to be content: he is forced to no new concessions and may apparently continue as before. In the following episode, the story of Ásbjǫrn selsbani, he is anxious not to break his settlement with Óláfr.

The relationship between long-term and short-term conflicts in this story is not entirely clear. Snorri is apparently more interested in dramatic episodes and "scenes" than in analyzing the reasons for the breach between Óláfr and Erlingr. The story of Ásbjǫrn selsbani, which ends in reconciliation, at least on the surface, is thus told in great detail, although the exact reason for the ultimate breach is not given at all. However, Snorri gives a quite reasonable sketch of the long-term conflict of interest between the two, which evidently forms the background of their dramatic clashes. Erlingr is in reality the king of Western Norway and consequently an obstacle to Óláfr's plan of becoming the real ruler of the country, which Snorri presents in other contexts. In Snorri's narrative, however, the issue is rather the more concrete conflict between Erlingr's quite reasonable claim on the *veitslur* he has held for a long time and Óláfr's insistence on the king's free disposition of them, a principle that is apparently legally well founded, whatever its merits from a political point of view. Snorri seems to imply, however, that such conflicts of interest do not inevitably lead to open enmity. This is more likely to be the result of more or less fortuitous events, which leave the protagonists no other choice but fighting for their relatives, their honor, and so forth. Though not explicitly stated, the selsbani episode seems to be an example of this.

A similar example is King Cnut's slaying of his earl Úlfr Þorgilsson. Úlfr served as Cnut's representative in Denmark while Cnut was in England. He then became involved in an attempt to make Cnut's son King of Denmark in his father's absence. The attempt failed and Úlfr became reconciled with Cnut (OH chap. 148). Some time afterward, Cnut is received by Úlfr at a *banquet*. Úlfr shows great hospitality and is in good spirits, but the king is silent. Later, a chess party leads to a quarrel. Úlfr leaves the king in anger, and the next day Cnut has him killed (OH chaps. 152–153, *Hkr,* vol. 2: 369 ff.). Cnut clearly regards Úlfr as a dangerous man after his attempt at rebellion, and their quarrel is a good pretext to get rid of him.

The same applies to most of the other conflict episodes we have considered so far. Þórir hundr becomes Óláfr's enemy because of Ásbjǫrn's death, but Snorri hints that his pride and independence as a magnate might have led to this in any case. The conflict between Óláfr and the Árnasons is clearly accidental, but does not lead to permanent enmity between the parties. Hárekr at Tjøtta's relations to Óláfr are strained through Óláfr's promotion of Ásmundr Grankelsson, which in its turn is part of Óláfr's policy of creating a counterweight against the mightiest magnates. Hárekr's final defection then takes place after his conflict with Ásmundr's father Grankell. Finally, Kálfr Árnason has good reasons for leaving Óláfr when his stepsons are killed, but his decisive motive seems to be self-interest. The episodes analyzed so far thus point to the conclusion that Snorri normally regards conflicts as the result of a combination of immediate clashes over concrete issues and conflicting long-term interests.

The Importance of the Interest Aspect

This conclusion receives further support from Snorri's description of the outbreak of the civil war in the 1150s, which presents the alternatives confronting the actors after an accidental clash. This passage is practically identical with those of *Fagrskinna* and *Morkinskinna* (*Ingi* chaps. 26–28; see also *Msk.*: 454 ff.; *Fsk.*: 352 ff.). The conflict between King Ingi and his brothers Sigurðr and Eysteinn, according to both Snorri and his predecessors, had its origin in Sigurðr's and Eysteinn's plan to depose Ingi, because of his bodily defects that made him unfit to be king. This agreement was concluded as part of a settlement after Sigurðr's killing of two of Eysteinn's men. The plan then became known to Ingi and his men. When Ingi and Sigurðr meet in Bergen in connection with a scheduled meeting between all three kings, their adherents quarrel. One of the housecarls of Grégóríús, Ingi's closest friend and the real leader of his faction, is killed. Grégóríús demands revenge but Ingi and many others are unwilling. Then one of Ingi's *hirðmenn* (retainers) is killed. At the following meeting between Ingi's adherents, Grégóríús and Ingi's mother Ingiríðr strongly urge Ingi to take action. Grégóríús bases his arguments on a "domino theory": if Ingi does not take revenge, their next step will be to kill a *lendr maðr* (landed man) and then gradually to decimate Ingi's adherents, until he is left alone and can be easily deposed. The "doves" in the assembly argue that Sigurðr will certainly offer indemnity. They are not heard, and Ingi and his men attack Sigurðr's hostel and kill him. When Eysteinn arrives shortly afterward, a new conflict is imminent. But men go between, and a settlement is reached. During the following two years there are frequent clashes and settlements, until full war breaks out and Eysteinn is deserted by his adherents and killed (*Ingi* chaps. 29–32).

This example shows in an unusually clear way the deliberations following an accidental clash, in which long-term interests determine whether or not it will result in a full-scale conflict. Although a similar conflict between Sigurðr and Eysteinn led to an alliance between them, the deaths of Ingi's and Grégóríús's men were exploited by the latter to launch a full attack on Sigurðr. Though there are numerous stories of accidental clashes in *Heimskringla,* it seems that in most cases they are not by themselves able to account for serious conflicts between the leading men in society. Competitions (*mannjafnaðr*) or quarrels over matters of prestige between kings or magnates or conflicts arising out of incidents between their men may lead to dramatic situations, but not to full-scale conflicts unless conflicting long-term interests are involved.[13] In the latter case, however, trivial incidents may lead to major conflicts.[14] Though Snorri clearly implies that honor, sudden anger, and the like were important factors, society had its mechanisms to prevent such clashes from leading to extended and violent conflicts. Friends, often older and wiser than the protagonists themselves, go between, and according to traditional law and custom almost any crime or dishonor could be compensated economically. The actors therefore had the choice between violence and negotiation, and this choice seems to a considerable extent to be determined by long-term interests.

Snorri's Politicians

The greater importance of long-term interests over accidental clashes is apparent from the fact that the former are by themselves sufficient to lead to a conflict whereas the latter are not. In contrast to the episode of the *mannjafnaðr,* the real feuds of the Eiríkssons are the results of conscious planning to get rid of rivals. They are ambitious and greedy, and being many, they have a difficult economy. This makes them pursue a ruthless policy of extermination against their rivals. Snorri opens their saga with a presentation of the *hǫfðingjar* (here: rulers) at the time (*HGráf.* chap. 1). Haraldr hárfagri's descendants Tryggvi Óláfsson and Guðrøðr Bjarnarson ruled respectively in Eastern Norway and Vestfold, both apparently as kings, whereas Earl Sigurðr of Lade (son of Haraldr hárfagri's ally Earl Hákon) ruled Trøndelag. The Eiríkssons themselves ruled Western Norway, like their predecessor Hákon. They came to terms with the other rulers during their first winter, allowing them to keep their territories in the same way as before. Peace did not last long, however. On one of their regular meetings, their mother Gunnhildr approaches the question of Earl Sigurðr, pointing out how small a part of the country her sons ruled. Although the two kings of Eastern Norway are kinsmen and thus ought to be tolerated, Sigurðr is not. It is a shame that Haraldr hárfagri would not have tolerated to allow him thus to keep a part of their paternal heritage (fǫðurleifð). Haraldr gráfeldr has no moral objections to this, but points to the difficulty of the undertaking, to which Gunnhildr replies that cunning is necessary. The result is that Sigurðr is killed by treachery (*HGráf.* chaps. 3–5). Some time later, the Eiríkssons suspect the kings of Eastern Norway of trying to ally themselves with Sigurðr's son, Earl Hákon; they attack them by surprise and kill them (*HGráf.* chaps. 9–10, 12).

The story of Earl Hákon's access to power (OT chaps. 9–16; I: 267–281) is also the story of a ruthless player in the political game, who pursues a consistent aim and outwits his rivals. It is not Snorri's own story, but taken over almost word by word from *Fagrskinna* (OT chaps. 9–15; see also *Fsk*: 58 ff.). Hákon has been expelled from his earldom in Trøndelag by the Eiríkssons and has been received by King Haraldr Gormsson in Denmark. When the story opens, Hákon is sitting in deep thought, barely eating and drinking, spending most of his time in bed, without being able to sleep. His problem is apparently how to win back his earldom. He is not completely inactive, however, but manages to spark off a rebellion against King Erlingr Eiríksson in Trøndelag by sending a messenger there. Then he is approached by his good friend Gull-Haraldr (Gold-Haraldr), the nephew of King Haraldr, a great Viking chieftain, who now wants a part of the kingdom to be able to settle in Denmark. He asks Hákon for advice in this matter, and Hákon advises him to go to the king and claim his part of the kingdom, which King Haraldr angrily refuses. Gull-Haraldr returns, in greater trouble than before: he is still without a kingdom, but has now incurred the king's disgrace. Hákon kindles the fire, pointing out that Haraldr is in great danger, but cannot give up his claim without shame. He admonishes him strictly to disclose these talks to no one. Next, King Haraldr comes to Hákon for advice. Hákon points out his dilemma to him: if he refuses Gull-Haraldr's claim, the latter will rebel against him and probably get considerable support. If he kills him, people will blame him for it. The king strongly urges Hákon to give him advice, and Hákon asks for a few days to think. He remains alone, and when the king comes back, he tells of his long hours of waking and thinking, which have finally led to a solution: the king should keep Denmark for himself, but let Gull-Haraldr have Norway. The king objects, pointing out that Norway is a difficult country to conquer and that King Haraldr gráfeldr is his foster-son, but Hákon insists that this is the only solution to the dilemma and finally manages to convince him. The plan is to entice Haraldr gráfeldr to come to Denmark and then let Gull-Haraldr kill him and take over the kingdom. The plan is disclosed to Gull-Haraldr, who agrees. Haraldr gráfeldr is invited to Denmark to receive *veitslur* there, and Gull-Haraldr leaves to attack him. Then Hákon makes his final move. He arouses the king's suspicion against Gull-Haraldr by telling him of Gull-Haraldr's plan to kill him for refusing to share the kingdom. Hákon offers his service, to kill Gull-Haraldr. The king accepts, Hákon departs, attacking and killing Gull-Haraldr shortly after the latter having killed King Haraldr gráfeldr. King Haraldr and Hákon then go to Norway and conquer the country, which Hákon is to govern as the king's earl. When King Haraldr tries to convert Hákon and the Norwegians to Christianity,

Hákon makes himself completely independent and later defends his country against Haraldr's son and successor Sveinn.

A third example of politicians consciously pursuing long-term interests is Einarr þambarskelfir's and Kálfr Árnason's activity during the reign of St. Óláfr and his immediate successors. Both had played a prominent part in the opposition against St. Óláfr. After his death, when the combination of Óláfr's reputation for sainthood and the unpopularity of the Danish regime had led to widespread opposition against the Danish King Sveinn and his mother Álfífa, Einarr and Kálfr became the leaders of the opposition and put Óláfr's son, the young Magnús, on the throne (OH chap. 240 ff.; MG chap. 1–5). Snorri explains this change of sides in an entirely logical way.

Einarr, having been pushed aside by St. Óláfr, sees his opportunity when Cnut approaches the Norwegian magnates. He is promised the position as the mightiest man in the country next to the king, with the title of earl, and joins Cnut in England. After Óláfr's exile, however, he is disappointed. Having learned that Cnut does not intend to keep his promise to him of making him earl, he prepares rather leisurely to go back to Norway, in case Óláfr should return: ". . . it occurred to him that it might be a wise course not to be in too great a hurry about his return journey; because if it came to a fight with King Óláf he might not have an increase in power any more than before."[15] Now Snorri once more describes Einarr the politician. After the battle of Stiklestad, he lauded himself that he had not fought against King Óláfr. Then he remembered that Cnut had promised him an earldom and not kept his promise. Finally, when there are rumors that Óláfr was a saint and increasing dissatisfaction with the Danish rule, Einarr comes forward as the first of the magnates to believe in Óláfr's sainthood and as the leader of the opposition against the Danes.

Kálfr Árnason, who was one of Óláfr's closest adherents, joined the king's adversaries, partly because of the latter having killed his two stepsons (OH chaps. 165–166), partly to serve his own interests. Concerning the stepsons, Kálfr is under pressure from his wife, the mother of the two young men. Besides, Kálfr is a rather cynical player, who acts according to his long-term interests. After Óláfr's exile, he is offered a leading position in the country by Cnut, succumbs to the temptation, and becomes one of the leaders of the army against Óláfr at Stiklestad. Like Einarr, he does not get the promotion he has expected and gradually joins the opposition against the Danes, though he has reasons to be more reluctant, as he had actively fought King Óláfr and even, according to some, had dealt him one of his fatal wounds (OH chap. 228: 494). Still, he has the same reason as Einarr to be dissatisfied with the new régime. Further, he has been Óláfr's old adherent and all his brothers are firmly in Óláfr's camp. His change of side is therefore also a reconciliation with his brothers (OH chap. 247). Accordingly, Einarr and Kálfr go to Russia and return with the young King Magnús, who receives overwhelming support. Sveinn then leaves the country and dies shortly afterward in Denmark (MG chaps. 4–5). During the following reign, Einarr and Kálfr are the real leaders, until Kálfr has to leave the country to avoid being killed by Magnús as a revenge for his father's death (MG chaps. 13–14). Einarr remains the most prominent of the magnates until Magnús's death, but falls from favor under his uncle and successor Haraldr harðráði and is killed by him. In Snorri's description, Einarr and Kálfr are thus power politicians who act out of self-interest. They change sides several times and their acts are all to be explained as means to further their own interests.

The Game of Politics

The ultimate object of the actors in the political conflicts is probably best defined as the greatest possible power and influence. In a rather loosely organized society such as Snorri's, this is not generally to be identified with any particular office or position. Kingship, of course, is the supreme position in society, and, as Snorri's work deals with kings, one of the most important objects of contest. This contest, however, is not open, as only a limited number of participants can aspire to this office. There are also other offices, such as those of earl or *lendr maðr,* which can be subject to contests, but this is exceptional. More often, conflicts are about rights, which may be of greatly varying importance in themselves, but which, through being contested, may lead to increased power and influence.

At first sight, the conflicts Snorri describes appear like a *bellum omnium contra omnes* in which the will to power is the only motive and strength the only resource needed. Though there is a strong element of political realism, even cynicism, in Snorri, this is not quite correct. Snorri is normally careful in presenting the legal claims of the factions in the conflicts. Aggressive and ruthless men like Eiríkr blóðøx and Earl Hákon of Lade, to some extent even the Eiríkssons, have some legal claims, or at least some particular reasons for their actions. When civil war breaks out after the death of King Sigurðr jórsalafari (1130), his half-brother Haraldr gilli has some excuse for breaking his oath of not claiming the kingdom as long as Sigurðr's son Magnús was alive, namely that he was forced to make it (MB.HG chap. 1: 316; see also *Msyn.* chap. 26). Magnús, in his turn, could use this oath as justification for claiming the kingdom alone after some years of co-rule with Haraldr

(MB.HG chap. 2: 317). Haraldr's murderer, Sigurðr slembir, has apparently a bad case, which is stated thus by the king's men and people of Bergen, who refuse to serve a man who had murdered his brother: ". . . and if he was not your brother, then you have not the birth to be king" (". . . en ef hann var eigi þinn bróðir, þá áttu enga ætt til at vera konungr," MB.HG chap. 16: 346; Holl.: 734). But Sigurðr can justify his action by Haraldr's refusal to let him prove his claims and his attempt on his life (MB.HG chaps. 14–15). In the 1150s, Sigurðr and Eysteinn use Ingi's physical disability as an argument for deposing him, whereas Ingi and his adherents use this attempt, together with accidental clashes between adherents of the factions, as excuse for a counterattack. When Ingi's adherents continue the fight after the death of their king (1161), they apparently have a weaker legal foundation. After all, their adversary, Hákon herðibreiðr, is undoubtedly the son of a king, whereas they are left without a legitimate heir. Their spokesman, Erlingr skakki, then gives another argument: it would not be safe for Ingi's former adherents to serve Hákon (ME chap. 1: 433 f.). In other words: "necessitas non habet legem." No one can demand that one should sacrifice one's life and honor for the sake of legitimate succession! Even the Danish King Cnut has some hereditary claim on Norway, which is one of his motives for the war against St. Óláfr (OH chap. 130).

Snorri rarely comments on the legitimacy of the claims, nor do pretenders or their adherents give detailed arguments to prove that they have better claims than their adversaries. St. Óláfr does so in one case, in a speech to the people of Trøndelag, in which he refers to the fact that Earl Hákon has given up his claim on Norway at his surrender some time before (OH chap. 40). This is probably more a tactical than a legal argument: when Hákon has resigned, there is no reason why the people of Trøndelag should not acclaim Óláfr. In his speech on behalf of King Hákon herðibreiðr before the battle of Göta Älv, Sigurðr from Reyr states Hákon's legitimate claim to the throne in some detail (*HHerð.* chap. 8). This is a battle speech, however, and not intended to convince anyone but those who were already on Hákon's side. Finally, King Magnús góði claims England in a letter, stating in detail his hereditary right. King Edward the Confessor answers in the same way, and Magnús finally decides to abstain from further claims. This is a rare example of a king who abstains from pushing his claims for ideological or legal reasons.[16] Conflicts are not usually decided on the basis of the legitimacy of the claims that are brought forward, nor does Snorri often refer to detailed discussions of such claims. Still, it would be wrong to dismiss them as mere pretexts for ruthless power politics. A sort of basic legitimacy seems to be a necessary condition for playing the game at all. As this condition is normally satisfied, Snorri does not comment very much

upon it. But the example of Sigurðr slembir seems to point to the conclusion that it is a very serious matter if it is not. Sigurðr has great difficulties in winning adherents, and though Snorri does not state so directly,
his cruel treatment when taken captive may have something to do with
his lack of legitimacy.[17] Legitimacy thus serves as a sort of "entrance
ticket" to the game. When this condition is satisfied, there is no question
of degrees of legitimacy; then intelligence, arms, and the ability to attract followers settle the issue.[18]

The question of legitimacy in Snorri's narrative is not primarily a
question of power versus right. It is rather an expression of the fact that
conflicts take place within a certain social order and in a rather static
society. There are great possibilities of conflicting legal claims and it is
often necessary to fight them out. Norms and exact rights are often
vaguely defined. Still, only a limited number of persons are allowed to
fight for the kingdom, and monarchy itself, though rather vaguely defined, contains power and resources that remain basically the same
throughout history. The game is a zero sum game within relatively fixed
limits and the fight is not a breach against the social order; it is part of it.

As often, the rule is best illustrated through its exception, Haraldr
hárfagri's conquest of Norway. This is a totally unprecedented undertaking, which cannot be explained in normal terms. How could Haraldr get
such an idea? Romantic legend provides the answer: Haraldr gets the
idea from a woman, Gyða, whom he wants as his mistress, but who
refuses him, because he is only a petty king. Haraldr then promises not
to cut his hair until he has conquered the whole of Norway (*HHárf.*
chaps. 3–4). The story is a traditional one and not Snorri's invention.
But there are numerous examples of Snorri "rationalizing" fantastic or
mythical explanations of earlier authors. When he fails to do so in this
case, the reason is most probably that Haraldr's undertaking was so
extraordinary that a "mythical" explanation seemed necessary. Snorri's
explanation is thus not simply evidence of a certain naiveté, but points to
the contrast between the normal working of the political game between
actors with more limited aims and the conception of an enormously
ambitious plan, which permanently alters the history of the country.

No other story of a conflict is entirely comparable to this. When later
kings and princes try to conquer the kingdom, they have Haraldr as a
precedent and most often can trace their hereditary claims from him.
Characteristically, the clearest examples of long-term political planning
concern quite well-defined rights. Eiríkr blóðøx is no doubt a ruthless
and aggressive person who does not shrink from killing his brothers, but
he has a legal claim to overlordship over the whole country in Haraldr's
decision (*HHárf.* chaps. 41, 43). The Eiríkssons have particular economic reasons for wanting the kingdom for themselves and eliminating

their rivals, and may even have similar legal arguments as their father, at least for eliminating Earl Sigurðr. Earl Hákon is in exile in Denmark and intrigues against Gull-Haraldr and Haraldr gráfeldr to regain his heritage in Norway, and Kálfr Árnason and Einarr þambarskelfir change sides in order to gain quite specific political positions. The actions of such men need not necessarily be explained from long-term planning; quite as often, they react to the opportunities that present themselves, such as King Cnut's offers or the change of opinion on St. Óláfr.

The conflicts between the king and individual magnates, which fill so much of the reign of St. Óláfr and are prominent in some other parts of *Heimskringla* as well, are more complex. There is no inevitable conflict of interest between a king and a magnate, as there is between two pretenders to the throne. Therefore, such conflicts are more often the result of accidental clashes. As already mentioned, the exact issues involved may differ considerably, from political interests of the first order, as in the case of Erlingr Skjálgsson's *veitslur,* to rather trivial matters, which gain importance through the rivalry over power and influence in general, as in the conflict between Haraldr harðráði and Einarr þambarskelfir. Or they may be strictly personal matters, as in the case of Hákon Ívarsson and Finnr Árnason, who fight to revenge the death of their kinsmen.

St. Óláfr is clearly the king who was involved in the greatest conflicts with his magnates. He is also the king who comes nearest to being a parallel to Haraldr hárfagri. First, his and his namesake Óláfr Tryggvason's Christianization of the country is something quite unprecedented. This, however, partly belongs to the supernatural sphere and is partly explained in familiar terms of power politics. On the purely political level, Snorri stresses the contrast between his strong monarchy and his predecessors', the earls', concessions to the leading magnates. There is also a considerable amount of long-term strategy in Snorri's decription of St. Óláfr's internal policy. Snorri's chronology, in letting Óláfr establish himself as king through acclamation at the popular assemblies and treaties with the leading magnates before his attempts at Christianization, is evidence of this. Snorri's references to Óláfr's alliances with a number of magnates, mostly of secondary rank, is probably intended as a description of a consistent policy directed against his rivals inside and outside the country (see Schreiner, 1926: 108 ff.). In the Bohuslän region, Óláfr allies himself with the mighty farmer Brynjólfr úlfaldi (camel) and makes him his *lendr maðr,* thus using him against the king of Sweden (OH chap. 61). In Opplandene he has a faithful adherent in Ketill kálfr (calf) of Ringnes, who uncovers the plot of the petty kings and is later married to one of Óláfr's half-sisters (OH chaps. 52, 75, 128). The Árnasons are his firm supporters in the Møre region, one of them, Kálfr, taking over the position of Qlvi at Egge after his execution, thus giving the king a foothold in the important region of Trøndelag (OH chap. 110). In Gudbrandsdalen he allies himself with Þórðr Guthormsson at Steig, possibly as a counter-weight against Dala-Guðbrandr (OH chap. 128; see also Schreiner, 1926: 121 f.). In the central region of Western Norway, he tries to use Áslákr fitjaskalli against Erlingr Skjálgsson, but fails (OH chap. 116). Finally, Grankell and his son Ásmundr are used to balance the power of Hárekr at Tjøtta in Northern Norway (OH chaps. 106, 140; see also above).

In the first half of the saga, Óláfr usually has the initiative, and Snorri's composition, which concentrates on Óláfr's successes in the first ten years of his reign, serves to create the impression of a king who systematically extends his power and pursues his policy in various fields. Having put Óláfr on the throne, Snorri describes his fullfilment of vari-ous aims: reconquest of the border regions toward Sweden and peace with the Swedish king, Christianization, subordination of the leading magnates, and increased control of the Norse settlements in the West. However, there is little real connection between the fields. When they are "interlaced" in the narrative, the purpose is not to present them in an overall perspective, but rather to fit them into Snorri's geographical and chronological schema.

For instance, there is a close chronological connection between Óláfr's victory over the petty kings of Eastern Norway and his negotia-tions with his namesake, King Óláfr of Sweden. Snorri even exploits the connection when letting the latter's daughter, Ingigerðr, compare the king of Norway's success in capturing five kings at one time to her father capturing five birds (OH chap. 89). But Snorri makes no at-tempt to draw the line between the situation in Sweden and that in Eastern Norway. Were the petty kings encouraged by Óláfr's difficul-ties in the border region? Was Óláfr eager to make peace with Sweden in order to be able to deal with the internal opposition? Did his victory in Eastern Norway bring in him a stronger position vis-à-vis the King of Sweden? The two stories are told without any consideration along these lines.

In the subsequent conflicts with some of the mightiest magnates, conflicting long-term interests are clearly involved. But it is nevertheless difficult to detect a consistent strategy on Óláfr's part. He clearly seeks to extend his power, but the actual conflicts concern rather limited is-sues. Óláfr does not maneuver to depose Erlingr Skjálgsson from his position in Western Norway, nor does Erlingr want to make himself totally independent of Óláfr or depose him—at least, not until King Cnut has entered the scene. In general, what binds the different conflict episodes together, is not a clear-cut opposition between Óláfr's attempts to create a strong monarchy and an aristocracy fighting for traditional positions, but the fact that the magnates gradually become involved through friendship or kinship with Óláfr's enemies. Though Snorri has done much through his chronological arrangement to create a coherent picture of Óláfr's reign, the king is not depicted as a great strategist aiming at changing society in accordance with some well-defined aim of aggrandizement of the royal power. The king clearly takes initiatives in various fields, but there is little connection between them. And a considerable part of his activity is simply reactions to issues that present themselves. To some extent, this is the consequence of the strictly personal character of the political game in Snorri: Óláfr does not fight for the monarchy, he fights for his own, personal interests. But it is also a consequence of the rather static character of Snorri's society. The conflicts take place within a society that is more stable than it appears at first sight. The game offers few opportunities for large-scale strategy; therefore, Snorri's politicians are tacticians more than strategists.

Success and Failure

Having established that politics in Snorri is primarily a game between individual actors who maneuver for gain, we next turn to the question of success and failure. How is the game won?

Óláfr's Conquest of Norway

Snorri's story of Óláfr's access to power may serve as an example. Óláfr arrives with two ships (knarrar, i.e., normally merchant ships) and 260 men (OH chap. 29). After several years as a Viking, with many victories and much booty, one would suspect that he also carried with him a lot of gold. This is confirmed by a scaldic stanza quoted by Snorri (OH chap. 30: 38 f.), but Snorri himself does not elaborate on the matter. Nor does he explain why Óláfr has such a small force, despite the fact that he must have been a prominent "war entrepreneur" during the fight over England in the previous years. By contrast, Snorri gives a vivid picture of the formidable opposition he was likely to meet on his return to Norway. The two leading magnates, Einarr þambarskelfir in Trøndelag and Erlingr Skjálgsson at Sola in Western Norway, have great resources. Before Óláfr's return, the earls have contracted marriage alliances with both of them and have them firmly on their side (OH chaps. 21–22, 31). Furthermore, the *lendir menn* are extremely powerful at this time and are wholly on the earls' side.

The actual conquest of Norway takes place in four steps:

1. Óláfr surprises and takes captive the young Earl Hákon and forces him to give up his claim to Norway (OH chap. 30).

2. Óláfr goes eastward to Opplandene to see his stepfather Sigurðr sýr and by his help manages to get the support of the Oppland kings. They in turn make the people of the region accept him (OH chaps. 32–37).

3. Óláfr goes to Trøndelag and is acclaimed king by the people there, but is attacked by his adversaries Earl Sveinn and Einarr þambarskelfir and has a narrow escape (OH chaps. 38–42, 44–45).

4. Óláfr's adversaries gather a large force against him, but are defeated in the battle of Nesjar. Óláfr is then acclaimed king over the whole country, and his adversaries either accept him or leave the country (OH chaps. 46–53, 56).

All the events of this story are taken from earlier authors. One is common only to *Fagrskinna* and *Heimskringla,* namely Óláfr's expedition to Trøndelag in his first winter (1014–1015, according to Snorri's chronology), but this is unimportant for Snorri's general view of the reasons for Óláfr's success. Snorri's most important changes are the following:

1. The religious aspect is toned down. In the clerical sagas, Óláfr's return to Norway is the result of God's direct intervention.[19] Snorri also mentions this, but purely political reasons are much more prominent. Characteristically, Snorri also omits the story in chapter 24 of the *Legendary Saga* that Óláfr tried to avoid fighting the battle of Nesjar on a Sunday.

2. The political explanation of Óláfr's success is largely Snorri's own creation. Snorri uses information on the earls and the mightiest men in Norway before Óláfr's arrival in an original way to create a precise picture of the political situation in the country, showing the difficulties he had to overcome, and then goes on to describe how he managed to change the loyalty of the magnates and the people. At this point Snorri differs equally from the clerical sagas as from *Fagrskinna.* The latter gives only the events, without explanation (*Fsk.* chaps. 26–27), whereas the clerical sagas give a religious explanation.

Like many other, similar stories in Old Norse literature, the story resembles the one of David and Goliath.[20] Óláfr manages to overcome a formidable opposition in a short time and wins a total victory. His luck (*hamingja*) is an important element in this. But Óláfr's victory is by no means described as a miracle. Snorri manages to give an explanation in social and psychological terms, showing how Óláfr step by step was able to gain the support of the magnates and people.

The crucial event in this context is Óláfr's meeting with the petty kings of Opplandene, to whom he presents his claims (OH chaps. 35–36). First, Óláfr addresses a forceful speech to his mother and stepfather, pointing to his right to the kingdom, his will to fight for it, and the people's wish to be delivered from foreign rulers. Sigurðr then agrees to support him and presents his case at a meeting of the Oppland kings. The decisive arguments in Óláfr's favor, as brought forward by King Hringr, are first, the ties of kinship that exist between him and them, and second, Óláfr's luck and impressive personality, which makes it likely that he will win in any case, so that it will be in the interest of the petty kings to support him as early as possible. Both the situation in general and other, similar cases, point to the conclusion that the latter argument is the more important. Óláfr's success so far, in capturing Earl Hákon, and his impressive personality speak in his favor. By contrast, there is no discussion of his legitimate claim to the kingship.

Óláfr's success at this meeting gains him the support that is necessary to win the battle of Nesjar. In this battle, which proves decisive, Óláfr is numerically inferior, but has excellent and well-equipped men in his army. This is probably an important factor behind his victory. Apart from that, Snorri does not explain why Óláfr won, and he is completely silent on his personal performance during the battle. However, he clearly indicates why this battle is decisive, namely because it gives him the people's support. Earl Sveinn goes to Sweden to prepare another attack with Swedish help. In the meantime Óláfr is able to travel around the country and be acclaimed king. Sveinn's adherents among the *lendir menn* either go into exile or make their peace with Óláfr. The latter group includes Erlingr Skjálgsson. Though Óláfr is luckily saved from a renewed attack by Sveinn's death the following year, these events clearly show the political consequences of victory.

Snorri has thus managed to give an explanation of Óláfr's apparently miraculous victory in terms of impressive military successes, diplomatic ability, and a charismatic personality. How far can this example be generalized? And which of these factors is in Snorri's opinion normally the most important?

The Means to Success: War

In contrast to modern, democratic politics, Snorri's politics—or at least the part of it with which *Heimskringla* is primarily concerned—is essentially military. The competition for adherents does not take place in the form of election campaigns or struggle for office. Admittedly, the king is elected, and Snorri lays some emphasis on this fact. The pretenders, however, do not confront each other at the popular assemblies, but on the battlefield. Snorri's conflicts thus normally involve violence, and the use or threat of it is the most important means of competing for power or political positions. This does not necessarily mean that *Heims-*

kringla is primarily concerned with battles or military action or that skill at arms is the most important quality in a successful politician.

Snorri's descriptions of battles are fairly stereotyped. In the earlier part of the saga, where his sources are scarce, he confines himself to some general remarks about hard fighting, often quoting scaldic poetry (e.g., HS chaps. 1–4 and *HHárf.* chaps. 5, 11–12, 17–18). Later, he mainly describes dramatic episodes and individual bravery.[21] Nowhere are "stance" and traditional chivalric virtues more prominent than in the battle descriptions. The outcome of the battle is usually only stated, not explained. Occasionally, special reasons for the victory of one party are given, either deliberate stratagems or arrangements that happen to surprise the enemy. When fighting the Eiríkssons with inferior forces, Hákon góði arranges his army in a long, thin line, to avoid being surrounded. This makes the enemy believe that they are being surrounded by a superior force, and they flee (HG chap. 24). Speeches of exhortation before the battles usually contain little information on strategy, while at the same time being rather poor agitation, in clear contrast to those of *Sverris saga* (Lie, 1937: 104 f.).

Strategy plays a more prominent part toward the end of the saga, in the part dealing with the civil wars from the 1150s. Describing the Birchlegs' attack on Nidaros in 1176, Snorri blames the defenders for retiring into the upper story of a house (lopt) instead of trying to defend the whole complex of buildings (garðr). If so, the townsmen would have come to their assistance (ME chap. 40). This is not a specifically strategic observation, however, but rather a case of the general rule of the importance of demonstrating strength in order to gain support. Snorri's greater emphasis on military matters during this period may have to do both with the more prolonged wars and with the fact that some of the protagonists at this time distinguished themselves as generals, namely Grégóríús Dagsson and above all Erlingr skakki. Grégóríús, who was the real leader of King Ingi's faction until his death early in 1161, is described more like the conventional warrior hero: strong, beautiful, brave, and generous to his men, whereas Erlingr, who succeeded him as faction leader and was the virtual ruler of the country until his death in 1179, is the cold, calculating politician and strategist. Erlingr's strategic ability is described for the first time during the battle of Göta Älv in 1159 in which he advises the king and the other leaders to attack downstream, to avoid using men to row, thus exploiting their numerical superiority (*HHerð.* chaps. 5–7; see also Bagge, 1986: 185). In the last battle of *Heimskringla,* the battle of Ré (1177), Erlingr's son Magnús defeats the numerically superior Birchlegs because the latter are hampered by the deep snow, whereas Magnús's men have packed down the snow to be able to move (ME chap. 42).

These are rather simple devices and not evidence of brilliant strategic thinking. More important is the fact that Snorri describes an increasing contrast between the discipline, strategy, and intelligent planning of Erlingr skakki and his faction, to which the majority of the aristocracy belongs, and the brave but unruly and ill-planned warfare of their opponents (ME chaps. 5–7, 12–13, 33, 36). This contrast, however, is not confined to military matters, but is a particular example of Snorri's general rule that intelligence and the ability to attract adherents and lead them are more important than reckless courage and that such qualities are more likely to be found among the established leaders of society.

The importance of warfare is difficult to detect from Snorri's battle descriptions, because he so rarely explains the reasons for victory and defeat in them. The picture becomes a little clearer if we also consider his descriptions of campaigns. Insofar as they more often involve political considerations, these are normally better than his battle descriptions. Both Haraldr hárfagri's and St. Óláfr's conquests of Norway are examples of this. Cnut's conquest may be placed in the same category. He prepares the ground through rich gifts to the Norwegian magnates, and when he actually arrives with his large force, he wins the country without battle (OH chaps. 130–131, 161, 170–171).

Normally Snorri describes the frequent movements of the armies without giving any reasons for them. To some extent, this may be explained by the fact that this was obvious to his readers. In medieval Norwegian warfare, fairly constant movement of armies was necessary simply to get provisions (Bagge, 1986: 184). Most of the country must therefore be covered within a relatively short time, at least if the army was large. The reason for moving to some particular place would either be to fight a battle with the enemy or to gain support from the population of the region in question. This strategic thinking can be illustrated in the deliberations at the court of King Magnús blindi in Bergen late in 1134 at the news of his rival, Haraldr gilli's, return to Norway after his defeat the previous autumn (MB chap. 5).

Magnús asks the *lendr maðr* Sigurðr Sigurðarson for advice. Sigurðr gives him the following suggestions, which are in turn rejected by the king: (1) open negotiations and offer to share the kingdom with Haraldr; (2) attack and kill the *lendir menn,* who have now refused their help, and raise new men to their positions who will be more trustworthy, and then mobilize all the forces he can get to attack Haraldr in the east; (3) withdraw to Trøndelag, which is densely populated, and assemble men there. Finally, he sees that Magnús has already decided to remain in Bergen to await Haraldr's attack. Warning him that this will lead to his fall, he leaves him.

The story is also found in *Fagrskinna* and may be ultimately derived from *Hryggjarstykki*. If so, we cannot exclude the possibility that it may contain some historical truth. But it is probably rather to be regarded as a preparation for a major event, the fall of a king. Despite Magnús's youth and cruel fate, Snorri shows scant sympathy for him. Consequently, a fitting prelude is not ill omens, but a dialogue that brings out the king's stupidity. The situation, however, is not dissimilar to that facing St. Óláfr after Cnut's attack. Óláfr also chose to remain passive, but Cnut, for some mysterious reason, did not attack him. Óláfr's passivity, however, cost him his kingdom. As Óláfr is one of Snorri's great heroes, Snorri does not construct a similar dialogue in his case or attempt to explain his behavior, but rather he tries to suppress the awkward fact of his passivity.[22] Both in Óláfr's and Magnús's case, the choice of strategy is posed more in political than in military terms. It is not a strategy of fixed armies, which move against strongholds or places of particular strategic interest, but rather a question of moving in a way that is likely to lead to maximum support.

Similarly, the real purpose of winning a military victory is to gain support. Whatever the reasons for initial support, early success or failure is normally decisive for the final outcome. Óláfr gains sufficient support to defeat his enemies through a combination of luck and charisma. Óláfr Tryggvason's coup in Trøndelag proves sufficient for him to gain the whole country (OT chaps. 47–49, 51). When the civil wars of the twelfth century start in 1130, neither of the two pretenders is a very impressive personality. Haraldr seems to have been personally the more popular, whereas Magnús to some extent could count on the loyalty people had felt to his father, King Sigurðr jórsalafari. At the start of the conflict, Magnús is able to assemble a largely superior force and defeat Haraldr. Haraldr flees, but returns with Danish support and is able to capture Magnús and win the country thanks to the latter's stupid behavior after his initial victory. During the war between Haraldr's sons, Ingi relatively soon wins the support of most of the magnates and thus of the people and is able to defeat his rivals (*Ingi* chaps. 22, 29–32). The exceptions to this are mainly campaigns in foreign countries, where one cannot usually count on support. Snorri's descriptions of these campaigns are normally rather pointless lists of raids and sackings, interrupted by battles, in which heroes and dramatic episodes are emphasized in the ordinary way. Haraldr harðráði's war with Denmark (*HHarð.* chaps. 29–35, 58–67, 71) and Magnús berfoetr's campaigns in Scotland, Ireland, and other regions of the west (MB chaps. 8–11, 23–25) may serve as examples. In the inner Norwegian conflicts, there are only two exceptions, the last phase of the civil wars which Snorri describes and above all Haraldr hárfagri's conquest. The latter is a prolonged struggle, lasting for ten years and with numerous battles.

Haraldr's conquest is clearly exceptional in other respects as well. Even in this case, however, Haraldr's victory is to a considerable extent determined by his ability to win support. Early in his account of the conquest, Snorri gives a sketch of his system of government, based upon a fixed number of magnates of higher rank (earls) and of lower (hersar) (*HHárf.* chap. 6; see also below), adding that many powerful men now entered Haraldr's service because it gave them more power and wealth than they had had as independent kings or rulers. In the following he gives examples of this, Haraldr's alliances with Earl Hákon of Lade and Earl Rǫgnvaldr of Møre, two of the mightiest men in the country (*HHárf.* chaps. 7, 10). Like Óláfr, Haraldr is a great hero, who wins against great odds, but his victory is no miracle. He can fight his adversaries one by one, and after some initial successes, he gets powerful allies and increasing support.

Why is Snorri such a poor military historian? I shall postpone the full discussion of this question. But part of the answer must be that he considers politics to be more important than warfare. A military victory is indoubtedly an important step toward the final success. But it can easily be destroyed by an incompetent politician, as the example of Magnús blindi shows. Further, a military victory is often the result of good political management in assembling a sufficient number of adherents and giving them the right inspiration. The military aspect is thus subordinated to the political one. To win a military victory is not sufficient in itself but is a means to win support and thus to gain the final victory. Success in this game is above all dependent on support, which in its turn is largely determined by success. In the same way as the protagonists in the conflicts, the magnates and people as a whole are rational actors, who act according to their own interests. Therefore they support the strongest; and therefore the combination of an impressive personality and an impressive victory is likely to lead to universal support.

The lesson to be drawn from these examples is thus that "nothing succeeds like success," and—corresponding to this—that "nothing fails like failure." This latter maxim is aptly illustrated by the words of the crippled King Ingi after the death of his closest friend and best warrior Grégóríús (1161), when his friends advise him to flee from the battle:

> I have often heard you say, and I think there was truth in it, that Eysteinn, my brother, was little favored by fortune, once he took to flight, and he was well equipped with the qualities that adorn a king. Now it is easy to see how, with my disability, I shall have little success, if I do what caused him so much trouble, considering the difference between us in health and strength in every respect.[23]

A consequence of this system, which at the same time contributes to its maintenance, is that the defeated faction is normally treated mildly. The rival and some of his closest adherents may be killed or exiled, but the rest of the faction not only save their lives and estates, but also their ranks and enter the service of the victor.[24] The working of the system is best illustrated by its exceptions. After Ingi's death, Erlingr skakki uses the danger to himself and his friends of accepting Hákon herðibreiðr as an argument to continue the fight under a new candidate. Snorri uses Erlingr's own harshness to his enemies as an explanation for their stubborn resistance and thus for the prolonged civil wars from around 1160.

Snorri's numerous examples of total victory may appear to contradict our impression of the rather limited aims of his political actors. Actually, however, there is a close correspondence between the two. Victory is total exactly because so little changes. One king is substituted for another, but monarchy remains largely the same throughout *Heimskringla*. Consequently, there is also a correspondence between the limited aims of the actors and Snorri's analysis of the political game. Like his actors, Snorri is a tactician more than a strategist.

The Means to Success: Diplomacy

Military success is thus mainly a means to win political support. How important is it compared to other means? The question may be put in the traditional terms of the contemporary mirrors of princes: what is more important for the prince, to be feared or to be loved? Some places Snorri refers to the general rule that people normally submit to superior forces. The leader of a burning and looting army normally has his will (OT chap. 87: 411; *Ingi* chap. 2: 352). But a much more common means to success is the use of gifts and concessions. There may be some social differences in this. Ordinary men are more easily terrorized, whereas it is necessary to win the friendship of magnates and mighty men. But the difference should not be exaggerated. In the long run, it is not possible to rule by terror and suppression. Those who try are deposed and killed, as the fate of numerous kings in *Heimskringla* demonstrates. In the saga of Haraldr harðráði this point is established as a general "law": when trying to persuade Haraldr to attack England in 1066, Earl Tósti points out that support from the magnates and the people is decisive in winning a country. Haraldr's predecessor Magnús succeeded in holding Denmark because he had this support, whereas Haraldr failed because he lacked it. Magnús did not try to conquer England because the people there wanted Edward as their king. Now, however, Tósti offers Haraldr the support of the majority of the magnates and people (*HHarð*. chap. 79). Snorri usually seems to imply that a conqueror, particularly a foreign one, will normally be unable to hold a country permanently through force. Though fear is not unimportant, Snorri thus seems to lay greater emphasis on love as a motive for obeying the prince.

"Love" in this context can be created in two ways, through an attractive personality (charisma) or by gifts, concessions, and so forth through which the king or pretender convinces people that it will be in their own interest to follow him. Snorri's speeches may serve as a clue to this. The importance of eloquence appears from the speeches at the meeting of the Oppland kings, from general statements to this effect in the characterizations of persons, and from numerous other speeches throughout *Heimskringla*. As we should expect, neither legitimacy nor ideological arguments play a prominent role.

The normal way of arguing is to start with a short presentation of one's claims and then to continue, either with an emotional appeal, or—more frequently—by appealing to the interests of the audience. When King Cnut presents his claim on Norway, St. Óláfr does not find it worthwhile to refute them in detail, but depicts Cnut as a man who tries to grasp everything that comes his way and declares his will to defend his claim on Norway with armed force (OH chap. 131). The Danish bishop Sigurðr's appeal to the army of Óláfr's adversaries before the battle of Stiklestad is also strongly emotional, depicting Óláfr as a Viking and robber. But the bishop soon turns to the questions of interest: who is without reasons for revenge? And what will be the consequences if Óláfr wins? The saintly king himself, in his speech before the same battle, also primarily appeals to his men's interests, though with more of the dignity and restraint of the future martyr (OH chap. 211). In the speeches in the Swedish assembly where St. Óláfr's peace proposal is discussed, interest is the most important argument brought forward by the peace party: war with Norway causes considerable damage and is against Swedish traditions, according to which expansion ought to take place in the Baltic region. By implication, this latter policy is considered to be in the people's interest, by giving booty and honor (OH chap. 80). Characteristically, the Swedish king, who is consistently depicted as an arrogant fool, brings no real arguments, only accusing his adversaries of treason. As we have seen, considerations of interest proved decisive to the petty kings of Eastern Norway when Óláfr presented his claims. Finally, Einarr's famous speech at the Icelandic *Álþingi* against ceding to King Óláfr's demand of Grímsey, an island off the northern coast, in return for his friendship, is entirely in terms of interest: doing this will give the Norwegian king a threshold, which may prove dangerous in the future (OH chap. 125: 274 f.).

There are thus two main sorts of arguments in the speeches, rational arguments intended to convince the audience that it is in their interest to support the faction in question and emotional arguments that serve to emphasize the charismatic personality of the speaker. The importance of appealing to people's interests can be demonstrated from numerous examples from practice. Hákon góði wins support through his promises of giving the people back their *óðal* (the right to own their farms) which Haraldr harfagri had taken away from them, and through his attractive personality (HG chap. 1; cf. 15: 189). Earl Hákon Sigurðarson of Lade has strong support in his home region Trøndelag and he has the luck that the harvests are good and there is plenty of fish during his reign. Moreover, he comes to Norway with the Danish king and a large army, having killed Haraldr gráfeldr. And finally, his adversaries, the Eiríkssons, are extremely unpopular (OT chaps. 16, 45; see also *HGráf.* chap. 2). Óláfr Tryggvason is lucky enough to arrive in Norway at the time of the rebellion against Earl Hákon and is acclaimed as a liberator (OT chaps. 49, 51). Cnut wins through his generous gifts of gold, his promises to the leading magnates of high rank in his service, and through Óláfr's increasing unpopularity (OH chap. 130; see also above). Magnús góði's success is due to a combination of his father's sainthood and opposition against the Danish rule, which is skillfully exploited by the two leading magnates, Kálfr Árnason and Einarr þambarskelfir. During the civil war of the 1150s, King Ingi is clearly the most popular of the three sons of Haraldr gilli. He shows the greatest generosity to the magnates, which explains his victory (*Ingi* chaps. 22, 30–31). The fate of his brother, King Eysteinn, shows how dangerous it is not to be generous. His men desert him when he mobilizes against Ingi, one of them with the words: "Let your chests of gold support you now and defend your land!" ("fylgi gullkistur þínar þér nú ok veri land þitt." *Ingi* chap. 31; see also below.)

The importance of charisma is less evident from the speeches, but appears from several stories. Winning the king's friendship is an important motive for conversion to Christianity, and although interests are clearly involved in this, it also has something to do with the attractive personalities of the two Óláfrs. Hákon góði's looks and personality are also able to impress the people, in addition to his promises. In accordance with Snorri's ideas of the human personality one should probably not distinguish too clearly between the kings' personalities and their successes. A man's personality is very much the sum of his acts. A man who has success is therefore by definition a great man, with an attractive personality. The importance of military victory for gaining support may be regarded in this light. It clearly has something to do with the traditional idea of *hamingja,* which frequently occurs both in Snorri and other historians. It is not easy to draw the line of division between the attraction of a charismatic personality and the desire for gain. Most of the alliances made at least by the great magnates of Snorri's society are easily explained through individual interests. But the emotional aspect, which emerges strongly from many of Snorri's stories and the scaldic stanzas that he quotes, should not be overlooked. Probably, there was a stronger connection between friendship as an emotional relationship between men and as the result of mutual interests than in our society.

In addition to these examples of the importance of giving a favorable impression and appealing to people's interests, we may point to the importance of diplomatic skill in general in Snorri. The embassy to the King of Sweden is a good example of this. Snorri describes vividly and in great detail the Icelander Hjalti's careful and gradual approach to the King of Sweden, first via Earl Rǫgnvaldr, then via the king's daughter Ingigerðr, and his attempts to gain the king's friendship by offering him silver, pretending it to be his payment of the tax (landaurar) when visiting Norway, thus recognizing him as king of the country. Finally, having spent a long time at the king's court, he takes the opportunity when the king is drunk and in good spirits to approach the subject of peace with Norway (OH chaps. 69–72). Though this approach eventually turns out to be a failure, Snorri's joy and admiration of Hjalti's diplomatic ability in this respect is evident from the story. Clearly, diplomacy is of greatest importance when approaching someone in a higher position than oneself. But it is also important for a king who tries to gain acceptance and defeat his rivals, as is evident from the story of St. Óláfr's conquest of Norway through his alliance with the Oppland kings, and Earl Hákon's, Kálfr Árnason's, and Einarr þambarskelfir's careful maneuvering in the political game. Further, Erlingr skakki's settlement with King Valdimarr of Denmark is presented as a diplomatic triumph, whereas King Eysteinn Magnússon achieves through gifts and diplomatic ability what his predecessors have attempted in vain by force, to attach Jämtland to Norway (*Msyn.* chap. 15).

An Exception to the Rule: Ideological Conflicts

Having considered the main pattern of conflicts in Snorri, I shall turn to the exceptions to the rule, the "ideological" conflicts, and examine how far they are real exceptions. There are three kinds of conflicts that may be termed ideological, the national, the religious, and the constitutional.

National Conflicts

Snorri's account of the battle of Svǫlð between the three Nordic kings (1000), in which Óláfr Tryggvason is killed, may serve as an example of his way of treating foreign policy (OT chaps. 89–94, 97–113). Óláfr's journey to Wendland, which gave his adversaries their opportunity to attack him, takes place in order to settle the problem of the goods of his wife, Þýri, who had been sent there to marry King Búrizláfr but had refused and gone to Norway and married Óláfr instead. Of his adversaries, Earl Eiríkr, the son of Earl Hákon, has clear political reasons to fight him, as he also aspires to rule Norway and has been exiled by Óláfr. Eiríkr is well received by the kings of Denmark and Sweden and marries a daughter of the former (OT chaps. 89–90). But the crucial event in concluding the alliance against Óláfr, is the marriage of King Sveinn of Denmark to Sigríðr stórráða (the haughty), the mother of King Óláfr of Sweden (chap. 91). Sigríðr is Óláfr's most bitter enemy, because he had refused to marry her, despite their engagement, and even slapped her face, when she did not accept Christianity. After this insult, Sigríðr says: "This may well be your death" ("þetta mætti verða vel þinn bani") (OT chap. 61). Sigríðr sees to it that her prophecy is fullfilled and instigates her husband to take revenge, in addition pointing to the humiliation he has suffered because of Þýri having shared Óláfr's bed without his permission. The result is an alliance between the kings of Denmark and Sweden, Sigríðr's husband and son, and Earl Eiríkr against Óláfr (OT chap. 98). At his return from Wendland, Óláfr is surprised by a largely superior fleet, fights heroically but is finally defeated and probably killed.

This is foreign policy at a very personal level. Both Óláfr's expedition and his enemies' alliance against him are the results of women's initiative and concern private property or hurt feelings. There is no strategic reason for Óláfr to go to Wendland, and though some of his adversaries have territorial ambitions, this is not a very prominent motive for their fight against him. In this respect, Snorri tells basically the same story as his two most direct sources, Oddr munkr and *Fagrskinna*.[25]

St. Óláfr's negotiations with his namesake, King Óláfr of Sweden (OH chaps. 67–72, 77–80, 87–94), which are intended to undo the consequences of the battle of Svǫlð, give the same impression. In the beginning, the Swedish king stubbornly resists Óláfr's peace proposals, brought forward by his messengers. Hjalti, together with the king's daughter Ingigerðr and St. Óláfr's friend Earl Rǫgnvaldr of Västergötland, then seeks the aid of Þorgnýr lǫgmaðr, who, with the support of the people, forces the king to conclude a peace treaty with his Norwegian namesake, giving him Ingigerðr in marriage. This takes place at an assembly at Uppsala. The king, however, fails to carry out his promise, marrying Ingigerðr to the King of Novgorod. Óláfr, who has traveled to the border to meet his bride, has to return empty-handed after a long period of waiting. However, some of his men manage to persuade another, illegitimate daughter of the king of Sweden, Ástríðr, to marry

Óláfr, and aided by Earl Rǫgnvaldr they carry her off against her father's will. The king of Sweden is furious, but is forced to a settlement when the people rebel against him.

The background to these negotiations, as far as it can be reconstructed from Snorri's narrative, is the following. After the battle of Svǫld, Norway was conquered by the kings of Denmark and Sweden, who set up the earls Eiríkr and Sveinn as direct rulers (OT chap. 113). Óláfr's conquest of the country was thus a direct challenge to the kings of both the neighboring countries. His one adversary, Hákon, joined King Cnut in England, whereas the other, Sveinn, went to Sweden after his defeat at Nesjar (OH chaps. 31, 54–55). A counterattack from Denmark and England or Sweden or both thus seemed likely. It therefore would appear quite obvious to a modern historian, if he were to reconstruct the story of Óláfr's negotiations with Sweden from Snorri's facts, that their main purpose must have been to break the alliance between Denmark and Sweden against Norway.[26] When Óláfr conquered Norway, in 1014–1015, according to Snorri's chronology, and some time after, King Cnut of Denmark was fully occupied in England. Óláfr's chance then lay in fulfilling the conquest of the whole country, including the border regions under Swedish control, and then coming to terms with the Swedish king before King Cnut was able to turn against Norway. This explains Óláfr's aggressive policy in the beginning and his eagerness to come to terms after having completed his conquest, as well as the Swedish king's unwillingness to negiotiate and reluctance in carrying out the terms of the treaty: he can afford to wait, Óláfr cannot.

In Snorri's story, however, the initial conflict is sparked off by the king of Sweden sending messengers to Óláfr to demand taxes. Óláfr rejects the claim with scorn, even hanging one of them, who has attempted to tax the country (OH ch. 59). He then manages to get hold of the border region in the southeast through a coup (OH chap. 61). The initiative to the peace negotiations then comes from the people in the border region. The king of Sweden's negative reactions to Óláfr's overtures are explained as haughtiness and stubbornness on his part, which eventually almost leads to his deposition.

To some extent, this way of presenting the story may be Snorri's way of covering up the fact that Óláfr suffers a considerable humiliation during this affair. He turns up at the border to wait for his bride, according to the treaty negotiated some time before, but waits in vain for the Swedish king and his daughter, only to learn some time later that she has been married off to the king of Novgorod. He then compensates his loss by marrying another, illegitimate, daughter of the Swedish king, Ástríðr, against her father's will. To be promised a legitimate daughter and then having to marry an illegitimate one is of course an extreme humiliation, which is actually implied in one of the speeches.[27] Besides, it is difficult to understand the point in Óláfr's actions. The real aim of the negotiations was a peace settlement with the Swedish king, and the marriage was a means to achieve this. What was then the point in marrying the king's daughter against her father's will? A possible answer might be that marriage created such strong bonds that a weddding, even against the will of the father, was likely to lead to peace. But the main explanation is probably Snorri's attempt to present Óláfr's humiliation as a victory by describing his wedding to Ástríðr as a result of his own initiative, which the Swedish king is forced to acknowledge, instead of an offer with which Óláfr has to be content.[28] Thus, Snorri's attempt to present the king of Norway in the best possible light prevents him from analyzing the story from the point of view of power politics.

Magnús góði's and Haraldr harðráði's conflicts with Denmark have their origin in the settlement between Magnús and Harthacnut, the son of Cnut the Great, that the one who lived longer should inherit the other (MG chap. 6). When Magnús inherits Denmark, he appoints Sveinn Úlfsson earl of the country (MG chaps. 22–23). Sveinn is the son of Úlfr Þorgilsson and related to the Danish royal house, and he uses this opportunity to claim the kingdom for himself and rebel against Magnús (MG chap. 25). He is repeatedly defeated by Magnús, but has somewhat greater success during Haraldr's reign, after Magnús on his deathbed gives Sveinn Denmark and Haraldr Norway (*HHarð.* chaps. 28, 31), and finally manages to make his peace with Haraldr and be recognized as king (*HHarð.* chap. 71). This is a conflict that more resembles the internal conflicts, both parties fighting for vital interests. In a similar way, Magnús berfoetr's conflict with the king of Sweden concerns the borderline between the two countries and thus resembles what one might call a "normal" conflict between two countries (MB chaps. 12–15). By contrast, no reason is given for his expeditions against the Western Islands and Ireland, except the king's wish to seek glory through foreign conquest (MB chaps. 8–11, 23–25; see also 26: 266). The actual campaigns are described as a series of battles and heroic acts, with no mention of a strategic plan, like most wars of *Heimskringla*.

The conflict with Denmark in the 1160s has its origin in Erlingr skakki's alliance with the Danish King Valdimarr, on the condition that Valdimarr help him against Hákon herðibreiðr in return for Viken, the part of Norway that had belonged to his ancestors Haraldr Gormsson and Sveinn tjúguskegg (ME chap. 2). Having gained Norway, Erlingr breaks his promise, which leads Valdimarr to invade Norway. The invasion is unsuccessful but Erlingr nevertheless finds it best to attempt a peace settlement. His wife Kristín, daughter of King Sigurðr jórsalafari and Valdimarr's cousin, goes to Denmark and is well received. The next year Erlingr goes to Denmark with few men, but well armed, enters King Valdimarr's hall and asks for a truce (grið). Erlingr is well received, hostages are exchanged, and peace negotations start. Erlingr declares himself willing to fulfil his promise, but suggests that Valdimarr appoint him earl to govern Viken on his behalf, which Valdimarr accepts. Erlingr has thus achieved both peace with Denmark and actual control over Viken (ME chaps. 23–30).

This story shows some similarity to Snorri's accounts of internal conflicts. Erlingr emerges as the great statesman and diplomat. First, he gathers the scattered remains of Ingi's faction and mobilizes the Danes to defeat his opponents. Then he skillfully exploits nationalistic sentiments, receiving popular support to refuse submission to Valdimarr.[29] And finally, having suppressed an attempted rebellion in Trøndelag and warded off the Danish attack, he shows himself conciliatory and concludes a settlement that helps King Valdimarr to save face but in reality leaves Erlingr in control of the whole of Norway. However, Snorri's story has some inconsistencies that, like the ones in the story of St. Óláfr's negotiations with Sweden, must be due to its covering-up purpose: if Valdimarr's expedition against Norway was a total failure, why did Erlingr go to such extremes to achieve a peace settlement? And was the idea of Erlingr becoming Valdimarr's earl actually his own ingenious solution to a diplomatic impasse, and not rather what Valdimarr had intended from the beginning?[30]

As analyses of politics, Snorri's descriptions of foreign policy generally seem less successful than those of inner-Norwegian conflicts. They have a certain romantic flavor, the code of honor and accidental clashes count for more and the conflicts are determined more by personal likes and dislikes than by objective interests. And whereas it is usually difficult to identify heroes and villains in internal conflicts, Snorri is much less objective in his descriptions of foreign policy, for instance in his portrait of King Óláfr of Sweden's stubbornness, arrogance, and irrational behavior. One reason for this may be that politics to Snorri is primarily a question of gaining support through a personal approach, not to act strategically in territorial terms. The game of politics is therefore most suited to a restricted territory, like one country. But the contrast between foreign and internal policy is probably also the result of a "nationalistic" tendency that is to be found in other passages of Snorri's work as well.

In Snorri's description of the battle of Svǫld, where both the Danish and the Swedish king fight together with Earl Hákon's sons against Óláfr Tryggvason, there is a scene where King Óláfr is watching his enemies approaching. When the Danes are pointed out to him, he declares that there is nothing to fear from them, because they lack courage. He has a similar comment regarding the Swedes. Finally, seeing the ships of Earl Eiríkr, the king comments: ". . . we may expect a smart fight with that force: they are Norwegians like us."[31] This is also brought out by the outcome of the battle, where Earl Eiríkr is the real victor. In the long war between Magnús góði and his successor Haraldr harðráði and King Sveinn of Denmark, the Norwegian kings win most of the battles and generally behave more bravely.[32] When Danish kings try to extend their sphere of influence during the Norwegian civil wars of the twelfth century, they meet with little success, and Snorri uses the opportunity to emphasize the courage and warlike manners of the Norwegians in contrast to the Danes.[33]

Snorri also implies that it is more difficult to gain and to hold important political positions in a foreign country than in one's own. Óláfr Tryggvason is promoted to a leading position in Novgorod, but is envied by men of the country, "as often happens when foreigners gain power or acquire such great fame" ("sem optliga kann verða, þar er útlendir menn hefjask til ríkis eða svá mikillar frægðar") (OT chap. 21). Óláfr therefore leaves the country to go back to Norway. Earl Tósti's words to Haraldr harðráði also imply that it is usually more difficult to be accepted as king in another country than one's own.

Nevertheless, the practical importance of these nationalistic sentiments should not be exaggerated. Though the idea of treason against the king occasionally occurs in Snorri, it apparently has nothing to do with loyalty to one's country. It seems quite normal to enter the service of another king or ally oneself with him against the king of one's own country, as do Finnr Árnason, Hákon Ívarsson, and the magnates who rebel against St. Óláfr. Personal interests frequently lead people to disregard this sentiment, and "national" conflicts are not depicted in a way that is fundamentally different from internal ones. Like the latter they are personal conflicts between the kings and are conducted in much the same way.

Religious Conflicts

As we have seen, the Christianization of the country is the clearest example of an ideological conflict. Though modern historians may regard even this as an example of power politics, Snorri does not. Still, he is not blind to the political aspects of the process. Above all, his description of the way in which the kings succeed in converting the people bears close resemblance to his descriptions of their victories in the political field.

Snorri clearly implies that it is more difficult to make people change religion than political allegiance. He even gives a psychological reason for this: when people could decide for themselves, they preferred the belief they had known from childhood (OH chap. 60: 87). This explains many cases of individual resistance, which made the kings use extremely harsh methods, such as torture. The saga of Óláfr Tryggvason contains some drastic examples of this (OT chaps. 76, 80). To break this resistance, the kings also receive help through divine intervention.

In most cases, however, people are converted in the same way as they change political allegiance. When most of the mightiest men in Viken favor Christianity, King Óláfr Tryggvason easily makes the rest of the people follow their example (OT chap. 53). In Hordaland, Óláfr converts the mightiest clan in the region, the descendants of Hǫrðakári, by giving Erlingr Skjálgsson his sister in marriage and thus succeeds in converting the entire region. When the use of force is necessary, a conspicuous demonstration of strength is often sufficient to achieve the aim. In Trøndelag Óláfr Tryggvason promises to sacrifice to the pagan gods and then threatens to sacrifice the leading men of the region (OT chap. 67). At the old pagan cult place Mære he kills the leading magnate Járnskeggi and destroys the idols, thus intimidating the people to accept Christianity (OT chaps. 68–69). In the story of Dala-Guðbrandr, which is told in great detail, St. Óláfr manages to destroy the idol of the people of Gudbrandsdalen at the right moment, thus securing total submission to Christianity (OH chap. 113). When converting the inner regions of Western Norway and Valdres, Óláfr succeeds through threats or cunning (OH chap. 121). In Voss, it is sufficient to arrange the army in battle array. In Valdres, he offers to settle disputes between people, which results in their turning against one another instead of him. When Óláfr's men then plunder and burn their farms, the farmers' army disperse and they are forced to submit. Without accusing Snorri of "secularizing" the conversion of Norway, we can therefore note that the main structure of these stories conform to those dealing with power politics in the secular field. Whether by natural or supernatural means, success is achieved through a power demonstration or by defeating or winning the support of a few top leaders.

By contrast, religious and "theological" discussions are rare. When Hákon góði asks the people of Trøndelag to accept Christianity, he just tells them what to do, giving no arguments to show that the new religion is better than the old one. Ásbjǫrn of Medalhus's answer is a defense of old customs and contains some "constitutional" principles, but no religious defense of the old faith. In one of his conversion stories, Snorri tells of some Icelanders, who go to mass and listen to the songs and bell-ringing. One of them, Kjartan, is impressed, while most of the others are not (OT chap. 82). Apart from this, Christian doctrine and liturgy are rarely mentioned; when people convert, they do it to gain advantages or avoid punishment, or because they are impressed by the power-ful personalities of the missionary kings (OT chaps. 56–57, 77, 83, 201, 204, 215). This is the case even with Kjartan: he converts in return for Óláfr Tryggvason's friendship (OT chap. 82).

Similarly, there is no mention of religious motives in Snorri's descrip-tions of crusades. King Sigurðr jórsalafari's expedition takes place when men come from Jerusalem and Constantinople and tell of their adven-tures and of the possibility of gaining wealth by entering the service of the emperor of Constantinople (*Msyn.* chap. 1). In the following story, Snorri's emphasis is on wealth, success, and honor, and he ends by stating that no more honorable expedition (virðingar-fǫr) had ever sailed from Norway (*Msyn.* chap. 13). Gain in prestige is also mentioned as the most important result of Erlingr skakki's crusade (*Ingi* chap. 17).

In addition to his analogies between the Christianization and secular politics, both the stories mentioned here and Snorri's description of Óláfr's suppression of pagan cult in Trøndelag through killing the local leader Ǫlvi at Egge demonstrates his awareness of the political conse-quences of the conversion (OH chaps. 107–110). Ǫlvi is the local leader in Northern Trøndelag and is executed as punishment for the pagan sacrifices that were still going on at Mære, despite the formal conversion of the region. Óláfr then confiscates his farm and gives it to Kálfr Árnason, to whom he also marries Ǫlvi's widow. The conversion thus often allows the king to gain a local foothold, either by replacing local leaders or by forming closer links with existing ones.

Constitutional Conflicts

My conclusion that the conflicts between the king and the magnates are feuds and not constitutional conflicts, and consequently that constitu-tional conflicts are not the central theme of *Heimskringla,* does not mean that such conflicts do not occur or that they are unimportant. The clearest examples of conflicts over constitutional principles in Snorri are the stories of Haraldr hárfagri taking the *óðal* (the right of property to their land) from the people and Hákon góði giving it back (*HHárf.* chap. 6; HG chap. 1), Ásbjǫrn of Medalhus's speech against Hákon góði's attempt to Christianize the country (HG chap. 15), Þorgnýr lǫgmaðr's (the Law-speaker's) speech to King Óláfr of Sweden concerning the peace negotiations between him and St. Óláfr (OH chap. 80: 142 f.), and Sigvatr's *Bersǫglisvísur,* in which he made himself the spokesman of the oppressed people and made King Magnús change his harsh rule and become known as Magnús góði (the Good). These are no doubt "consti-tutional" conflicts in the sense that they involve the rights of the people versus the king, partly also in that the popular assemblies are described as representing "popular" opposition—with magnates as leaders—against the king. The fact that most of these stories seem to be Snorri's invention or much expanded by him, may also indicate special interest in such questions.[34]

However, it must be pointed out that the general constitutional significance of these episodes is not necessarily the same to Snorri and his readers as to us. For instance, the similarity between Ásbjǫrn from Medalhus's speech against the attempt by Hákon góði to introduce Christianity and Þorgnýr lǫgmaðr's speech against King Óláfr of Sweden seems obvious to us, and has been duly noticed by modern scholars: in both cases a king who tries to introduce novelties is met with resistance from a strong magnate, who speaks on behalf of the people and successfully defends traditional rights and customs (Sandvik, 1955: 29 ff., 44). Though Snorri and his readers may also have seen the similarity, the contrast between these episodes is likely to have struck them more. In the first case some stubborn and ignorant peasants prefer their pagan superstition to the true faith, which they reject as a strange novelty. In the other the people react against a haughty and unwise king, who conducts a meaningless war against his peaceful neighbor in the west instead of winning honor and riches in the Baltic region as his predecessors have done. Further, it is evident from Snorri's description of Óláfr Tryggvason's and St. Óláfr's use of the popular assemblies to introduce Christianity and for other purposes that Snorri is more interested in the reality of the issues than in the "constitutional" point of the competence of the assemblies. Popular opposition is here overcome by cunning or violence, without Snorri considering the "constitutional" aspect of the matter. The assemblies are clearly a political reality in Snorri's society, but his interest in them from a constitutional point of view may be doubted.

This does not mean, however, that conflicts between the king and the people are unimportant. The two other examples quoted above are probably a better illustration of the sort of constitutional conflicts which seem most important to Snorri, those directly related to the people's interests. Hákon góði becomes immensely popular by giving back the óðal and easily manages to defeat his brother and rival Eiríkr blóðøx. In Sigvatr's *Bersǫglisvísur* the scald describes the people's reaction against royal oppression and manages to make him abstain from it. To these can be added the numerous examples of the kings' need for popular support and the characterizations of kings, which attach great importance to their popularity and behavior toward the people. Snorri is thus clearly interested in constitutional problems, but he is concerned with interests more than formal political structures. The people do not react against royal decisions that take place outside the popular assemblies and without their cooperation but against royal decisions that are contrary to their interests. We thus have to do with the same informal structure as in the feuds between the leading members of society and the same description of political decisions based on interests. The king's power is not restricted by formal rules or constitutional assemblies, but by what the people are willing to accept from him. The constitutional conflicts are thus not very much more ideological than the feuds: they are not between permanent parties and do not concern formal political structures. Rather they serve to bring home the same lesson as the conflicts between kings and magnates, that people normally act according to their interests and that the political game is a game aimed at winning universal support.

Conclusion: Ideology and Politics

Though there are clearly conflicts in Snorri which may be termed ideological, the similarity between such conflicts and the normal ones, the feuds, is striking. Conflicts between countries are mainly regarded as personal conflicts between their kings, religious conflicts are conducted in much the same way as feuds, and constitutional conflicts concern similar kinds of interests as those between individuals. The ideological conflicts thus serve only to modify, not alter, the impression from the previous analysis of the feuds. Comparing the three categories of ideological conflicts, the amount of national ideology is perhaps the most striking. Snorri shows less objectivity toward the external enemies of the Norwegian king than toward his internal ones, the political issues are often camouflaged behind romantic and nationalistic stories, and his normal rule, that an impressive victory is sufficient to achieve general support, does not apply. He thus seems to have some idea of a national community uniting the contending groups and individuals (see below). Though the ideological element is equally strong or even stronger in the religious conflicts, their relative conformity to the normal pattern is more striking against a medieval background. The explanation to this should perhaps be sought more in Snorri's definition of the theme of his history than in his attitude to religion, though the two cannot be completely separated.

The relative importance of ideology is well illustrated through the comparison between St. Ólafr and his half-brother Haraldr harðráði (*HHarð*. chap. 100). When hearing people stress the difference between them, Halldórr Brynjólfsson, an old follower of both kings, points to their essential similarity in character: no two men were as similar. Halldórr attributes to them the conventional virtues of warrior kings and then goes on to describe their deeds as kings. Ólafr forced people to become Christians and punished severely those who did not obey. He was then killed by his own people, who did not tolerate his justice. Haraldr used violence to force people to submit under his dominion and tried to extend it as far as possible and died in the attempt to win another king's country. This description rather seems like a contrast than a similarity. One might even suspect that it was ultimately derived from an ecclesiastical source—ecclesiastical authors were negative to Haraldr[35]—who wanted to point out the contrast between the good king, using violence in God's service, and the evil one, who used it to extend his own dominion. However, though Snorri clearly sees the contrast, the main purpose of his comparison is to emphasize the similarity. Therefore, his view of similarity in this case must be different from ours, that is: the fact that both kings were great warriors who used violence to further their ends is more significant than that the one's end was to introduce Christianity and uphold justice, whereas the other's was to extend his own dominion. This accords well with the importance Snorri attributes to power politics in other contexts and thus confirms my impression that power politics and human character are a more important aspect of the conflicts between the king and the magnates than ideology or principles of division of power within society.

3

The Society

Introduction

Going from the analysis of conflicts to society as a whole, we take a step away from Snorri's explicit ideas to his basic assumptions based on a common *mentalité*. Although the conflicts are his main interest, Snorri is no sociologist and does not attempt to analyze Norwegian society. In his narrative, however, he inevitably reveals some kind of social organization, though we must have in mind that his exclusive interest in conflicts and dramatic events may distort the picture of the normal functioning of society.

In studying society on the basis of Snorri's narrative, we have to consider two kinds of social organization: first, the groups that are opposed to one another in the struggle for power, and second, the way in which individuals are ranked in the social hierarchy. In modern industrial societies we expect some kind of correspondence between the two but this need not be the case in more traditional societies. Let us start with the first kind of organization.

The Factions in the Conflicts: Family Clans or Ad Hoc Groups?

The discussion in the preceding pages has led to the conclusion that Snorri's conflicts are mostly feuds, not conflicts over ideology, constitutional principles, or class interest, and further that the feuds, though often sparked by accidental clashes, usually involve conflicting long-term interests between the actors.

Though the conflicts may be termed personal rather than ideological or social, it remains to consider more closely the formation of factions and consequently the lines of division within Snorri's society. Norwegian and Icelandic society of the eariler Middle Ages is often referred to as a "society of kindreds," without a very precise definition of the term (e.g., Johnsen, 1948; Andersen, 1977: 70 f., 185 f., 247 f., 336 ff.). By contrast, authors who have attempted a more exact analysis of the kinship system have generally concluded that it was bilateral and thus not likely to form the basis of extended clans and that it was fairly early surpassed by other forms of social organization. This impression is based on comparative analyses of the laws, but no examination of the whole material according to modern anthropological principles has been carried out. Above all, the sagas and documentary sources have been relatively neglected.[1] It is evidently outside the scope of the present work to analyse the kinship system in full. I shall confine myself to Snorri and to the political relevance of the system.

The Importance of Kinship

The kindred (ætt) is frequently mentioned in *Heimskringla*. Relatives can give important support. When a man is killed, it is the duty of his relatives to take revenge or seek compensation. It is a laudable act to perform this duty and dishonorable to shrink from it.[2] Conversely, one should not kill one's own relatives. The English Earl Tósti even declares that he prefers to be killed by his brother Harold Godwineson rather than to kill him, despite the fact that they are enemies (*HHarð*. chap. 91). Haraldr gilli's treatment of his nephew Magnús blindi, which seems to us an example of the utmost cruelty, may be explained in this way. Magnús was blinded, castrated, and had one of his feet cut off. The purpose of this is clearly stated: he should not be able to be king any more (MB.HG chap. 8). Being unable to see or to walk in a normal way, he cannot lead an army. As a castrate, he cannot have offspring, apart from the fact that he has lost his power as a man and is thus hardly fit to be a leader of other men. Magnús's fate may appear worse than death and be considered—as has often been done—an act of sadism. Though there are indications that people thought like this in the Middle Ages as well,[3] the aftermath of the story shows that he was still dangerous and thus that the most prudent thing would have been to kill him—if there were no moral objections to it.[4] Snorri's story of King Hroerekr, who was also blinded but whom St. Óláfr did not want to kill, seems to confirm that this was the case.[5] An Icelandic example points in the same direction: Sturla Sigvatsson in 1236 tried and partly succeeded in blinding and castrating his cousin Óroekja, Snorri's son, but did not attempt to kill him (*Sturl.* I: 485; see also Heusler, 1912: 36). Though there are examples of near relatives being killed, this mostly happens in battle and not at the direct order of their kinsmen. This applies among others to Ingi's brothers Sigurðr and Eysteinn. The former was killed by arrows in the battle in Bergen following the conflict between him and Ingi (*Ingi* chap. 28), whereas the latter was taken captive by a former adherent and killed (*Ingi* chap. 32). Though this was hardly against Ingi's will, he could not be blamed directly for carrying out or ordering the execution. King Eiríkr blóðøx, who killed two of his brothers (*HHárf.* chaps. 35–36) is a more direct exception to the rule. But Eiríkr was an extremely cruel and violent man, whose acts Snorri describes with some disapproval. By contrast, Erlingr skakki, who was a hard man and ruthlessly exterminated all potential rivals of his son Magnús, is no real exception, because none of the men he killed were his blood relations.[6]

How far do these ties of kinship extend? According to the laws, both the Norwegian and Icelandic ones were fairly extensive, but the practical importance of the rules there may be doubted. According to Gaunt (1983: 206), who quotes Johnsen (1948: 76 ff.), there are few examples in the sagas of revenge for other than very close relatives, such as fathers or brothers. This is not quite the impression we receive from *Heimskringla,* which does give examples of revenge or attempts at revenge for more distant relatives. When Haraldr harðráði has killed Einarr þambarskelfir and his son Eindriði, he fears the revenge of Hákon Ívarsson, the grandnephew of Einarr's wife, whose father was thus Eindriði's cousin. Þórir hundr revenges his nephew Ásbjǫrn selsbani (OH chap. 133). Erlingr Skjálgsson, who risks a major conflict with the king for Ásbjǫrn's sake, is also his uncle—Ásbjǫrn's mother is Erlingr's sister (OH chap. 117: 242). In some other cases, the degree of kinship is not indicated. Erlingr Skjálgsson is revenged by a man called Vígleikr Árnason, of whom nothing else is known (OH chap. 178). It has been suggested that the duty of revenge did not depend on the degree of kinship but that it pertained to the heir (Sommerfelt, 1974: 144 f). This fits in well with the example of Hákon Ívarsson.[7]

Whether or not to take revenge, however, is hardly a question of duties only. Individual interests also come into consideration. For a king or magnate to abstain from revenge without compensation is clearly out of the question, as this normally means loss of honor and consequently of political influence. There are indications both in the laws and the Icelandic sagas that it is considered more honorable to take revenge than to receive compensation.[8] However, these alternatives are not strictly opposed; there is a sort of sliding transition between them: if the compensation is sufficient, it may be an honorable alternative. This is expressed in the institution of *sjalfdoemi*, that is, that the offended party becomes judge in his own case. Economically, he may seek any compensation he wants, and politically, he has forced his adversary to total capitulation.[9]

The negotiations between King Haraldr harðráði and Hákon Ívarsson after Einarr þambarskelfir's death at Haraldr's hands may serve as an example (*HHarð*. chaps. 45–47). When Finnr Árnason as the king's representative offers compensation in case Hákon is willing to abstain from revenge, Hákon first points to his duty to revenge his kinsman Eindriði, Einarr's son. Finnr tempts him with a large compensation—he may ask the terms he likes—and threatens him with punishment or dishonor for treason against the king. Hákon then asks for the daughter of King Magnús góði in marriage, thus seizing the opportunity that the king's offense offers him to further his own interests.

Hákon's willingness to reach an agreement may be explained either from the fact that it was a question of a relatively distant relative or from political reasons, or—of course—both. The way Snorri tells the story points to the political reasons as the more important, but we cannot exclude the possibility that the relevance of the degree of kinship was evident to Snorri's readers and thus implied. As Snorri is mainly interested in conflicts and therefore rarely quotes examples of peaceful settlements, general rules of behavior in such cases, including the importance of the degree of kinship for the course of action that was taken, can hardly be reconstructed from his examples. Generally, given the importance of individual interests in Snorri, he probably regards them as more important than the degree of kinship. Further, the story of Magnús góði shows the conflict between political considerations and the wish for revenge. When Magnús grows up, he persecutes his father's enemies, helping Ásmundr Grankellsson to kill Hárekr at Tjøtta (MG chap. 12), forcing Kálfr Árnason to leave the country (MG chap. 14), and confiscating the property of many men who had fought against Óláfr in the battle of Stiklestad (MG chap. 15). This leads to opposition against him, and he mends his ways and becomes the good king Magnús (chap. 16), though Kálfr remains in exile till after his death (*HHarð*. chap. 51) and Snorri does not mention what happens to the confiscated property. Though Snorri is fairly vague on this point, the story clearly suggests that it is necessary for a king to show moderation in carrying out revenge.

Although there seems to be a certain logic in the duty of revenge being coextensive with the right to inherit, the ban against killing relatives may well have had a wider application. To abstain from killing is clearly less to ask than the active solidarity implied in the duty to take revenge. Erlingr Skjálgsson was quite a distant relative of Áslákr—they were second cousins (OT chap. 54)—but Áslákr is nevertheless blamed for killing him. In the case of St. Óláfr and King Hroerekr, Snorri confines himself to stating that they were both descended from Haraldr hárfagri, which probably means that Óláfr's father and Hroerekr were second cousins.[10] The kinship between Óláfr Tryggvason and Hárekr at Tjøtta, which is one of the reasons for Óláfr to release Hárekr (OT chap. 75: 392), was equally distant.[11] There are thus at least some indications of quite extensive kinship ties in Snorri's society. Their practical and political importance, however, is another matter. Halvdan Koht tried to demonstrate the importance of kinship for faction formation during the inner conflicts from the tenth century until the first half of the thirteenth century (1921: 114 ff.; 1936: 89–104). He managed to show that the divisions that Edvard Bull (1917: 177 ff.) had regarded as the result of regional differences were better explained by kinship or marriage alliances (see Bagge, 1986: 160 ff.). His attempt to explain the political conflicts through a long-term opposition between kindreds was less successful, however, because he did not cross-check his material by examining (1) how many equally near relatives were on the opposite side; and (2) how many adherents of the respective factions had family backgrounds that were irrelevant to their choice of sides. Nor did he distinguish between kinsmen and in-laws. Admittedly, marriage probably created strong ties. But since marriage is the result of a choice, faction adherence may equally well be its cause as its effect. Finally, in analyzing Snorri, we may note that he does not always state the genealogies explicitly, so that they have to be reconstructed laboriously, a fact that indicates that Snorri was not particularly concerned with kinship ties as the explanation to faction loyalties.

More specifically, the following arguments may be adduced against Koht's results. Koht attaches great importance to the generation-long conflict between Haraldr hárfagri's kin and that of the earls of Lade, which is quite correct. He can also show that many of the magnates who rebelled against St. Óláfr and his successors were related by blood or marriage to the earls. But some of them were related to the kings as well, such as Hroerekr and Hárekr at Tjøtta. Moreover, many of them were not consistent enemies of the kings, as they ought to have been if the conflicts were along kinship lines. Men like Einarr þambarskelfir, Kálfr Árnason, and to some extent Finnr Árnason were power politicians who changed sides according to their interests, not consistent opponents of the royal family.[12] Further, the inner conflict until the time of Haraldr harðráði cannot be summarized as a conflict between the royal line and that of the earls of Lade. First, the two kins were themselves related. King Haraldr hárfagri married one of his daughters to Earl Hákon Grjótgarðsson of Lade, whereas the earl's son, Sigurðr, married

one of Haraldr's granddaughters. Earl Hákon Sigurðarson was thus
Haraldr's great-grandson, descending from him both through his mother
and father (*HHárf.* chaps. 9, 37; HG chap. 11), and equally related to
the royal line as Hárekr at Tjøtta to the earls of Lade. Second, the
conflict was as much between members of the royal family as between
the kings and the earls. Nor was there perfect unity and harmony within
the earls' line: Grjótgarðr betrayed his elder brother and rival Sigurðr to
the Eiríkssons and was in turn killed in battle by his nephew Hákon
(*HGráf.* chaps. 4–5, 15). There are also other examples of relatives
belonging to different factions or rivalry between them.[13] As for the
connection between this period and the civil wars of the twelfth century,
the fact that both Grégóríús and Erlingr skakki were probably descended from the earls of Lade is less significant than the former's close
friendship with King Ingi and the latter's marriage to the daughter of
King Sigurðr jórsalafari (see Koht, 1921: 118 ff.). Though kinship ties
were not unimportant, there is thus slight evidence for faction divisions
being consistently determined by them. It was probably more usual that
relatives belonged to the same faction than to different ones, but exceptions to this were sufficiently numerous to make it difficult to regard the
factions simply as family clans.

Rather, we have to make a fundamental distinction between particular duties between kinsmen on the one hand and active solidarity and
faction formation on the other, that is between grid and group (see
Douglas, 1970: viii ff.). In a bilateral kinship system such as the Norwegian and Icelandic ones, only very close relatives, that is, siblings of the
same parents, belong to exactly the same kindred. Consequently, there
is no rule that determines the loyalty of an individual in a conflict between two of his kinsmen, who may themselves be unrelated to one
another. Thus, though there may be strong solidarity within the smaller
family unit, larger factions are likely to be formed through ties other
than those of kinship, or individual interests may determine the choice
(see n. 1).

The actors in the political game very often seem to be heads of house-
holds who are supported by sons and brothers. Erlingr Skjálgsson's sons
play an important part in his struggles with St. Óláfr, among other things
in the story of Ásbjǫrn selsbani. Þorbergr Árnason turns to his brothers
for help in his conflict with the king. The role of women can also be
regarded in this context. To Snorri, women are not normally actors in
the political game, as they do not take part in war. But they may play an
important indirect role, by influencing their husbands, sons, brothers,
and so forth. Their most important role in *Heimskringla* as in the saga
literature in general is that of inciters. They bring pressure on their
reluctant male relatives to take revenge rather than reaching a peaceful

settlement. Examples of this are Þórir hundr's sister-in-law and Kálfr Árnason's wife, both named Sigríðr. There has been some discussion whether this role corresponds to historical reality or whether it is a literary phenomenon, inspired by the negative picture of women in contemporary clerical literature.[14] Though I do not want to express a definite opinion on this question with only Snorri as a source, this role of women certainly makes sense in the political game as described in *Heimskringla*. To women, who are not constant participants in the political game, the ties of kinship and the loss of a dear relative are the most important consideration, whereas long-term political interests often make men seek another solution.

However, this is not the only role of women in *Heimskringla*. They may also act in the interest of peace or to help their male relatives, such as the Swedish Princess Ingigerðr or Kristín Sigurðardóttir, Erlingr skakki's wife. Or they may use their influence to serve their own interests, revenge insults against their honor or improve their position. Sigriðr storráða seeks revenge against Óláfr Tryggvason for his insult against her and gets her husband and son to make war against him and defeat him in the battle of Svǫlð. At the court of the young King Magnús góði, his mother Álfhildr and the Queen dowager Ástríðr compete for prestige, and the former's behavior serves to illustrate the general "law" that people who come to great power often grow arrogant (MG chap. 7). But women rarely pursue long-term political aims in the same way as the male protagonists in the game. One who does is Queen Gunnhildr, the moving force behind the ruthless policy of the Eiríkssons (see Christophersen, 1987). In one particular context, Queen Ingiríðr, King Ingi's mother, acts in the same way, being one of the "hawks" in the assembly that decides to fight King Sigurðr in Bergen in 1155. And Queen Ástríðr, St. Óláfr's widow, plays an active role to secure the throne for her stepson, Magnús, who is a minor. These are exceptional cases, however. Generally, women are more closely linked to family and kinship in two ways. They normally act through their male relatives and their aim is often, though not always, to strengthen or protect the ties of kinship.[15]

Patronage and Marriage Ties

Similar ties of loyalty as those between kindreds existed between a king or magnate and his men. The duty of revenging "friends" or lords/clients is apparently the same as the duty to revenge kinsmen. St. Óláfr's intended execution of Ásbjǫrn for killing his *ármaðr* Selþórir is quite explicable in these terms. He also claims compensation for his *hirðmaðr* Karli, who was killed by Þórir hundr in revenge for Ásbjǫrn, by humiliating Þórir and forcing him to buy his peace for an enormous amount of gold. King Ingi feels obliged to revenge his friend Grégóríús and gives this as one of his reasons for not withdrawing from battle. The provision in the laws of a special fine for killing the king's men, which in *The King's Mirror* is pointed out as one of the advantages of entering the king's service (*Kgs.*: 41, lines 20–21), may be regarded as a formalization of this solidarity between the king and his men. Conversely, it is the duty of *hirðmenn* or housecarls of great men to revenge their lord, as is evident from the episodes when this duty is not carried out because of the panic caused by the loss of the leader.

Snorri gives no clear indication of the relative importance of the loyalty between a lord and his men and that between kinsmen. As in the case of kinship, he clearly indicates that interests may lead men to break the ties of loyalty to their leader, though the ethical evaluation of this depends on social status. The ties of loyalty between a king or magnate and his men are thus not necessarily stronger than those of kinship. Nevertheless, the former ties are probably more important for faction formation, first, because they do not present the same obstacles to group formation, and second, because they are more likely to serve individual interests. Depending on the distance in power and status between the partners and on benefits bestowed and received, alliances based on friendship, loyalty, or mutual interests could be created that were stronger than those forged by kinship ties.

If we look at the reality behind the apparently chaotic picture Snorri gives of respect and disregard of kinship ties, a certain pattern seems to emerge: kinship ties are weakened by concentration of power. Kinsmen offer valuable protection against aggressors and may be allies in struggles for power and influence, as Snorri repeatedly demonstrates.[16] But kinsmen are probably more difficult to command than nonrelated clients, at least with the kinship structure that prevailed in medieval Norway and Iceland. Consequently, they become a hindrance rather than an asset to really mighty men. The development of office points in the same direction. Although private property was normally divided between heirs, kingship and the office of *lendr maðr* were not, at least not in the same sense. Heirs to the kingdom might stick together against nonrelated rivals, like the Eiríkssons, but generally, they were rivals rather than allies.

Within the royal line conflicts not only occur, but seem to be the normal way of things. According to Gurevich, the explanation for this is a hereditary damnation deriving from an episode in the Ynglinga period (Gurevich, 1971: 49 f.; see also Sørensen, 1977: 165). From a modern point of view, the obvious explanation is that kingship is an office, which cannot be divided as easily as private property and, more generally, that the concentration of power in connection with the unification of the kingdom worked against solidarity between the members of the royal family. It is difficult to tell how far Snorri was aware of these facts. However, though he may have intended the episode in the *Ynglinga saga* as an explanation when he wrote it, his narrative as a whole and his general analysis of politics suggest that he regarded conflicts over power and resources as a normal phenomenon, even between kinsmen, and did not really need a "mythical" explanation like the one in the *Ynglinga saga*.

Lower offices, like that of earl or *lendr maðr,* are in principle treated in the same way as kingship. Only one member of a family is normally appointed, and he is in a superior position compared to his brothers. In this way the Eiríkssons can play off Grjótgarðr against his brother Sigurðr. Þórir hundr is in greater esteem than his brother Sigurðr because he is a *lendr maðr,* and Sigurðr's son Ásbjǫrn's hospitality is an attempt to rival him. The case of Erlingr Skjálgsson is particularly instructive. He belongs to the mightiest kindred in Southwest Norway (Rogaland, Hordaland), whose members seem to act together as a clan. Erlingr is chosen to marry King Oláfr Tryggvason's sister. He is appointed *lendr maðr* by the king, receives great *veitslur,* and becomes the real ruler of Western Norway, thus changing the collective leadership of his family into a personal principality. Consequently, his kinsman Áslákr fitjaskalli becomes his greatest rival and ultimately kills him. However, rivalry between kinsmen is not the normal way of things within the aristocracy to the same extent as within the royal family. Members of the aristocracy were in greater need of allies on their own social level, and their position in society did not depend on holding an office in the same sense as that of the king.

My last example raises the question of marriage ties, which in feudal Europe seem to have become relatively more important in the high Middle Ages with the change from extended family clans to lineages, and in connection with this the introduction of primogeniture (Duby, 1977: 59 ff., 149 ff;, and 1985: 92 ff., 227 ff.; Freed, 1986: 560 ff.). Such a radical change did not take place in Norway and Iceland, though there were tendencies in this direction.[17] Nevertheless, marriage seems to have been able to forge important political ties, equally important, if not more, than kinship (see Sigurðsson, 1989: 108 f. on Iceland). This seems likely enough in a bilateral system such as that of Norway and Iceland. Moreover, marriage ties are more easily adapted to new realities, since they can be used to strengthen alliances that are the results of political interests. Marriage ties may therefore well have been strengthened while kinship ties were weakened. In any case, marriage plays a prominent part in Snorri. Alliances between great men are often confirmed through marriage. Haraldr hárfagri's alliance with Earl Hákon Grjótgarðsson of Lade, which is of fundamental importance for his conquest of Norway, is confirmed by Haraldr marrying the earl's daughter (*HHárf.* chaps. 7, 9). Earl Hákon Sigurðarson's best friend is his brother-in-law, to whom he also marries his daughter (OT chap. 19). Óláfr Tryggvason uses his two brothers-in-law, together with his maternal uncle and stepfather, to make the people of Viken accept Christianity (OT chap. 53). Erlingr Skjálgsson's marriage to Óláfr Tryggvason's sister brings Western Norway to Óláfr's side while at the same time laying the foundation of Erlingr's greatness. The earls who rule the country after Óláfr's death link the leading men of the country, Erlingr Skjálgsson and Einarr þambarskelfir, to their cause through marriage alliances (OH chaps. 21, 31). The story of St. Óláfr's negotiations with the king of Sweden may also be understood in this perspective. Most of Koht's examples of alliances based on kinship during the civil wars of the twelfth century (1921: 118 f.) are actually marriage alliances, which give the impression that the factions were built up systematically through intermarriage.

The normal pattern of marriage alliances seems to be that if the partners have different rank, the woman has the higher, as is also the case in feudal Europe (see Duby, 1985: 143 f.). The king marries the daughter of another king, whereas the king's daughters or sisters marry magnates within the country or their sons.[18] Female members of the royal house are thus an important resource in building up a faction around the king, and the alliances formed in this way very often seem to last.[19] The kings' concubines and illegitimate sons serve to form alliances in a similar way, as does the institution of fostering.[20] This development is quite logical. On the one hand, politics is based on personal relationships. On the other, the permanent ties of kinship are often opposed to individual interests (see Wolf, 1982: 93 ff.; Verdery, 1988: 268). The logical solution is to create bonds between men that resemble family ties, but which are the result of their deliberate choice. The ties of loyalty between a king or magnate and his men may be regarded in the same way. They imply much the same duties as between kinsmen and have similar emotional overtones, while at the same time being stronger because they take into account individual interests.

The examples quoted above cannot without reservations be considered evidence of an actual historical development. On a priori grounds, however, it seems likely that change along these lines should have taken place, given the apparently rather loose kindred structure at the outset. But as some form of principalities may have existed long before the unification of the kingdom in the late ninth century, the alternatives, solidarity within the kindred or individual assertion, may have presented themselves long before Snorri's time. Nor is there any evidence that

Snorri regarded these alternatives in the perspective of a historical development. However, he obviously did reflect on the problem.

In the discussion between the petty kings of Eastern Norway over St. Óláfr's claim to the throne the kings Hringr and Hroerekr represent diametrically opposed attitudes on one point, namely on kinship. Hringr regards it as a promotion for the whole kindred if one of its members ascends to the throne, whereas Hroerekr thinks strictly in individual terms, seeing no reasons for supporting Óláfr other than personal gain. Snorri's own point of view does not emerge from the speeches. On the one hand, Óláfr is the great hero of the saga, and Hringr is thus on the right side; on the other hand, Hroerekr is an excellent analyst of politics and, as far as the interests of the petty kings are concerned, ultimately turns out to be right. The most probable conclusion is that Hringr represents the ideal of kindred solidarity, whereas Hroerekr better reflects the way people actually behaved, as is evident in Snorri's numerous examples of rivalry between kindreds and the pursuit of individual glory and power.

Snorri's particular interest in the problem may be explained from personal experience. Snorri lived through the greatest period of power concentration in Iceland and took active part in the process. In these struggles, his own kinsmen were as much his rivals as allies. In the 1230s his own brother and nephew even became his most bitter enemies. Though the Sturlungar may have been exceptional in this respect, it is easy to imagine that the emergence of larger and stronger principalities led by individual magnates might result in increased rivalry within the kindreds.

We may then conclude from the preceding analysis of the conflicts and the present one of the ties of loyalty within the factions that Snorri's society is neither a society based on group or class solidarity, nor a society of kindreds. It is primarily a society of individual kings or magnates competing for power or resources, where clashes or revenge are more pretexts than real reasons for conflicts, and where alliances are the results of personal interests.

Society as a Whole: Conflict or Harmony?

From a modern point of view, the society depicted in Snorri's narrative resembles sheer anarchy. Armed conflicts, mostly between individuals and alliances based on kinship or mutual interests, are quite normal, and they are conducted in a way in which most means are allowed that may lead to victory, the "rules of the game" being few and vaguely defined. Consequently, very little seems to tie this society together. This impression, however, is only partly correct. Snorri focuses on armed conflicts, whereas the elements that unite the members of society are only mentioned occasionally. First, peaceful means of solving conflicts are clearly underrepresented in the sagas, as they do not lead to important events. Second, in Snorri's society as in many other traditional societies (see Gluckman, 1965: 140 ff.) armed conflicts are not necessarily against the social order. They are part of it and may even serve to preserve it, in a similar way as the political conflicts that are conducted by peaceful means and according to strict rules in modern society.

This sense of the fundamental unity of society despite internal conflicts is expressed in Snorri's comment on the measure Erlingr skakki got passed against his adversary Earl Sigurðr, the leader of the young King Sigurðr Markúsfóstri's faction. After Erlingr's victory over King Hákon herðibreiðr renewed the conflict, but had small support and mainly conducted guerilla warfare, to the detriment of the people of Viken. At a popular assembly Erlingr had his adversary condemned to the devil. Snorri is evidently shocked at such unprecedented harshness and calls it an abominable act (ME chap. 10). The reason for this reaction is probably a fundamental distinction between conflicts "within" society, such as conflicts between pretenders and the—very rare—conflicts when society as a whole must defend its fundamental values. To use the sanctions meant for this last category of enemies against one's normal adversaries is such a horrible break against the rules of the game that it deserves the strongest condemnation in the whole of *Heimskringla*. By placing his adversaries outside society, Erlingr has broken one of its fundamental rules, the one that unites both parties in a conflict in a fundamental community.[21] Snorri's reasoning may be compared to the basic idea of modern democratic politics of a consensus concerning the fundamental values of society and politics, despite the constant struggle between different parties.

Apart from such extreme cases, the unity of society is not often focused in Snorri's narrative, probably because it is taken for granted. But Snorri clearly has an idea of Norwegian national unity as opposed to other countries. He frequently expresses nationalistic bias when describing conflicts with other countries and he mentions as a fact that it is usually difficult for a foreigner to be accepted in another country, in particular for a king to conquer another country than his own and be accepted as its ruler. His most important expression of this idea, however, is indirect, consisting in the kind of conflicts that do *not* occur. As we have seen, a conflict is not a *bellum omnium contra omnes,* but takes place within particular layers of society, whose members are allowed to claim the positions that may lead to major conflicts. Total victory or defeat has dramatic consequences for the chief participants but does not change very much. That is: the fundamental order of society is not really affected by the conflicts. The warring factions are united by a common social order and common values, which are implicit. In contrast to what is often the case in modern society and what has often been stated about medieval society, this social order with its inequality and hierarchy is not subject to conflicts but taken for granted, the conflicts taking place between people who belong to approximately the same order, usually at the top.

The Hierarchy of Society

In his analysis of Snorri's view of society, Gudmund Sandvik points out a tripartite structure: king, magnates, people. In terms of political tension or conflict, however, the line of division goes between king and magnates, whereas there is complete solidarity between magnates and people, the two terms often being synonymous. To Sandvik, Snorri's view of society is essentially aristocratic. Though the magnates ulti- mately have their basis of power in the people, they are not its represen- tatives in the strict sense. They take the political decisions, and the people automatically support them. When their leader is killed, the people are normally helpless even when they are numerically superior. Similarly, discussions in the popular assemblies are solely between mag- nates or between the magnates and the king, and the people are easily lead by the strongest or most influential person (Sandvik, 1955: 45 ff.).

In its main outlines, this description seems correct. Although Snorri mentions quite a number of social categories, from the king at the top to the slave at the bottom of the social ladder, his main line of division goes between these three. Slaves and freedmen are mentioned, but play no great part, at least not from a political point of view. Though there must have been distinctions of wealth and influence within the people, Snorri treats it as one group, and in fact rarely mentions its individual mem- bers. Nor are the magnates clearly distinguished from the people.

The usual Old Norse term for the people, which is also common in Snorri, *bóndi,* pl. *boendr,* has no exact English equivalent. It is derived from *búa* (= to live at or inhabit a place) and is used of ordinary, free men who lived on farms that they owned or rented, whatever their wealth and position in society. It may thus include very prominent men, who were in reality magnates. Þorgnýr lǫgmaðr, one of the mightiest men in Sweden and the leader of the opposition against King Óláfr of Sweden, is called *bóndi,* and even uses the term for himself (OH chap. 80). So is Járnskeggi, the leader of the people in Trøndelag and Einarr þambarskelfir's kinsman (OT chap. 66; see also *HGráf.* chap. 14). When Ragnhildr, the daughter of the late King Magnús góði, refuses to marry

Hákon Ívarsson, one of the mightiest men in the country, she calls him *bóndi* (*HHarð.* chap. 48: 142). The term is thus synonymous with *útíginn maðr* (a man not holding a *tígn*, i.e., high rank, usually that of king or earl), which is used both in this and other contexts (ibid.; see also OT chap. 56 on Erlingr Skjálgsson). Nor is the distinction between king and magnates entirely clear. From the time of Haraldr hárfagri there had normally been one or more persons to claim the right to rule the whole country, usually with the title of king. Besides, there were petty kings until the reign of St. Óláfr. As appears from Óláfr's saga, their position was not fundamentally different from that of the mightiest magnates. The title of earl could even be used for the ruler of the whole country, as in the case of Earl Hákon. For the most part, however, Snorri distinguishes relatively clearly between the person or persons claiming the lordship over the whole country and the rest of the aristocracy. His definition of the aristocracy, however, is more problematic.

The Aristocracy

Snorri gives several titles for members of the aristocracy, both before and after Haraldr hárfagri's conquest of the whole country. Having described this conquest, he gives a brief account of Haraldr's system of government: Haraldr put one earl in each district called *fylki* as its supreme judge, who was to have one-third of the royal incomes in his district. Under him there were to be four magnates of lower rank (*hersar*) with fixed *veitslur*—twenty marks—in income. Both the earls and the *hersar* were required to muster a certain number of men for the king's army. According to this description, the aristocracy consisted of royal officials, organized as a hierarchy (*HHárf.* chap. 6). Later he tells that this arrangement was upheld for a long time, and that Earl Hákon of Lade had sixteen earls under him (OT chap. 45—with reference to a scaldic stanza). Under Haraldr harðráði he refers to a custom, introduced by St. Óláfr and Magnús góði, of having only one earl at a time in the country (*HHarð.* chap. 48). Though this alleged rule may be introduced for the sake of the story Snorri was just then telling, it conforms better with Snorri's account of actual practice than the system of one earl in each *fylki*, as he only mentions a small number of earls at any one period (see Bøe, 1962: 560 f.). Nor does the number of *hersar* in Snorri's story actually conform to the enormous number that must have existed if Haraldr's rule had been practiced. To Snorri and other Icelandic saga writers, the term *hersir* seems to have been equivalent to *lendr maðr*, which is the usual term from the saga of St. Óláfr on (Bøe, 1965: 498 ff.). Snorri implies that these positions were not hereditary, although custom favored certain kins.

The real aristocracy is not confined to men with these titles. In his narrative, Snorri repreatedly refers to men as esteemed, mighty, and so forth, who have a strong position in their regions and act as spokesmen for the people and local leaders. Such men may or may not be attached to the king's service as *lendir menn*. The term "magnate," which I have used frequently above, is meant to include these men as well as those holding formal titles. In this way, the aristocracy is vaguely separated from the king on the one side and the people on the other. Though titles are not without importance, they are clearly insufficient to distinguish Snorri's aristocracy from the rest of the population. We may note, however, that in contrast to the office of *goði* in the society to which Snorri himself belonged, medieval Iceland, there was no formal office for local leaders, except those distributed by the king.

Despite the rather vague lines of distinction between the categories, there is no real doubt of the tripartite structure in itself. As is evident both from the discussion above and from Sandvik's analysis, the magnates are the clue to the whole system. They are the intermediate category, with connections to the king above them and the people below. Sandvik emphasizes their function as leaders of the people in opposition to the king, in my opinion too strongly. As we have seen, his and Koht's picture of an almost constant conflict between the latter and the people is hardly correct. Still, the contrast between the magnates' almost completely harmonious relationship to the people and their frequent conflicts with the king is striking and demands an explanation. Before we turn to that, however, we shall have a closer look at the foundation of their power.

We can distinguish between four elements as the foundation of a magnate's power: (1) kin; (2) wealth; (3) charisma; (4) office bestowed by the king. All four can be illustrated in the person of Erlingr Skjálgsson. Erlingr was a descendant of Hǫrdakári, who was an important man in Western Norway in the mid-tenth century, and whose kinswoman Þóra became Haraldr hárfagri's mistress and the mother of King Hákon góði. His son, Klyppr hersir, killed King Sigurðr Eiríksson for having raped his wife (*HGráf.* chap. 14). Snorri gives Erlingr's genealogy in connection with Óláfr Tryggvason's visit to Western Norway to convert this region. Hǫrðakári's kin is presented as the mightiest there (OT chap. 54). Under their leader Ǫlmóðr, they agree in accepting Christianity on the condition that Erlingr is married to Óláfr's sister, a marriage that makes Erlingr the most prominent man of the region.

Erlingr is thus elected to succeed Ǫlmóðr as the leader of the clan. He is the grandson of Hǫrðakári's second son, whereas Ǫlmoðr is Hǫrðakári's fourth son, probably the only one surviving at this time. His grandson, Áslákr fitjaskalli, later becomes Erlingr's enemy and kills him. Theoretically, this might indicate some sort of primogeniture within each generation of the clan. But there is no trace of such principles in Snorri's own Icelandic society (see n. 16), nor does Snorri refer to it in this case. He clearly states that Erlingr is elected because of personal qualities, that is, *charisma*.

Snorri normally seems to imply that the magnates have inherited their position, and he often gives their genealogies, usually when introducing them. Sometimes he does so in order to trace the descent of men who have played an important part recently or in his own time, such as Archbishop Eysteinn and his own friend Duke Skúli (*HHarð*. chaps. 37, 98: 219). Modern scholars, who have tried to establish genealogies on the basis of Snorri and other historians, have succeeded in linking together a number of leading magnates from various epochs, which gives the general impression that there was a considerable continuity in the aristocracy from the time of St. Óláfr until the latter half of the twelfth century.[22] The self-esteem of the old aristocracy is evident from the reaction of Hárekr at Tjøtta against King Óláfr's promotion of Ásmundr Grankellsson, which in Hárekr's opinion means reducing the status of the old aristocracy in favor of a "new man."[23] In the same way, the position of the low-born Selþórir is an extreme provocation of Erlingr Skjálgsson. But Snorri does not always point out the links that must have existed, which indicates that he is less interested in genealogy than in other criteria of aristocratic status.

There is some connection between *charisma* and descent: noble blood will normally produce a noble character. The idea is directly expressed by Earl Rǫgnvaldr of Møre, who says to his son Einarr that he will hardly bring any honor to his kinsmen, because his mother was a slave.[24] In this case, Rǫgnvaldr is actually proved wrong: Einarr defeats the Vikings who have driven his half-brother away from the Orkneys, establishes himself as earl there, and becomes a mighty ruler. His words do not therefore necessarily express Snorri's own opinion. Snorri even gives an example of a slave becoming king by rebelling and deposing the right king.[25] However, Snorri's characterizations are best interpreted in the light of some belief in a general connection between noble blood and noble character, though Snorri does not necessarily mean that this always holds true: this idea is balanced by a rather matter of fact consideration concerning courage: younger and less established people with more to gain are likely to be braver than the great magnates (OH, chap. 90: 167).

With the relatively vague distinction between the magnates and the rest of the population, what kind of blood is considered noble? When Snorri refers to a man as *gǫfugr* (great, prominent) or *ættstórr* (high-born) he probably refers to the fact that his ancestors have been wealthy and mighty men in a particular region over some generations. One qualification, however, seems to be particularly important, namely connection with the royal family. In his remark on the great power of the *lendir menn* at the beginning of St. Óláfr's reign, he explicitly mentions that many of them were descended from kings or earls (OH chap. 46). This is borne out by individual examples of men who are related to the king or the earls of Lade through kinship or marriage, such as Erlingr Skjálgsson, Einarr þambarskelfir, and Hárekr at Tjøtta. When the latter complains about Óláfr's promotion of the "new man" Ásmundr Grankellsson, he may very well have this in mind. Ásmundr's father is characterized as an *auðigr bóandi* (a wealthy farmer), a former Viking chieftain and a *hermaðr mikill* (a great warrior) (OH chap. 106), whereas Hárekr is himself something of a newcomer as far as wealth is concerned (OH chap. 104). The great difference between the two is apparently that Hárekr is related to the royal family, whereas Ásmundr is not. Membership in the royal family is in itself a sign of prominence, whereas families who rise to prominence through wealth and their own efforts will sooner or later end up with being married into it.

Snorri repeatedly refers to Erlingr's great wealth. Erlingr is sufficiently wealthy to be the leading man in Western Norway even without the king's *veitslur* (OH chap. 22). His wealth evidently consists in large estates, to which Snorri refers in the story of his allowing his slaves to buy themselves free through extra working (OH chap. 23; see also chap. 117). In one sense this is a further indication of the importance of birth for aristocratic status, as landed estates were hereditary. But Norwegian and to some extent Icelandic rules of divided inheritance made it less likely than in systems of primogeniture that the position of a particular family or kin would be maintained (see n. 15). Besides, Snorri also mentions other methods of acquiring wealth, above all Viking expeditions. Though one probably had to hold a prominent position within one's region to become the leader of such an expedition, its success or failure very much depended on luck and personal ability. Such expeditions must therefore have contributed to some degree of social mobility. The civil wars of the late twelfth and early thirteenth centuries may have had the same effect.[26] Even landed estates might be acquired through personal efforts, as the example of Hárekr at Tjøtta shows.[27] In Erlingr Skjálgsson's case, Viking expeditions compensated for his loss of royal *veitslur* after the death of Óláfr Tryggvason. Politically, wealth served two purposes: to keep a numerous and well-equipped army of retainers and to attract adherents and allies through generosity.

The importance of *charisma* appears from Snorri's description of Erlingr, which makes him a sort of popular hero among Snorri's readers even today. His old kinsman Ǫlmóðr calls him the most beautiful young man in Norway and Óláfr Tryggvason points out his beauty to his reluctant sister (OT chap. 56). Snorri repeatedly stresses his skill at arms, bravery, and attractive personality, which makes him a number of friends. His last battle is one of the great "scenes" of *Heimskringla,* with Erlingr standing alone on his ship after all his men have been killed, defending himself "so nobly that no one could remember any one man having stood off the attack of so many so long" ("svá prúðliga, at engi maðr vissi doemi, at einn maðr hefði staðit svá lengi fyrir jammargra manna atsókn") (OH chap. 176: 405). In his narrative, Snorri often implies that a magnate's ability to win adherents and thus to improve his position in society depends on qualities like eloquence, wisdom, bravery, and so forth.

Erlingr's position under the earls and Óláfr serves as an example of a magnate managing to be extremely powerful even without the king's support. This should not, however, be taken as evidence that the king is normally of marginal importance for the position of the magnates or that there is usually a conflict of interest between them. Snorri clearly implies that Erlingr is an exception in this respect. His counterpart in Trøndelag, Einarr þambarskelfir, is apparently without *veitslur* after his reconciliation with Óláfr. He is still a very rich man but plays no political role until after Óláfr's exile (OH, chaps. 121, 144, 171, 194). In other cases, such as in most of Óláfr's alliances with "new men," the king's support is decisive in promoting people to high rank in society, though it is clearly not a question of raising men from the dust. Snorri even expresses this point in a more general way: Haraldr hárfagri's conquest and his new arrangement of government gave his "officials" more wealth and power than the petty kings had had before, thus leading many magnates to Haraldr's service. Even Erlingr is to a considerable extent an example of a man promoted by the king. During the negotiations between Óláfr Tryggvason and Erlingr's kinsmen about his marriage with Óláfr's sister Ástríðr Ástríðr, first refuses to marry Erlingr because he is an *útíginn maðr,* that is, a man without aristocratic rank. Óláfr offers to make him earl, but Erlingr refuses, not wanting a higher name than that of his kinsmen before him, who have been *hersar.* But he wants Óláfr to make him the mightiest *hersir* in the country, which Óláfr in fact does. Erlingr in reality becomes the prince of most of Western Norway and is able to maintain this position against Óláfr's successors. Even great magnates, like Þórir hundr and Hárekr at Tjøtta, to some extent owe their position to the king.[28] Another interesting example is Kálfr Árnason, whom Óláfr gives the estate of the former local leader Qlvi at Egge and who has apparently no difficulty in maintaining his position as the leading magnate of Inner Trøndelag.

It is difficult to form an exact opinion on the relative importance of Snorri's various criteria for aristocratic status. Snorri does not treat the question systematically, nor is he sufficiently specific in his detailed narrative to allow us to weigh their importance, for instance the size of income derived from royal *veitslur* versus "private property," the importance of hereditary position versus "appointment" by the king or the people. The previous examples are, however, sufficient to reject Sandvik's view of the magnates as exclusively popular leaders. Snorri implies that they derive a considerable part of their power from the king: to be appointed *lendr maðr* by the king means a clear promotion compared to other men of equal wealth and status and even gives considerable economic resources. And membership in the royal family by kinship or marriage is the highest expression of aristocratic status. Snorri thus regards the magnates as mediators between the king and the people rather than exclusively popular leaders.

The King

The ideology of the Norwegian monarchy of the thirteenth century, as expressed in the official sources, notably *The King's Mirror,* was derived from the European and Christian idea of the king as God's representative on earth: the king holds his office from God. He has duties to perform on God's behalf, above all in the field of justice. He is given extensive power by God in order to perform those duties, the most important check on him being that he is not allowed to reduce his power. And finally, he rules a hierarchically organized society, whose members owe him loyalty and obedience, the more so the higher their rank (Bagge, 1987*b*: 22 ff., 50 ff., 153 ff., 205 ff.).

As might be expected from my previous analysis of the conflicts, Snorri's picture of the king differs from this ideology on most points. As for legitimacy, both the traditional Christian idea of the king as God's representative on earth and the more recent idea of the king as the representative of the state, are largely absent from Snorri's work. Although the latter is not very surprising, the former idea is found in Norwegian sources long before Snorri's time and is clearly expressed by the clerical historians of the late twelfth century.[29] Snorri's picture of St. Óláfr as the *rex iustus* belongs to this tradition but, as we have seen, it is of minor importance in Snorri's overall view of his reign.

The supernatural aspect of kingship in Snorri is rather an example of what Max Weber calls *charismatic lordship* ("charismatische Herrschaft"), which includes both particular powers inherent in the royal blood and impressive personal qualities (Weber, 1964, I: 179 ff.). Though Snorri most probably believed in supernatural qualities inherent in the king, especially the king's luck, his main emphasis is on charisma in the sense of ordinary, human qualities that make the king attractive to other men.

The idea that the king should belong to the royal line of descent may possibly be derived from the belief in particular powers inherent in the royal blood. Sigurðr slembir, who was the most able of the pretenders in the first phase of the civil wars, had serious difficulties when he could not persuade people of his royal blood. Even Magnús Erlingsson's claims on the throne were allegedly dubious because he only descended from the royal line through his mother (ME chap. 21: 462). However, royal descent apparently plays no role for the magnates who rebel against King Magnús berfoetr under the leadership of Sveinn Haraldsson, a man of Danish noble descent, whose genealogy Snorri does not attempt to trace (MB chap. 4).[30] Nor does Snorri reflect on the legitimacy of Earl Hákon Sigurðarson's ascent to rulership over Norway after the fall of King Haraldr gráfeldr or Haraldr hárðráði's claim while his nephew, King Magnús, was still living.[31]

Snorri's inconsistencies at this point probably reflect actual historical development. Royal descent became progressively more important and the way the kingdom was transmitted from one generation to the other was more clearly defined.[32] Snorri and other thirteenth-century sagawriters seem generally to express the stricter attitude of their period, and there are reasons to believe that some of their royal genealogies of the early period are actually constructions. Occasionally, however, the realities of the earlier age appear in their narrative. Thus, although it is possible though not usual for "new men" to achieve aristocratic status and relatively easy to succeed a local leader without being blood related to him, the qualifications for kingship seem to be stricter.

In the official ideology of the Norwegian monarchy, God's election of the king is expressed through hereditary succession (Bagge, 1987b: 39 f.). This may even suggest that the idea of hereditary succession is not derived from the traditional belief in the powers inherent in the royal blood, but is of fairly recent and Christian origin. This is not a necessary conclusion, however. What is characteristic of thirteenth-century ideology is not hereditary succession as such but its restriction to one person in each generation and the very definite rules for selecting this person. This idea is in turn combined with the legal or quasi-legal idea of the kingdom as the hereditary property (óðal), of the royal line (Bagge, 1987b: 31 ff.). By contrast, Snorri seems to believe in particular powers inherent in the royal blood, at least in the sense that royal descent is more likely to produce the qualities needed in a king than descent from ordinary men. But such powers evidently belong to all the king's descendants, not only to one heir. Moreover, they are probably not qualitatively different from the ones belonging to other great men. A man's descent is important for his personal qualities. The king ought to be the best man in the country, and the chance for this is better if he belongs to the royal line.

There is little trace in Snorri of the ecclesiastical and monarchical idea of the king holding an office on God's behalf (see Bagge, 1987b: 25 f., 194 ff.). Snorri does not refer to the king's position as an office (embætti etc.), nor does he distinguish between the king's person and his position within society. His position is to be regarded as a social role rather than as an office in the modern or contemporary ecclesiastical sense: to be king is first of all a personal performance, and it is difficult to distinguish between the royal person and the royal office. However, his position is an office in the sense that he is formally appointed to it, through election at the popular assemblies; that there is normally only one holder of it at a time—if there are more, this is a problem that needs a special solution—and that certain rights and duties appertain to it. In this way, the king's position differs from that of the magnates. Though most magnates are also formally appointed to an office, that of lendr maðr, this is not as essential to their position as the king's ascendance to the throne.

The idea that the king has his legitimacy from the people is expressed in his formal election at the popular assemblies which is frequently mentioned in the sagas. This popular right of election was progressively restricted during the high Middle Ages and had degenerated into acclamation by the latter half of the thirteenth century (Helle, 1974: 60 ff., 115 ff., 136 f.; Bagge, 1987b: 40; see also NG chaps. 4–8, L part 2, chaps. 3–6, H chaps. 2–10). Snorri seems in this respect to reflect the more "democratic" attitude of the earlier Middle Ages, usually mentioning with great care the kings' acclamations at each particular assembly. As nearly all pretenders are acclaimed at least at some assemblies, however, the real decision between rival pretenders is not taken there, but in more informal encounters between them and their adherents, and ultimately at the battlefield. However, this is also a kind of "democratic process," as success in such encounters depends on the ability to attract adherents. Thus, although Snorri tones down the mystical and magical aspect of charisma and its hereditary character (in Weber's terminology, "das Erbcharisma"; see 1964: 183 f.), he lays great emphasis on its personal aspect. The king is supposed to be an impressive personality. As rival pretenders are all of royal blood, and it is impossible on the basis of heredity alone to decide which one of them has the best right, personal qualities are usually decisive. Wealth has a similar importance. Gifts are necessary to attract adherents, and the king must therefore be both wealthy and willing to spend his wealth.

In the version of the Christian ideology of the rex iustus that was shaped by the thirteenth-century Norwegian monarchy, jurisdiction is the single most important duty of the king; in The King's Mirror it even seems to be his only duty (Bagge, 1987b: 51 ff., 156 ff., 189 ff.). Through its insistence on the king's position as the supreme judge of the realm,

The King's Mirror also lays the foundation of a theory of his legislative authority, though this is first explicitly stated in the laws of the second half of the century (Bagge, 1987*b*: 156 ff., 174 n. 28, 189 ff.; see e.g., L Prologue, part 2, chap. 8).

This picture of the king is occasionally found in Snorri. In the competition between the kings Sigurðr and Eysteinn, a fairly long passage is devoted to the performance of the two kings in the field of justice and administration (below, chap. 4). Snorri's picture of St. Óláfr's daily life as king resembles that of the *rex iustus* in *The King's Mirror:* he rises early, attends mass and the canonical hours, and spends his day in meetings and in settling peoples' issues (OH chap. 58; see also *Kgs.*: 92, lines 8–34, 97.12–98.19 and Bagge, 1987*b*: 90 ff.). He is also a great legislator, in accordance with contemporary tradition, which attributed much of the existing legislation to him (see Blom, 1981: 61 ff. with ref.). Further, Snorri often refers to the king's duties as a judge and legislator in his characterizations of other kings. King Hálfdan svarti was a just man who issued laws and respected them himself and who stipulated the fines for various offenses according to the rank of those involved (HS chap. 7: 95). He was thus apparently the inventor of the system of fines that still existed at Snorri's time. King Haraldr hárfagri made arrangements for the governance of the country, including the judicial administration (*HHárf.* chap. 6), but apart from this, nothing much is said of his judicial activity. By contrast Hákon góði was the great legislator, who issued the *Gulaþingslǫg* and *Frostuþingslǫg* (HG chap. 11) and organized the *leiðangr* (the popular levy) (HG chap. 20). After his "conversion" Óláfr's son and successor Magnús becomes a wise king and a great legislator, the author of *Grágás,* which was still the law of Trøndelag at Snorri's time (MG chap. 16). Haraldr harðráði is above all a warrior king but is also mentioned as a strong ruler within the country (*HHarð.* chap. 36). Among later rulers Snorri praises Erlingr skakki for his strong rule, which probably includes judicial activity, and for his effort in maintaining internal peace (ME chap. 37; see also *HHerð.* chap. 9; ME chap. 10).

In practice, however, we rarely meet the king in what in thirteenth-century ideology appears as his normal capacity as judge and internal administrator. This is natural insofar as the sagas are interested in extraordinary events, not in normal routines. Therefore, the king's function as war leader is more prominent than his function as judge, administrator, and legislator. This applies not only to Snorri but also to the sagas dealing with the period after 1177, such as *Sverris saga* and *Hákonar saga.*[33] What is somewhat more surprising is the fact that so few of the conflicts Snorri deals with arise out of such activities.[34] By contrast, in the Icelandic sagas we are constantly reminded of the chieftains' position as great farmers and local leaders and mediators through the kinds of conflicts in which they are engaged (Byock, 1982: 39 ff., and 1988: 113 ff., 168 ff.). As we have seen, the king in *Heimskringla* is mainly a great magnate, who tries to extend his sphere of influence by outmaneuvering his opponents and gaining adherents through generosity, patronage, and so forth. Though Snorri no doubt takes into account the official thirteenth-century picture of the king as a judge and administrator and the representative of an impersonal justice, it is not really integrated in his narrative.

As for the king's government, Snorri's description of Haraldr hár-fagri's appointment of earls and *hersar* in each district after his conquest of the country seems to imply some kind of bureaucratic structure. However, the importance of this should not be overrated. First, the system appears more like a regulation of the traditional system of government than as an entirely new one, and the new officials seem largely to be recruited from the old class of magnates and to govern much in the same way. Second, Snorri rarely refers to the system after Haraldr's own time.

However, Snorri frequently refers to the king's local representatives, particularly from the period of St. Óláfr onward. There were two kinds of such men, the mighty and high-born *lendir menn,* who seem to be the king's allies more than his officials, and the *ármenn,* who were of lower rank, though not necessarily descended from slaves, like Selþórir.[35] The *ármenn* administered the king's farms but also had "public" duties in the district, such as jurisdiction, as appears from the examples of Selþórir and Bjǫrn. A *lendr maðr* was assigned a particular part of the royal demesne as *veitsla* for life, an arrangement resembling the European fief. In addition, he performed duties on the king's behalf, similar to those of the *ármaðr.* Snorri sometimes implies that the *lendir menn* had regular districts, called *lén* or *sýslur* (e.g., OH chaps. 116, 123, 167; see also Hertzberg, 1893: 307 ff., and Lie, 1907: 22 ff.). This is an administrative system similar to the one found in Norway in Snorri's own lifetime, which had a quasi-bureaucratic character and in which the officials were clearly subordinated to the king and served as his representatives.[36] However, we rarely come across this system in practice in Snorri's narrative. There the *lendir menn* are mainly the king's local allies, whereas the *ármenn* are his personal servants.

Snorri's attitude to bureaucracy is well illustrated through the conflict between St. Óláfr and Erlingr Skjálgsson over Selþórir, Óláfr's *ármaðr* at Avaldsnes, that is, within Erlingr's "kingdom" of Western Norway. In one of their encounters Erlingr expresses his willingness to obey the king, but flatly refuses to submit to the low-born Þórir.[37] Selþórir is not described as an attractive person, and Erlingr probably has Snorri's full sympathy. To some extent, this controversy can be regarded as a conflict between the old system of personal loyalty between the king and the magnates who were his local allies and a bureaucratic system of local officials. But this aspect should not be overrated. All magnates had low-born men in their service, whose prestige reflected that of their master. The mightier the magnate, the more low-born creature could he afford to use against his rivals. Characteristically, when Þórir is killed, Óláfr is not concerned with the fact that he is a royal official, but with the offense against his own honor, because the killing took place in his presence.[38] A parallel case is that of Einarr þambarskelfir, who risks a conflict with King Haraldr harðráði to save a thief—the most despicable of all men—from execution, because the man had been in his service. Moreover, Snorri evidently does not regard Selþórir as representative of Óláfr's normal way of building up his power at the local level. Óláfr did try to curb the power of the great magnates, but his usual method was to use men of approximately the same rank or slightly lower as their rivals.

Rather than building up a bureaucratic or quasi-bureaucratic apparatus, Snorri's kings rule by establishing personal connections, through gifts, concessions, and—not the least—through marriage, sexual relationships, or fostering. Haraldr hárfagri marries most of his daughters to his earls (*HHárf.* chap. 42) and lets his sons grow up with their mothers' kin (*HHárf.* chap. 21). In accordance with his policy of promoting second-rank men, St. Óláfr marries his female relatives to such men instead of trying to win the greatest magnates over to his cause in this way.[39] His half-brother, Harald harðráði, coming from abroad and apparently lacking a strong kindred—and female relatives?—goes to the fairly unusual step of marrying the Norwegian magnate Þorbergr Árnason's daughter Þóra (*HHarð.* chap. 33). During the civil wars, the most prominent members of the factions are normally related to the royal family through kinship, marriage, or fostering.[40] Given the importance of such relations for aristocratic status, this is probably an important instrument for the king in linking the magnates to his service. Another such instrument is membership in the king's *hirð*, a community that bears some resemblance to a kindred or a family: the members share the same house and table, are obliged to keep peace between them and to avenge one another.[41] When one member of a kindred is included in the *hirð*, the whole kindred or at least some of its members may be drawn into the king's sphere of influence. The story of Grankell and his son Ásmundr is an example of this.[42]

The importance of such personal links between the king and his servants clearly indicates that the people as a whole have few obligations to the king. Admittedly, Snorri agrees with royalist ideology in not defining any constitutional checks on the king's power. Although in the latter this is combined with rather explicit statements of the king's competence and the respect and obedience the people owe to him (Bagge, 1987*b*: 22 ff., 156 ff.), there are few such statements in Snorri. The idea of treason against the king is expressed in Óláfr's words to Erlingr Skjálgsson after his surrender in the last fight between them: "A mark he shall bear, the betrayer of his king ("merkja skal dróttinsvikann," OH chap. 176: 406). In a similar way Finnr Árnason warns Hákon Ívarsson that he will be called a traitor if he rebels against the king and defeats him (*HHarð.* chap. 47). Óláfr's severity against offenders against him may also be intended as an illustration of the idea of the king as representing impersonal justice and therefore refusing to accept indemnity for men like Ásbjǫrn selsbani and Þórir Ǫlvisson. Though Snorri clearly knows these ideas and occasionally refers to them, they are of minor importance in his actual narrative. Usually, the king is an actor in the political game like everyone else, and Snorri rarely expects the other actors to take into consideration his exalted position as God's representative on earth. Although the king's men are obliged to serve their lord and avenge him if he is killed, the people as a whole have few such obligations. When one king is defeated and killed, they usually acclaim the victor as his successor—their refusal to acclaim Sigurðr slembir is exceptional.[43] To get support, the king must do two things. He must rule in such a way as to promote the interests of the people, or at least not counteract them. As we have seen, Snorri gives several examples of kings being deposed or killed for not respecting the rights and interests of the people. And he must form links to the leading magnates—make them his clients—so that their clients in turn will support him.

There is thus very little qualitative difference between a king and a magnate. The king is the magnates' superior, but he depends on their support in the same way as they depend on the support of the people. Although there are no constitutional checks on him, he cannot claim special protection from rebellion and opposition by appealing to God's election. Snorri most probably believes in particular powers inherent in the royal blood, but such powers are not qualitatively different from those of the magnates. The king is a *primus inter pares* who depends above all on his personal ability to be able to rule. The qualities demanded of him differ more in degree than in kind from those demanded from the magnates, as is evident from the characterizations. There are traces of the contemporary monarchical ideology in Snorri's reference to the king's duties as a judge and legislator, but generally, he performs much the same functions as the magnates. Rather than a bureaucratic apparatus, he must use a net of personal alliances with more or less prominent magnates to be able to rule.

The Magnates Between the King
and the People

By and large then, there is a close similarity between the king and the magnates. Both have largely the same foundation of their power, both have to rule by gaining followers through gifts and personal attraction, and the magnates do not regard the king as qualitatively different from themselves.

Admittedly, Sandvik is correct in pointing out the contrast between the magnates' frequent conflicts with the king on the one hand and their undisputed position as popular leaders on the other. There is, however, another explanation to this, namely that Snorri is primarily interested in kings—in fact, *Heimskringla* is strictly speaking a series of royal biographies, not what we would call a national history. Consequently, conflicts below the royal level are uninteresting. This suggestion receives some support from Snorri's casual references to conflicts between magnates that did not directly involve the king, as the one between Hárekr of Tjøtta's and Ásmundr Grankellsson's kinsmen (MG chap. 12). The background to the story of Ásbjørn selsbani points in the same direction. Ásbjørn's generosity has a political background. He tries to win adherents in order to become the leading man in the region in competition with his uncle Þórir hundr (OH chap. 117). Snorri evidently does not regard local society as a society of perfect stability under the leadership of magnates with a fixed position. Rather, he implies that there is rivalry and competition between the leaders there in the same way as in the country as a whole. Even a "constitutional" conflict between a magnate and the people does not seem entirely out of question. Besides being the ruler of the whole of Norway, Earl Hákon of Lade was also the local leader of Trøndelag and derived much of his strength from this position. But it was the people of this region that eventually deposed and killed him. The reason for this, his behavior toward their women, is quite the sort of oppression one might expect from a local leader who grows too self-confident.

The contrast between the relationship between the king and the magnates on the one hand and the magnates and the people on the other is therefore of less importance than appears at first sight. Nor are there sufficient reasons to believe in a constant conflict between the king and the magnates. The magnates should rather be regarded as a group between the king and the people, depending on support from both and having an important function for both. Admittedly, it seems likely that a magnate may control his people more easily within his smaller region than the king who tries to establish his dominion over the whole country and that Snorri had this in mind when telling his stories. We need not necessarily imagine the same loose organization on the local level as in society as a whole. Kinship, personal acquaintance, and personal loyalty may account for more there and thus create more stable relationships. The fact that men of lower status are supposed to show greater loyalty to their superiors than the great magantes also point in this direction.

The difference is, however, rather one of degreee than of kind. Basically, both the king and the magnates have the same foundation of their power: they have some hereditary claims, but these are insufficient without popular support, which is obtained through generosity, success, and charisma. Society is loosely organized and support is easily lost or won. No strong organization for control over the country exists, and military means are clearly insufficient for a real conquest. Military victory is a means to win support, not an end in itself. This is the lesson that can be drawn from Óláfr's and Cnut's conquests of the country, from Ásbjǫrn selsbani's desperate attempts to maintain generosity, and from the dramatic clashes between the king and the people at the numerous popular assemblies.

An Aristocratic Society?

From a modern point of view, it is not difficult to agree in Sandvik's description of Snorri's society as an aristocratic one. It is commonplace in *Heimskringla* that the people are helpless without their leaders. When the king manages to kill the local leader in battle or through a coup, popular resistance is impossible. Even if they are numerically superior, the people are unable to avenge their leader, as the case of Einarr þambarskelfir's fall and numerous other examples show (*HHarð.* chap. 44; see also Sandvik, 1955: 49 ff.). During the civil wars, the great magnates are the most able leaders, and the faction that has the support of the majority of them is most likely to win. At the popular assemblies, there is always a magnate to speak for the people, and the magnates' opinions are decisive for the final outcome of the deliberatons (Sandvik, 1955: 45 ff.). When St. Óláfr offers the Icelanders his friendship in return for Grímsey, an uninhabited island off the coast of the country, Guðmundr Eyjólfsson at Mǫðruvellir almost persuades the assembly to grant the king his prayer, until his brother Einarr stands up and speaks against the demand in a way that turns the opinion entirely against the king (OH chap. 125; see also Sandvik, 1955: 33 f.).

The opposition against the Danish rule after the death of St. Óláfr is in one sense an exception to this (OH chaps. 247, 250–251; MG chaps. 1–5). The Danes are very unpopular, and the widespread belief in Óláfr's sainthood serves to strengthen the opposition. After the young King Magnús's arrival in Trøndelag, King Sveinn tries to mobilize the people of Western Norway at an assembly in Sunnhordland. But few men appear, and King Sveinn and his Danish adherents receive little acclamation at their speeches and some even speak against them. In a short speech, Sveinn draws the conclusion that those who are not present or have not spoken in favor of Magnús will hardly be more trustworthy than those who have and decides to return to Denmark. Snorri tells the episode rather briefly, neither naming the leaders of the opposition nor stating their arguments in direct speech. This may indicate that they were not magnates in the real sense, though they may well have been prominent men at the local level. The fact that he refers to them as *boendr* (commoners) is less significant from this point of view. Though this is hardly an example of a spontaneous, popular uprising, it shows local society in opposition against the ruler. But Snorri seems to imply that it is rather exceptional that ordinary men dare to speak against the king in his own presence.

Taken as a whole, however, Snorri's account of the rebellion against the Danes clearly emphasizes the role of the two magnates Einarr þambarskelfir and Kálfr Árnason more so than those of his predecessors. Einarr, who is disappointed at not being rewarded as he was promised, begins early to exploit the rumors of Óláfr's sainthood. A meeting between him and Bishop Grimkell results in Óláfr's canonization. Later he allies himself with Kálfr Árnason, and the two of them become the leaders of the opposition and later bring Óláfr's son Magnús back from Russia and make him king.

On the explicit level, Snorri attaches great importance to the aristocracy. When we read his text as a whole, however, the importance of the people is equally striking. This is above all evident through a comparison with contemporary European sources. In European historiography of the period the people are hardly mentioned at all, whereas in *Heimskringla* and other sagas they are constantly present. Against a contemporary European background, Snorri's constant reference to the popular assemblies, both concerning royal elections and other matters, is more remarkable than the fact that the people at the assemblies are normally led by their superiors. The difference becomes even more striking when we consider the interest aspect of the policy of the kings and magnates.

One of the reasons why Snorri implies that there is normally no conflict between the magnates and the people is that the magnates become leaders largely by serving the interest of the people. The magnates who stand up against the king at the assemblies, like Ásbjǫrn of Meðalhús, Þorgnýr lǫgmaðr, Einarr Eyjólfsson, and Sigvatr skáld, articulate common interests. The kind of interests that is most frequently in focus is peace. Snorri generally assumes that the people want peace, and thus peaceful kings are more popular than those who conduct an aggressive foreign policy, like Haraldr harðráði and Magnús berfoetr (*HHarð*. chaps. 36, 99; MB chap. 26; see also above). A magnate like Erlingr skakki, who is the real ruler of the country in the 1160s and 1170s, is popular with the people because of his ability to create internal peace through suppressing the raiding groups of the opposite party. Peace negotiations are very often the result of initiative from the people. This applies to the conflicts between St. Óláfr and King Óláfr of Sweden and between Earl Hákon of Lade and the Eiríkssons (OH chap. 68; *HGráf.* chap. 6). In these cases the magnates are often the people's spokesmen before the king.[44] Second to peace, the people want good years and low taxes. They support the rulers they think are able to help them to achieve this, and, led by the magnates, they rebel against those who are not. Finally, the people are usually conservative, for instance in religious questions. Led by the magnates they oppose the kings' attempts at conversion. But when the magnates convert, they usually follow. Dealing with politics at a high level and with dramatic episodes, Snorri usually focuses on the magnates' role as leaders in the conflicts that result from these events. Occasionally, however, he alludes to the magnates' more normal function of leadership, as offering hospitality (e.g., Qlvi at Egge and Ásbjǫrn selsbani, OH chaps. 107–110, 117) and protecting their clients or adherents. His reference to what was probably a very important aspect of leadership, settling legal issues between people, is more vague, but he does mention their judicial functions in connection with their conflicts with the kings. Erlingr Skjálgsson appropriates the fines in his district whether the rulers agree or not (OH chap. 22; see also chap. 116) and Einarr þambarskelfir's conflict with King Haraldr harðráði takes place at a popular assembly and concerns legal matters (*HHarð*. chaps. 43–44).

Snorri thus represents an aristocratic view in the sense that he considers the common people unable to articulate their own interests, but not in the sense that their interests are unimportant. Admittedly, aristocratic, self-interest can easily be presented as the common good of society. Snorri, however, presents both popular interests in such a concrete way and so frequently refers to the people and their opinions that he clearly represents a different and more "democratic" historiography than the one current in contemporary Europe.

Snorri distinguishes between two types of kings, the warrior hero and the peaceful ruler, the latter of which is clearly the more popular with the people. To some extent, the same distinction may be made concerning the magnates. In economic terms, the king or magnate may spend his surplus in two distinct ways in order to get support, either on an army of retainers or on ordinary people. Snorri sometimes points to the generosity of kings to their *hirð* as opposed to their harshness toward the people. Although he mentions magnates, such as Erlingr Skjálgsson and Grégóríús Dagsson, with large armies of retainers to whom they are very generous, the distinction seems less relevant in their case. All together Snorri's description of the road to victory clearly implies that exclusive reliance on an army of retainers is not sufficient, but is more likely to lead to disaster. Popular support is necessary, to kings as well as to magnates.

Against this background we must see the "constitutional" conflicts we have considered above. Given his view of the political game as a question of winning support, Snorri evidently regards it as very important for a king to treat the people in the right way and finds it natural that they react against hard exactions, such as Haraldr hárfagri confiscating their *óðal*, Sveinn and Álfífa's taxes and strict laws, and Magnús góði's harsh measures before his "conversion." To Snorri the people are both strong enough and sufficiently organized to react against royal oppression. But this does not mean that he regards such conflicts as the main theme in his history. They are rather one of several kinds of conflict, and, to judge from their relative infrequency, hardly the most important.

The Social Order

The difference between Snorri's idea of society and that of the contemporary Norwegian monarchy becomes evident through a comparison with sources like *A Speech Against the Bishops* (c. 1200) and *The King's Mirror* (c. 1255). *A Speech Against the Bishops* is the product of the violent conflict between King Sverrir (1177–1202) and the Church toward the end of his reign. Its author sets out to prove from "the holy writs," that is, ecclesiastical authorities contained in Gratian's *Decretum,* that the king should have a leading function within the Church. Although this source deals explicitly only with the Church, it contains an overall view of society which is relevant in other contexts as well.

This view is most directly set forth in the image of the human body, which represents the Church, that is, the Carolingian ecclesia, comprising both ecclesiastical and secular society (Holtsmark, 1931: 1, line 11–2, line 7; see also Gunnes, 1971: 50 ff., 73 ff.): Christ and his holy Church are one body, and the author then goes on to describe how the various limbs and organs, which represent clerical and secular ranks and offices, take care of different functions. The difference between the clergy and the laity is fairly clear, the former representing the senses and the organs of digestion and serving to give the body spiritual nourishment and guidance, whereas the latter represents the skeleton and the muscles and should defend the body. A strict hierarchy prevails within this part of the body. The king is the chest and the heart and consequently the real governor. The rest of the aristocracy is ranked according to its proximity to the king. Earls and "great princes" (stórhǫfðingiar) are the shoulders and the back, the *lendir menn* are the upper arms, *hirðmenn,* knights, and other military men are the forearms and hands, and finally, the people are the legs and feet.

Such representations of society as the human body were very popular at the time, and many others are preserved in European sources (Gunnes, 1971: 73 ff., 367 ff.; Struve, 1978: 123 ff.). However, it is not just a question of an illustration or representation, such as may occur in our time as well, but of the idea that society is a phenomenon of the same kind as the human body, that is, there is no fundamental distinction between nature and society. The image of the human body is thus an expression of a basic idea in many traditional societies of an order that manifests itself in the whole known world, that of nature as well as that of men, and to which men have to adapt themselves. Admittedly, they do not always do so, and a given society may even over a longer period depart from this order.[45] But this is fundamentally a moral problem. The point of "constitutional" thought, as expressed for instance in the mirrors of princes of the period, is to make the various individuals and groups acknowledge their place within this order and act accordingly. If not, the body of society is ill, as is demonstrated by the author of *A Speech Against the Bishops,* who explains this illness by the errors of the clergy (Holtsmark, 1931: 2, lines 8–3; line 18; see also Gunnes, 1971: 83 ff.).

The medieval constitutional thought derived from the clerical tradition differs from the modern one in its idea of the constitution as belonging to an eternal order, ultimately sanctioned by God, to which men must conform. Constitutional struggles are therefore not the expression of conflicting class or group interests or ideas, based on empirical observations, as to what sort of government is most suitable to society as a whole. They are interpreted in moral terms, as a question of conforming to God's will concerning social or political arrangements. However, this by no means prevents conflicting opinions or interests regarding constitutional arrangements.

In *The King's Mirror,* this view of constitutional arrangements is directly used to attack the old social order—the one that is largely represented by Snorri. Using an image of famine, in which the author compares a country ridden by civil war with a farm affected by famine, he contrasts the right social order, with a strong monarchy and public justice, with the chaos, dissolution, and feuds prevailing when the kingdom is divided between several petty kings. Then rivalry arises between the kings, they try to attract adherents from one anothers' territory, including criminals, who then escape their just punishment. This in turn leads to general disregard for law and order, people demand compensation or take revenge for kinsman who are killed for their crimes. This leads to feuds, which ultimately lead to full civil war (*Kgs.*: 51, line 1–55, line 30).

What the author does here, is to present the traditional social order, according to which killing and violence are matters between the parties concerned and feud is a legal way of seeking compensation, as a deviation from the right, divinely instituted order (Bagge, 1987*a*: 43 ff.; 1987*b*: 81 f., and "Science and Political Thought"). We thus have a clear example of a "constitutional" debate, expressed in the terms of an eternal order. This implies a concept of society which is in one sense closer to modern ideas in emphasizing that society is arranged in a particular way and at least to some extent regarding this arrangement as the subject of conflicts. Nevertheless, the "constitutional" thought of these authors is fundamentally different from the modern one. The right social order is not established empirically, it is the eternal order of things. Admittedly, it may be supported by empirical arguments, as is done in *The King's Mirror*, but this is less necessary than in modern constitutional thought.

This idea of society is to be found more implicitly in historical works such as "the Norwegian synoptics" and *Fagrskinna*. A characteristic example is Theodoricus Monachus's reasons for ending his work at the death of King Sigurðr jórsalafari (1130): he does not want to tell of the crimes, murders, violations of women and sacred places, and so forth that took place in the subsequent period.[46] To Theodoricus, armed conflicts are not part of the social order; they are its direct antithesis and against the will of God, who wants *pax* to prevail on earth and in society. The use of arms is only permitted for a good and just cause. Although this statement by Theodoricus seems to suggest a neutral attitude to the civil wars,[47] his basic idea could also be used for political purposes. As a matter of fact, it became prominent exactly when the civil wars were at their most fierce. First Erlingr skakki and his faction and then Sverrir maintained that they were fighting for God or the just cause and that their adversaries were evil men who opposed the right order of society. This ideology led to Erlingr skakki's condemnation of his enemies, which shocked Snorri so much.

This moralistic attitude to internal conflicts is more prominent in the Norwegian tradition than in the Icelandic one. Theodoricus and the other historians belonging to the milieu around the archiepiscopal see of Nidaros consistently classify the kings as good or evil according to the ecclesiastical schema of the *rex iustus/iniquus* and carefully expose the moral relevance of their acts. The author of *Fagrskinna*, who is in one sense equally "secular" as Snorri in avoiding nearly all references to religious matters and supernatural phenomena, is nevertheless closer to this tradition. Though both Snorri and many other Old Norse historians have a nationalistic bias, *Fagrskinna* goes further in this direction, in celebrating Norwegian deeds at the cost of the country's enemies and in derogating the Danes (Indrebø, 1917: 260; Jakobsen, 1970: 101 f.), and above all in its selection of materials. *Fagrskinna* is about one-fourth of *Heimskringla*'s length and contains almost as much material on foreign policy, whereas inner Norwegian conflicts are treated more briefly (see Indrebø, 1917: 257 ff.). Very few feuds are mentioned. The conflicts that are mentioned are often of a constitutional or ideological character. Though Snorri often pays exceptional attention to such conflicts whereas the author of *Fagrskinna* refers to them rather briefly, there are indications that the latter also takes a different attitude.

Like the other sagas, *Fagrskinna* classifies the kings as good or evil, but is usually more reluctant in blaming them (Indrebø, 1917: 198 f., 223 ff., 226 f., 275 ff.). In the saga of St. Óláfr, the conflict between Óláfr and the magnates, which is also there in the earlier sagas, is made the main theme. In *Fagrskinna* the magnates take the initiative to get Cnut's support against Óláfr, whereas their rebellion is the result of Cnut's gifts in the earlier sagas. Both in the saga of St. Óláfr and in that of Haraldr harðráði, the author of *Fagrskinna* refers to the great power of the magnates and their unwillingness to submit to the king as a reason for conflict. In the case of St. Óláfr, their rebellion is aimed at his strict justice. In the reign of Haraldr harðráði, his conflict with Einarr þambaskelfir, which is presented as a feud in *Heimskringla,* is a rebellion against the king in *Fagrskinna.*[48] Thus, the author of *Fagrskinna* focuses on Norwegian national unity versus other countries and on the kings as representing this unity.

This attitude in *Fagrskinna* is largely the result of the author's connection with the Norwegian royal court (Indrebø, 1917: 275 ff.). He may be influenced by Sverrir's struggle with the majority of the Norwegian aristocracy, but probably above all by the attempts of the contemporary monarchy to suppress feuds and strengthen public justice. Still, it would be an exaggeration to see this "constitutional" struggle as the dominant theme of *Fagrskinna.* His portrait's of kings are by no means always favorable, nor does he consistently side with the king in internal conflicts.[49]

Unlike modern historiography committed to particular constitutional or political ideas, the development of this social order and its conflict with other ways of organizing society are not traced through history. It is an absolute norm, from which deviations are presented in moral terms. Although a certain pro-monarchical tendency can be detected in *Fagrskinna,* this ideology does not necessarily force its author always to side with the king. The fact that individual kings may occasionally lapse from their moral responsibility does not affect divinely instituted monarchy. Nor are historical arguments necessarily very effective from a propagandistic point of view.

In contrast to works like *A Speech Against the Bishops, The King's Mirror,* and contemporary European mirrors of princes and political treatises, the social order is rarely mentioned explicitly in *Heimskringla* and nothing is said about its divine origin. This evidently does not mean that there was no such order, but rather that it was taken for granted. The apparently war- and faction-ridden society was held together, not only by a common nationalistic sentiment directed at outside attacks or by occasional explicit or implicit rules of "fair play," but by a social order that was generally accepted and not subject to conflict. There was a social hierarchy, not very strictly defined and with some mobility upward and downward, but with generally accepted rules as to who should lead and who should obey and who were allowed to fight for supreme power in society. However, this model of society gives no room for a bureaucracy, whereas the royalist model analyzed above is easily compatible with it and may even be said to include the idea of such an organization. And while the king in *Heimskringla* is superior in rank to the magnates, his actual power is vaguely defined and to a large extent depends on his own personality. The leaders have the right to rule by virtue of their descent, wealth, and personal qualities but they are also supposed to rule in the interest of their inferiors. As they depend on the latter for support, they are easily deposed if they do not. Thus the conflicts take place within a fairly stable, harmonious, and "democratic" society. The basic features of the social order are not contested, and victory or defeat in the conflicts between the rulers does not lead to great changes. The really important aspects of the social order are therefore left implicit in Snorri's narrative.

Finally and most important: the basic idea of society in *Heimskringla* corresponds fairly well to the picture in *The King's Mirror* of a society afflicted by famine. Feuds and revenge are taken for granted, and a man is largely valued according to his ability in conducting such conflicts. Snorri's view of society is thus in clear contrast to the royalist one. His censure of Erlingr skakki's condemnation of his adversaries may even appear like its direct refutation. Nevertheless, Snorri also shows traces of the opposite view, notably the picture of St. Ólafr as the *rex iustus* and the explicit explanation of his fall as the result of his strict justice.

It is not quite easy to grasp the relationship between these two views of society in Snorri. It is hardly a question of explicit royalist ideology versus traditional ideas of society as an implicit or unconscious framework. The view of society which I have traced in this chapter may be implicit in the sense that Snorri does not regard it as an ideology as opposed to other ideologies, but hardly in the sense that he is unable to draw explicit consequences from it. Quite the contrary, Snorri uses it systematically to analyze human behavior and manages to create a largely consistent picture of politics and society in older Norwegian history. His explicit references to the *rex iustus*-ideology and the hierarchically organized society propagated by the contemporary Norwegian monarchy are rather to be explained as respect for King Óláfr's reputation as a saint or as concessions to Snorri's Norwegian public. Evidently, Snorri has not been fully aware of the contrast between the two ideologies. This may seem strange to us, but is more understandable in a society and political milieu in which one was not accustomed to thinking in different political ideologies. However, he may have been well aware of particular consequences of the royalist ideology which he found unacceptable, such as Erlingr skakki's attempt to use religion to crush his adversaries or arrogant and authoritarian behavior from the kings, which would inevitably provoke rebellion, and may partly have intended his work as a warning against this and more generally as an education for a politician in the fairly "democratic" and loosely organized society with which he was familiar.

4

Morality and Human Character

Introduction

In the present chapter I shall attempt to draw the conclusions from Snorri's treatment of conflicts for his ideas of morality and human character, thereby directly addressing the question of "political man" mentioned in the introduction. I shall treat Snorri's ideal king and aristocrat and the norms they are supposed to adhere to, compared to those of the contemporary European aristocracy. Finally, I shall deal with Snorri's concept of human character. This analysis will, I hope, contribute to the discussion between the adherents of Elias's evolutionary perspective of political man and those who follow Bailey in assuming a fairly universal political game between rational actors.

The Ideal Man

The qualities Snorri expects from his kings and magnates are summarized in his numerous characterizations of various great men. These characterizations correspond to the two types of ancient rhetoric, which were still fairly widespread in the middle ages, the *notatio,* a general characterization that usually serves as the introduction of the person in question, and the *elogium* or *epilogus,* which comes after his death and lays particular emphasis on the deeds he has performed (Kirn, 1955: 41 ff.). The most detailed characterizations, however, are to be found in the competition between the kings Sigurðr and Eysteinn (the *mannjafnaðr-* comparison of two men, *Msyn.* chap. 21), which seems a fitting starting point for an analysis of Snorri's ideas of royal virtues.[1] The two kings and their men drink together while taking *veitslur* at Opplandene. The beer is not good and the men are quiet. Then Eysteinn suggests a game to cheer up the party: as is often done in drinking parties, the men would compare themselves to others. Eysteinn challenges his brother, and the kings compare their skills and deeds. They start with their athletic skills, go on to their bodily size, strength, and beauty, then to their eloquence and skill in handling legal and other cases, until the competition reaches its climax in the comparison of their deeds: Sigurðr's expedition to Palestine against Eysteinn's building and peaceful activities at home.

The kings' appearances are often described in great detail. To some extent the descriptions contain characteristic features that have a realistic ring and may ultimately be derived from observation, as when Haraldr harðráði is said to have had one eyebrow that was higher than the other (*HHarð.* chap. 99: 220) or Erlingr skakki (crooked-neck) is said to have had a long and narrow face, hair that grew grey early, and of course a crooked neck, which earned him his sobriquet (ME chap. 37). St. Óláfr's medium height, blond hair, and ruddy complexion also give an impression of authenticity. But the characterizations must primarily be understood against an ideological background, as expressions of an ideal of masculine beauty which ought to be found in a king or a great magnate.[2]

Size is very important. "A man who is to be the leader of other men should be tall . . . so that he is easily seen and recognized when many men are together," says King Sigurðr in the *mannjafnaðr*. If a king is not tall, this is often compensated for by other qualities, as in St. Óláfr, who is unusually broad and strong, or Eysteinn, who is very handsome and considers this equally important as his brother's size and strength. The crippled King Ingi, who is small and whose body is the very opposite of the ideal of bodily strength and beauty that becomes a king, has an exceptionally beautiful face (*Ingi* chap. 21). Beauty is only vaguely defined. There is evidently some connection between beauty and strength and masculinity, but they are not synonymous. King Sigurðr jórsalafari was masculine, but not beautiful. As might be expected, beauty has to do with harmonious proportions. King Haraldr hárðráði's hands and feet were large—that is, probably too large to be really handsome—but well-shaped (*HHárf.* chap. 99: 220). Sigurðr Haraldsson, nicknamed munnr (mouth), was handsome in other respects, but had an ugly mouth (*Ingi* chap. 21).[3] Apart from these rather vague hints, the criteria of beauty that are most frequently mentioned are beautiful eyes and hair. St. Óláfr had very beautiful eyes, which were so sharp that people became frightened when they looked him in the eyes and he was angry (OH chap. 3). The earls of Lade were exceptionally beautiful. The young Earl Hákon, who is taken captive by St. Óláfr, is the most beautiful man people have ever seen. He wears his hair long, it is fine as silk, and he has a golden ribbon around his head. The king directly comments on his unusual beauty (chap. 30). The beauty of long, golden hair is frequently mentioned and seems to be the feature that is most admired by Snorri and his readers.[4] Beautiful hair is normally fair and most kings belonging to the Norwegian dynasty are also fair.

Though Snorri probably finds some rough correspondence between outer and inner qualities, this is not the main reason for his great interest in the kings' looks. Outward appearances are not primarily symbols of inner qualities; they are important qualities in themselves. When King Sigurðr insists that a king should be taller than other men and King Eysteinn that he should be more beautiful, it is not just empty phrases in a drinking party, it is a succinct expression of the idea of charismatic kingship. The same idea is expressed when Hákon góði returns to Norway and people say to one another that he must be King Haraldr hárfagri who has become young once more (HG chap. 1). Similarly, people are impressed by Óláfr Tryggvason's strength and athletic ability (OT chap. 85; see also 77, 82–83) and by St. Óláfr's worthy and kingly appearances and sharp and strong eyes. The king is above others not because he has a higher office but because he is literally a better man. This must be expressed in appearances, inner qualities, and above all ability to perform great deeds. Hereditary kingship is evidently not always able to produce such kings, but there is a clear connection between noble or royal blood and the corresponding qualities. There are always some good and noble qualities in a king; his noble blood guarantees that. Snorri has therefore always something positive to say about his kings, though in some cases he has to confine himself to the most conventional phrases.[5]

From the physical appearances Snorri normally goes on to athletic ability. The *mannjafnaðr* devotes a large section to this. Sigurðr emphasizes his strength and Eysteinn his suppleness, and they compare their skill in swimming, skiing, skating, and shooting. As in the characterization of St. Óláfr, athletic abilities often receive attention in the characterizations of kings, especially those that are most important in war. The description of Óláfr Tryggvason's abilities is unusually detailed, as he, together with Hákon góði, was the greatest athlete in Norwegian history (OH chap. 106). Strangely enough, there is no comparison of the two kings as warriors, nor are such abilities very prominent in the other characterizations. The explanation is probably that they were included in the athletic abilities, which largely had a military purpose. Toward the end of the discussion, Sigurðr's battles against the Saracens during his journey to the Holy Land are compared to Eysteinn's peaceful activities at home. Generally, military exploits are prominent in enumerations of kings' or great men's achievements. Next, the two kings turn to a long comparison of their legal knowledge, their eloquence, and their way of treating people who bring their cases before them. There are also numerous other references to the kings' ability in this field. Eloquence, which is of course important in a legal context, is important in other contexts as well and frequently mentioned in the characterizations. Its importance is further enhanced by Snorri's examples of kings or pretenders who are able to gain adherents through their speeches and by his numerous speeches and quotations of famous words (see above; also, Lie, 1937: 83 ff., 100 ff.). The latter was evidently highly admired in Snorri's society, and numerous such words and sentences are quoted by Snorri and other saga writers.

Another important virtue, with which kings and rulers are normally credited, is intelligence or wisdom.[6] Virtues like legal knowledge and the ability to speak convincingly are often regarded as its practical application. Another application is the ability to find a solution in difficult situations, which is explicitly mentioned as an example of King Haraldr harðráði's great intelligence (*HHarð.* chaps. 36, 99–100). In general, intelligence is a practical quality, which enables a man to solve the political or military problems he is facing.[7]

A quality that is not directly mentioned in the *mannjafnaðr* is generosity. In spite of this, there can be no doubt of its importance, which is evident from frequent references in the characterizations, and the political consequences, not least of which is its absence. Snorri's explicit denial that Earl Hákon and St. Ólafr were deposed because of lack of generosity, seems to indicate that he regards this as particularly shameful.[8] A related quality, pomp and magnificence, seems to be implicit in much of the *mannjafnaðr*: who is most prominent, most conspicuous, has most royal dignity, and so forth? Eysteinn directly draws attention to his beautiful clothes, in addition to his good looks.

The story of King Sigurðr's *jórsalaferð* is a particularly good example of the importance of wealth and magnificence. When arriving in Constantinople, the king waits half a month for sidewind before sailing into the city, so that his sails, adorned with velvet, will appear at their best.[9] Snorri occasionally mentions valuable objects, particularly arms, and kings' or other great men's magnificence and lavish spending,[10] but he rarely gives elaborate descriptions of dress, buildings, ceremonies, and so forth. Mostly, such descriptions occur when they are necessary to make the action intelligible.[11] The contrast between Snorri's reticence here and his often vivid descriptions of men and their actions is striking. The only really detailed description of this kind is the one of St. Ólafr's reception by his mother and stepfather when he comes to claim the

throne. Here Snorri describes the decoration of the houses, his stepfather Sigurðr sýr's clothes, the number of housecarls and domestic
servants, the banquet in Óláfr's honor and the food served him and his
men during their sojourn there.[12] Though this scene shows the importance Snorri attaches to outward splendor, its main purpose is to create
the right atmosphere around the young pretender's meeting with his stepfather and the decisive discussion whether or not to support his claim.
This is achieved both through the description itself and through the
technique of retardation.

Another related quality, popularity with people and the ability to
attract friends, plays some part in the discussion on legal questions:
Sigurðr accuses his brother of promising too easily without keeping his
promises very well. Eysteinn replies that he wants to satisfy people as far
as possible, whereas Sigurðr is harsh and stern and promises evil to
everyone so that no one complains if he does not keep his promises.
Such qualities play considerable importance in the characterizations and
often serve to distinguish between good and bad kings.

Finally, the two kings compare their deeds. The importance of this is
evident from Eysteinn's words when Sigurðr brings forward his journey
to the Holy Land: "Now you come to the point. I would not have started
this controversy if I did not have an answer to that" ("nú greiptu á
kýlinu; eigi mynda ek þessa roeðu vekja, ef ek kynna hér engu svara,"
Msyn. chap. 21: 293; Holl.: 703 f.). This emphasis on deeds as opposed
to "inner" qualities is in perfect accordance with Snorri's description of
the political game, according to which virtues serve as means to success
and, as we shall see, with his view of human character. A man is above
all valued through his deeds, virtues being of no avail if they are not
shown in the corresponding deeds, or rather: they do not exist except as
summaries of deeds.

Snorri's picture of the ideal king in the *mannjafnaðr* and the various
characterizations can be described as secular-heroic. There are religious
elements in his descriptions of the missionary kings, notably St. Óláfr,
and King Eysteinn boasts about the churches he has built in the
mannjafnaðr, but apart from that, neither piety nor other aspects of the
rex iustus-ideal play a prominent part, in clear contrast to the descriptions of the kings in the clerical chronicles. Snorri's emphasis on the
kings' legal abilities shows some connection with the aspects of this ideal
that were emphasized by the contemporary monarchy. But, as might be
expected from his treatment of the king's functions, there is no great
similarity to the ideal king of *The King's Mirror* or similar sources.[13]

Rather, in its broad outlines, Snorri's ideal corresponds to that of the
European aristocratic chronicles. Snorri's ideal king or chieftain is the
aristocratic hero, who is tall, strong, handsome, brave, magnificent, and

generous. There are, however, some differences. There is little trace of the courteous ideal that became prominent in feudal Europe from the twelfth century, emphasizing polite manners, courteous behavior toward women, and romantic love.[14] As for individual virtues, the most striking difference is that Snorri is less concerned with pomp, ceremony, and lavishness, which are often extremely important in European aristocratic literature. This corresponds to the fact that Snorri's heroes are somewhat more concerned with ordinary, practical tasks than their European counterparts. Thus, besides all his warlike virtues, St. Óláfr was "skilled and had a sure eye for all kinds of handicraft work, whether he made the things himself or others did."[15] His stepfather, Sigurðr sýr, whose peaceful habits and agricultural interests form a prosaic contrast to the brilliant young warrior, is nevertheless depicted as a man of great wisdom, who proved essential in gaining Óláfr the necessary support to be acclaimed as king and win the battle of Nesjar. Similarly, it is perfectly normal for a magnate in *Heimskringla* to take part in trading expeditions, as for instance Þórir hundr during his expedition to Bjarmaland, in which Óláfr's *hirðmaðr* Karli and his brother Gunnsteinn participated, the former as his master's partner.[16] Thus, as we should expect from Snorri's description of society, the norms concerning aristocratic behavior differ less from those of ordinary people than the corresponding ones in feudal Europe. Finally, Snorri lays greater emphasis on eloquence, intelligence, and political maneuvering than his European contemporaries. This emphasis may even to some extent explain his way of treating other qualities, such as generosity and magnificence: Snorri clearly understands the importance of pomp and lavishness for gaining adherents and political influence, but he does not take the same pleasure in describing such things as do his European contemporaries. The same applies to the other aristocratic virtues: they are means to achieve political success, not an end in themselves.

One Ideal or Many?

Having analyzed Snorri's description of the ideal king as it is found in the *mannjafnaðr* and other places, I shall now discuss it within a wider context. Two questions then present themselves: (1) how far does this ideal differ from his ideal of man in general? and (2) how is Snorri's ideal of man and king related to his idea of the game of politics?

Concerning the first question, the qualities required in a king in the *mannjafnaðr* and other characterizations do not give the impression that the king's duties differ radically from those of other great men or that there are virtues that are specifically royal. Rather, Snorri describes a heroic-charismatic ideal of a king, according to which he should excel all others in bodily beauty, bravery, generosity, wisdom, eloquence, and so forth. As the theme of *Heimskringla* is the game of politics, and virtues and vices are closely related to this, we could hardly expect such a distinction. All the characters Snorri describes are politicians, and though some are more prominent than others, basically the same qualities are needed to succeed in the game. The distinction between kings and ordinary men is rather expressed quantitatively.

Very few of the large number of persons mentioned in *Heimskringla* are characterized. A somewhat larger number are presented through their genealogies. As might be expected, there is a connection between characterization and social status. Kings are normally characterized, often in some detail. So are usually the greatest magnates, whereas men of lower status are not, though they may play an important part in the saga.[17] Characterizations of women are short and extremely stereotyped. Women whom the kings fall in love with or marry are usually described as beautiful but nothing more is said about their appearances.[18] We are thus left entirely in the dark concerning Snorri's ideal of feminine beauty, whereas his descriptions of men's appearances are often detailed. Occasionally, Snorri makes some references to inner qualities of women, wisdom, pride, and so forth.[19] But even here, it is difficult to detect a clear picture of the ideal woman which may be compared to the one of the ideal man which I have already discussed. The reason for treating women in this way is most probably their indirect or secondary role in the political game.

There also seems to be a general correspondence between a person's standing and importance and the length of his characterization. Characterizations of men who are not kings are often confined to qualities that are relevant in the particular context in which the person appears. The characterization of Hárekr at Tjøtta as a prudent man who is able to further his interests comes in connection with the description of how he gathers wealth by buying land from small farmers (OH chap. 104). Einarr þambarskelfir is described as a man who knows the laws and is able to speak at the popular assemblies in the introduction to his conflict with King Haraldr at a particular assembly (*HHarð.* chap. 43).

Very few magnates receive characterizations that are as complete and detailed as those of the kings. Of Norwegian magnates this applies only to Earl Hákon, Einarr þambarskelfir, Erlingr Skjálgsson, and Erlingr skakki. Of the four, the first and last were the real rulers of the country for a considerable period, whereas the two others ruled important parts of it and were prominent allies or rivals to more than one king. Then Snorri gives exceptionally detailed characterizations of two Icelanders who served under Haraldr harðráði, namely Halldórr Snorrason and

Úlfr Óspaksson (*HHarð*. chaps. 36–37), above all of the former. The reason for this is probably that Halldórr was one of Snorri's ancestors and even one of his sources (cf. *HHarð*. chap. 9). The latter played a prominent part as Haraldr's *stallari* (constable) and became the ancestor of Archbishop Eysteinn. The difference between kings and other men is particularly striking concerning the *elogium*. Only two of the above-mentioned magnates receive this, Earl Hákon and Erlingr Skjálgsson. Erlingr skakki might possibly deserve it, but he was still living at the end of *Heimskringla*.

The characterizations of kings may also be of quite varying length. This may have something to do with the distance between their times and Snorri's and thus with the amount of information at his disposal, but above all with their importance. Óláfr Tryggvason, St. Óláfr, and Haraldr harðráði are described in great detail, whereas for instance Óláfr kyrri, Magnús blindi, Haraldr gilli, and Hákon herðibreiðr are dismissed in a few sentences. While the great kings receive both *notatio* and *elogium*,[20] those of minor importance receive only one characterization, normally *notatio*. But there is no exact correspondence between a king's importance and the length of his characterization. Magnús góði, who is one of the kings that most conforms to Snorri's picture of the ideal king and is credited with some of the greatest external successes in *Heimskringla,* receives no *notatio* and only a short, though very favorable *elogium* after his death (*HHarð*. chap. 30). By contrast, the two Magnússons, Sigurðr and Eysteinn, who are certainly great kings, but whose reigns are not among the most important, are described in great detail; actually, their saga is largely composed around their contrasting characters. The three sons of Haraldr gilli, who are all fairly insignificant as persons, are also described in some detail, though without an *elogium,* apparently because their characters serve to explain the result of the war between them (*Ingi* chaps. 21–22). The characterizations thus show a fairly clear consciousness of social status, which is also evident in Snorri's description of society. This status distinction corresponds very well with the heroic-charismatic ideal of the king: the king is not qualitatively different from other great chieftains, but he should represent the heroic ideal more completely than they.

Morality and the Political Game

As for my second question, the analysis of the game of politics in chapter 2 gave a fairly clear picture of the kind of person who was most likely to survive in this game, namely the astute, careful, and rather cynical politician who is able to use both force and diplomacy. How far can this picture be generalized? Does Snorri's description of morality and human character confirm it, or are there also other ideals of human behavior in *Heimskringla?* Lie (1937: 94 ff.), as an example of Snorri's general inclination toward antithesis, points to his contrast between the egotist and the idealist, illustrated for instance by the contrast between Hroerekr and Hringr, Haraldr harðráði and his brother St. Óláfr, and Kálfr Árnason and his brother Finnr. The contrast is too sharply drawn. Idealists in the real sense are rare in Snorri; most men fight for their own interests, even saints like King Óláfr. At least apparently, however, there is a contrast between politicians such as Einarr þambarskelfir and Kálfr Árnason, who consistently maneuver for gain, and men who remain faithful to their masters whatever happens or who distinguish themselves through bravery and heroic qualities. I shall refer to them as respectively politicians and heroes.

The general difference between heroes and politicians can be illustrated through the contrasts between Erlingr Skjálgsson and Einarr þambarskelfir and between Grégóríús Dagsson and Erlingr skakki. The former embody all the traditional and heroic virtuse, whereas the latter are cold, calculating politicians. An even clearer contrast is the one between Bjǫrn stallari and Kálfr Árnason. Both have been promoted by King Óláfr but desert their master after his exile. But Bjǫrn does this in a momentary weakness, repents his sin, and joins King Óláfr in Russia and is killed in the battle of Stiklestad (OH chaps. 185–186, 228: 493). Kálfr, however, becomes one of the leaders of the army that defeats King Óláfr, and there are even rumors that he dealt him one of his wounds. When he eventually returns to the cause of his former master and brings his son to the throne, it is clearly to serve his own interests.

Among kings, perhaps the two Óláfrs could be used to illustrate the difference. Óláfr Tryggvason is above all the great athlete and warrior hero (OT chap. 85), whereas St. Óláfr is the wise governor and the good politician. Snorri does not mention the former's eloquence and intelligence, but he lays great emphasis on the latter's. The saga of Óláfr Tryggvason is also one of the most romantic ones of *Heimskringla,* in which the protagonists act more out of regard for chivalry and splendor than as politicians maneuvering for gain. Rather than contrasting St. Óláfr and Haraldr harðráði, who are after all said to be essentially similar despite apparent differences, one should point to the contrast between Haraldr, the politician, and Óláfr Tryggvason, the chivalrous hero; St. Óláfr is in an intermediate position, having something in common with both, although he is closer to his half-brother than to his predecessor. Haraldr harðráði is described as an exceptionally intelligent man, who is always able to find a solution in a difficult situation (*HHarð* chaps. 36, 99–100). This corresponds very well to his acts. Another quality, which is not mentioned explicitly in the characterization, but which repeatedly occurs in individual episodes, is his ability to suppress anger and conceal his feelings. He gives way to his young nephew Magnús, who is outraged when he finds Haraldr's ship at his place in the harbor (see above and n. 13), and he is completely calm when the old and captive Finnr Árnason directs the most extreme insults against him (*HHarð.* chap. 66). This quality also gives him an unusual talent for treachery, which is demonstrated in several episodes.

How great is the actual difference between heroes and politicians? The most serious problem is the contrast between Bjǫrn stallari (the constable) and Kálfr Árnason. On the one hand, Snorri seems to suppose that most men act according to their own interests and easily change sides if it can serve this purpose. On the other hand, Bjǫrn is depicted as a repentant sinner and together with some other characters serves as an example of loyalty to one's lord and master.[21] It would be too easy to describe this difference as the contrast between ideal and reality or to assume that Bjǫrn is an example of the right way of behaving, whereas Kálfr is not. Snorri's numerous examples of changing loyalties to serve one's own interests in the political game make this suggestion unlikely. In this particular case, though Bjǫrn and Kálfr are different characters, the former's repentance is not quite independent of political calculation, as it conveniently takes place when he has received the news that Óláfr's rival, Earl Hákon, is dead and the country is without a ruler. Further, we can point to the discussion between the Árnasons after the conflict over Steinn Skaptason of whether or not to accept King Óláfr's peace proposal (OH chap. 138; *Hkr.* vol. 2: 319 f.; see Lie, 1937: 96, 98). Kálfr is here the most negative, refusing to swear an oath to the king and only declaring himself willing to serve him as long as it serves his own interests. Finnr may perhaps be considered an idealist, though he later shows that his loyalty to his king and master is not unconditional, but generally, the discussion is not in terms of interest versus loyalty or idealism. Þorbergr finds his interests best served by remaining on Óláfr's side, whereas Árni wants to follow Þorbergr.

There is no reason to suppose that Snorri is always consistent. Though friendship in his opinion is primarily a political relationship, it is not devoid of the emotional aspects with which we associate it. The main explanation to this difference, however, must be sought in different kinds of relationships between men. One does not have general duties to other men, whether loyalty to the king or the duty to be a good man or citizen and treat other men decently. Duties, loyalty, and so forth depend on some kind of special relationship, kinship or its equivalent, membership of the *hirð* or household of a master. It is difficult to trace exactly Snorri's view of the kind of obligations one enters by becoming a *hirðmaðr* or *lendr maðr,* but there is clearly some distance between

Snorri's attitude and the sort of total submission demanded by contemporary royalist ideology, as expressed in sources like *The King's Mirror* (Bagge, 1987*b*: 26 ff.). Basically, to become another man's "man" is to enter a contract, with mutual rights and duties and with the possibility of ending the relationship if it does not turn out to be satisfactory. The exact obligations may vary. An oath of submission or loyalty creates very strong obligations, but Snorri seems to regard this as unusual, even between the king and his men. The general rule determining a man's loyalty to his master or superior is best illustrated by the parable in the New Testament concluding that the one who has had the larger debt annulled will also love his benefactor most (Luke, 7: 41–43). It is the same logic as in the exchange of gifts. A gift presupposes a return of equal value. If a man cannot return the gift with material values, he owes service to the giver (Hamre, 1960: 653 f.; Bagge, 1986: 154 f.). Consequently, a man of low status or a man who has been promoted by a benefactor is bound to serve him loyally, whereas the one who is his equal is not.[22] From this point of view Kálfr Árnason is possibly morally reprehensible, as he had been promoted by Óláfr, whereas Erlingr Skjárgsson, who also joined King Cnut against him, is not, and appears as the perfect example of a hero.

A Good King Is a Successful King

As for Kings, the *mannjafnaðr* presents two ideals, which are to be found throughout *Heimskringla*. The first is the mild lover of peace, who is popular with the people and excels in the administration of justice and other peaceful activities and is moderate in his demands on the people. The second is the warrior, strong-willed and aggressive. The contrast is particularly striking in the case of the peaceful Óláfr kyrri and his warlike father and son, Haraldr harðráði and Magnús berfoetr. Snorri apparently shows no consistent preference for either type. On the one hand, Óláfr kyrri, in spite of his good looks and popularity, is a rather dull and insignificant person. On the other hand, Snorri explicitly mentions the heavy burdens Magnús berfoetr laid on the people because of his wars (MB chap. 26) and he is no uncritical admirer of Haraldr harðráði. Probably his ideal king should be a mixture of both types. Hákon góði and Magnús góði, after his "conversion," come very near to fulfilling this ideal. Both are extremely popular and manage to keep internal peace, while at the same time being great warriors and fighting external enemies. Haraldr harðráði is also a great king, though too much on the harder side. To some extent, this even applies to the two main heroes of Norwegian history, the Óláfrs.

Whereas the good kings more or less conform to the ideals described in the *mannjafnaðr,* the bad ones depart from it in one way or another. Eiríkr blóðøx and his sons are strong, beautiful, and brave but ruthless and cruel. The reign of the Eiríkssons is one of the worst periods described in *Heimskringla* because of the kings' greed and lack of respect for the laws. Among the kings of the later period Magnús blindi, Sigurðr munnr, and Eysteinn Haraldsson belong to the same category. They are characterized as cruel, ruthless, and unfriendly. Other kings are weak and insignificant, such as Haraldr gilli, who is easily led by his friends. He is described as a slightly ridiculous person, with his bad mastery of the Norwegian language and his foreign habits. Before his accession to the throne, he receives little respect at the court, and on one occasion he is nearly hanged by his adversaries in a quarrel (*Msyn.* chap. 29). A man against whom his subordinates dare to do such things is evidently no great king. Nevertheless, Haraldr's character enables him to gain more friends than Magnús and he is ultimately successful. Another king who is depicted as rather weak is Ingi Haraldsson, who is crippled and thus prevented from being an actual leader in war, but who is a mild and friendly man, who easily attaches friends to him. Though Ingi is not a great king, Snorri's picture of him is fairly sympathetic. He even gains heroic dimensions toward the end of his life, when he dies in battle, fighting to revenge his friend Grégóríús. Snorri thus seems to be more indulgent toward weak kings than toward those who are ruthless and aggressive.

The reason for this preference, however, is not Christian ideas of clemency as a virtue for the prince, but political realism. Snorri's real criterion for a good or bad king is not morality but success. A good king is a successful king, a bad king is a failure. The Eiríkssons are clearly and Earl Hákon to some extent depicted as bad rulers. But it does not follow from this that Snorri regards their means to achieve power as evil. In the case of Earl Hákon, Snorri rather seems to admire his cunning than to condemn his treachery. His double-dealing and his feigned worry on behalf of both King Haraldr and Gull-Haraldr is described with considerable humor. Moreover, in his final characterization Snorri describes Hákon as a great man and a magnificent chieftain, whose fall was not primarily caused by his own shortcomings, but by ill luck and unforeseen circumstances (chap. 50). And though Hákon to some extent was to blame, the reason for this was not his treachery and political cynicism but his behavior toward the wives and daughters of the farmers of Trøndelag, which led them to rebel against him (chaps. 45, 48).

Moreover, there is little difference between Snorri's heroes and villains regarding their means to achieve power. The Eiríkssons' treachery against Earl Sigurðr is hardly more reprehensible than Haraldr harðráði's against Einarr þambarskelfir or even the acts of the Óláfrs against some of their adversaries. Óláfr Tryggvason lures the leader of the people of Trøndelag, Járnskeggi, away from his men under the pretext of wanting to see the *hof* and then kills him, admittedly for the noble purpose of introducing Christianity (OT chap. 69). St. Óláfr kills the leader of his adversaries in Ránríkí (Bohuslän) at a negotiation meeting (OH chap. 61). His capturing Earl Hákon by ambush without any declaration of war or feud is also morally objectionable by contemporary European standards, although there is nothing to suggest that this was the case in Snorri's society. Snorri occasionally lets St. Óláfr, as a good Christian, repent his sins, and even, in his last days, show consideration for his adversaries, but there is no indication that the king's conscience was particularly burdened by such treacherous acts. Thus, the real reason for the condemnation of rulers like the Eiríkssons and Earl Hákon is not their treacherous acts, but their failure. The former are even blamed for suppressing paganism, which is highly laudable when the Óláfrs do it. Magnús blindi's great fault was to spoil his victory and drive his friends away by stupid and arrogant behavior. In Snorri's characterizations he appears in a worse light than his adversary, Haraldr gilli. The contrast between the two is not, however, borne out by the actual events. Magnús's cruelty is only a general assertion; all actual cruelties in the conflict between them are committed by Haraldr.[23] Magnús seems to be condemned mainly because he was a failure.

Snorri's characterizations of the kings thus confirm our impression from the conflicts: you can do anything, if you can only get away with it. But as ultimate success depends on general support and the prize of the battle is not primarily wealth or fixed social positions and offices but influence over other men, there are certain limits to what you can actually get away with. Excessive aggressiveness or cruelty is counterproductive. The worst thing a king can to do is to be mean and tyrannical; this will inevitably cost him his throne. This is evident from the case of King Erlingr Eiríksson, who is killed by the people of Trøndelag because of his harsh taxation, and from other kings, who meet resistance from the people in the "constitutional" episodes. By contrast, weakness is not good for one's honor and reputation and may place one at risk of being a king in name only, but it is less dangerous. Consequently, Snorri shows more sympathy for a weak and insignificant king like Haraldr gilli than for his unsuccessful adversary.

The Problem of St. Óláfr

The great problem from this point of view is of course the reign of St. Óláfr, which was an ultimate failure, as he was killed in battle by his own people. Admittedly, other great kings were also defeated and killed in battles, such as Hákon góði, Óláfr Tryggvason, Haraldr harðráði, and Magnús berfoetr. When such a battle takes place against a foreign enemy, who is greatly superior in number, it is a fitting end to a great hero. The problem in Óláfr's case is that he is deposed by his own people. The rebellion against Óláfr thus becomes an equally great problem from a secular as from a theological point of view, a problem that Snorri strictly speaking is not able to solve. Considering his real as opposed to his ideological explanation of Óláfr's fall, one gets the impression that Óláfr ought to have been able to overcome the opposition through some diplomatic ability, negotiating a compromise with some of his enemies and outmaneuvering others. Actually, in dealing with the magnates Óláfr appears to commit almost all possible blunders, provoking and humiliating them by defending his own rights to the bitter end. From a political point of view, some of the episodes that occur between Óláfr and the magnates may be well suited to launch an attack against a mighty rival. But it is sheer folly to provoke so many of them at one time, particularly when they have a potential ally in King Cnut. Thus, at a time when Cnut prepares himself for attack and has secured himself allies among the mightiest Norwegian magnates, Óláfr risks losing his best friends and allies, the Árnasons, for the sake of revenging a minor servant. At about the same time, he provokes Hárekr at Tjøtta by supporting his enemy Ásmundr Grankelsson in the dispute between them. And even worse: immediately before Cnut's massive attack Óláfr kills two of Kálfr Árnason's stepsons, thus contributing to bringing him into the opposite camp. Nor is Óláfr's behavior in the conflict arising out of the episode of Ásbjǫrn selsbani a model of political wisdom. Though there may perhaps be something to be said in favor of a hard line against Erlingr Skjálgsson at a time when Óláfr is in a strong position, and Ásbjǫrn's failure to fulfil his promise certainly calls for revenge, Finnr Árnason's behavior toward Þórir hundr is bound to give Óláfr another dangerous enemy at a time when he is in great need of friends.[24]

Thus, by reading Snorri's account of Óláfr's fall, it is difficult to avoid the impression that it is largely the result of his own political incompetence. To say so explicitly, however, would not be acceptable to Snorri's public and may even have been a difficult conclusion for Snorri himself to draw, given Óláfr's well-established position as a saint. Consequently, Snorri is in great need of a different kind of explanation, which he finds in the ecclesiastical picture of the *rex iustus,* who is deposed because of his strictly impartial justice: Óláfr's intransigent behavior is the result of his insistence that offenses should be strictly punished and that it should not be possible for mighty men to buy themselves off. Though Óláfr's practice of this principle is at best highly selective, it serves to explain some of his acts which seem otherwise incomprehensible. Further, in complete contrast to Snorri's normal way of thinking, Óláfr's apparent failure is depicted as in reality a success: by resigning the earthly kingdom he prepares himself for the heavenly, and through his death at Stiklestad he wins the country for Christianity and becomes its eternal king. By means of Christian ideology and the traditional legend of St. Óláfr, Snorri is thus able to show that the great king was after all successful. Though Snorri in his description of St. Óláfr's fall clearly departs from his normal criteria for evaluating kings, his very problem with this case serves to confirm the preceding analysis of his attitude toward virtues and morality, that virtues are important insofar as they are means to success.

Means and Ends

Consequently, the difference between the contrasting ideals we have considered on the preceding pages should not be exaggerated. Both heroism and political ability are means to the same end. An attractive personality, outward splendor, and lavish generosity are important in gaining adherents. On the other hand, Snorri has little sympathy with a leader who acts foolishly. Magnús blindi, who fights a greatly superior force instead of fleeing, might easily be depicted as a tragic hero, but Snorri has only scorn left for him. The constrast between the warrior king and the peaceful ruler may be regarded in the same light. A successful king must be able to win the support of powerful and influential men in the country. The warrior hero is more likely to win it among his own men, the *hirð*, the peaceful ruler from the people as a whole. Ideally, however, a king should be able to satisfy both groups. In a similar way a good king or leader should be able to maneuver for gain, find the best solution in a difficult situation and be sufficiently eloquent to convince other men that they ought to follow him. But he is more likely to be successful in this if he also possesses virtues like bodily strength and beauty, courage, and athletic abilities.

From this point of view we can distinguish between the conventional heroic virtues, such as beauty, courage, skill at arms and athletics, which are important for one's esteem among people, that is, they belong to the charisma of the leader, but are not of great importance in themselves. To lack courage is a shame, and to accuse another person of doing so or in general to be "unmanly" is a great offense against his honor and has to be revenged (Sørensen, 1983). However, though the leader's bravery in battles is often underlined, it rarely appears to be decisive for the outcome of the battle, and even less for success in general. Other virtues are more directly important for success, such as generosity, which is essential for attracting friends and adherents. But the single most important

virtue is intelligence. This is important both in war, in diplomatic negotiations, in justice and administration, and in general in the political game
that consists in winning adherents and outwitting one's adversaries. As is
evident from numerous examples, such as Óláfr's conquest of Norway,
his negotiations with the King of Sweden, and Magnús blindi's defeat
against Haraldr gilli, this is the virtue that is most often decisive for
success in the game.

It is tempting in this context to quote Machiavelli's dictum that it is
more important to appear to have the virtues, than actually to have them
(*The Prince,* chap. 18). It is doubtful, however, whether Machiavelli is
quite appropriate or useful in understanding Snorri, as he presupposes a
clearer distinction between the "inner" and "outer" side of the human
personality than is actually to be found in him.

Dignity, Self-Control, and the
Code of Honor

According to Elias (1977, vol. 1: 65 ff.) there is a fundamental difference between the modern and the medieval personality, which is determined by a corresponding one between the respective societies: to the
simple, loosely organized medieval society corresponds a spontaneous
personality, whereas modern man is bound by innumerable restrictions,
which are integrated in his personality and which enable him to function
in our highly specialized and complex society. In Elias's opinion, the first
breakthrough for the modern personality came in the court milieus created by the early modern, absolutist state. In accordance with this general view, Elias depicts medieval aristocrats as primitive and uncivilized,
both concerning table manners, attitudes to bodily functions, sexuality,
and cruelty and aggressiveness. This picture is based partly on descriptions in the sources of cruelty and aggressiveness; and partly on hand-
books on manners and behavior at court and in higher circles, which
contain elementary rules like the ones addressed to children in modern
society, such as to wash one's hands before a meal, not to blow the nose
at the table—with the hand, because one did not use handkerchiefs
and—not to dry one's hand—which was used for eating—on the clothes
during the meal (Elias, 1977, vol. 1: 79 ff.). From a political point of
view, Elias's aristocrats are far removed from the cold, calculating courtier of the absolutist age, who behaved with impeccable politeness and
amiability to his most dangerous rivals, while at the same time planning
their downfall (Elias, 1977, vol. 2: 351 ff.; see also 1975: 139 ff.).

Elias's theory of a unilinear civilizing process is probably too crude:
there is no particular reason to believe that cruelty and aggressiveness
belong to human nature in its "unrefined" form and are modified with

the progress of civilization. It is probably more a question of adaptation to different circumstances. His picture of the Middle Ages is also somewhat one-sided. Though there are numerous examples of aggressiveness and cruelty in the sources, he generalizes too much from them.[25] There is also another side to the picture. First, the ideal of the courtier is hardly as alien to the Middle Ages as Elias assumes. Though its circulation and practical importance should not be exaggerated, it can be traced back to the German imperial court of the tenth and eleventh centuries, and it became gradually more prominent in the following centuries with the influence from ecclesiastical and classical sources and the growth of the royal court and administration (Jaeger, 1985: 101 ff., 196 ff.). Second, and most important, Elias underestimates the importance of the aristocratic concept of honor and the rules of chivalrous behavior.[26]

Chivalrous behavior means that one should be able to control fear or anger and treat one's enemies amicably and honorably. It was considered disgraceful to flee, and there are numerous examples in the sources of men who for honor's sake prefer to fight against a superior force.[27] During conflicts there were fairly strict rules of "fair play," for example, against treason or ambush or against taking advantage of the enemy's momentary weakness, such as to attack him when unarmed, exploiting one's own numerical superiority, and the like.[28] Finally, aristocratic prisoners—as opposed to ordinary ones—were normally treated honorably and released against ransom. Very often they were released before the ransom had been paid against their word of honor.

The difference between these two kinds of aristocratic behavior may to some extent be explained as the difference between ideal and practice and individual differences. But the most important explanation is no doubt the exclusive character of the feudal aristocracy. The aristocratic code of honor that was developed from the twelfth century on was applied mainly to members of the aristocracy, whereas the rest of the population could be treated at will.[29]

The code of honor, which evidently demands considerable self-control on some occasions, serves to modify Elias's picture of the spontaneous medieval aristocrat. Medieval aristocrats could even behave with greater self-control than modern men in some respects, for example, in sustaining pain. Further, when medieval aristocrats behaved irrationally according to modern standards, attacking the enemy under unfavorable circumstances instead of planning carefully or awaiting reenforcements, this was not necessarily a result of spontaneous impulses, but might be directed by the aristocratic code of honor. In a similar way, the love of pomp and splendor, generosity, and lavish spending is not necessarily evidence of a personality unhampered by capitalistic and puritan norms of saving and thinking of the future, but can as well be regarded as an expression of the entirely different norms of chivalrous behavior.

It may be objected both to the picture of the spontaneous and the chivalrous medieval aristocrat that numerous examples can be found in the sources that are best explained as the result of strategic behavior. Modern studies of individual politicians or of warfare in general (e.g., Smail, 1956; Beeler, 1971) have detected strategic plans, which cannot be easily dismissed as modern constructions. Further, we may suspect that apparently naive and straightforward accounts of chivalrous warfare often cover a rather cynical game, as in Villehardouin's story of the conquest of Constantinople as a noble undertaking, which the good men among the crusaders managed to carry out in spite of opposition from evil men who wanted to destroy the plan, or in Froissart's descriptions of the many great deeds performed during the Hundred Years War.[30] Such strategic thinking is not incompatible with the chivalrous code of honor. Feudal warfare and politics is a game, which the actors want to win. The difference is that the game is played according to fairly strict rules, which the actors generally obey, even if they risk to lose. At least, this is the picture we get from the narrative sources.

Though these sources no doubt contain idealizations and exaggerations, the most likely explanation to their general picture of chivalrous behavior is that it bears some resemblance to reality. This seems gradually to have become a fairly widespread opinion among scholars (Painter, 1940: 39 ff.; Keen, 1984: 3; Duby, 1986: 91 f., 115, 149 ff.; see also Gillingham, 1988). Given the existence of the rules, we can also point to the rationality in obeying them. In many preindustrial societies, there is no distinction between "soft" values in the cultural and social field, such as honor, and the "hard" ones of the political and economic field. Consequently, generosity, reckless bravery, chivalrous behavior toward the enemy, or other kinds of apparently unselfish behavior may actually be a kind of maximization of the kind of "profit" that is most highly regarded in a particular society (Bourdieu, 1977: 177 ff.; see also below), whereas failure to obey them may lead to sanctions in the form of loss of honor.

Despite these objections, Elias's basic assumptions deserve close examination and may even be largely correct. The idea of a correspondence between table manners, attitude toward the body, and rules of daily life and social change seems fruitful and may be able to explain important features in the evolution of modern society.[31] Though the aristocratic code of honor of the Middle Ages does not generally allow people to indulge in their immediate impulses, it accords better with a spontaneous personality than with the modern ideal of self-control. First, it is in complete opposition to the modern ideal of the rational politician who acts to further his own long-term interests. One should act so as to impress other people and acquire fame, and every offense against one's honor must be punished immediately (see Brandt, 1966: 110 ff.). The code of honor demands that one should act according to certain specific rules, whatever its consequences for one's own interests and welfare. The ideal man is not the one who plans in advance and acts strategically and prudently but the one who acts according to some specific rules in every situation, whatever the consequences for his own interests and welfare. Though it is not irrational to behave according to such norms the systematic pursuit of long-term aims as opposed to obedience to norms that dictate behavior in each particular situation is likely to make considerable difference.

Second, according to the modern ideal of the civilized man, self-control is more or less an ideal in itself, to be exercised all the time, whether one is alone or together with other people. This has to do both with the modern ideal of the individual personality as clearly distinct from its surroundings and with the importance of discipline and long-term planning in modern civilized society, which necessitates suppression of immediate impulses. By contrast, the medieval demand for self-control was directly related to other men: it was necessary to suppress certain impulses in certain circumstances to avoid losing face or to maintain "stance," in Brandt's terminology (Brandt, 1966: 114).

Chivalry and the Code of Honor in Snorri

As we have seen, long-term interests play a more prominent role in *Heimskringla* than in contemporary aristocratic European chronicles. This is also evident in Snorri's attitude to honor and the rules of chivalry. The European chivalric romances may serve as examples of literature in which "pure" honor plays an overwhelming part. In Chrétien de Troyes's *Erec et Enide,* for instance, the protagonist is exclusively concerned with honor. After his marriage to Enide, he is so happy for a while that he forgets his real task, to perform honorable deeds. Having been reminded of this, he sets out do it, only accompanied by Enide, fighting numerous other knights and distinguishing himself (*Erec,* verses 2430 ff.). His adversaries are completely unknown to him and no reason is given for their conflict. Erec is apparently wholly uninterested in the material advantages he may gain from victory; his sole concern is honor. Thus, to Chrétien, pure honor gives nothing but honor. This is an extreme example, which is certainly not representative of actual behavior. Nevertheless, it belongs to the kind of literature that was popular in aristocratic circles and may be considered an extreme example of the chivalrous ideals of this milieu, which can be contrasted with the ideals of Snorri's society.

The importance Snorri attaches to honor can be illustrated through one of the miracle stories: Guthormr Ketilsson had been on a Viking expedition with the king of Ireland. On their return from the expedition, the king demands all the booty for himself. Guthormr is in a desperate situation, having only five ships against the king's sixteen. On the one hand, fight seems to be impossible, on the other, it is dishonorable to give away the booty without a fight. Trusting in St. Ólafr, Guthormr decides to fight and wins a complete victory (*HHarð.* chaps. 54–55). Honor is thus the most important consideration. In this case, however, great material interests are also at stake. This seems generally to be the case in Snorri: honor is related to material and other interests.[32] First, wealth is essential for honor and for furthering one's political interests. Snorri often refers to the material foundation of his characters' power and influence, and the idea that one can be a great hero without wealth and thus that nobility is an "inner" quality does not seem to have occurred to him. Second, honor is a reward for success. Admittedly, the tragic hero, who dies fighting an overwhelming number of enemies, is not unknown to Snorri—Ólafr Tryggvason is an example of this—but he more often refers to the honor that is the result of a successful action and the scorn and dishonor following defeat.[33] Finally, honor is a means to success. It is dangerous not to fight for one's interests. This point is occasionally made by Snorri's persons, for instance by King Ingi when refusing to flee for his enemies: it is dangerous to show weakness, for it is likely to lead to the desertion of one's friends. It may therefore be rational to act in sudden anger to revenge one's friends or subordinates or protect one's interests, however small. But the next step is carefully to consider whether one's interests are better served by accepting an offer of compensation from the opposite party or by using the opportunity to launch an attack in the hope of gaining a decisive victory. Whether a particular course of action is honorable or not ultimately depends on its success. Thus, there is no point in provoking a dangerous conflict over a trivial matter if there is little to gain from it.

The difference between Snorri's concept of honor and that of the contemporary European aristocracy is therefore not that honor is less important, but that it has another meaning. This also seems to be the solution to the modern discussion on the importance of honor in the sagas. Honor is the fundamental value in the sagas, in the sense that one's value as a person depends on other men's esteem, but not in the sense that the man who goes to the most extreme length in revenging insults, taking risks, and so forth is also the most highly esteemed. Honor is not incompatible with prudence or moderation. On the contrary, if such qualities are likely to lead to success in the long run, they also promote honor.[34]

Consequently, whereas "pure" honor in European aristocratic ideology is crystallized in fairly detailed rules, which should be observed whether they lead to victory or defeat, honor in Snorri's society is mainly a consequence of success, and few means are banned which may lead to that. The examples mentioned above of treason and ambush are in clear contrast to the detailed rules of "fair play" of the European aristocratic ideology. Further, Snorri often refers to discussions before battles whether or not to fight against an overwhelming majority. The matter is usually decided by the king or another person of heroic inclination, who points out that it is a shame to withdraw from battle (e.g., HG chaps. 23, 28; OT chap. 102; *HHarð.* chaps. 61, 88). A battle is then fought and normally won. However, there are frequent examples of heroic kings withdrawing from battles, though with no direct discussion of the decision.[35] The norm that it is a shame to withdraw from battle should therefore not be taken too seriously, it is rather a piece of rhetoric that can be invoked when suitable.

To release prisoners against ransom was apparently not normal practice in Snorri's society, though it is occasionally mentioned.[36] The rule seems to have been that captives belonged to the victors, who decided their fate, either to kill them or give them *grið*. In the latter case they were released completely, but normally against a promise not to fight against their victor any more or to join his faction.[37] Though there was no code of honor obliging the victor to do the one thing or the other, there were clearly general criteria for the choice. Erlingr skakki, who was a great politician and a hard man, gives the following answer to his son Magnús, who has asked him to save the life of a potential pretender: "You will not govern your kingdom in peace for long if you only yield to counsels of mercy" ("þú munt lítla hríð ráða ríkinu í frelsi, ef þú skalt heilhugaráðum einum fram fara"; ME chap. 35, *my translation*). Though Erlingr was harder than most against his adversaries, his advice here was certainly in accordance with normal practice. Direct rivals in conflicts over the throne were normally executed, if they were not killed in battle. St. Óláfr apparently behaved with the utmost clemency when he allowed the young Earl Hákon to survive against promising to leave the country and not to fight against him any more (OH chap. 30). In most cases it seems to have been considered too dangerous to let such rivals survive. However, this rule might contradict another one, namely the rule that one should avoid killing close relatives. Revenge was clearly also a motive for killing one's adversaries, though in the case of kings this seems to have been subordinated to political considerations.

In the case of adversaries who were not direct rivals, the decisions seem less predictable. Magnús berfoetr kills the leaders of the rebellion against him. Snorri refers in this case to treason against the king (MB chaps. 6–7; see also below). When Steigar-Þórir, who has instigated the rebellion, is hanged, the king is so angry that none of his men dare to ask for pardon. It appears, however, that he had wanted them to do so. Þórir's fate was thus more the result of unfortunate circumstances than political calculation. The scene of the captive *jómsvíkingar* after the battle of Hjǫrungágr gives a similar impression (OT chap. 41). The captives are sitting in chains on a log, waiting to be executed. Sigurðr Búason, the son of one of the leaders, has barely escaped the first blow of the axe, when Earl Eiríkr passes by, asks the name of the young man with such unusually beautiful hair, and gives him *grið*. Shortly afterward, another of the leaders, Vagn Ákason, manages to kill his personal enemy Þorkell leira, who is about to kill him, and is also pardoned. Eiríkr is apparently impressed by his adversaries' courage, beauty, or ability to act in a difficult situation to save their lives.[38] In one of his first battles during the conquest of Norway, Haraldr hárfagri takes King Grýtingr of Orkdalen captive, pardons him, and allows him to enter his service (*HHárf.* chap. 5). Earl Eiríkr pardons Einarr þambarskelfir after the battle of Svǫlð, marries his sister to him, and makes him his closest ally (OH chap. 21). St. Óláfr offers Erlingr Skjálgsson pardon after defeating him in their last encounter (OH chap. 176), but Áslákr fitjaskalli kills him. The king's words to Áslákr, that he had struck Norway out of his hands,[39] succinctly expresses the political aspect of this pardon: to kill Erlingr would mean to have his numerous kindred and friends as enemies, to pardon him would at least mean a possibility of having him as an ally. The example of Einarr þambarskelfir shows that such an alliance could be very close. Apparently, the *grið* created a bond of gratitude similar to the ones established through gifts. Though one could never trust one's allies in the game completely, there seems to have been fairly good political reasons for pardoning most of one's adversaries after a victory, except one's most direct rivals.

There seems to have been a similar respect for oaths in Snorri's Icelandic society as in feudal Europe (Sigurðsson, 1987: 150 ff.). It is difficult to tell exactly how far this respect goes in *Heimskringla,* as there are not many examples of oaths. Earl Hákon breaks his oath to St. Óláfr not to fight against him any more, but is severely blamed for it (OH chaps. 130, 146, 161). Haraldr gilli swears not to demand the kingdom as long as King Sigurðr and his son Magnús are alive (*Msyn.* chap. 26). When he breaks the oath, it is justified by the fact that he was forced to take it (MB.HG ch. 1). Thus, though oaths are not always kept, there seems to be considerable respect for them. But they are apparently not much used. St. Óláfr does not demand an oath from Ásbjǫrn selsbani when he allows him to go home before taking up his position as *ármaðr*, despite the fact that it would be difficult to catch him in Northern Norway. When Óláfr demands an oath from the Árnasons as part of the settlement between them, this seems to be a drastic step, which meets with strong resistance from Kálfr. The rare use of oaths thus seems to confirm the suggestion that to swear an oath means to take on a very heavy responsibility. But just because of this respect for oaths, it is difficult to demand it from other people. With some reservations, we may therefore conclude that the respect for oaths is the nearest parallel to the European code of honor. One should as far as possible avoid oaths, but if one does, it is difficult to avoid blame if it is not kept.

Another point on which similar rules of chivalry as in feudal Europe seem to apply in Snorri's society is the treatment of women. At least women of high rank, who are mentioned by name in *Heimskringla*, seem to be perfectly safe in the hands of the enemies of their male relatives, as for instance in the example of Kristín konungsdóttir, Erlingr skakki's wife, who remains in Oslo after King Ingi's death and defeat to take care of the dead bodies and who is able to inform her husband of the enemy's plans (*HHerð.* chaps. 18–19). There are examples of sexual assault on women, which may create serious political repercussions, but women are not regarded as actors in the political game and accordingly not subject to revenge or violence. This seems to be the general rule in other Icelandic and Norwegian sagas as well (Heusler, 1912: 40 f.).

The different attitude to the rules of chivalry once more illustrates the greater importance Snorri attaches to political maneuvering. The difference between Snorri's society and the one described in the chivalrous literature of feudal Europe does not lie in the different importance of honor, but in the fact that honor is more directly related to success in Snorri's society. Honor is primarily a political reality. Snorri's aristocrats are thus more "modern" in the sense that they act according to their long-term interests and are less concerned with the norms of chivalry. Does this mean that they have also a less spontaneous personality than their European contempories?

Self-Control or Spontaneity?

The immediate impression of Snorri's aristocrats is that they bear close resemblance to the Olympic Gods. One is almost reminded of Winckelmann's famous characterization of Greek art: "Edle Einfalt und stille Grösse." The impression is enforced by the famous drawings of the 1899 translation. Such an impression, however, can easily be misleading. Elias's picture of the spontaneous medieval personality is not as a rule derived from the kind of historical writings Snorri represents, which often tends to heroize and tells little of the situations in which the modern ideal of the civilized human being is most clearly expressed, daily manners, attitudes toward the body, and so forth. However, the short glimpses Snorri gives confirm the impression of Elias and others of physical intimacy among men and a matter-of-fact attitude to bodily functions and sexuality. Kings and great men sleep together, often in the same bed (e.g., OH chap. 83: 151, 85). There are occasional, though rather discrete references to urination and defecation (e.g., OH chap. 83: 151; MB.HG chap. 14: 343). To be a great womanizer, is entirely compatible with being a great chieftain, and Snorri gives fairly direct references to kings' and other great men's affairs with women, though he is more discrete in this respect than some of his predecessors, often omitting words and episodes that may appear indecent (Nordal, 1973: 202 ff.). His main criterion, however, is more probably political relevance than decency.[40] He casually mentions drinking parties and people who get drunk (e.g., OT chap. 43; OH chaps. 72, 83; MB.HG chap. 16; *Ingi* chap. 28; *HHerð.* chaps. 11, 12). In contrast to European aristocratic literature, he rarely mentions differences in manners and behavior between members of the aristocracy and ordinary people.[41]

Kings' and great men's anger is often mentioned. St. Óláfr was apparently known for his hot temper, which even made his men afraid of waking him when his newborn son was about to die unbaptized (OH chap. 122). Snorri several times mentions his anger (OH chaps. 90, 108, 119, 165). Anger evidently belonged to a forceful personality. Some of the conflicts are also the result of sudden anger, but, as we have seen, this is not the normal way of things. Generally, Snorri does not approve of decisions taken in sudden anger. Nor are Óláfr's harsh measures the result of this.

In a similar way, personal hatred does not seem to play an important part in *Heimskringla*. The wish for revenge and the duty to carry it out is evidently an important factor, but is apparently not often associated with strong hatred.[42] When some member of the aristocracy is killed, the killer and his victim ususally behave with the same restraint. Torture is occasionally mentioned, notably as a means to force people to accept Christianity (OH chaps. 76, 80). For the purpose of revenge, however, as in the case of Sigurðr slembir, it is highly exceptional. Snorri tells that the chieftains wanted to kill him at once and went away when he was tortured (*Ingi* chap. 12), thus apparently expressing disgust at such cruelty. Killing people may be necessary and even laudable, but Snorri seems to condemn cruelty without purpose. His attitude appears to be in general accordance with that of contemporary Norwegian and Icelandic society.[43]

Thus, Snorri and his milieu appear more "civilized" in this respect than contemporary Europe. However, the idea that cruelty is characteristic of "primitive" people is one of the most controversial aspects of Elias's theory. It is probably more characteristic of certain levels of "civilization," during which terror was used to create respect for the norms of society and keep the common people in their place. The relative absence of cruelty in Snorri's society may thus be evidence of less conflict, violence, and social stratification than in contemporary Europe rather than of a particularly "civilized" mentality in the upper classes. At least in Snorri's case, however, there seems to be a connection between his attitude on this matter and his general view of political behavior: violence is a means in the political game, which should not be used more than strictly necessary.

Snorri quotes several examples of almost incredible self-control during danger or physical pain. The highest form of such dignity seems to be the ability to deliver a casual, even humorous remark in the face of death. After the battle of Stiklestad, St. Óláfr's scald Þormóðr kolbrúnarskáld, is treated for his wounds by a woman. He asks her to cut in his breast to remove an arrow. Then Þormóðr takes her pincers and pulls out the arrow:

> It had barbs on it, and there were fibers of his heart in it, some red and some white; and when he saw that he said, "[Well has the king fed us.] I am fat still about the roots of my heart." Thereupon he leaned back and was dead.[44]

King Eysteinn Haraldsson, who is otherwise neither a great king nor a sympathetic person, is praised for dignity in the face of death (*Ingi* ch. 31). And Sigurðr slembir, who is a violent and not very successful pretender and war leader, gains heroic dimensions through his incredible self-control when tortured to death.[45] In a similar way, confrontations between Snorri's heroes take place in an atmosphere of calm dignity.[46]

Examples similar to those mentioned by Snorri of self-control and heroic behavior can easily be found both in contemporary Icelandic (see e.g., Foote, 1984: 51 f.) and European sources. The difference from the corresponding modern ideal is also evident: these examples show the heroes acting on the stage before their fellow men. Characteristically, Snorri normally accords his praise through the mouths of other men: "It was said," "most men thought," and the like. This is not to be understood as modesty or discretion on the part of the author, but rather as an expression of the fact that morality is directly a question of what people thought. Just as a man's personality is what appears to other people, so morality is what people think is good, and other men's reactions represent the standard to which one must adjust one's behavior, that is,

Snorri's culture is a culture of "shame," not of "guilt."[47] These examples
of self-control are thus expressions of stance and different in purpose,
partly also in kind, from the modern concept of internalized self-control
in all situations in life. Shame and honor are not connected to the
difference between nature and culture or privacy and the external world,
but to other men's esteem. Self-control is not an instrument to keep
oneself intact versus the world and nature, but a means to win other
men's recognition. These ideas are in turn closely connected to Snorri's
almost exclusive interest in the social aspect of men's character and
behavior.

There are, however, occasional examples of self-control which do not
quite fit into this picture. Some of Snorri's most astute politicians,
Haraldr harðráði and Erlingr skakki, distinguish themselves by an unusual ability to conceal their feelings.[48] Halldórr Snorrason, who accompanied Haraldr harðráði on his adventures in Byzantium, is described as
a man who was able to control himself in all situations:

> Halldórr was very tall, strong and handsome. That testimony King
> Haraldr bore him that he was one of those among his followers who was
> least disturbed when anything terrible and unforseen occurred. Whether
> danger threatened or good news was brought, or whatever peril there was,
> he was neither gladder nor sadder, nor did he sleep more nor less, nor eat
> nor drink otherwise than was his custom. Halldórr was a man of few
> words, and gruff, outspoken, stubborn and obstinate.[49]

Snorri clearly considers Halldórr an unusual person. Does he also admire him? The answer probably lies in the concluding remark, which
shows him as an introverted and rather difficult man, who was no success at King Haraldr's court. Snorri adds that the king did not like him
and sent him away. Further, Snorri points to the contrast to Haraldr's
other follower, Úlfr Óspaksson, whom Haraldr loved greatly and who
was the kind of joyful, extroverted and eloquent person who is likely to
impress other people and be a political success (*HHarð.* chaps. 36–37).
Self-control and the ability to think clearly in difficult situations are no
doubt valuable qualities, but Snorri seems to think that Halldórr's extreme self-control is won at a rather high price. An example that points
in the same direction is the story of Earl Hákon's intrigues during his
exile in Denmark. Hákon is not the polished courtier, who plans and
carries out his plots while conversing amiably with other men, including
those whom he intends to deceive. He pretends to be ill, eats and drinks
little, and isolates himself from other people, probably because it must
have been impossible to conceal his plans during the intense social life
and frequent drinking parties of the court. Self-control and the ability to

conceal one's feelings are valuable assets in Snorri's milieu, but he does not expect his characters to have too much of these, nor does he consider them worth having at any price.

To some extent Snorri's characters excel in self-control in the same way and for the same purpose as their European counterparts: they are brave, able to sustain pain and face death with dignity for the purpose of impressing other men. They are extremely concerned with honor and shame and seem to act as if on a stage before their fellow men. Nevertheless, the importance of the political game in Snorri means that his characters are relatively more concerned with the long-term effects of their acts and with achieving success in the long run rather than doing the adequate thing in each particular situation. To some extent, self-control serves this purpose. One should avoid excessive cruelty and one should kill or conduct feuds not because of sudden anger or to seek vengeance but to further one's political interests. Deception, treachery, and cunning are necessary means in the political game, and self-control makes it easier to deceive one's opponents. Though it may be difficult, it is often necessary to control one's immediate impulses, such as anger or sexual desire, not because it is shameful to indulge in them but because it is likely to endanger one's interests in the long run.

Norms and Society

Though it should not be exaggerated, there is clearly a difference between Snorri's ideas of virtue as means to achieve a political purpose and the complex code of honor of contemporary European aristocratic society. This difference may possibly be explained by an analogy to Mary Douglas's analysis of rules concerning purity and pollution in different societies. She points out that there is no unilinear development from detailed and mechanistic rules to the emphasis on inner attitudes and flexibility commonly associated with modern society. Rather, apparently very "modern" attitudes can be found in quite primitive societies. The decisive factor is therefore not the complexity or modernity of a particular society, but the "tightness" of the society and the need for its members or particular classes of them to protect themselves against "contamination" from other peoples or from lower classes within their own society (Douglas, 1970: 99 ff., 125 ff.; see also 1966: 109 ff.). This seems to fit in well with the contrast between Snorri's society and that of his European contemporaries. The aristocracy of feudal Europe was more segregated from ordinary people than that of Snorri's society, and its members were probably also in closer contact with one another, both in conflict and friendship. Consequently, a detailed code of honor that served to distinguish this class from the rest of the population and to regulate its behavior was likely to develop.

We can also point to reasons for the particular rules of this code of honor. When stance and heroic behavior were more highly valued than success, it may have to do with the fact that the stakes were relatively low in most internal conflicts within feudal Europe, that the possibilies of total victory were small, and that a large number of the warriors had no great interest in the outcome of the conflict.[50] In some cases—though evidently by no means always—it might even be rational for the individual actor to behave according to the code of honor rather than to win, for example, to fight bravely and be captured instead of fleeing, not to take advantage of the momentary weakness of an adversary but give him a fair chance, and so forth. The adversary of today might be the ally of tomorrow, and to an ordinary member of the aristocracy, the considerable financial loss of being taken prisoner might be worthwhile if he could then be "discovered" by some great prince and enter his service.[51] By contrast, in Snorri's society chivalrous behavior was clearly not rational. The stakes were high, one fought to win, and the participants, at least the aristocratic ones, had great interests in the outcome of the conflict.

However, the greater emphasis on the ability to play the political game is not necessarily evidence of a very advanced society. Though I do not intend to deny that modern society and in some respects also modern man are radically different from all that has existed before, there is apparently no unilinear "Prozess der Zivilisation" from the Middle Ages and other traditional societies to our own. There is probably a difference in degree concerning the ability to suppress immediate impulses in favor of long-term gain between modern men and those of less complex societies, but there seems to be ample evidence of quite "rational" political behavior in "primitive" societies (Barth, 1981: 72 ff.; Bailey, 1980: 37 ff.; 86 ff., etc.). The difference between the political behavior of Snorri's society and that of our own is not so much the difference in rationality as the lack of distinction between the political sphere and other spheres of life. "States have no friends, only interests" is the maxim of classical diplomacy and foreign policy. Though Snorri's characters clearly had interests that they sought to further, it was not possible to distinguish so clearly between interests and friendship in a society where politics was mainly conducted at the personal, face-to-face level. This meant that personal friendship or enmity could influence political alliances much more than is the case in our society, but also the opposite. Consequently, though the politics of Snorri's society is in one sense less "rational" than in ours we are equally justified in saying that private life was more "rational."[52]

Modern and Medieval Ideas of the Personality

It is commonplace that modern, Western culture is extremely concerned with the individual. Institutions and professional groups (psychologists, psychiatrists, etc.) are devoted to the care of the individual. Our official ideology, expressed explicitly or implicitly in political agitation, definitions of human rights, laws, speeches at solemn occasions, the teaching in the schools, and so forth regards individual rights as sacred and encourages individual assertion and self-realization. In addition, numerous biographies, autobiographies, novels, films, and theatre and television productions testify to the interest and importance of the individual in modern culture. It is equally commonplace that this concern with the individual is a specifically modern and Western phenomenon, though there are reasons to believe that the development that has culminated in the nineteenth and twentieth centuries actually started in the Middle Ages.

The modern idea of the individual, as expressed among other things in the biographical literature, both fact and fiction, is both historically and logically intimately connected to historicism (Weintraub, 1975: 821 ff.; see also Olney, 1980: 3 ff. and Gusdorf, 1980: 28 ff.). It rests on two foundations, the uniqueness of the individual and the ideal of historical development. As for the first, this is not necessarily opposed to the idea of man as a social being, nor does it mean that each individual is intrinsically different from all others. On the contrary, both our ideas of human rights and our highly organized society presuppose some sort of common human nature. The individual represents a unique combination of common human qualities. Further, the uniqueness of the individual is not only a biological or psychological fact, it is an ideal. Every human being should find his or her own identity, expressed in personal taste, interests, career, ways of behavior, religious or political opinions, and even to some extent moral norms. Finally, this combination is largely the result of his or her contact and interaction with other individuals. This again means that there is a close connection between the first and the second foundation: the individual becomes unique largely because of unique experience, that is, a sort of historical development. Like the history of society, the modern idea of the individual personality implies organic growth. Our idea of the uniqueness of the individual is based on evolution, which is a combination of constancy and change: everything is in constant change, which is not predictable, but, however, neither total nor unintelligible. The individual is formed through choices, events, reactions to other people, and so forth. New situations occur, and his or her reactions to them affect the personality. Nevertheless, the reactions are specific to that particular individual, as is also the change and development. The changes take place "in character."

The modern concept of the personality presented above was developed in the nineteenth century and may be considered passé by avant-garde authors and philosophers. I nevertheless believe it to be sufficiently widespread as an ordinary, more or less implicit idea to form a useful contrast to medieval ideas on the subject. Besides, there is a difference between deliberately rejecting this concept and never having heard of it. Though both ideas of the personality and ways of describing individual persons differed considerably in the Middle Ages, a common medieval attitude can be defined negatively in opposition to the modern one. Much less importance was attached to the uniqueness of the individual person, and the idea of evolution, combining change and constancy, did not exist or was at least far less prominent than in our time. In contrast to modern, historicist thought, there was a clear opposition between constancy and change.

The ideas of the human personality found in learned or clerical milieus are derived from Greek thought and tend to emphasize constancy rather than change. There were two such theories, which may be termed respectively materialistic and idealistic. The materialistic one imagines a correspondence between outward appearances and character, based on the four temperaments, which correspond to the four elements. From a Christian point of view, however, this theory presented a threat to the doctrine of free will and the superiority of the soul over the body. It was therefore not acceptable in its extreme form, but in a moderate one, that is as a tendency for persons to behave in a certain way under the influence of certain fluids, which could be counteracted. By contrast, the idealistic doctrine, mainly of Platonic origin, was more acceptable in a Christian context. This view is based on a clear difference between "substance" and "accidence," which is again ultimately based on the Platonic "realistic" philosophy. In contrast to various other philosophical schools in antiquity, the Platonists maintained a clear distinction between body and soul and regarded the latter as a nonmaterial entity (Armstrong, 1952: 3 ff.). This doctrine was adopted by most of the Church Fathers and became universally acknowledged in the medieval Church. Behind the outward appearances of a man, there was thus a constant, inner nucleus.

Although the doctrine of the four temperaments describes types rather than individuals, the idealistic theory, at least theoretically, opens the possibility of describing unique individual characters, as Christian doctrine maintained that each soul was unique, created directly by God, in contrast to the human body, which was only indirectly created by him, through natural procreation. Similarly, its insistence on each human being's responsibility for the choice between eternal life and damnation evidently implied some emphasis on the uniqueness of the individual. The practical consequences of this, however, should not be exaggerated. The saints' lives, which are the best example of the clerical view of the human personality in practice, are mostly stereotyped and make disappointing reading from the point of view of modern psychology. This is a result of their purpose, which is not to describe individual character but to demonstrate general truths within the framework of the life of an individual: the life of the saint is an imitation of that of Christ, it shows God's works in human life and serves as an example of Christian virtues (see Børtnes, 1988: 26 ff. with ref.). This emphasis on the general rather than the individual has to do with the character of medieval morality, which is very different from the modern one: there are always clear answers to the question of right or wrong and there are fixed models of behavior to which each individual should conform, according to his or her position in society.

Further, most of the Church Fathers and their successors adopted the static view of the human personality that was current in antiquity. Admittedly, the great biographer Plutarch pointed to the variety and inconstancy of human character (see Kirn, 1955: 108), and in his works are several nuanced and complex descriptions of individual character. Nevertheless, the normal way of explaining change in character was to explain it away, as for instance in Polybios's famous portrait of Philip V of Macedon and Tacitus's of Tiberius. Both these rulers were excellent in the beginning and later changed into tyrants. To Polybios and Tacitus the tyrannical character was their true self all the time and gradually became manifest as they became established as rulers (Kirn, 1955: 110 ff.). To some extent, the idea of a fundamental moral choice, in ancient thought expressed in the story of Heracles at the crossroads (Kirn, 1955: 109), might modify this. This idea was further developed in the Christian doctrine of conversion. Augustine's *Confessiones* is a famous example of this doctrine leading to a detailed and nuanced description of a fundamental change in character. But Augustine was not only unique against an ancient background, he was without real successors among the Christians, until the high Middle Ages. In the saints' lives, the heroes are normally perfect Christians from the time of their birth, or, if they are converted at adult age, it happens all of a sudden, with no real psychological explanation. Change was thus not integrated into a concept of the individual personality. On the contrary, insofar as one was interested in describing one particular person, his or her constant qualities were emphasized. Being the essence of a person, the personality could only be changed with great difficulty, normally only through drastic interference from the outside, through God's grace or seduction by the Devil. Nevertheless, the Christian idea of conversion and individual choice between salvation and damnation did eventually encourage interest in change in character.

In contrast to the idealistic theory the materialistic-biological seems more modern in the sense that it integrates the idea of change in the form of the seven ages of man. This, however, was not understood as organic growth but as a series of successive stages (Ariès, 1973: 1 ff.).

Whereas the saint's life was a well-established literary genre, which produced an enormous number of works, the secular biography appears later, is more difficult to classify within one genre, and contains fewer examples. Though the norms themselves are different, the secular authors take approximately the same attitude to the individual as the clerical ones, that he or she should conform to a fixed pattern. In contrast to the clerical view, this ideal is expressed in outward acts rather than in the inner nucleus of the personality. A man's virtues are the sum of his actions. Not only the "inner nucleus" of a person, his inner thoughts and motives, is irrelevant, but the individual himself. As the purpose of these works is mainly to describe and evaluate individual heroic acts, there seems to be no particular reason for giving a coherent picture of each character that performs them (see also Brandt, 130 ff.; Archambault, 1974: 68).

The most important explicit model of a secular biography in the middle ages was Suetonius's biographies of the Roman emperors. Suetonius distinguished clearly between biography and history (Townend, 1967: 82 ff.). In biography, chronology was looser than in history, and great events were described only if they were able to throw light on the person in question. But in contrast to his Greek counterpart, Plutarch, whose Platonistic view of the personality was similar to that of the saints' lives and may even have influenced them, Suetonius did not try to create a coherent picture of an individual character. His method may rather be termed impressionistic. It consists partly of characterizations inserted at appropriate stages of the emperors' careers, partly of vivid snapshots of them in particular situations. Suetonius is thus less concerned with the "inner nucleus" of human beings than with their outward activity and the impression they make on other men. Though Suetonius does not seem to have been very well known in the Middle Ages, some authors have been directly or indirectly influenced by him, such as Einhard, in his biography of Charlemagne (Beumann, 1969: 1 ff.; Smalley, 1974: 67 ff.), William of Malmesbury (Townend, 1967: 98 ff.; Southern, 1963: 326; Gransden, 1974: 171), and Otto of Freising and his successor Rahewin (Lönnroth, 1965: 81, 96 f.).

I believe it is important to underline the general difference between medieval and modern concepts of the personality. On the other hand, there was clearly a change in the modern direction in the high Middle Ages, which may even justify the expression "the discovery of the individual" of the changes that took place during the Renaissance of the twelfth century (cf. Morris, 1987; Hanning, 1977; Bynum, 1980: 1 ff.; Morris, 1980: 195 ff.; Benton, 1982: 263 ff.; Radding, 1983: 587 ff. and 1985: 196 ff.). On the theoretical level, this is expressed in an increasing number of works dealing with the soul (De anima), originally in French Cistercian monasteries and later in the universities, which attempted, first, to bridge the gap between body and soul that had developed in the early Middle Ages, by using a moderate version of the doctrine of the four temperaments to understand human psychology: the humors of the body influence the soul but do not determine character. The wise man and good Christian is able to counteract evil influences of the body upon the soul. Second, they tried to reach a more nuanced understanding of the various faculties of the mind, the relations between intelligence and will, and so forth (Webb, 1962: 3 ff.; Lottin, 1942: 393 ff., 505 ff.). This theoretical interest in psychology corresponds to an increasing practical interest in individual character expressed in biographies, autobiographies, and so forth from the late eleventh century onward (Lehmann, 1953; Misch, 1959; Southern, 1966: 320 ff.; Benton, 1982: 269 f.). These works show tendencies toward a more nuanced description of the individual human being, more interest in describing emotions and inner deliberations, and attempts to explain great changes in a person's life, such as a conversion, in psychological terms. Further, the interest in motives is a characteristic feature, not only of literature but also of moral theology and jurisprudence, which in turn influenced legislation and jurisdiction. This seems a quite logical consequence of the idealistic view of human character, which emphasized the "inner nucleus" of the personality rather than outward acts. Nevertheless, it was largely a novelty in the twelfth century that these consequences were actually drawn.

Examples of this new trend are Abélard's autobiography (Misch, 1959: 523 ff.; McLaughlin, 1967: 463 ff.; Southern, 1970a: 86 ff.; Hanning, 1977: 17 ff.; Benton, 1982: 265 f.), Eadmer's biography of St. Anselm of the twelfth century (Misch, 1959: 220 ff.; Southern, 1966: 314 ff.), Gerald of Wales' historical and autobiographical writings of the early thirteenth (Kirn, 1955: 179 ff.; Misch, 1962: 1297 ff.), and Joinville's biography of St. Louis of the early fourteenth (Southern, 1966: 336). There is also an increasing sense of psychology and development of character in the romances of the late twelfth and early thirteenth centuries (Scholes and Kellogg, 1966: 167 ff.; Hanning, 1977). Two of the most interesting descriptions of change in character are Adam of Bremen's biography of Archbishop Adalbert (late eleventh century), a great archbishop and great man who was ruined through his own ambition (*Gesta* book 3; see also Kirn, 1955: 119 ff.; Misch, 1959: 168 ff.; Smalley, 1974: 125) and Thomas of Celano's first Life of St. Francis from the first half to the thirteenth century. In the latter we have to do with the static character of the worldly and shallow youth in the beginning and the equally static picture of the ascetic and God-loving saint in the later and larger part of the vita. In between, however, there is a conversion story of considerable psychological interest, describing Francis's growing disappointment with the life he has led hitherto and his search for a new and better life in God's service.[53] Though the modernity of these works should not be overrated, they indicate new trends in the concept of human character in the high Middle Ages.

Snorri's Ideas of the Personality

As is evident from the analysis of Snorri's ideas of morality, he belongs to the secular tradition. Further, he shows similarity on several points to the classical tradition derived above all from Suetonius. Both the contents of his characterizations, the distinction between *notatio* and *elogium,* and his various ways of placing the former conforms to this tradition (Lönnroth, 1965: 90 ff.). By contrast, there is little to suggest that he was influenced by the Platonist doctrine of the soul that dominated medieval clerical historiography. He shows little concern for the inner nucleus of the human personality. As in the Icelandic sagas, Snorri's persons are nearly always regarded from the outside. The character sketches usually start with a quite elaborate description of the person's appearances, and the subsequent description of his mental qualities mainly deals with what may be observed by other men, such as eloquence, courage, generosity or greed, temper or normal way of behaving. In his direct narrative, Snorri very rarely "looks inside" his persons to tell of their thoughts and feelings. Motives, plans, and reflections are normally expressed in the speeches and dialogues. Or they are expressed through dreams, such as Óláfr's deliberations on whether or not he should return to Norway, or indirectly, as when Earl Hákon in his exile in Denmark isolates himself from other men to deliberate, and the results of these deliberations are gradually disclosed in the events that follow.

This form of narrative is fairly familiar to readers of the twentieth century, as many modern authors, like Hemingway, have deliberately adopted it, leaving their readers to draw their conclusions as to the "inner" side of the persons' actions. As Steblin-Kamensky has pointed out (1973: 69 ff.), the narrative of Snorri and other Icelandic authors is hardly to be understood in the same way, though he probably goes too far in stating that this narrative style was the only one available to them. The contemporary clerical style, even in the North, was very different and there is evidence that the "objective" saga style was the result of a gradual evolution and thus not a spontaneous expression of primitive mentality. Nevertheless, given Snorri's and other saga writers' ideas of morality, it seems reasonable to regard this style as the expression of a mentality in the sense that it is mainly concerned with the outward aspect of the human personality: Actions are more important than inner qualities, and it is of primary importance to his characters to impress other men. The same point of view is to be found in the older Norwegian and Icelandic laws, which are concerned with outward acts and mete out punishment according to the damage caused by them, completely disregarding motives, in clear contrast to the new jurisprudence introduced by the Church (see Bagge, 1987*b*: 66 ff.).

As for the theories of a constant human character referred to above, Lars Lönnroth has suggested that the contrast that is often found in the Icelandic sagas between men who are dark, ugly, quarrelsome, and difficult on the one hand and those who are fair, beautiful, generous, and amiable on the other may ultimately be derived from the "materialistic" doctrine of the four temperaments, the former character corresponding to the melancholy temperament, the latter to the sanguine.[54] There are traces of this contrast in Snorri, notably in his description of the earls of the Orkneys: Þorfinnr was large and strong and ugly, and while he grew up, one could easily see that he was an avaricious man, hard, cruel, and very wise (OH chap. 96). The following description of the two brothers Einarr and Brúsi contain the same contrast in character but nothing is said of their appearances (OH chap. 97).[55]

Very few of the kings Snorri describes are dark. Hálfdan svarti, Haraldr hárfagri's father and the first great conqueror, is named after his dark hair but nothing much is said of his character apart from the fact that he was greatly loved by the people (HS chaps. 1, 9). Haraldr gilli, the foreigner, was dark and apparently not handsome but his character was the exact opposite of the hard, introverted melancholic. He was cheerful, weak, friendly, and easily led (*Msyn.* chap. 27; MB.HG chap. 1). By contrast, his adversary Magnús, who was exceptionally beautiful and thus probably fair, was just the sort of cruel, unfriendly, and introverted person that corresponds to this prototype (MB.HG chap. 1). Haraldr's son Eysteinn, who was also dark, corresponds better, as he was wild and aggressive and above all avaricious and mean (*Ingi* chaps. 21–22). Similarly, there is some correspondence between King Eysteinn Magnússon's beauty and his mildness, friendliness, and easy manners in contrast to his brother Sigurðr, who was more harsh and warlike and lacked beauty. Haraldr harðráði, whose character bears some resemblance to the melancholic type, as he is hard against his adversaries and—as appears from several descriptions of individual episodes—unusually able to conceal his feelings, has fair hair and beard. The contrast between fair and dark thus seems to be of no great consequence to Snorri, apart from the fact that he clearly prefers fairness for aesthetic reasons. All his great kings are also handsome and strong, most are also tall. But there are handsome kings who are not great, such as the Eiríkssons and Magnús blindi, and there are kings who although not handsome or even strong, are at least better than their appearances, such as Ingi, Haraldr gilli, and Sigurðr jórsalafari. Snorri is therefore hardly influenced by the doctrine of the temperaments in the form Lönnroth refers to. There are somewhat better reasons for thinking that he believed in a correspondence between outward appearances and inner qualities in general. The clearest expression of this is his reference to St. Óláfr's exceptionally strong and beautiful eyes, which frightened his enemies when he was angry. It is a widespread assumption that the eyes are the mirror of the soul, and Snorri seems to share this idea (Lönnroth, 1963–1964: 43 f.). More generally, Snorri's great interest in outward appearances and his description of physical and mental qualities in the same way and the same context indicate that he did not distinguish very sharply between them.

This admittedly rather vague correspondence between inner and outward qualities indicates a belief in some constancy of the human character. So does the fact that Snorri does not confine himself to describing his persons in action, but regularly gives fairly detailed characterizations of the most important of them. As we have seen, the two do not always correspond. Nor is it easy to see how Snorri manages to reconcile the constant and changing features of the personality. His way of coping with this problem is best illustrated in his largest and most detailed biography, of the greatest king in Norwegian history, St. Óláfr.

The Biography of St. Óláfr

The life of St. Óláfr represents a real challenge to a biographer: a man who started as a Viking, raiding the Baltic and the Christian countries of Western Europe, then became the great Christian king of Norway and a strong ruler, and finally found his death as a saint and martyr. Moreover, Snorri's oral and written sources presented him with a wealth of material on all aspects of the king's activities, from his performances on the battlefield to his miracles. From a modern point of view, Óláfr's life would make the ideal *Bildungsroman:* how did the Viking chieftain develop into the Christian king? And how did the Christian king, cleansed through sufferings and adversities, change into the saint and martyr? Snorri's life of St. Óláfr has in fact been interpreted in this way and been regarded as his greatest achievement as a psychologist (Storm, 1873: 151 ff.; Paasche, 1916: 377 ff.; Nordal, 1973: 181 ff.).

Compared to his predecessors, Snorri does emphasize the changes in Óláfr's life through a more orderly chronology, above all concentrating most of his miracles and religious life to the period after his exile. But Snorri does not describe a development. He describes three successive characters with no real link between them.

Óláfr's saga starts with a characterization of him as a quite young man (OH chaps. 1, 3). As usual, Snorri gives a detailed description of his appearance: he was not very tall, but broad and strong, with blond hair and ruddy complexion. His eyes were exceptionally good and beautiful and sharp, so as to frighten people when he was angry. He grew up early, both in wisdom and strength, was wise, eloquent, good at sports and in the use of arms and in handicrafts. He was well liked by all and he was ambitious, wanting to be the first in all things—as he ought to be, Snorri adds. Already in his early years, Óláfr's ambitious, warlike character is contrasted to that of his stepfather, Sigurðr sýr, above all in the story of Óláfr saddling a he-goat for him when asked to saddle his horse (OH chap. 2). This characterization serves as a useful introduction to the following story of Óláfr as a Viking and his numerous victories and heroic deeds. In accordance with Snorri's normal practice concerning military matters, he lays particular emphasis on Óláfr's intelligence, that is, his ability to find a solution in a desperate situation.[56] This is also an important aspect of his success at the beginning of the next phase of his life, the conquest of Norway. During these events, Snorri further underlines Óláfr's strong and ambitious character by once more pointing out the contrast between him and Sigurðr sýr and by letting Hroerekr describe him as a dangerous man for the petty kings.

After Óláfr's conquest of Norway, Snorri once more stops to give a picture of his daily life as a king (OH chap. 58). He rises early, dresses, and washes his hands, goes to church to attend mass and the early canonical hours, and then spends his day on meetings, solving conflicts between people, judging and other necessary matters, and on legislation. Snorri describes him as a man of high moral standing,[57] wise, controlled, quiet, a man of few words, generous but at the same time fond of money. In other words, the aggressive and ambitious Viking chief has become the wise and moderate statesman and a good Christian. The same picture emerges from Snorri's *elogium* on Óláfr, in which he emphasizes his strict justice, which led to his fall (OH chap. 181; see also above).

How has the change come about? As his predecessors, but in contrast to the saga of Óláfr Tryggvason, Snorri does not tell of Óláfr's conversion. He accepts the Icelandic tradition that he was baptized at the age of three and had Óláfr Tryggvason as his godfather (OT chap. 60). He is then completely silent about Óláfr's Christianity until he tells of his plans to go to Jerusalem, a plan that is not carried out because of a dream, in which a man tells him to return to his *óðal* to become king eternally (OH chap. 18). Though not directly stated, this must be seen against a Christian background. There was no reason for Óláfr to go to Jerusalem unless he was a Christian, and the dream is evidently to be regarded as a sign from God, prophesying Óláfr's future as the eternal king of Norway. Characteristically, however, Snorri does not make Óláfr follow the advice of the dream immediately, and when he does, he has also more secular reasons for returning. In political terms, Snorri is able to give a convincing explanation of Óláfr's return, but his change in character remains a mystery.

Snorri is more explicit concerning the next change. Having brought Óláfr in exile to Russia, he turns to the changes that now took place in the king's life and character:

> We are told that King Ólaf led a pure life and was diligent in his prayers to God all the time he lived; but when he found his power diminishing and his opponents waxing strong, he concentrated all his mind on serving God. Then no other concerns kept him from that, nor such efforts as he had before been busy with. Because during the time he was king he had labored with what he considered most requisite, first, to pacify the land . . . then to convert the people . . .[58]

The opening of this passage reads like a rather banal modern psychologization: troubles in this life make people more prone to seek consolation in religion, a psychologization that has its counterpart in traditional Christian ideas of God using adversities to make men turn to him. We may note, however, that Snorri only points explicitly to a chronological connection between the two, not a causal one. His causal connection follows in the next passage: when Óláfr was free from his duties in Christianizing and governing Norway, he could spend all his time in prayers and religious contemplation. What occurs, is not strictly speaking a change in character, but only a change in the circumstances of life.

The question of change or continuity between the three phases of Óláfr's life must ultimately be answered from Snorri's description of his deeds. How different are actually the Viking chief, the king, and the saint? In his speech before his mother and stepfather when returning to claim Norway (OH chap. 35), Óláfr expresses some regret concerning his earlier life: while in exile from his lawful inheritance, he has been forced to seek his living at the cost of others, many innocent men having lost their properties and some even their lives. As a confession from a saint and future martyr, this is not very impressive. Óláfr concedes that plundering innocent people is not a very praiseworthy activity, but after all, one has to live. The real blame is directed at the men who have usurped Óláfr's inheritance, thus forcing him to gain his livelihood in this way.

Another possible example is Óláfr's patience at the humiliation he suffers during the negotiations with the King of Sweden. Is this an example of the moderate statesman, suppressing his pride for the sake of long-term gain, having replaced the aggressive young Viking chief? This is unlikely for two reasons. First, Snorri does his best to cover up the fact that Óláfr is actually humiliated. And second, the story is not at all representative for Óláfr's behavior as a king. On the contrary, he is usually quite uncompromising in his confrontations with the Norwegian magnates. We may thus safely conclude that the difference between the Viking chief and the king is much less in practice than appears from the characterizations.

The difference between the saint and the king seems somewhat greater. Whereas Óláfr hardly makes a miracle during his period as ruling king, several miracles occur during his exile and on his way to Stiklestad, and these are more integrated in the story than miracles usually are. Óláfr's piety is emphasized in several episodes. He punishes himself for working on a Sunday by burning the slivers he has cut from a piece of wood while sitting in deep thought (OH chap. 190). He refuses to burn the farms in Verdalen on his way to Stiklestad (OH chap. 205). He accepts only Christian men in his army (OH chaps. 201, 204). And he gives silver for masses for the souls of those of his adversaries who will be killed in the battle, no masses being needed for his own men, who will enter heaven as martyrs (OH chap. 207). Óláfr's inner life also receives more attention in this part of the saga. He has dreams and visions, which point to his future death and his position as the eternal king of Norway,[59] and Snorri often refers to his deep thought and deliberations. His deliberations before his decision to return to Norway to fight for his kingdom are told in great detail, in contrast to his original decision. The decisive argument for returning to Norway, brought forward by Óláfr Tryggvason in a dream, is also derived from the Christian idea of the king as God's representative on earth, who is not allowed to leave his office (OH chap. 188).

However, the contrast between the new and the old King Óláfr should not be exaggerated. Óláfr's new mildness, in forbidding his men to burn the homes of farmers, is in clear contrast to his harshness during his two previous "lives." But his reason for showing moderation now does not imply a confrontation with his former behavior: previously, he had burned farms to force the people to accept Christianity; now, as he is only fighting for his own kingdom and punishing his adversaries for betraying their king, he will abstain from such means and show mercy toward his enemies. Nor does Óláfr repent his burnings and lootings during his two earlier lives which were not for the sake of Christianity (see OH chaps. 5, 7, 15, 68, 89). Further, Óláfr has a more down-to-earth reason for not burning: he does not want to destroy his and his men's booty in case they should win! In a similar way Óláfr's last speech before the battle of Stiklestad (OH chap. 211) contains some pious references to God's providence and his and his men's just cause. Apart from that, however, it is an ordinary battle speech, appealing to luck, promising rewards—of an entirely earthly nature!—in case of victory, urging the men to fight bravely and outlining the tactics.

As in the case of the change between the first two "lives," there is thus no direct comparison between then and now. There are some short glimpses of Óláfr looking back on his former life. When deliberating whether or not to return, Óláfr reflects on the fact that his first ten years as a king were successful but that luck had then changed and he had experienced increasing difficulties the following five (OH chap. 187). This is not a biographical reflection, however, but a part of the discussion whether or not to trust luck so much as to return to Norway. Óláfr's dream, in which he sees the whole country and remembers that he has often been happy (*glaðr*) there (OH chap. 202) is evidence of the close connection between the king and his country, which is now going to be permanent but is even less relevant from a biographical point of view.

Finally, there is a characterization of Óláfr which sums up his whole life, the comparison between him and his half-brother Haraldr (*HHarð.* ch. 100), which points to their essential similarity as great warriors and strong, proud, and ambitious kings, despite the different purposes of their activities, Óláfr fighting for Christianity and justice, Haraldr for his own glory. As this comparison is intended to show the similarity, not the difference between them, the heroic ideal seems more important to Snorri than their different aims. This then points to the essential unity of Óláfr's character. After all, the qualities Snorri describes in his initial presentation of the young Viking chief remain throughout the three successive "lives."

There is thus a considerable tension between continuity and change in Snorri's biography of St. Óláfr. In most of the general characterizations and in some of the stories he appears as three different characters succeeding one another, while in most of the narrative he is essentially the strong, warlike, and ambitious leader. This evidently reflects the different traditions Snorri had before him, the saint of the clerical vitae, the great ruler and legislator of the contemporary royalist ideology, and the hero of the many stories that had survived in oral and written traditions. Particularly the first tradition, to some extent also the second, were alien to Snorri's normal way of thought and are therefore less successfully integrated. Snorri's "real" Óláfr is thus most probably the one who appears in the first and the last characterizations and the numerous confrontations with his rivals among the magnates.

Continuity and Change in Human Character

Although the particular arrangement of the biography of Óláfr may thus be explained from the sources at Snorri's disposal, his way of solving this problem also throws a more general light on his concept of human character. Clearly, both the modern concept of the evolution of a personality, which is expressed in the *Bildungrsroman* and the historical biography originating in the eighteenth and nineteenth centuries, and its medieval predecessors were alien to him. In contrast to Thomas of Celano, who tries to explain the transition from the one life of St. Francis to the other, Snorri describes St. Óláfr's three successive lives without reflecting on the change from the one to the other. How does he then conceive of the relationship between constancy and change in human character? And how is it possible to combine essential unity of character with the description of three successive personalities that are basically different? The problem has to be solved along two lines.

First, there is a close connection between social role and personality. Although Snorri has no concept of the royal office in the modern sense, he has fairly clear ideas of a royal personality. One is king all the time, and to be so, one has to have certain qualities. Admittedly, not all kings fulfill these demands, but it seems entirely conceivable that a man could change sufficiently to conform to the ideal. In Óláfr's case, the role of king may be compared to that of saint. To us there is a fundamental distinction between them. To be a king is to be appointed to a certain office, which may clearly mean new demands and duties but which need have no consequences for one's personality. By contrast, to be a saint is exactly a question of personality. Snorri's description of Óláfr as successively a king and a saint shows that he makes no real distinction between the two roles. In both cases, it is a question of being a particular kind of person.

Second, Snorri's characterizations do not aim at a "total" representation of character, but confine themselves to particular features that seem striking. Nor are they concerned with the "uniqueness" of the particular person. Rather, the characters are valued according to a fixed scale, which is in turn determined by the game in which they take part. What Snorri describes is the various persons' amount of beauty, strength, courage, intelligence, and other qualities that serve to gain support and ultimately success in the political game. These qualities are all easily observed by other men; hidden qualities are irrelevant from a social point of view. Further, the qualities are not only observable, to a large extent they summarize the deeds the person in question has performed: to be brave means to have performed brave deeds, to be intelligent is to have been able to find the correct solution in difficult situations, and so forth. This is evident both from the way the descriptions of persons are arranged, such as in the *mannjafnaðr*, and from numerous examples that show that a man's honor and reputation is dependent on his acts and may change accordingly.

This conclusion receives further support from a comparison between the characterizations and the actual narrative. The characterizations are often vivid and detailed, particularly the descriptions of outward appearances, more so than European descriptions in the rhetorical style (Lönnroth, 1965: 71 ff.). Compared to the narrative, they are nevertheless fairly conventional. Nor are they intended to be objective descriptions of the persons in question. Both their occurrence or not and to some extent also their contents are determined by status. Occasionally, they may differ considerably from the impression we get of the persons in the narrative, notably in the case of Magnús blindi and Haraldr gilli. The best descriptions of human character are usually found in the narrative and not in the characterizations. We are more impressed by the descriptions of Haraldr harðráði's maneuvers to save himself in difficult situations or to suppress his enemies (*HHarð*. chaps. 45, 52) and by the scenes between him and Magnús (*HHarð*. chap. 27) and Finnr Árnason (*HHarð*. chap. 66) than by any general assertion that he was an intelligent man, who was able to conceal his feelings. And many of Snorri's best descriptions of politicians are found entirely in the narrative.

To Snorri, man is thus the sum of various amounts of individual characteristics and—above all—actions, that may be observed by other men. Admittedly, a modern characterization or biography, which aims at depicting the uniqueness of a particular character, must also necessarily describe degrees of various qualities. After all, there are no words in the language for qualities that are unique to one particular human being. But we have an idea, which was apparently alien to Snorri and his contemporaries, of a combination of qualities and a particular relationship between them, that is unique to each particular human being. The question of change versus continuity is therefore not the same as in modern discussions of character. When a man's character is basically the sum of his acts, each new act may in principle change it. Sudden, radical changes of character are thus in principle no problem. King Magnús góði changed from a tyrannical and vindictive king to one of the best rulers the country had known, who was loved by the whole people. This happened all of a sudden as a result of Sigvatr's *Bersǫglisvísur*. Earl Sigurðr, the leader of the party of the pretender Sigurðr Markúsfóstri, was not considered a brave man. Before his last battle against Erlingr skakki, he commented on this himself and promised to fight bravely and urged his men to do the same. He kept his promise and fell honorably in the first battle at Ré in 1163 (ME chaps. 13–14). Earl Hákon was most of his time a great chieftain and a successful and popular leader, but changed toward the end of his life, notably because of his lusting after women, which led him to an ignominious end. Nevertheless, his achievements before this were sufficient to earn him a great name.

This conclusion serves to confirm our impression of the similarity between Snorri and the tradition from Suetonius. Both his way of characterizing his subjects by showing them in action and his lack of interest in creating a consistent picture of their essential character are similar.[60] However, there is a considerable difference between the style of Suetonius and other Roman historians and the Old Norse sagas (Amory, 1979: 68 ff.). And Suetonius's interest in biography as opposed to history, that is, describing character instead of giving a continuous narrative of events, has no parallel in Snorri. There is no direct evidence that Suetonius was known in Iceland in the Middle Ages, though this is not impossible. But other Roman historians were, and Old Norse historians may have been influenced either by them or by medieval authors who in their turn had borrowed from Suetonius.[61] Characterizations in the classical style are fairly widespread in medieval historiography, and though the kind of impressionistic and indirect descriptions of individual characters in action are less frequent, they do occur.[62]

However, Snorri and his contemporaries hardly chose this way of describing persons solely in order to adapt to foreign models, but because it suited their purpose. Snorri's concept of human character is ultimately determined by the political game he describes. Modern man can play and normally does play a number of different games, as a politician, scholar, industrialist, artist, lover, father or mother, and so forth, and the particular aims or combination of them pursued by each particular person is an important feature in a biographical description. Even within the game of politics, which is of primary concern in our context, there are a number of different aims. Though there are no doubt "pragmatic rules of the game" (Bailey, 1980: 4 f.) that are common to all politicians and which aim at gaining important positions, no modern politician would survive without pursuing—or at least pretending to be pursuing—long-term aims. By contrast, there is for all practical purposes only one game in *Heimskringla,* that of winning power and honor among other men. There may be differences as to the extent of one's ambitions, such as between St. Óláfr and his stepfather Sigurðr, but basically, most men described by Snorri are politicians whether they like it or not and have to try to win the esteem of their fellow men. In some marginal cases, it may be a question of playing or not, as when a king's son, having grown up outside the court and the royal family, deliberates whether or not to claim the throne. If he decides not to do so, he becomes uninteresting and is hardly likely to be mentioned at all in *Heimskringla.* Occasionally, Snorri hints that there may be other games, such as being a saint and abandoning earthly power and glory, which Óláfr to some extent does. But this is very exceptional and is of little consequence to *Heimskringla* as a whole.

We can then conclude that Snorri's biographies and characterizations of his subjects do not represent a particularly "advanced" psychology or an anticipation of the modern historical biography. On the contrary, they are less "advanced" than some of the works associated with "the discovery of the individual" in the twelfth and thirteenth centuries, such as the autobiography of Abélard and Thomas of Celano's biography of St. Francis. Nor does Snorri seem very much influenced by contemporary explicit theories of human character. He may have some idea of a correspondence between a man's personality and his outward appearances, but he does not adhere to this doctrine in its more extreme form. He is even less influenced by the idealistic or clerical theory of "the inner nucleus" of the personality. Rather, his basic ideas of human character resemble those of contemporary aristocratic thought, both in the North and in feudal Europe: a man is what he appears to other men.

On one point, however, he may be influenced by clerical thought, namely in his interest in motives. He is the only one of the authors whose works are extant to mention Óláfr's deliberations before his return to Norway, though Theodoricus also mentions the dream (chap. 18). He explicitly states Cnut's motives for conquering Norway (OH chap. 130: 282 f.). He mentions that Einarr þambarskelfir remembered King Cnut's broken promise to him and delayed his return to Norway to avoid taking sides in the fight between him and King Óláfr, whereas earlier extant sagas are completely silent on Einarr þambarskelfir's shifting loyalties and his motives for this. *Legendary Saga* mentions Kálfr Árnason's apostacy from Óláfr's cause and his subsequent conversion on the battlefield of Stiklestad after Óláfr's death, but regards it entirely in religious terms (*Leg. Saga:* 76, 79, 88 f.). *Fagrskinna* gives the bare facts of Kálfr's alliance with Cnut and his subsequent change of sides in leading the rebellion against the Danes, but gives no motives (*Fsk.* pp. 178 f., 191 f.). Further, apart from these rather rare direct references to motives, Snorri makes more direct use of speeches and dialogues to analyze motives than his predecessors (Lie, 1937: 85 f.; Knirk, 1981: 142 f.). In his interest in motives Snorri also distinguishes himself from aristocratic authors of contemporary Europe.

Though we cannot exclude the possibility that Snorri may be influenced by clerical historiography or thought in general, it is important to note that his purpose in analyzing motives is very different. Snorri is not concerned with the inner soul of his characters, but with making them intelligible in terms of the political game. In attaching greater importance to long-term interests, Snorri also has to analyze motives. Motives are the "inner" side of human acts and can be fairly easily reconstructed, as most men act according to their interests. As Snorri, in contrast to European aristocratic chroniclers, is less interested in the intrinsic value of the individual act, according to the code of honor, than in his characters' ability to achieve the aims they have set for themselves, motives become more important to him. A good politician must be able to understand other people's motives, and he must plan his own actions in advance and maneuver carefully to carry out his plans. Consequently, analyses of motives become an important part of the political game.

Though Snorri is not very "advanced" in his descriptions of human character and his reputation as a psychologist is somewhat exaggerated, he nevertheless compares favorably by modern standards to most—though not all—of his contemporaries through his vivid snapshots of characters in action. From a literary point of view, this is not difficult to understand. A modern literary public is much more likely to be impressed by such descriptions than by long discussions of what a particular person really was like behind the façade. Snorri's "nominalistic" idea of man as a sum of his actions, in addition to his considerable literary talent and understanding of the political game, enables him to excel in this in a way that impresses even modern readers, despite his generally static view of human character and his lack of ability to analyze change and development. His psychological insight is thus not derived from an "advanced" theory of human nature, but from his practical experience as a politician.

Conclusion

There is thus a correspondence between moral norms and the general concept of character in Snorri, both being determined by the game of politics. Though Snorri seems to represent a more advanced stage than his European contemporaries according to Elias's evolutionary schema of political man, this is to some extent an illusion. His "machiavellian" attitude to politics has its parallels in fairly "primitive" societies and is thus probably more the result of actual conditions in his rather loosely organized society than an anticipation of modern political thought. And his psychological insight, which is in one sense impressive, is not derived from a particularly modern or advanced theory of the human personality, but is rather to be understood in a similar way, as derived from practical experience in the game of politics. This indicates, as we should expect, that Elias's theory needs considerable modification, though it does not contradict his general assumption of the uniqueness of the modern personality and the connection between "private" norms, attitudes to the body, and so forth, and modern, complex society.

5

The Historian

Introduction

Having analyzed Snorri's descriptions of conflicts, man, and society, I shall now examine his own way of finding order and meaning in the phenomena he is describing, that is, I shall deal more directly with Snorri as a historian. Though this includes a variety of subjects, I shall confine myself to the following three, which I consider most important: the idea of development and periodization, the purpose of history, and historical causation.

Historical Development and Periodization

One of the most distinctive traits in Koht's theory of Snorri as a conscious historian with an overall interpretation of Norwegian history lies in attributing to him the idea of periodization. According to Koht, the constant struggle between the monarchy and the aristocracy falls into distinct phases, in which now the one, now the other of the antagonists gains the upper hand, until King Sverrir—in the period immediately after the one covered by *Heimskringla*—manages to curb the aristocracy and finally establish the strong monarchy that took its first beginnings with Haraldr hárfagri's conquest (1921: 81 ff.). Sandvik (1955: 57 ff., concl.: 94 f.) and Beyschlag (1966: 59 ff.) think in approximately the same way.

This sort of periodization, or "linear" view of history, has often been considered a unique feature of the modern sense of time, which developed in close connection with the emergence of modern historiography, mainly from the eighteenth century on. There is no general agreement on this, however, and claims for a "linear" view of history have been made for the Renaissance (Kelley, 1970: 303 ff.) and even for the Jewish-Christian view of history from late antiquity and the Middle Ages (Nisbet, 1969: 62 ff.; Funkenstein, 1965: 93 ff., 116 ff. and 1974: 3 ff.). As for the Middle Ages, Christian eschatology no doubt offered a sort of basic periodization, which was expressed in the current theory of the seven ages of world history. But this periodization was mainly an abstract schema that had little relevance to most events that were treated by historians. After all, nearly all history contained in the works of medieval historians took place in the sixth age, the period from the birth of Christ till the present day. And the ages did not usually "grow out" of historical events, but were "imposed" from the outside, through divine intervention.

There are, however, exceptions to this, notably from the twelfth century on. Eschatology did not always confine itself to the idea of Christ's return as God's sudden interruption into history. A more "organic" idea was also developed, according to which Christ's return was provoked or at least prepared by the evolution of human history. The most well-known and perhaps also the most important example of this is Joachim of Fiore's theory of the three ages of ecclesiastical history, leading up to Christ's return in 1260 (Reeves, 1969: 295 ff.; see also Funkenstein, 1965: 105 ff. and 1974: 10 ff.). Second, there are traces of the idea that laws and institutions must change according to changing historical conditions among theologians, lawyers, and political thinkers, probably stimulated by the search for eternal truth as opposed to merely human traditions in the Investiture Contest and above all by the codification of ecclesiastical and later also secular law (Gagnér, 1960: 185 ff., 228 ff., 341 ff.; Klinkenberg, 1969: 157 ff.). Some twelfth-century theologians, notably Hugh of St. Victor, used history as a basis for their theological thinking and to some extent explained differences between authorities through historical development (Chenu, 1954; Southern, 1971: 163 ff.; see also Ehlers, 1973: 67, 71 ff., 77 ff., 169 ff.).

We cannot therefore completely exclude the possibility that Snorri had an idea of historical development. But such an idea is less likely to occur in a historian, above all a secular one, than in a theologian, lawyer, or philosopher. Some clarification seems necessary here. What is characteristic of the modern sense of history is not only a specific concept of time, but also of human nature and society. Change is conceived as a normal and inevitable phenomenon, but also one that can be understood in rational terms. That is to say: it cannot be predicted, only be explained afterward. History does not move according to a fixed set of rules, it is the result of human activity and—partly at least—human will. Change may go in different directions, but not in any direction; there is always some connection between the present and the past which makes change intelligible, though not predictable. There is therefore a logical connection between this sense of history and secularization in that history is understood as the result of human activity. In a similar way, it is logically connected to a certain relativism in the concept of society: not only the actors in the game and their actions change, but also the game itself and its rules. In practice such a change in historiography is probably brought about by the development of larger and more complex political units and by a further development of the concept of the rational political agent which we have found among other places in Snorri (see Koselleck, 1981: 166 ff.).

This means that statements to the effect that certain customs were different in the past and that certain institutions were introduced at a particular time for a particular purpose, which are occasionally found in Snorri and other medieval historians,[1] are not in themselves evidence of a modern "linear" concept of history. The traditional, static view of history did not imply that everything was the same throughout history. Changes could and did take place, but they were not the normal order of things. Further, although the modern idea of historical development implies constant change, which culminates in certain crucial periods, change is never total. There is always some element of continuity, which makes explanation possible. By contrast, total, inexplicable change was possible according to medieval ideas. What did not exist was the idea of a development in a certain direction and consequently of periodization in the modern sense, that is, as "growing out" of history itself. However, we cannot always distinguish clearly between traditional and modern concepts of history. There are intermediate forms. Consequently, though it seems a priori fairly obvious that Snorri had a traditional and not a modern concept of history, we need not dismiss the problem so easily, but must go on examining the exact contents of this concept.

Modern periodizations of older Norwegian history are to a considerable degree based on Snorri. Many nineteenth-century historians shared the interpretation of history which Koht attributes to him, of a continuous struggle between monarchy and aristocracy:[2] The struggle started with Haraldr hárfagri's conquest, through which the monarchy established itself over the whole country by suppressing local magnates and centers of power. In the following period there was a continuous struggle between the centralizing monarchy and magnates wanting to be independent, which reached its climax in the reign of St. Óláfr, whose struggle for a strong monarchy went hand in hand with his Christianization. The monarchy then emerged victorious under his successors, but in the following period, a strong aristocracy emerged, no longer consisting of independent magnates, but an "aristocracy of the realm," which sought to control the monarchy. The renewed conflict between the monarchy and this aristocracy then led to the second long period of internal strife, the "civil wars" from the 1130s, which reached their climax under Sverrir (1177–1202).

As we have seen, it probably needs modern concepts of classes and political structures in conflict to read this development out of Snorri. Snorri's conflicts take place between individuals, within a rather static system of society. Nevertheless, we cannot exclude the possibility of some sort of periodization. To a certain extent, Haraldr hárfagri's conquest represents a turning point, admittedly not quite as much to Snorri as to modern historians. Snorri regards the event more in a dynastic than in a national perspective. Queen Ragnhildr's dream, prophesying the event, is concerned with Haraldr's numerous descendants and the glorious future of many of them, not with national unification.[3] Nor is the event quite as unique in a dynastic perspective as in a national one, as the dynasty had previously governed a great kingdom, Sweden.[4] Nevertheless, the event is sufficiently singular for Snorri to need a "mythical" explanation to account for the fact that Haraldr conceived such an extraordinary idea as to conquer the whole country. The conquest itself is also described in a different way from the normal conflicts within the system. To some extent then, the conquest represents something radically new, which permanently changes the course of Norwegian history.

The radical novelty of this event, however, gives direct evidence of the contrast between Snorri's periodization and ours. In the modern "myth" of the "unification of the kingdom" (rikssamling), this crucial event is the result of a long development in which the political unification is the manifestation of an inherent tendency toward unity, which has previously been expressed on the geographical, cultural, social, and economic level.[5] The unification of the kingdom is a watershed in Norwegian history and may certainly be considered a unique event. But it is entirely explicable in terms of previous development, and there is thus no need for a "mythical" explanation of Haraldr's plan. When Snorri needs such an explanation, it is because he sees no such organic connection and accordingly has a conception of historical change that differs radically from ours.

His continuation of the theme of the united monarchy versus government by local rulers is of somewhat greater relevance. Having described Óláfr's suppression of the petty kings of Eastern Norway, Snorri comments that Óláfr was now the only one who bore the name of king in Norway.[6] As a matter of fact, the petty kings were finally suppressed. Though the country was divided several times in the following period, such divisions were either the result of civil war or temporary arrangements between pretenders belonging to the ruling dynasty. Nor does Snorri refer to magnates with the same power and resources as Erlingr Skjálgsson or Einaar þambarskelfir or the same ambitions to remain independent of the king after the fall of the latter.[7] Though such differences are certainly very significant from a modern point of view, the importance Snorri attaches to them should not be exaggerated. After all, the game is basically the same throughout *Heimskringla*. The disappearance of the petty kings should be considered against the fact that the power and influence of the magnates are more important than their titles. The difference between Erlingr Skjálgsson and Einarr þambarskelfir and their counterparts in the twelfth century is one more of degree than of kind. And when some modern historians point to the difference between the struggles between strong kings and magnates of the first half of the eleventh century and the civil wars of the mid-twelfth century, which were largely waged between strong *lendir menn* with kings as figure heads (see, for example, Sandvik, 1955: 73 ff.), Snorri's explanation to this is certainly not different political structures, but the different characters of the kings.

One turning point in particular is conspicuous through its absence: the death of King Sigurðr jórsalafari in 1130, which marked the beginning of a period of more than a hundred years of recurrent internal wars, lasting until 1240. To most modern historians this epoch stands out in contrast to the peaceful periods before and after, and the explanation of this change has been one of the classical themes of scholarly discussion.[8] The origin of this discussion can be found already in the Middle Ages, within the clerical tradition in Theodoricus and within the royal one in *The King's Mirror* and some diplomas (Bagge, 1987b: 47 ff.).

By contrast, Snorri narrates Sigurðr's death and Magnús's and later Haraldr's succession in the same way as any other succession and later refers to several peaceful periods after 1130.[9] His only possible reference to a turning point around this time is his story of King Sigurðr's dream, prophecying the advent of Haraldr gilli (*Msyn.* chap. 25; also in *Msk.*: 395 f.). The king dreams of a tree, drifting ashore from the west and being shattered so that its parts spread all along the coast, most of them small, but some large. The dream makes the king sad and might easily be interpreted as a reference to the civil wars. Snorri's explicit interpretation, however, as put in the king's mouth, is that the shattered parts are Haraldr's numerous offspring and their different fate. Admittedly, dreams in Snorri normally signal turning points or great events. Snorri therefore most probably regards Haraldr's advent as a turning point, but from the point of view of the dynasty more than for the country as a whole. The king's sadness is easily explained through the consequences of Haraldr's advent for his own offspring. To the dynasty as a whole, Haraldr's advent marks the beginning of a series of important events, because of his numerous descendants and their different fate and mutual rivalry.

There is, however, another difference between the later phase of the civil wars, that is, from about 1160, and almost all earlier conflicts that Snorri describes, namely the prolonged struggles between the factions and the rather fixed lines between them. A conspicuous success is no longer sufficient to bring about the final victory by causing mass defections from the opposite faction. That is: the game has changed. In the contemporary sagas, starting with that of Sverrir, the descriptions of conflicts differ considerably from those of Snorri. Snorri seems to some extent to have noticed the fact, but explains it in terms of character more than in terms of structural change: Erlingr skakki was a hard man, who did not easily pardon his enemies. Consequently, they fought to the bitter end, thus causing prolonged wars (ME chap. 37). Erlingr's extraordinary measure, condemning his enemies to the Devil, is also regarded in personal terms instead of being linked to the ideological change that took place at the time. There is thus room for the changes in this phase of the civil wars within Snorri's general "model" of history. After all, "laws" of history, both those of Snorri and those of modern historians, are full of exceptions. Individuals like Erlingr skakki and later King Sverrir may act in a different way from most men, without this leading to a fundamental change in the rules of the game.

The kind of modern periodization assumed by Koht and others thus turns out to be an anachronism. But that does not mean that Snorri has no periodization at all. Opposing the attempts to attribute to Snorri a modern, linear view of history, A. Ya. Gurevich finds a cyclical pattern in *Heimskringla:* one king is raised to power by the people, then grows tyrannical and is replaced by another, who develops in the same way, and so forth (1971: 42 ff.; see also 1969: 48 ff.). In a more general analysis of medieval concepts of time—including those of Snorri and his milieu—Gurevich points to its concrete character and close connection to human actions and the rhythm of nature (Gurevich, 1983: 98 ff.). Snorri's periodization is cyclical in the sense that there is no progress and the same things recur. But it is difficult to find such a regular pattern as Gurevich assumes, and there is hardly evidence for attaching so great importance to "constitutional" struggles.

In contrast to Gurevich and Steblin-Kamensky, who in a certain sense are heirs to the Germanistic tradition of the last century, Gerd Weber places Old Norse historiography, including Snorri, within a European Christian framework: his periodization is based on Christian typology and serves to link the history of the Nordic people to the general history of the world, governed by God (Weber, 1987: 109 ff.).

There is one clear example that Snorri uses the introduction of Christianity as a principle of periodization. When commenting on the fall of Earl Hákon, he states that one reason for this was that "the time had come when heathen worship and idolators were done away with and the sacred faith and the right morals took their place."[10] There is no reason to doubt that Snorri here accepts a Christian interpretation of history and divides his chronology accordingly. Nor is this an isolated example in Snorri's thought, as he expands on such ideas in his *Edda*.[11] In *Heimskringla,* however, this statement stands fairly isolated and cannot be used as evidence for Snorri's general principles of periodization or interpretation of history. It belongs to exactly the same category as the one concerning Haraldr hárfagri. It is an example of a force outside the normal chain of events, in this case God's direct intervention. Further, its function is strictly confined to explaining the fate of Earl Hákon. There is no preparation of the new epoch in terms of an increasing number of conversions, dissatisfaction with the old religion, and so forth. On the contrary, the change is mainly brought about through the efforts of the two great kings, Óláfr Tryggvason and St. Óláfr, in a way that does not differ fundamentally from the normal way of gaining power within the existing political system. Nor is there any logical connection between Hákon's paganism and his fall. He was deposed by the thoroughly pagan population of Trøndelag, who admittedly turned to the Christian Óláfr Tryggvason, but certainly not because of his Christianity. Finally, the introduction of Christianity does not constitute a new epoch within Snorri's main story of secular history. Admittedly, there is a change on the supernatural level, in that most examples of witchcraft belong to the pagan period and are substituted by the miracles worked by the Christian kings. There may be some hints at a logical connection between monarchy and Christianity in Snorri's description of King Hálfdan and King Haraldr's "enlightened" attitude to religion and in Óláfr Haraldsson's combination of Christianity and the new unification of the kingdom.[12] Generally, however, religion plays a subordinate part in Snorri's actual narrative both before and after the introduction of Christianity, and it is difficult to find any real change within the field that is Snorri's main interest, the game of politics.

It is also strange that Snorri attaches so little importance to linking his history of the Norwegian dynasty to world history. Admittedly, he places the original residence of its founder, Óðinn, on the map of ancient geography, in Asia north of the Black Sea (Great Svitjod, *Yngl.* chap. 1; see also Weber: 114). But this is very much in the periphery of the ancient world, in the realm of the barbarians. Snorri regards Óðinn's reign as roughly contemporary with the Roman conquests (*Yngl.* chap. 5) but does not seem interested in establishing any chronological link between these events and the history of the North. Neither the reign of Augustus nor the birth of Christ is mentioned, though Snorri refers to this in his *Edda*.[13] Snorri's reference to the Roman conquest may be regarded as a sort of *divisio imperii:* Óðinn was foresighted and versed in the art of magic. He knew that his descendants were to live on the northern half of the earth and acted accordingly, conquering these regions and setting his sons up as rulers.[14] Having made this division of the world, Snorri completely loses interest in the main events of European history, except insofar as they are directly relevant to the history of the Norwegian kings. As we have seen, he is not even interested in pointing out the chronological links between their reigns and those of contemporary kings in other countries. This is in clear contrast to the learned or ecclesiastical tradition of the North, as for instance Theodoricus Monachus and the Icelandic annals.[15] Thus, though Snorri may have known ecclesiastical divisions of world history and even occasionally made use of them, there is little to indicate that such divisions governed his historical narrative.

The reference to the introduction of Christianity does not stand completely by itself, however. Snorri distinguishes between "the age of creation" (bruna-ǫld) and "the age of burial mounds" (haugs-ǫld).[16] Within this schema, the introduction of Christianity probably forms the third period. Whether this is a kind of learned periodization dating from Snorri's time, or it is a popular way of referring to the very distant past, perhaps derived from grave monuments that were visible at the time, is difficult to tell. It apparently corresponds to no traditional or ecclesiastical division of time (see Hastrup, 1985: 17 ff.). As a practical means of periodization it is a little better than the six ages of traditional Christian historiography, but hardly adequate for Snorri's purpose. The shift from the first to the second age took place in the distant past, long before the majority of the events Snorri is telling, and the shift to the third one in the late tenth century or well within the first third of Snorri's work. Admittedly, this shift was not completed until after the battle of Stiklestad, thus including by far the largest of Snorri's sagas. Nevertheless, it seems of little relevance to most of Snorri's material. Further, Snorri only indirectly refers to the transition from "the age of cremation" to the "age of burial mounds" in *Ynglinga saga* and does not even indicate when it took place.[17]

In Gurevich's opinion, this is an archaic periodization, which differs from that of contemporary clerical historiography, in that "*ǫld* is not a chronological course of time, but a qualitative and precise condition of the people" (1969: 49). Taking its starting point in human activity, this periodization changes from people to people: the age of burial mounds started earlier in Denmark than in Sweden and Norway. Though the characterization is quite correct, this is hardly evidence of a specifically archaic mode of thought, as periodization in modern archeology (bronze age, iron age, etc.) is of exactly the same kind.

It is quite possible that this three-fold division of time is of learned or Christian origin and that the comment on Earl Hákon's fall is thus less isolated in Snorri's narrative than it appears at first sight. On the other hand, its practical importance in *Heimskringla* as a whole should not be exaggerated. It is a kind of superimposed periodization with little connection to the actual events. This feature makes it less important to Snorri than to clerical historiography. This is the same difference as the one we found by comparing their chronological principles: in the absolute chronology of the annalistic clerical chronicle, the logical order is created by the orderly division of time, regardless of the connection between the events. The clerical chronicler regards human history *sub specie aeternitatis*. This gives him fixed principles of chronology, periodization, and historical causation, which are derived from the eternal order of the universe, created by God, and are superimposed on human events. By contrast, Snorri's relative chronology is subordinated to the events, serving to underline their inner, logical connection.

By insisting on explanation in purely human terms and on linking together events in a logical way, Snorri appears more familiar to modern readers of history than his clerical contemporaries. But his modernity is from one point of view an illusion: the events are linked together in a short-term perspective, one conflict within the game of politics, at most the reign of one king, as in the case of St. Óláfr. It is thus not the kind of long-term planning of political action, which accompanied the rise of the early modern, absolutist state and in its turn led to the modern, linear view of history (Koselleck, 1981: 174 ff.). In this perspective clerical historiography is the more modern, in its insistence on a universal history, with a strict chronology and periodization, despite its lack of "inner" connection between the events.

This difference between Snorri and clerical historiography corresponds to the one we have found regarding the life of the individual, the tendency toward vivid narrative and impressionistic glimpses on the one hand and all-embracing, abstract principles on the other. Snorri occasionally adopts the clerical schema, as in the biography of St. Óláfr, where he divides the life of the king into three periods and to some extent describes three different persons. But these three characters only cover a limited part of Snorri's real Óláfr, who is mostly found in vivid descriptions of the king in action and encounters with other persons. Like individual characters, history to Snorri is a series of actions and events, which to some extent can be linked together into chronological and causal chains but which do not form a coherent whole. History has really neither beginning nor end, nor a fixed periodization. Individual life admittedly has both beginning and end and even some sort of "natural" periodization, but from point of view of Snorri's interests, political action, this plays a relatively subordinate role. In both cases, Snorri focuses on events and the short-term perspective. And though he occasionally borrows the chronological framework of clerical historiography or other sources, this does not really form an organizing principle.

The Purpose of History

Explicit statements on the purpose of their works are rare in Norse historians, except for the clerical authors, who refer to the usual moral reasons of European historiography. In his prologue, Snorri is solely concerned with the problem of arriving at the truth about the past and thus takes for granted that this truth is worth knowing. The question of his purpose must therefore be answered from the work itself.

This question began to be asked in connection with the increasing emphasis on his original authorship, in the modern sense, above all by Koht. In attributing to Snorri "an overall interpretation of history," Koht distinguished between an implicit aspect, of which Snorri was not conscious, but which made him describe the past according to models taken from society as he knew it in his own time, and explicit evaluation of men, actions, and ideas. Koht's reinterpretation of the sagas was above all concerned with the former aspect. But it had important concequences for the latter as well. First, his description of Snorri's "overall view" of Norwegian history implies a wish on Snorri's part to explain history in a similar way as that of a modern historian. Second, Koht finds a close connection between historiography and political propaganda under Sverrir and his successors, which makes it possible to identify the "party label" of any particular author and thus implies that political propaganda was an important purpose for the historians. Finally, though Koht makes a clear distinction in principle between implicit models of the world and society and explicit propaganda purposes, this distinction is not always clear in practice. After Koht, there has been a certain trend among historians to detect "bias" in the saga writers and classify them accordingly. The philologists, however, have sometimes protested against this, stressing the "objectivity" of the saga writers and the purely literary purpose of their works.[18] Paasche in particular has given some, in my opinion largely, convincing arguments against Koht's (Paasche, 1967: 56 ff.).

Koht's and other historians' view of the propagandistic purpose of the sagas is intimately connected with their belief in an ideological or class struggle and with their implicit assumption that Snorri and his contemporaries had similar ideas of historical development as we have. As we have seen, the "developmental" perspective, which is so natural to us, is largely absent from Snorri's work, and history cannot therefore be intended to explain how the present "grows out" of the past. Rather than asking the "modern" question of the importance of the past, we must therefore ask what was interesting in the kind of stories told in *Heimskringla* and similar works. Whether they had happened recently or long ago was of minor importance, as the sort of events they dealt with could happen at any time, and many of the protagonists were the ancestors of Snorri's contemporaries, or even his own.

From this point of view the answer to the question of the purpose of history becomes very simple. In a society where a man is what he has achieved in the eyes of other men, it is essential, both from point of view of the actors themselves and society as a whole, to record and make known the achievements of great men. The sentiment behind this may be illustrated through an episode from *Sturlunga saga,* quoted by Paasche to illustrate this point. In 1252 Þorgils skarði is taken prisoner and expects to be executed. When asked by another man why he is so silent (i.e., sorrowful), he replies: "I am thinking of how evil it seems if there will be no story to tell of me before the end of my life."[19] This importance of one's reputation after death is further emphasized in the famous words of *Hávamál,* which are echoed in *The King's Mirror:* All men die, but their memory survives, for good or evil. Consequently, one must live in such a way as to be remembered for great deeds (*Hávamál* verses 76–77; see also *Kgs.*: 56, lines 1–7 and Holm-Olsen, 1970: 106 f.). From point of view of the public, the stories of great men were of course entertaining. But they also fulfilled an important function in confirming and strengthening the fundamental values of society. And from a practical point of view: how could a man be expected to perform heroic deeds if there was no one to tell about them?

This important function can be carried out in different ways in different societies. In feudal Europe, at least in the later Middle Ages, there were heralds present at battles, who reported outstanding performances and whose reports were probably among the sources for later chronicles (Keen, 1982: 405 ff.). There is no evidence of this in Norway and Iceland at Snorri's time. A more informal and far more widespread means is the drinking parties in the mens' houses and similar places, which are known from societies all over the world, including Homeric Greece.[20] This is also to be found in Snorri's society. When Ásbjǫrn selsbani returns to Avaldsnes after his ill-fated expedition to revenge the shame Selþórir has brought upon him, he finds that there is a drinking party going on. He enters the house and discovers Þórir standing before the king's seat and telling a story (saga)—the one of his encounter with Ásbjǫrn the year before! When Þórir tells that Ásbjǫrn was crying when his sails were confiscated, Ásbjǫrn is unable to control himself, rushes forward, and kills Þórir (OH chap. 118, *Hkr* vol. 2: 253 f.). Similarly, the winter before, when Ásbjǫrn has returned defeated and empty-handed, he is unable to invite guests for the customary party at Christmas, and he also refuses his uncle Þórir hundr's invitation. This man, who has spent so much effort in being able to entertain other men with lavish hospitality, thus prefers to sit alone during the Christmas celebration—and must even endure further scorn because of this, when Þórir hundr comments on his refusal in the following way:

> There is . . . a great difference between us kinsmen of Ásbjǫrn in the honor he does us, and he makes that plain, seeing the effort he put forth this summer to visit Erlingr and his kin at Jæren; whereas now he disdains to come to me who lives next door to him! I don't know but he fears that Seal-Thórir be there on every islet.[21]

Evidently, Ásbjǫrn cannot support the thought of having to sit together with other men at the drinking table, listening to their jokes over his unsuccessful expedition. The drinking table is the great tribunal, where a man's deeds are evaluated. Characteristically, the *mannjafnaðr* takes place at such an occasion, and quarrels starting here may lead to armed conflict.

To what extent the stories told in *Heimskringla* have actually been told at drinking parties and how great similarity there is between oral and written versions is of course difficult to tell, but this is of less importance in this connection. What is essential is that the saga literature performs the same *function* as this storytelling. Thus, Snorri's battle descriptions mostly consist of examples of individual brave deeds and he often goes out of his way to report heroic behavior, even from minor characters. This function must have been taken for granted by the saga writers and their public to such an extent that they hardly reflected on it and hence felt no inclination or need to give explicit reasons for why their stories were worth telling. The saga thus represents, in a much more direct sense than modern historiography "the judgment of history."

This is also the main explanation to the "objectivity" of the sagas. Evidently, the sagas are not objective in the sense that they do not accord praise or blame, but they contain no consistent party bias. The sagas more resemble heroic poetry (see Bandle, 1969: 1 ff.) than the ideological historiography of nineteenth-century Norway with which Koht and other modern historians were familiar. Their storytelling is the expression of a society of shared values. One does not fight for ideas or group interests, one fights one's own or one's leaders' personal enemies, who belong to the same social stratum and share the same values as oneself. Of course, one may be tempted to present the enemy in a bad light, as the cause of the quarrel or as performing less well than oneself or one's ancestors. But it does not always serve one's own reputation to detract one's enemies. After all, there is no glory in defeating a coward or a bad warrior. Nor is it of great importance to have the right cause, if we are to judge from Snorri and other saga writers. An even more important argument for some amount of "objectivity" is the fact that the conflicts do not normally take place between permanent groups, which last for generations. Though there may be bias in favor of particular kindreds, it is hardly likely that the tradition was usually formed by one particular kindred in isolation. Rather, it was formed in public, where men from different kindreds and different factions of the countries in question, Norway and Iceland, met. The tradition is thus the result of stories told before men who for the most part did not favor any particular party in the conflicts, that is, before the "objective tribunal" of the drinking parties.

Admittedly, this situation did change with the later phase of the Norwegian civil wars, which were to some extent ideological, and with the rise of a new monarchy, propagating its quite explicit ideology, which was definitely not shared by everyone. This monarchy took historiography into its service, and sagas like *Sverris saga* and *Hákonar saga* and to some extent *Fagrskinna* bear the stamp of monarchical ideology. Nevertheless, the heroic tradition of the early saga telling lingered on and must be the main explanation for the amount of objectivity with which even the authors of these sagas treated the adversaries of the dynasty.[22] Though it is not unreasonable to see some connection between the composition of *Heimskringla* and Snorri's contact with Norway, this work seems relatively unaffected by ideological bias, and may, despite its late date, be considered one of the best examples of the "heroic" and "objective" tradition in storytelling and saga writing. This is no doubt a consequence of its Icelandic origin, as there was no parallel to the Norwegian ideological conflicts and rise of the monarchy in the Icelandic struggles of Snorri's time.

Though the "publication" of heroic deeds was the *raison d'être* of the whole genre of saga writing, the past also had other functions in Snorri's society, which are evident in its use by several of his characters. Most commonly, the past serves as a justification, either in the legal or quasi-legal sense of legitimizing claims to a kingdom, special rights, and so forth, or more generally in pointing to the behavior of people in the past as a norm for the present. The past is frequently invoked in the long story of the conflict and negotiations between St. Óláfr and his Swedish namesake. Brynjólfr úlfaldi refers to the ancient borderline between Norway and Sweden and to the difficulty for the people of Ránríki to maintain their Norwegian allegiance and then, somewhat illogically, as Lie points out (1937: 103), declares his support for the king of Norway (OH chap. 61). King Óláfr of Sweden gives a long historical exposition in response to Hjalti's careful attempt to take up negotiations between Norway and Sweden (OH chap. 72: 117 ff.). Its main purpose is to demonstrate the superiority of the Swedish kings over the Norwegian ones and to justify Óláfr's own right to rule Norway, which he has won from Óláfr Tryggvason in the battle of Svǫlð. In these cases history, or rather the past, comes close to having its normal legal function as the justification of claims on property. Other examples of this are St. Óláfr's speech when claiming Norway (OH chap. 35), Hárekr at Tjøtta on the traditional rights of the *lendir menn* (OH chap. 123: 268), Óláfr in response to King Cnut's claims on Norway, when he contrasts Gormr, who was content with ruling the whole of Denmark to his succcessors who seek to rule countries belonging to other kings (OH chap. 131: 285).

In their "constitutional" speeches Ásbjǫrn of Medalhus and Þorgnýr lǫgmaðr appeal to the past as a norm. Ásbjǫrn defends the faith of their fathers and ancestors, which the people maintained from the "burning-age" and through the present age, the "mound-age," "and they were better men than we, and yet this faith has served us very well."[23] Þorgnýr compares the present king of Sweden—unfavorably—to his ancestors and contrasts his attempt to win Norway with the traditional Swedish policy of conquering land in the Baltic region (OH chap. 80: 142 ff.). The opposition against Magnús góði's harsh rule in the beginning of his reign also appeals to the past, though less explicitly (MG chaps. 15–16). In the standard discussion on whether to fight or flee when the enemy is approaching, appeal is often made to the past, for example, by the old Egill ullserkr when Hákon góði is surprised by the Eiríkssons (HG chap. 23).

An example of a strong fascination with the past is the story of Óðinn's visit to Óláfr Tryggvason on the king's journey in Western Norway to convert the people there. Óðinn is an old and wise man and the king asks him about King Ǫgvaldr, after whom the farm where King Óláfr is staying, Avaldsnes (Old Norse: Ǫgvaldznes) has got its name. Óðinn tells him this and many other things from the past. Óláfr is so fascinated that he cannot leave him, but the bishop—who apparently suspects the identity of the stranger—eventually manages to part them (OT chap. 64). This story is not Snorri's own invention but is taken almost word for word from Oddr munkr.[24]

The examples above, which can be divided into three groups, the past as legitimation of rights, as norm for behavior, and as mysterious wisdom, are all closely related to the idea underlying the heroic stories. As in most societies, modern society included, people's rights in Snorri's society are based on tradition, but in Snorri's society they are exclusively so. There are no general human rights and no divine right of the kind which according to ecclesiastical thought regulated the position of the clergy and partly of the king. Similarly, the values of Snorri's society are not abstract norms derived from a few fundamental principles as in Christianity and other philosophical and theological systems, they are implicit in the way people normally act. Just as inspiration for heroic behavior must be sought in the deeds of other men, that is, in the past, the decision concerning particular rights or ways of acting in particular situations must be sought in the past. This also explains Óláfr Tryggvason's fascination with Óðinn's stories. In one sense this example seems different, in presenting the past as something mysterious, which arouses fascination and curiosity. However, the story hardly implies that the past is qualitatively different from the present. Knowledge of human affairs is knowledge of the past. Óðinn is wise because he knows things that are hidden from most people. This is the enormous attraction of his wisdom, but it is not qualitatively different from that of ordinary human beings. As in the original Greek—of which Snorri and his contemporaries evidently had no knowledge—history thus means knowledge. Through his conversation with Óðinn, Óláfr is able to acquire all the wisdom and knowledge that is accessible to man.[25]

Another, and less frequent use of history is the pragmatic. King Hroerekr's speech at the meeting of the Oppland kings to discuss the election of Óláfr is an example of this. Hroerekr recapitulates Norwegian history from the time of Hákon góði to the present and analyzes it from the point of view of the petty kings. His way of doing so is in clear contrast to modern historicist thought: his concern is not to show how the present—and the future—"grows out" of the past. Using the past as a collection of examples of the results of various regimes, he tries to determine the likely result of a particular choice in the present. The choice is between a descendant of Haraldr hárfagri and a foreign king, and Hroerekr shows the results of similar choices in the past. One passage sounds like a "law" on the advantage of foreign kings: it is better to have a king that is far away, for he will not interfere with the independence of the petty kings.[26] However, not all the examples support this generalization, and Hroerekr's explicit conclusion is only that the present conditions are satisfactory, and that a change may easily be for the worse. Hroerekr's speech is therefore less an example of history as material for generalizations than of the fact that men usually act out of experience. Characteristically, Hroerekr's examples are confined to what may possibly be his own lifetime.[27] Another example of a similar type is Sigurðr sýr's speech in response to Óláfr, when he comes to claim the kingdom: Óláfr is a brave man—too much so in Sigurðr's opinion—

and he will have great difficulties in fighting the kings of Denmark and Sweden. In spite of this, he will probably have popular support, for the people always want something new. This was also the case with Óláfr's predecessor, Óláfr Tryggvason, who was universally acclaimed at his arrival. But his rule did not last long (OH chap. 35: 49).

The general idea underlying this use of history may be illustrated by the comment on the use of biblical examples in *The King's Mirror:*

> The world is now so ancient that, no matter what comes to pass, one is likely to find that similar events have occurred before; and nothing is likely to happen of which a learned man can find no examples.[28]

In *The King's Mirror* the examples serve a legal and moral purpose: the king should learn from them to pass the appropriate judgment on those appearing before his tribunal, considering all relevant circumstances behind their acts, above all the intention (Bagge, 1987*b*: 53 ff.). This is also the most common function of pragmatic history in European sources, although the question of the most useful way of arranging things gradually receives more attention, above all with the revival of Aristotle's political thought from around 1260.

This pragmatic use of history is not fundamentally different from the ones we have considered so far. After all, if one is to learn from experience, one must have some criteria for applying the examples derived from the past to the present situation. Nevertheless, there are more or less explicit ways of using such examples. The general trend, with the development of scholasticism and university education, was in the direction of explicit use of examples that were strictly relevant to the general statement they were intended to prove or illustrate. Within the mirrors of princes, the change from the loose, anecdotal use of examples in John of Salisbury's *Policraticus* to their strict submission to the general argument in Aquinas's *De regno* is a case in point.[29] Though Snorri evidently does not belong to the scholastic tradition, in this particular field he moves in the same direction compared to his predecessors. Both the examples quoted above are taken from passages that are in all likelihood composed by Snorri himself. Another characteristic feature of Snorri's, related to this, is his many generalizations: people normally submit to a superior army. Many kings with large *hirð*s are a great burden for a country and may cause famine, which explains people's belief that the king is responsible for the harvests. The people are helpless when their leader is killed. People who come to great power often grow arrogant (MG chap. 7). In addition to his explicit generalizations we may note his implicit ones, which are evident in his analyses of the political game and which allow him to reconstruct the intentions of men like Einarr þambarskelfir and Kálfr Árnason. Men normally act to further their own interests. Changes in loyalty can easily be explained in this way, as can success and failure in the political game. Thus, his way of describing politics is much more consistent and explicit than that of his predecessors. He often changes the traditional stories in a way that makes the actors appear as rational politicians according to Snorri's standards. And his concept of historical causation clearly emphasizes the importance of choosing the most prudent course of action. In sum: Snorri's *Heimskringla* represents a development from its predecessors in two related ways, from individual heroic acts to the game of politics and from history as stories illustrating implicit values to a more deliberately pragmatic historiography.

Snorri and the Supernatural

In Snorri's account of the rise and fall of St. Óláfr, we have noticed a strong tendency to play down the supernatural explanations of his predecessors in favor of natural or human causes. This is a general feature of Snorri's work.

Snorri's "rationalism" has been pointed out by several scholars. Edvard Bull even claims to find Snorri's own doubt in Queen Álfífa's skeptical words concerning the miracle that Óláfr's hair and beard had grown after his death: "Mighty little do bodies decompose when buried in sand. It would not be the case if he had lain in earth."[30] This is clearly wrong, both the context and Snorri's numerous stories of miracles show that the words are meant to characterize Álfífa's stubborness, not Snorri's own opinion.[31] It is correct that Snorri includes relatively fewer miracles than earlier historians,[32] and there are a few examples that he gives less fantastic versions of the ones he includes. Whether this is evidence of a rationalistic attitude that differs from that of his predecessors, however, remains to be examined.

The saga of Óláfr Tryggvason is the one in *Heimskringla* that contains most miracles and supernatural events. These stories in turn form a selection from Snorri's source, Oddr munkr's *Saga Óláfs Tryggvasonar* (see Andersson, 1977). Snorri makes occasional changes in the stories he does derive from Oddr, of which the following are of relevance for his belief in the supernatural. In the story of Óláfr's opponents at the popular assembly in Rogaland, who were suddenly unable to speak, Snorri omits Oddr's explanation, that St. Martin had visited Óláfr in a dream the night before, promising to help him on the condition that his toast was substituted for that of the pagan gods at the traditional celebrations (*SagaOT:* 94 ff.; see also OT chap. 55). Oddr further emphasizes Óláfr's special relationship to St. Martin in the statement that the saint spoke through the king's mouth when he propagated Christianity, thus enabling him to convert his audience (*SagaOT:* 113). In the story of Eyvindr kelda's attempt to kill Óláfr, Snorri differs to some extent from Oddr, but both stories contain supernatural elements. According to Oddr, Eyvindr and his men became blind when seeing the church (*SagaOT:* 134 ff.), whereas in Snorri's version, they used magic to cast darkness over their enemies, but were trapped by their own devices (OT chap. 63). Further, in the story of Eyvindr kinnrifa, who is tortured to death by Óláfr for refusing to convert to Christianity, Snorri omits most of Eyvindr's account of his origin. But he retains its essential contents, that Eyvindr was a spirit, brought into a man's body through Finnish magic and therefore unable to accept Christianity (OT chap. 76; see also *SagaOT:* 139 f.). Finally, Snorri omits the story that a hart runs out of the body of the dead Þórir hjǫrtr (hart), which is then killed by Óláfr's dog Vígi.[33] Only the last change definitely makes the story more rational. In the other cases, Snorri gives less detailed accounts of supernatural phenomena, but hardly less fantastic. The sudden silence of Óláfr's adversaries at the popular assembly is clearly presented as a miracle whether or not St. Martin had promised to perform it beforehand. It does not matter greatly from this point of view whether a sorcerer is blinded by seeing a church or through his own devices or whether an evil spirit in a man's body tells of his origin in more or less detail.

Nor is it easy to give a general explanation of Snorri's criteria for including Oddr's stories or not. Snorri omits the following of Oddr's miraculous stories: the story of Sunnefa and the Seljumenn, the Irish refugees who found their death at the Western coast of Norway and whose bodies were discovered through a miracle (*SagaOT:* 96 ff.), of God revealing himself to Óláfr, who is carried away from his men in a supernatural way (ibid.: 151 ff.), of Óláfr's meeting with the pagan god Þórr (ibid.: 173 f.), of some of Óláfr's men witnessing a meeting of trolls, complaining at their vain attempts to seduce the king (ibid.: 174 ff.), and of Óláfr's escape from the battle of Svǫlð, his life as a saint in Palestine, and the miracles he performed after his death (ibid.: 240 ff.).

In this last case, Óláfr's escape, which strictly speaking does not have to do with the supernatural, Snorri refers to the story but does not go into details, quoting a stanza by Hallfrøðr, who refused to believe in such rumors. There were different opinions on this point among Snorri's contemporaries,[34] and when Snorri even had at his disposal a contemporary witness who did not believe in it, he had good reasons to be skeptical. This evidently has nothing to do with his belief in the supernatural. Nor is skepticism toward supernatural phenomena necessarily his reason for omitting the rest of Oddr's stories, though some of them are fairly fantastic. After all, if one can believe in an evil spirit incarnating itself into a man's body through Finnish magic, why not also in a hart running out of a dead man's body or trolls discussing their failure to seduce King Óláfr?

Snorri's criteria for including such stories or not probably have to do with relevance rather than trustworthiness. This clearly applies to the story of the Seljumenn, which is of little relevance for the life of Óláfr. The stories of Óláfr's revelations and of the trolls mainly concern the king's inner life, which is not of great interest to Snorri. Finally, there was little reason for Snorri to tell the story of Þórr when he had already included a similar story of Óðinn. By contrast, all the miracles Snorri does include have to do with Óláfr's Christianization of Norway, which is one of the main themes in his saga.[35] Though Snorri's conversion stories generally bear considerable resemblance to his normal description of the political game, the introduction of Christianity has a supernatural dimension and is thus the field *par excellence* of divine intervention. Therefore, Snorri includes the miracles that take place in this connection and omits the rest.

The miracles of St. Óláfr start toward the end of the king's life and then occur regularly throughout *Heimskringla*, without any connection with the sagas in which they are placed.[36] In Snorri's original arrangement, however, they were placed together after Óláfr's death in the *Separate Saga* (vol. 1: 627 ff.). In defending these miracles as authentic writings of Snorri, Gustav Storm tries to show that Snorri's exactness and critical attitude is at work even here: he supplies names and places, apparently from his own interrogations at the places, and he accepts only the most trustworthy of the numerous accounts of miracles worked by the saintly king.[37]

A comparison with Snorri's direct or indirect sources shows that he has indeed been very restrictive. He includes almost all of the small number of miracles mentioned by Einarr Skúlason in his *Geisli* (strophes 20–62, *Skjalded.* vol. A 1: 462 ff., vol. B 1: 432 ff.) and then selects a few that are found in the *Legendary Saga,* Styrmir Kárason's saga of St. Óláfr, and *Passio Olavi.* The criteria for his choice are more difficult to detect. Miracles are by definition inexplicable and are therefore difficult to classify as more or less probable. Most of St. Óláfr's miracles are healings of men or women who are blind, deaf, dumb, or crippled, and there is no great difference between the miracles that are included and those that are not. One story in *Passio Olavi* seems more fantastic than the rest: a farmer was falsely accused of theft, hanged, then for nine hours miraculously supported by an invisible beam and, when finally cut down, fell down a steep cliff with a heap of sharp stones below, from which he was also saved by Óláfr's intervention (*Passio:* 83 ff.). Snorri omits this miracle, but he does include stories of people who have had their tongue cut off or eyes put out and are completely healed (*Msyn.* chap. 30; *Ingi* chaps. 24–25).

A more exact criterion for believing in a miracle or not is how well it is attested. It is fairly usual to refer to witnesses when reporting miracles, and Snorri is no exception.[38] But he is not consistent in this respect, nor is it possible to explain his including a particular miracle or not from such considerations. Some miracles that are included happen to anonymous persons, are undated, and only vaguely located and not confirmed by witnesses or testimony (e.g., *HHarð.* chaps. 56–57; *HHerð.* chaps. 20–21), whereas others that are well attested are not.[39] Snorri's critical attitude is therefore hardly his reason for including so few of Óláfr's miracles. Moreover, such an assumption is in itself unlikely. St. Óláfr was recognized as the great saint of the Nordic countries and his shrine was sought by a large number of people, often coming from far away, and numerous miracles performed by him were officially recognized by the Church and included in written accounts. Can one then really believe that Snorri made an independent examination of his sources to find out what to include and what not? There is nothing in Snorri's text to suggest this. Quite the contrary, he refers to the enormous number of miracles performed by Óláfr, of which the most important had been written down (OH chap. 245), clearly implying that his own stories were only a small selection.

Once more, then, Snorri's selection must be based on relevance and not trustworthiness. His exact criteria are difficult to ascertain but some general observations are possible. First, he omits all or almost all miraculous stories in Óláfr's lifetime before his exile from Norway. These stories are not numerous, only five in the fragments from Styrmir. Four of them take place before Óláfr's arrival in Norway,[40] and only one concerns his Christianization of the country, the subject Snorri most often associates with miracles. This one story deals with Óláfr's meeting with Óðinn (*Separate Saga:* 771 f.) and may have been omitted because it was fairly similar to the story told of Óláfr Tryggvason (OT chap. 64). As for the last period of Óláfr's life, Christianity and the supernatural play a major role, and Óláfr works several miracles. The few stories missing from this part of the work are fairly similar to those already found there and may have been omitted for this reason.[41] Except for Óláfr's intervention in favor of his son in the battle of Hlýrskógsheiðr (MG chaps. 27–28) and his appearance before him in a dream, giving him the choice between death and committing a mortal sin (*HHarð.* chap. 28), the miracles taking place after Óláfr's death are completely without relevance for the sagas in which they are told. If one is to guess why Snorri has picked out just these stories, his main reason seems to be, first, some need of variety concerning the kind of healing (eyes, ears, tongue, legs, etc.) and second, their location, which shows the spread of Óláfr's cult to Denmark, England, France, and even Byzantium. Further, some stories may have been chosen because they were particularly famous, such as the early "classic" stories, immediately after the battle of Stiklestad, that eventually led to Óláfr's canonization, others because they were recent, known in great detail and concerned well-known persons, such as the one of the priest Ríkarðr.

Taken together, these observations suggest the following conclusion. Normally, Snorri wishes to keep separate the natural and the supernatural level. In most of his stories of Óláfr's life, he attributes his successes to his own skill or luck and stresses the secular aspect of his career, thus omitting not only divine intervention but also most references to the king's piety and religious interpretations of the events. In the field where the supernatural is normally most prominent, the conversion stories, there were virtually no miracles to report. Thus, Snorri confines his reports of miracles to his hagiography toward the end of the king's life and to the ones taking place after his death. The latter are the sort of events that are not normally included in *Heimskringla*. Given Óláfr's reputation as a saint, Snorri has nevertheless found it necessary to do so, but has confined himself to a few examples.

At first sight, Snorri uses different criteria in the case of the two Óláfrs, including the miracles that are most relevant to his story in the case of the former and those which are least relevant in the case of the latter. On a closer look, however, his basic principles are the same in both cases. Miracles belong to the supernatural sphere. The reign of Óláfr Tryggvason is the great breakthrough of Christianity in Norway, that is, a change that takes place on the supernatural level and through God's direct intervention. Here miracles are clearly relevant. On the other hand, Óláfr Tryggvason was not canonized and did not become the eternal king of Norway, which means that there was no particular reason to emphasize the miracles worked by him. By contrast, St. Óláfr's special position necessitated just this, whereas miracles concerning the king's work for the Christianization of the country had to be excluded for lack of material. In both cases, Snorri concentrates his miracles in contexts that clearly belong to the supernatural sphere, while describing the kings' normal political activity in secular terms.

Consequently, Snorri's selection of miracles is not in itself evidence of a more critical attitude or of beliefs that differ from those of other medieval authors. What is different, however, is his distinction between the miracles and the rest of the story. Snorri usually confines God's intervention to the miracles, whereas human action or natural causation are invoked to explain the events that form the main theme of the story.

And when God is occasionally invoked even here, there is normally also a natural explanation.[42]

Snorri is probably not in doubt that God stood by Óláfr when he returned to Norway and won the kingdom. He mentions Óláfr's dream, in which he was told to return to his country to become king there eternally,[43] but also gives other, more secular motives for his return. A pious interpretation of the following events might detect God's finger in Óláfr's victory, as the clerical authors actually do, but although Snorri probably held the same belief, he manages to give an entirely natural explanation. When Óláfr after his expulsion from Norway decides to return, his final decision is reached after God's revelation in a dream (OH chap. 188). This dream also occurs in Theodoricus (chap. 18; MHN: 34 f.), though in no other extant source.[44] Snorri may possibly have taken it from Styrmir. Since we do not know exactly his sources, it is difficult to tell how he has formed his own version of the dream, but a certain "rationalization" seems evident.

Having told of the arrival of Bjǫrn stallari with the news that Earl Hákon is dead, Snorri presents Óláfr's deliberations, which—quite unusually—take the form of an "inner dialogue." He has three alternatives. The first is King Jarizleifr's offer of becoming the ruler of Bulgaria, the second to go to Jerusalem or some other holy place to serve God as a monk, and the third to try to regain Norway. Both Óláfr and his men prefer the last alternative, but Óláfr fears the difficulties involved. He can see no clear solution, but leaves the matter to God. Then Óláfr Tryggvason visits him in a dream, blaming him for failing to see that it is his duty and God's will to maintain the kingdom that God has given him and thus to regain it, even at the risk of his life. Óláfr now decides to do what he had wanted most, convincing himself that the country, lacking a prince, will be easy to conquer.

Such a dream is of course easily explained in terms of modern psychology: the dream is the result of Óláfr's deliberations, the subconscious part of his mind coming to the aid of his wish on the conscious level. Snorri most probably did not think in such terms. Nevertheless, the dream is not a manifestation of a *Deus ex machina,* but rather the final step in Óláfr's own reflections. Moreover, God's messenger, Óláfr Tryggvason, does not simply order Óláfr to return, but gives arguments. The dream thus serves to confirm a decision that Óláfr already wanted to take and to point out arguments that he ought to have seen in the first place. From a literary and historiographical point of view it is rather to be regarded as a dramatic embellishment of the story than as Snorri's real explanation of Óláfr's return to Norway.

The dream is also an expression of the fact that this part of the saga is in reality a saint's vita, and is thus another example of supernatural phenomena being placed outside the normal narrative. However, important events are often foretold in dreams, which may or may not be explained as a result of divine intervention. Examples of this are the dreams of Magnús góði before the battle of Hlýrskógsheiðr (MG chap. 27) and before his death (*HHarð*. chap. 28). These are clearly of divine origin. In the dreams of Ragnhildr, Hálfdan svarti, and Sigurðr jórsalafari, there is no direct mention of divine intervention, nor in the dream of Karkr before he kills Earl Hákon (OT chap. 49). The defeat and death of King Haraldr harðráði in the battle at Stamford Bridge is prophesied by St. Óláfr, visiting him in a dream, and by various signs and portents (*HHarð*. chaps. 80–82, 90). Generally, dreams that are clearly the expression of supernatural interventions relatively rarely change the course of events. They may signify death or defeat and the course of new generations, which are largely outside ordinary human control. But the large majority of decisions in *Heimskringla* are reached without aid from supernatural powers.

In his account of the miracles following Óláfr's death, Snorri, as we have seen, remains the pious believer. There is, however, a remarkable passage, which apparently presents a larger problem than Álfífa's skepticism, that is, Snorri's account of Einarr þambarskelfir's "conversion." In Einarr, Snorri gives one of his best portraits of a politician. Having described the first rumors of Óláfr's sainthood, Snorri immediately turns to Einarr, describing his disappointment when not being given the promotion King Cnut had promised him and his increasing lack of enthusiasm for Cnut's cause. Snorri then adds laconically: "Einarr was the first until then of the chieftains to maintain that Óláfr was a saint" ("Einarr varð fyrstr til þess ríkis-manna at halda upp helgi Óláfs konungs," OH chap. 241—*my translation*).

Is this simply a naive statement of fact or is it deliberate irony? As Snorri is generally not naive and has a keen awareness of the political game, the latter alternative clearly seems the more probable. Moreover, Snorri has changed earlier accounts of the events after Óláfr's death exactly in order to emphasize the role of the two magnates Einarr and Kálfr Árnason in using popular resentment against the Danish rule to further their own interests. His account of Óláfr's canonization and victory after his death thus becomes a curious mixture of a saint's legend and political cynicism. Einarr sees clearly that he can further his own interests by promoting belief in Óláfr's sainthood. Shortly afterward he stands forward as a pious believer, blaming Queen Álfífa for her skepticism. Is he a hypocrite? Is Einarr's self-interest one of the causes of Óláfr's canonization? These are obvious questions to a modern observer, but not necessarily to Snorri himself. To him, Óláfr's sainthood is an undisputed fact. His primary interest as a historian, however, does not lie in saints and miracles, but in secular politics. Without in any way disbelieving it, he can regard Óláfr's sainthood and the popular belief in it as political fact, which can be used by astute politicians as any other fact. Once more, we see a clear distinction between the natural and the supernatural and Snorri concentrating on the former.

Witchcraft

In Snorri's opinion witchcraft is linked to the pagan religion. Óðinn, the founder of the dynasty, who was worshiped as a god after his death, was also the great teacher of various arts (íþróttir), including magic. This art (seiðr) is the one that gives the greatest power, enabling its possessor to know things that will happen in the future, to kill or harm people, or to take reason or power from one person and give it to another. But "it is accompanied by so much *ergi* (shame, perversity) that men could not be associated with it without shame, and that is why this art was taught to the goddesses (gyðjur)."[45]

Witchraft is thus highly efficient but shameful, one of the few examples of a means that is disgraceful despite the fact that it serves to win the game. The stories of witchcraft are far more numerous in the pagan period than the Christian. There are a number of examples in *Ynglinga saga*. From the period of Hálfdan svarti, the members of the dynasty are rarely associated with it. Haraldr hárfagri helps a Finn who is a practitioner of witchcraft and is helped by him in return (HS chaps. 8–9) and his son Eirík blóðøx marries Gunnhildr, a woman who has been taught witchraft by the Finns (*HHárf.* chap. 32). Haraldr is seduced by the beauty and charm of Snæfríðr, a Finnish woman, marries her, and forgets everything about his kingdom. This is evidently a result of witchcraft (*HHárf.* chap. 24). One of his sons by her, Rǫgnvaldr réttilbeini, becomes a *seiðmaðr* (magician) when he grows up. But both Haraldr and Eiríkr dislike *seðmenn,* Eiríkr even killing his brother with eighty other *seiðmenn* (*HHárf.* chap. 34). Nor does the great pagan ruler Earl Hákon seem to be a great adherent of *seiðr,* though in one case he possibly uses magic against his enemies: there were rumors that he had sacrificed his son to win the battle of Hjǫrungavágr and that this caused the hailstorm that turned the battle (OT chap. 42). The great battle against the *seiðmenn* is fought by Óláfr Tryggvason, who kills a large number of them (OT chaps. 62–63, 76–80). After the conversion to Christianity there are few examples. Þórir hundr uses magic against the *bjarmar* (Permians) (OH chap. 133: 295) and wears a jacket of reindeerskin, which the Finns have treated with their magic art, as armor in the battle of Stiklestad and is not wounded (OH chap. 193, 228). Some of the Wends who attack Konghelle are also protected from weapons by magic arts (MB.HG chap. 11: 335). Sigurðr slembir has the Finns make ships for him, which are extremely fast (*Ingi* chap. 6). Given the latters' reputation, this may possibly be a reference to witchcraft. Finally, there are rumors that Hákon herðibreiðr's foster mother has hired a witch to bring Hákon victory in the battle near Oslo, where King Ingi is killed (*HHerð*. chap. 16), a rumor that Erlingr skakki later uses in his propaganda against his adversaries (ME chap. 12). Snorri's statement that *seiðr* is shameful for men implies that this means is primarily used by women, persons of low status or in the margin of society. The group most associated with it are the Finns, a term that includes both the modern Finns and the Samis. Most magicians who are directly mentioned are Finns. People of Northern Norway are far more inclined toward witchcraft than people of other regions. Characteristically, Þórir hundr, the only magnate among St. Óláfr's adversaries to use magic, is the one who lives farthest north. The most drastic episodes in Óláfr Tryggvason's crusade against witchraft and paganism also take place in the north. The women of the royal house who are associated with or practice magic are either of Finnish descent (Snæfríðr) or have Finnish connections (Gunnhildr).

In the Christian period, Þórdís skeggja, the witch who allegedly caused King Ingi's death, is a person of whom nothing else is known and who therefore hardly belonged to the upper classes. But Gunnhildr, Hákon's foster mother, who commissioned her, was a person of some standing, having been married to Símun, a "mighty man" (ríkr maðr), though a commoner (bóndi) (*Ingi* chap. 18). Hákon herðibreiðr's men were apparently not marginal in the sense that they were generally recruited from the lower classes, as has often been suggested by modern historians,[46] but they were mostly unsuccessful and unable to defeat their adversaries even when numerically superior (*HHerð*. chaps. 2–11). This may possibly explain their resorting to witchcraft.

In stating that witchcraft is shameful for men, Snorri implies that it is primarily practiced by women. As women are physically weaker and never directly involved in battles or violence in *Heimskringla,* this seems quite logical. However, it is not actually borne out by Snorri's text. Given the association with Finns, members of the royal house who practice witchcraft are likely to be women: no male Finn belongs to the dynasty! Apart from them, however, most practitioners who are directly mentioned are men. Some of them are even quite prominent, like King Haraldr's son and the magnates of Northern Norway who are defeated by Óláfr Tryggvason. Thus, Snorri may be suspected of exaggerating the marginality of the practitioners of witchcraft in his general statement.

In addition to witchcraft, there are less disreputable kinds of supernatural phenomena. The art of foreseeing the future is included in

Snorri's description of witchcraft in the *Ynglinga* saga. The diviner (spámaðr), whom Óláfr Tryggvason visits on the Silcly Isles, is perfectly respectable, probably a Christian hermit, whose prophecy leads to Óláfr's conversion (OT chap. 31; see also *SagaOT:* 43 f.). Before the attack on Konghelle by the Wends, Snorri refers to portents, dogs growing mad and attacking people, women aborting, and so forth. (MB.HG chap. 9). The disastrous result of Haraldr harðráði's expedition to England is also prophesied by dreams and portents (*HHarð.* chaps. 80–82, 90). Some of the dreams in *Heimskringla* are interpreted as the result of divine intervention but this is by no means always the case. Though they are not incompatible with a Christian interpretation, the dreams of the pagans Queen Ragnhildr and King Hálfdan svarti and the Christian King Sigurðr jórsalafari of the future of the dynasty may equally well be understood against a secular background. Haraldr himself is warned by his saintly brother King Óláfr before leaving for England, and a man in the army dreams of a witch, riding on a wolf before the army, and feeding it with dead men's bodies, a traditional sign of death and defeat.[47] Nor do Snorri's dreams very often carry a moral message, in contrast to those of his nephew Sturla Þórðarson's *Íslendinga saga.*[48]

There is no reason to doubt that Snorri believed in the existence of such phenomena,[49] but this does not prevent him from skepticism on particular points. In the case of Hákon herðibreiðr he refers to the rumor but explicitly states that he does not know whether it is true or not.[50] His skepticism may have something to do with the fact that Erlingr skakki, who was quite ruthless in his propaganda against his adversaries, deliberately used this rumor against them. He expresses a similar reservation in the case of Earl Hákon. Having described the battle, he adds that "it is men's saying (sǫgn manna)" that Hákon sacrificed his son (OT chap. 42: 337).[51] No such reservations are expressed concerning the stories in *Ynglinga saga* and Óláfr Tryggvason's saga, which are also integrated in the narrative. The connection between witchcraft and the pagan gods is clearly expressed in the latter saga. According to a widespread opinion in the Middle Ages to which Snorri at least occasionally seems to adhere, the pagan gods were not only human beings who existed in the past, they were still existing as demons and able to help their adherents through magical means, or they were used by the Devil to seduce men.[52] But their "black magic" is of no avail against the far stronger "white magic" of Christ.

Thus, a change takes place in this respect with the advent of Christianity. On the supernatural level there is clearly an evolution in Snorri's picture of history. At the same time, there is a close parallel between his understanding of the supernatural in the pagan and the Christian period. Such phenomena do occur, though not all reports of them are true, and they may occasionally intervene in men's lives. But this happens relatively rarely and does not reduce the importance of normal, rational planning and intelligent exploitation of the political game.

Luck

Whereas God's intervention is for the most part outside the normal narrative, luck is sometimes invoked as the explanation of important events. To Charles M. Radding the development of the concept of chance was one of the great advances of the intellectual revolution of the eleventh and twelfth centuries. People were now no longer, as before that time, forced to seek an inherent justice, sanctioned by divine powers, in everything that happened. This had the important consequence of weakening belief in ordeals, and—potentially, at least—of making historians less inclined to appeal to God's providence as the explanation of human events (Radding, 1985: 63 ff., 250 ff.).

Radding is probably right in regarding the more widespread use of *fortuna* as a kind of secularization, but he identifies it too easily with the modern concept of chance.[53] In medieval historiography, *fortuna* appears as an active force, a kind of secular providence (Hanning, 1966: 126; Green, 1972: 116 f.; Skinner, 1978: 97 f.). Or it is identified with the general tendency for things to change into their opposites, from success to failure and vice versa, as in the image of the wheel of fortune, derived from Boethius, which is found among others in Otto of Freising.[54] Or it depends on astrology, which gave a rational and even predictable account of human events in which the actors' will and intentions play a subordinate part (Green, 1972: 33). Finally, *fortuna* often has the tendency to favor certain men and not others,[55] that is, it represents the exact opposite of the concept of chance in modern statistics, according to which everyone in equal circumstances has the same possibility. The concept of luck is therefore not necessarily an anticipation of modern, secular thought but is rather to be regarded as an example of some kind of supernatural or at least nonhuman force in history that is not identified with the Christian God. Admittedly, it seems difficult from a modern point of view to distinguish luck from personal qualities on the one hand and God on the other. A logically consistent theory of such phenomena is hardly to be expected from medieval popular thought, nor from modern popular thought for that matter. But we can try to make some distinctions on the basis of the practical use of the various concepts.

Snorri refers to fate as an explanation, but only as one out of several.[56] His reference to the power of soothsayers also implies the idea that everything is prearranged: Óláfr Tryggvason asks such a man of his future and receives an exact description of what is going to happen to him immediately afterward (OT chap. 31). The same applies at least to some of his dreams, such as the ones prophesying the future of the dynasty (see Turville-Petre, 1972: 32; Glendinning, 1974: 25). The dreams and portents before Haraldr harðráði's expeditions to England all suggest disaster. Nevertheless, it apparently occurs neither to Haraldr nor to the other Norwegian magnates to cancel the expedition (*HHarð.* chaps. 80–82; see also chap. 90). The idea of an all powerful fate, which determines everything, occurs in a number of other passages in Old Norse literature, but it is difficult to tell how far this determinism really goes (Hovstad, 1948: 131 ff.; Maurer, 1965, vol. 2: 162 f.). In any case, it is not very prominent in Snorri's actual narrative. Men's decisions, ability, and so forth normally seem to be the most important factors in his explanations, whereas luck, or fate, serve to explain the aspects of events which men cannot control and which modern historians explain by chance or structural conditions. Snorri gives no precise definition of his concept of fate, nor does he connect it to astrology, of which he gives no explicit mention.

In most cases, luck or *hamingja*[57] in Snorri, as in other Old Norse sources, is not an impersonal fate, governing human events, but rather a force inherent in particular persons, notably kings and great men (see Grønbech, 1955, vol. 2: 108 ff.; Gurevich, 1971: 44 f.). Except for his last days, Earl Hákon Sigurðarson is a great chieftain, distinguished among other things by his *hamingja* in defeating his enemies (OT chap. 50). During his Viking expedition in Finland, St. Óláfr's *hamingja* proves stronger than the Finns' magic (OH chap. 9). Starting his dangerous expedition to Sweden, Hjalti asks Óláfr to give his *hamingja* to himself and his companion.[58] In their discussions, the petty kings of Opplandene refer to Óláfr's *hamingja* (OH chaps. 36, 74), whereas Óláfr himself boasts that his *hamingja* is superior to that of his adversary, Earl Hákon Eiríksson (OH chaps. 30, 180). In addition, *hamingja/ úhamingja* can simply refer to the good or bad result of an action, as in modern terminology (Hallberg, 1973: 154 f., 156 f.).

According to traditional opinion, represented among others by Grønbech (1955, vol. 2: 108 ff.), the belief in luck was a central element in Nordic religion and mentality, which survived into the Christian period. More recent scholars, notably Walter Baetke (1951: 47 ff., 1973: 345 ff., 1964: 19 ff.) and Lars Lönnroth (1963–1964: 29 f. and 1986: 76 ff.) have pointed out that the idea of luck mainly occurs in late and Christian sources, whereas it is not to be found in the Edda and is very rare in the early scaldic poems. Consequently, this idea must be the result of Christian influence. A number of other scholars have attempted to defend the traditional opinion.[59]

Baetke's approach has both the strength and the weakness of the traditional source criticism. His demonstration of the late occurrence of the idea of luck is certainly worth careful consideration, and he shows convincingly that many of the great constructions of ancient Germanic royal ideology rest on shaky foundations. However, he does not really analyze the various sources and situations in which the idea of luck occurs, nor does he demonstrate the logical connection between these ideas and contemporary Christianity. Though these sources are late, we cannot exclude the possibility that they reflect general attitudes that may originate in traditional society, the less so as the authentic sources of the pagan period are so few that it is risky to exclude the possibility that ideas that are not found there did not exist. Both the references to popular ideas of luck as pagan superstition in Christian sources of the later Middle Ages (Gunnes, 1971: 32; Hallberg, 1973: 143) and Hallberg's statistics, showing that the various terms for luck occur far more frequently in the secular literature of the high Middle Ages than in the typical clerical sources (1973: 161 ff.), make an exclusively Christian origin of these concepts unlikely.

The question of origin cannot be solved from an analysis of Snorri alone, nor is it very relevant in our context. However, we can and must address the question whether Snorri's ideas of luck are derived from the Christian doctrine of God's providence or they must be understood against a different background. There seems to be no logical connection between Snorri's idea of luck and Christian thought. As we have seen, there is a clear difference between Snorri's idea of charismatic kingship and the doctrine of kingship by the grace of God propagated by the contemporary Norwegian monarchy: whereas the former is based on the king's personal qualities, attractiveness, and so forth, qualities that are not specifically royal but in which the king is supposed to surpass other men, the latter emphasizes the radical difference between the king and all others. This also applies to the king's luck. Luck does not only belong to the king, nor necessarily to all kings, nor to one king all the time. By and large, however, the king needs more luck than ordinary men to be able to rule and easily loses his power if luck deserts him.[60]

Though Baetke is right that the concept of luck is particularly prominent in the sagas of the two missionary kings, the Óláfrs, there is nothing to suggest that it is synonymous with God's providence. In the story of Óláfr's dream in which he is told to return to Norway (OH chap. 187), both concepts occur, and it is not easy to distinguish logically between them. In pondering over the difficult decision, Óláfr reflects on the fact that the first ten years of his reign have been successful, whereas afterward everything has gone wrong and the *hamingja* has been against him. He then asks himself whether it is advisable to trust the *hamingja* once more and finally leaves the matter to God. One might solve the difficulty by assuming that God is ultimately behind *hamingja/úhamingja* or that the concepts in this case are only synonyms for success and failure. But there is no direct evidence for this in Snorri's text.

Snorri's explanation of the fall of Earl Hákon seems to imply a closer connection between God and the *hamingja*. The greatest *úhamingja* led to the fall of the great chieftain, says Snorri. And the principal reason for this was that the time had now come for pagan cult to give way to the true faith and right customs. Hákon seems to have been struck by God's providence and God thus to have been behind his *úhamingja*.

The comment on Hákon's *úhamingja* comes as a kind of modification after the description of him as a great and successful chieftain and is probably also intended as a further explanation of his fall, as told by Snorri immediately before.[61] In this story, Hákon is extremely unlucky. His plan of enticing Óláfr Tryggvason to Norway to kill him, ought to have every chance of succeeding. Hákon's position in Norway is very strong as the result of his victory over the *jómsvíkingar* in Hjǫrungavágr the year before, according to Snorri's chronology. Óláfr has a small army and does not expect serious resistance. Then suddenly, a rebellion breaks out in Trøndelag and Hákon is forced to flee. Admittedly, Hákon himself has caused the rebellion because of his offenses against the women of the region, but Snorri hardly regards this as sufficiently serious to cause his fall. It is Hákon's bad luck that this happens just when Óláfr is on his way to Trøndelag. Hákon has to hide and would normally have saved his life but for the fact that he is killed by his own house-slave, a person one would normally be able to trust. Finally, Hákon is unlucky not only in being defeated and killed but in suffering such a shameful death, being killed by his own slave in a pigsty.

In one sense, this is just an example of how the *hamingja* works: even when acting prudently, one can never be certain of the outcome. But this story clearly is in conflict with Snorri's normal ideas on the matter. The *hamingja* tends consistently to favor some men, and it tends to accompany wisdom, courage, and so forth—the qualities that normally lead to success in the game of politics. For both reasons, it ought to have favored Earl Hákon, whose earlier career has been an example of the combination of luck and great qualities as a leader. There must be a special reason why the *hamingja* suddenly deserts him, and Snorri finds this in divine intervention. Such an intervention is clearly extraordinary, being confined to matters regarding Christianity in the stricter sense. God does not usually cause the fall of pagan chieftains, but in this case, he had decided that time had come to convert Norway to Christianity. It was Hákon's bad luck that he happened to govern the country just at this time. The general conclusion therefore seems to be that *hamingja/úhamingja* belongs to the normal working of nature, whereas God's providence intervenes on special occasions. This is quite compatible with Snorri's general view and with contemporary theology and philosophy.

Another difference between Snorri's concept of *hamingja* and the Christian idea of providence is that the former has little to do with morality. Snorri's comment on the fate of Earl Hákon may serve as an example: his *úhamingja* was not the well-deserved punishment for his bad deeds, as in the clerical historians (Theod. chaps. 5, 10; HN: 111, 115; *Ágr.* chaps. 13–14), on the contrary, it is the explanation why this great man came to such an ignoble end.[62] Thus, there is little to suggest that Snorri's concept of *hamingja* is derived from Christian thought.

Snorri's "law" that nothing succeeds like success probably has something to do with the belief in particular persons', notably kings', luck. The idea is among other places expressed in King Hringr's speech at the meeting of the petty kings of Eastern Norway: Óláfr's *hamingja* will decide his success or failure and has already been demonstrated through his capture of Earl Hákon and his other victories so far. Therefore, the best thing to do is to support him as early as possible to receive the greatest rewards. According to Mary Douglas, such ideas of luck are exactly what we should expect in a society like Snorri's, which is loosely organized, in which important positions are open to competition, and success or failure in this competition determines one's rank in society (Douglas, 1970: 129 f.). We cannot tell from Snorri's text how old the idea of *hamingja* is, but there is every reason to believe that it reflects common attitudes in his society and is not only an imported literary idea.

Although chance is evidently a necessary and commonly acknowledged concept in modern thought, it is not very popular with historians, as it does not allow explanations. That is to say, it is satisfactory enough concerning mass phenomena, which can be treated statistically. Concerning individual events, however, one usually prefers deliberate action or structural conditions to such explanations as the sudden death of a particular king leading to defeat or change of policy or good or bad weather deciding the success or failure of a battle or a military expedition. We cannot exclude the possibility that such factors may be of decisive importance, but the prestige and importance of historiography as a science in some way or other rests on the assumption that there is an order and regularity in society and human behavior (see Koselleck, 1985: 116 ff.). This idea of rationality is further confirmed by the assumption that chance in the long run is likely to be evenly distributed between the actors, so that skill, superior organization, or material resources and so forth will eventually be decisive.

In medieval historiography, the concept of luck, although no doubt having the merit of emancipating the historian from religion, seems even more of an obstacle to rational explanation. To have luck means to have success. If luck is made the only explanation, every success is strictly speaking self-explanatory. As luck is not evenly distributed, it is moreover likely to be as decisive as human and material resources. Consequently, all that is left to the historian is to register the bare facts. In a similar way as in modern historiography, the rational element depends on the degree to which human thought and action are used as explanations, or more so, as modern historians much more frequently than their medieval counterparts use structural factors that do not depend on individual men's will.

Snorri's response to this problem seems to be some rationalization of the concept of luck. Though his law that "nothing succeeds like success" is clearly connected with the belief in luck, this does not prevent Snorri from explaining its existence in terms of psychology and social structure: most men act out of self-interest. They have few fixed loyalties in political matters and consequently shift their allegiance to the one who is most likely to be successful. In a similar way he assumes that luck normally accompanies intelligence, skill, personal attraction, and other qualities that serve to win the game. A general statement illustrates this. King Óláfr's mistress, Álfhildr, is pregnant and suddenly gives birth to a son, who is about to die. The king is asleep and has expressly forbidden his men to wake him up, for whatever reason. No one dares to do so. However, the child must be baptized, but who dares to give it a name without asking the king? Finally, the king's scald Sigvatr takes responsibility and names the child Magnús after Charlemagne. When the king wakes up, he is at first furious, but is finally appeased by Sigvatr's explanations. He then comments:

> You are a very lucky man, Sigvat; it is not to be wondered that luck should accompany wisdom. But it is strange that, as sometimes happens, luck attends unwise men so that a foolish counsel turns out to be fortunate.[63]

It is not quite clear whether King Óláfr regards Sigvatr as an example of both luck and wisdom and adds the last sentence as an afterthought, or whether he considers him an extreme example of luck in that even his foolish counsels turn out well. What is important in our context is the statement that luck normally accompanies wisdom, which is clearly Snorri's own view of the relationship between the two, as is amply brought forward in the narrative.[64] As we have seen, Snorri generally explains success and failure in terms of his actors' wise or foolish decisions.

In a similar way he tries to give a rational explanation to the idea of the king's luck manifesting itself in good years. Admittedly, he describes without further comment both Hálfdan svarti, Hákon góði (HG chap. 11), and Earl Hákon as rulers who were known for bringing fertility to the country. King Hálfdan was so famous for this that his dead body was cut into four pieces and buried in four different regions so that they could all take part in his power (HS chap. 9). Earl Hákon brought good years after the period of famine under his predecessors, the Eiríkssons, and continued to do so during most of his reign.[65] However, when refering to the bad harvests during the reign of the Eiríkssons as one of the reasons for their unpopularity (*HGráf.* chap. 2), which earlier historians mention without further comment (*SagaOT:* 3; *Ágr.* chap. 9; HN: 108; *Fsk.*: 53), Snorri attempts an explanation: the kings were numerous and each of them had his own *hirð*. They therefore had high expenses and needed great incomes, the more so as they were also greedy. Consequently, they appropriated so much of what the peasants produced that it lead to famine. Snorri uses a similar explanation in another context.[66] Are these reflections "rationalistic" comments to ideas derived from an authentic pagan belief in a sacred king, who was held responsible for the fertility of the land? Or should they be understood in a Christian context, as a demonstration of the inadequacy of what learned Icelanders of the thirteenth century believed to be the ancient pagan religion, whereas the actual idea of the king bringing fertility to his country is of Christian origin?[67] The fact that the otherwise fairly secular Snorri is the only historian to make such comments, whereas decidedly clerical ones do not, is to me a strong argument for the former position. Further, though Snorri clearly regards the missionary kings as specially favored by God, he never refers to their or to other Christian kings' influence on the harvests.[68] Nor do such ideas seem very prominent in the contemporary clerical picture of the *rex iustus*.[69]

Snorri's concept of luck therefore most probably corresponds to traditional Nordic ideas, whether or not they are derived from pagan religion, and is not an example of Christian influence. He may possibly be influenced by contemporary European thought, though there is some difference between his personal concept of luck and European historians' *fortuna*. This makes it even less adequate than *fortuna* as a means to rational understanding of history. Snorri's *hamingja* is rather to be classified with miracles and witchcraft as the expression of mysterious forces influencing human history. Snorri, however, goes further than his predecessors in linking luck to a rational interpretation of history, by emphasizing the connection between luck and intelligence and other qualities that normally lead to success in the game.

Snorri's Ideas of Causation

On the preceding pages we have seen that Snorri is definitely not a modern rationalist. He believes in miracles and witchcraft and his concept of luck does not correspond to the concept of chance in modern statistics. Nevertheless, the traditional idea of Snorri's rationalism is not entirely wrong. The supernatural plays a subordinate part in his actual narrative, and, above all, he tries to give a rational explanation of historical events. This rational explanation is for the most part derived from his view of the political game. Men normally act to further their own interests, and their abiliity to do this, by the appropriate combination of force, diplomacy, generosity, and an attractive personality, explains the outcome of the conflicts. A comparison with his predecessors clearly shows how much Snorri has "improved" their accounts in this respect.

To Bull and other Norwegian scholars, this kind of explanation in Snorri is evidence of a specifically Nordic attitude, little influenced by Christianity.[70] We cannot exclude the possibility that the peoples of the North may have been less inclined toward fantastic manifestations of the supernatural than some other peoples, for instance the Celts, as a comparison of their myths might perhaps suggest. "Secularization" in this sense is not necessarily a modern phenomenon. According to Mary Douglas, inclination toward the supernatural is the expression of strong group solidarity or more generally of a society in which the members' relations to one another is very important. By contrast, a more loosely organized society is less likely to develop such ideas. Consequently, we find very secularized attitudes in primitive societies of hunters and gatherers.[71] Though Snorri's Icelandic society was not primitive in this sense, it was relatively loosely organized and with a fairly scattered population. This may also have applied to Norwegian society of the pagan and early Christian period. How far this actually corresponded to a pagan religion in which the supernatural played a subordinate role remains to be considered.

Before we can answer the question of Snorri's "uniqueness," we have to find out how he actually differed from his European contemporaries. Snorri does not differ from his aristocratic contemporaries in playing down the supernatural, for this normally plays a fairly subordinate part there as well, but in his concern for explanation. To quote Brandt (1966: 88), the aristocratic chronicler seeks to "celebrate, not to explain." As we have seen, the concern with honor and stance in this literature precludes the kind of analysis of the political game that is found in Snorri. Nor does Snorri strictly speaking differ from his clerical contemporaries in not believing in the supernatural. The difference is that he usually distinguishes between the natural and the supernatural and bases most of his explanations on the former. There is a clear tendency in the same direction in twelfth-century clerical historians (Partner, 1977: 212 ff.). Nevertheless, the supernatural continued to be more integrated in their narrative than in Snorri's. And most important: ordinary, "natural" explanation plays a less prominent part (Southern, 1970, 181 f.; Partner, 1977: 194 ff.).

One of the great changes, from the twelfth century onward, in European theology and philosophy, perhaps even in common mentality, was an increasing distinction betweeen the natural and the supernatural. In contemporary science, the normal working of nature—according to the "laws" that God had laid down at creation—was distinguished from his extraordinary intervention through miracles, and the concept of miracle was more clearly defined (Radding, 1985: 250 ff.; Ward, 1987: 4 ff.). A practical example of this new attitude is the growing disbelief in ordeals from the twelfth century, which led to the ban against clerics contributing to them in 1215 (Radding, 1985: 5 ff. with ref.). In the thirteenth century, the distinction between the natural and the supernatural is a characteristic feature of the philosophy and theology of Aquinas and is moreover expressed in fields like ethics, law, and political thought. The emergence of a more secular historiography in Italy in the fourteenth and fifteenth centuries was partly a consequence of this distinction. What happened was not that historians stopped believing in miracles and the supernatural, but that they increasingly distinguished between the natural and the supernatural and strictly confined God's intervention to the miracles (Green, 1972: 132 ff., 145 ff.) in a similar way as Snorri. The problem is therefore not that Snorri represents a different philosophical attitude from the one current in contemporary Europe, but that so few other historians applied this attitude to their historical work. The solution to this problem is more likely to be found in different interests and purposes than in different philosophical attitudes.

To understand this difference we must have a closer look at the kind of explanation offered by the medieval clerical chroniclers. As an example of this, Brandt refers to Matthew Paris's account of the dramatic events at the beginning of the Barons' War in 1258 (Brandt, 1966: 49 ff.; see *Chronica majora* book 5: 695–703). Here Matthew describes in some detail the Parliament of Oxford. After some entries dealing with completely different matters, he returns to English politics to tell of the Poitevins leaving England, without mentioning the fact that this was the direct result of the barons' action against them at Oxford. Thus, Matthew entirely fails to establish the obvious causal connection between two events that were close in time. To a modern reader, this means that he misses the point of the whole story. By contrast, medieval chroniclers see connections that appear utterly fantastic to the modern mind.[72] Though this is not all there is to be said about explanation in medieval clerical historiography, Brandt certainly points to a characteristic trait and his examples can easily be multiplied.

To Brandt this reveals a "mode of perception" that is totally different from our own. Explanation meant classification within a static system; in history, to explain an event was to find its analogy, without regard for proximity in time or space (1966: 33 ff., 59 ff.). To some extent, this points to characteristic traits in medieval mentality. But it is very much regarded from the modern point of view and makes medieval man appear fairly irrational. Moreover, if we have to do with a "mode of perception" and not only with a way in which intellectuals organized their narratives or expositions of natural phenomena, we meet with serious difficulties. If men in the Middle Ages had no idea of causation behind human acts, how were they able to act rationally? If Matthew failed to see the causal connection between these events because of a common medieval "mode of perception," how could the actors themselves see it? And if they did not see it, was there any connection at all? To introduce a distinction between a specifically clerical mentality among persons confined to the ivory tower in contrast to the active politicians of the period is hardly very helpful. Medieval clerics were not necessarily cut off from secular politics, and even if they were, ecclesiastical politics was not fundamentally different from secular. Political actions may have been different in the Middle Ages from those in our time, and it may well be that impulses, norms "ranking" acts according to fixed criteria for behavior leading to high or low esteem, and so forth counted for more than consistency in pursuing definite aims for politicians of the period. Still, the code of honor is not entirely incompatible with rational deliberations in order to win the game and it is a priori difficult to believe that medieval politicians generally acted without considering the consequences of their acts or without taking into account loss or gain. Obviously, Brandt does not think so either. He clearly supposes that there was a causal link between the Parliament of Oxford and the Poitevins leaving England.

Moreover, medieval clerical chroniclers were not unable to see the causal connections that Brandt misses in Matthew Paris. Analyses of the political game, similar to Snorri's, are occasionally found in the European chronicles. According to Brandt, aristocratic chroniclers are sometimes able to give a quite complex description of the political game, resembling the game of chess, which was very popular among the aristocracy of the Middle Ages (1966: 103 f.). A clerical author like William of Malmesbury often shows an acute sense of people's egoistic motives, as for instance when explaining the unrest in England that started early in King Stephen's reign (*Historia Novella* chap. 467): Stephen was able to attract a large number of adventurous knights who gathered around him to share in his riches. But such men are never content. They always demand more, and if their demands are refused, they create disturbances, which can only be settled through new gifts. Consequently, when they had emptied the royal treasury, they turned to ecclesiastical property. After rumors of opposition against Stephen, they pressed their demands further and Stephen had the choice between ruining himself or losing the kingdom. A similar picture of society as Snorri's underlies both this statement and much of William's subsequent description of the war between Stephen and Mathilda: most people are without strong loyalties and change sides according to their interests. Medieval clerical historians were thus not unable to analyze politics in a "rational" way, but they were apparently not interested or rather, more interested in other aspects of human activity.

The "mode of perception" which Brandt describes is not simply a barrier against a rational understanding of the world; it is a system with its own rationality, which even, to most men at the time, seemed superior to the system of historical analysis preferred by modern men. It is based on allegorical or typological interpretation, that is, events or phenomena are classified according to their intrinsic meaning, not according to their proximity in space or time.[73] Symbols, analogies, and so forth are therefore highly significant, whereas the sort of mechanistic causal connection between the phenomena of this world with which we are primarily concerned is of secondary importance. "Symbolic" connections, such as the one between Frederick Barbarossa's coronation and his namesake's consecration as a bishop (Otto of Freising, *Gesta* book 2, chap. 3) are thus more important than the connection between the Parliament of Oxford and the exile of the Poitevins. Though Brandt's statement that this "mode of perception" has nothing to do with Christianity may be correct in the sense that it is not ultimately derived from Christian thought and may be found within other religions as well, I believe that medieval men saw a close connection between it and Christianity. Through this system, the world received meaning only by being related to God. Consequently, the study of both nature and human history must therefore ultimately be a study of God, even if this is not explicitly mentioned in the texts. In short, the fault in Brandt's otherwise excellent account of the medieval world view is that he regards it as an unsuccessful attempt to answer the same questions as we pose. In reality, it was intended as an answer to different questions.

Then, why did the contemporary clerical chroniclers continue to pose such questions and analyze historical events in this way instead of turning to the modern, "rational" explanations that are to be found in other disciplines and are represented by Snorri, among others, in history? I believe that there are two reasons for this. The first is the relative decline of historiography in the thirteenth century. Either, history and the "humanities" in general were excluded from the university curricula and replaced by logic and the philosophy of nature—which in turn prepared the students for the even more important studies of the higher faculties, law and theology (see, e.g., Leff, 1968: 120 ff.), or they were more strictly subjected to philosophy and theology than had been the case in the twelfth century.[74] The new ideas about natural causation were thus applied to subjects other than history. This in turn has to do with the fact that a real explanation in medieval philosophy should be a priori. Such explanations could only with difficulty be applied to the apparently chaotic events of human history.[75] Instead, intellectuals interested in analysis of social phenomena turned to law and political thought, both subjects having a marked revival in the second half of the thirteenth century.

The second reason has to do with morality. To find general laws in history was not only difficult, it might even be dangerous, because it came into conflict with the Christian idea of free will and the individual's responsibility for his acts.[76] Further, there is a close connection between interest in morality and realistic philosophy. First, morality, at least according to Christian thought of the high Middle Ages, concerns the "inner" aspects of human actions: the act itself and the intention behind it are more important than its consequences. Thus, descriptions of human acts in history are not linked together to form a causal chain in the modern sense but are intended as characterizations of the persons who performed them. Second, concern with morality makes the metaphysical world more relevant to the historian. The historical actors are responsible to God, and history becomes morally relevant when the historian is able to detect God's finger in it. It was common belief in the Middle Ages that God rewarded the just and punished the wicked, not only in the next life but also in the present one, though it was not always possible to see how he did so. However, by looking for signs of divine intervention in history, the historian might find a moral explanation to events that would otherwise seem inexplicable. The question of meaning, explanation, and rationality in history was therefore likely to be posed in moral and metaphysical terms. The common statement in the prefaces that the historian's purpose is to depict good and evil acts to make people abstain from vice and pursue virtue is not just a series of pious phrases but usually covers the author's intentions quite well. In their selection of materials medieval clerical historians are extremely concerned with morality.[77]

When William of Malmesbury, despite his ability to make the same kind of political analyses as Snorri, does not make such explanations the basis of his historical thought, the reason must be sought in his concern with morality. In contrast to Snorri he strongly condemns political opportunism and depicts his hero, Earl Robert of Gloucester, as a man who is entirely different in his unswerving loyalty to Queen Mathilda, and an example for others to follow. William is thus more interested in the moral aspect of history than Snorri. This is also evident from his selection of material. He treats the legal and moral aspects of the English civil war in great detail, both in explaining the motives of his hero Robert of Gloucester and in referring to the meetings and discussions while he pays relatively little attention to the conduct of the war.[78] Similarly, in summarizing the events of the period 1075–1152 and again in his description of Frederick Barbarossa's heroic acts, Otto of Freising is constantly emphasizing the moral aspect.[79] Numerous other examples can be found. This also means that the difference between the clerical and the aristocratic chronicle is less than may be assumed in the first place. Both are concerned with morality, though the norms for what is the good and appropriate way of acting differ. In addition, the clerical chronicler tries to fit his praise and blame of human acts into a consistent religious world view. But the difference between celebrating and explaining should not be exaggerated.

Returning to Snorri, we can now see that his attitude to morality is the very clue to his "rationalism" and lack of interest in the supernatural. We know little of Snorri's personal attitude to Christianity and the contemporary clerical world-picture,[80] but he certainly did not have much use for such ideas in his actual historical narrative. The lesson to be learned from it is not that God will reward the just and punish the wicked, but that it is necessary to act with great foresight and prudence if one is to have success in this world. Consequently, miracles have no purpose in Snorri's narrative, although he must surely have believed in them. God may occasionally intervene in human history, and there are also other supernatural forces that may thwart human efforts and expectations. Normally, however, success is the result of prudent behavior, and if Snorri has an explicit purpose behind his work, it is most probably to teach future politicians this kind of prudence. The question remains, however, why his interests differ so much from those of his contemporaries. To explain this, we shall have to compare his milieu and society to contemporary Europe.

Conclusion

This examination of Snorri as a historian has once more demonstrated the importance he attaches to the game of politics. Though occasionally referring to the division of long stretches of time according to schemas superimposed on the events, notably the ecclesiastical division between the pagan and the Christian period, he is mainly interested in individual human actions in a short-term perspective. This means that his view of human nature and society is static, not evolutionary or teleological. Therefore, examples from the past can easily serve as lessons for the present. In this respect, Snorri continues the "heroic" tradition of historiography in the North, though giving it a more deliberately pragmatic character through explicit generalizations and by arranging the narrative in such a way that it may serve as an example for future politicians.

Within this static system, the game of politics thus serves as a general framework of explanation. There is no reason to doubt Snorri's belief in miracles and God's intervention in history, nor in magic or other supernatural phenomena. But such phenomena play a subordinate part in his actual narrative because his main interest lies in the aspects of life which can be controlled by human effort and intelligence. Accordingly, Snorri gives by modern standards a more rational explanation of the events than most of his European contemporaries.

6

The Context

Introduction

In this last chapter, I shall deal with Snorri's context. What are the similarities and differences between him and his Nordic and European contemporaries, and how can his historiography be explained from the literary milieu and society to which he belonged—and in turn throw light on them? I shall start with his relationship to other Norwegian and Icelandic historians, above all those who are his sources.

Snorri and His Predecessors

The question of Snorri's originality has two aspects, his use of his sources and his ideas and general approach to history versus that of other Old Norse authors. Earlier research has done much to solve the first problem and has shown that Snorri directly or indirectly has drawn information from a number of sources, including most extant works by his predecessors. However, not all of these are equally relevant to the second problem. Snorri belongs to the secular tradition in Old Norse historiography, and it is here we must look for his intellectual ancestors.

First, Snorri's predecessors within the secular tradition share his "rationality" in the sense of avoiding the supernatural. *Fagrskinna* is almost as restrictive in this respect, whereas *Morkinskinna* tends a little more to pious legend and considerations. *Fagrskinna* treats the Christianization of Norway very briefly and is not much concerned with religion (Indrebø, 1917: 251 ff.). Other sagas belonging to the secular tradition, such as *Sverris saga* and *Sturlunga saga,* take a similar attitude. The former is relatively very concerned with God and the supernatural as a part of Sverrir's ideology (Holm-Olsen, 1953: 61 ff., 91 ff.). However, it is the only one of the kings' sagas that can be compared to Snorri in its rational explanation of success, failure, and events in general. The other saga writers appear to have basically the same ideas as Snorri but are less consistent in their attempts to explain, often confining themselves to mere description.

Second, the secular tradition arranges narrative according to relative and not absolute chronology, thus emphasizing human events rather than God's providence. Finally, these works have in common the "objective" style, in which the author remains in the background whereas any comments, reflections and explanations are normally expressed by the actors themselves in the form of speeches and dialogues. Though this may be partly a literary device; it is also an expression of the shared, implicit values of the secular aristocracy, which differ from the explicit and systematically expressed ideology of the Church. This is above all evident in the ideas of morality and human character. Snorri's method of characterization is very similar to that of other authors within this tradition, to a great extent even the characterizations themselves. So is also the "objective" style, the description of people in action rather than constant characters and the lack of interest in the "inner" aspect of their personality. When Snorri departs from his predecessors, he does so in the "modern" direction, referring occasionally to what his characters thought and showing greater interest in motives. Above all, both in his description of individual human action and the game of politics in general, Snorri makes more efficient use of the two means he had in common with his predecessors, relative chronology and speeches and dialogues. He creates a largely new picture of the political game conducted by kings like Haraldr hárfagri and above all St. Óláfr by constructing a consistent chronology. The saga of the latter is also the best but far from the only example of his use of speeches to uncover his actors' motives and their way of influencing one another.

In many cases, Snorri's authorship has mainly consisted in arranging, editing, and omitting materials from his predecessors. Quite frequently, he copies directly from his sources. Speeches and to some extent dialogues are more often Snorri's own invention. As has been shown by earlier scholars, Snorri often "improves" the earlier texts, clarifying chronology, removing logical inconsistencies, and creating a clearer picture of events and political arrangements. From our point of view the most important feature is that he rearranges his material so as to emphasize the political game. Numerous examples of this have been given in the preceding pages, such as his treatment of Óláfr's accession to power and his fall and the intrigues of the Eiríkssons and Earl Hákon.

In his description of the period 1030–1177, which is more a rearrangement of the narrative contained in *Morkinskinna* and *Fagrskinna* than an independent work of history, it is not always possible to explain why Snorri omits or includes particular stories. Generally, he is more restrictive in this part of *Heimskringla* than in the saga of St. Óláfr (Nordal, 1973: 209). All taken together, however, a comparison with his predecessors indicates that Snorri emphasizes the political game and long-term interests more strongly. A few examples, in addition to the ones quoted above, may serve to illustrate this.

In the story of Haraldr harðráði's return to Norway, Snorri differs from *Morkinskinna* and *Fagrskinna* in omitting Haraldr's first meeting with Magnús, in which the magnates, at Einarr þambarskelfir's instigation, make Magnús refuse to share the kingdom with Haraldr (*Msk.*: 88 ff., *Fsk.*: 234 ff.; see also *HHarð.* chaps. 18–22). This then explains why Haraldr allies himself with King Sveinn of Denmark against Magnús. It is probably also intended as an explanation of the bad relationship between Haraldr and Einarr þambarskelfir. In this way, both *Fagrskinna* and *Morkinskinna* give a more favorable picture of Haraldr than *Heimskringla*. However, there is nothing in Snorri's saga of Haraldr to indicate that he is interested in giving a negative picture of him, so this is hardly the reason for his omission. Snorri may simply have done it for the sake of brevity, but it is worth noticing that this omission to some extent serves to emphasize the picture of politics as a game between actors who try to further their interests at the expense of one another, rather than explaining political conflicts as the result of direct personal clashes. According to Snorri, Haraldr finds it unlikely that his nephew will share the kingdom with him unless he is forced to do so and acts accordingly. His later conflict with Einarr þambarskelfir is a conflict of interests, which can be explained without reference to previous personal antagonism.

In the following account of Haraldr's reign as sole king, there is a clear difference between *Morkinskinna* and *Fagrskinna* in that *Fagrskinna* omits several of *Morkinskinna*'s stories of the rivalry between Haraldr and the magnates (*Fsk.*: 264 f.; *Msk.*: 171–80; see also Indrebø, 1917: 198 ff.), in accordance with its author's "ideological" interpretation of the conflict (see above, chap. 3 n. 46). Snorri follows *Fagrskinna* in omitting *Morkinskinna*'s episodes, but not in its ideological explanation, and presents the conflict between Haraldr and Einarr in terms of power politics: the conflict is not the result of accidental clashes but of diverging long-term interests. In contrast to the two earlier sagas, Snorri also links the story of Haraldr and Einarr to that of Hákon Ívarsson, thus presenting it in a wider political perspective.[1] In accounting for the outbreak of the civil war between the sons of King Haraldr gilli, the most important difference between *Heimskringla* and *Fagrskinna* on the one hand and *Ágrip* and *Morkinskinna* on the other is that the former omit the long story of Geirsteinn and his sons, which leads to the enmity between Grégóríús and King Sigurðr (*Ágr.* chap. 60; *Msk.*: 448–453; see also *Fsk.*: 352 ff.; *Ingi* chaps. 26–27). Though we cannot be sure of the reason,[2] the effect of this omission is that the personal enmity between Sigurðr and Grégóríús is played down in favor of political considerations: Grégóríús wants to kill Sigurðr, not primarily because of his hatred of him, but because of his analysis of the situation, which tells him that Sigurðr is dangerous.

However, it is not a question of a radical difference between Snorri and his sources. The story of Earl Hákon's intrigues is a direct copy of the one told in *Fagrskinna*. The reasons for the outbreak of the civil war in 1155 are exactly the same in *Morkinskinna* and *Fagrskinna*. Clearly Snorri's predecessors were able to make the same combinations as he did and emphasize the political game in the same way. But whereas Snorri almost constantly takes this attitude, there are only scattered examples in his predecessors. There is a similar contrast between *Heimskringla* and the largely contemporary collection *Sturlunga saga* in this respect. In the latter, it is quite clear that politics is essentially maneuvering for gain, and the authors are very frank about the material interests involved for instance when the cheiftains interfere in law suits (e.g., *Sturl.* vol. 1: 165, 168). Nevertheless, it is often impossible to guess the motives of the actors in the almost endless conflicts that are the subject of the saga. Either the authors must have taken for granted that their audience knew what it was all about, or they may have reckoned that they were not interested. In describing the conduct and outcome of the conflicts, Snorri is similarly far more explicit than his predecessors, in pointing to the selfish motives and changing loyalty of most men and in emphasizing the "law" that nothing succeeds like success. His story of St. Óláfr's conquest of Norway may serve as an example of this. Though they may occasionally be more inclined toward emphasizing idealistic motives, there is nothing to suggest that the authors of *Morkinskinna* and *Fagrskinna* had a fundamentally different opinion on this point. *Fagrskinna* explains Haraldr hárfagri's success in conquering Norway by a combination of force and victory in war and gifts and generosity which attached the great men to him, just like *Heimskringla* (*Fsk.*: 13, see also above) and takes a similar attitude to the depositions of Eiríkr blóðøx and Earl Hákon. Both *Fagrskinna* and *Morkinskinna* imply basically the same attitude in the population when describing the conflicts between Magnús góði and Haraldr harðráði, Magnús blindi and Haraldr gilli and the sons and successors of Haraldr gilli. Nor do Snorri's predecessors attach greater importance to military success or analyze military matters more adequately. The only real exception is the author of *Sverris saga,* who was probably both an Icelander and a cleric. His ability in this respect may be due to his oral sources and to the fact that the protagonist of his saga was a brilliant strategist and the great innovator in the military field in Norwegian medieval history (Gathorne-Hardy, 1956: 171 ff., etc.; Lunden, 1977: 101 ff.; Bagge, 1986: 184 ff.).

Concerning society in general, we have already noted Snorri's aristocratic bias: the people are normally helpless without their leaders, and when there is popular opposition against the king, the magnates are the real agents. This is above all evident in the rebellion against the Danes who ruled Norway after their victory of Stiklestad, which Snorri largely regards as the result of the maneuvers of the two magnates Einarr þambarskelfir and Kálfr Árnason. By contrast, both Theodoricus, *Fagrskinna,* and *Morkinskinna* explain it as a spontaneous popular reaction against the Danish oppression and the belief in Óláfr's sainthood. The "people" are the active force, whereas Einarr þambarskelfir and Kálfr Árnason are the instruments. Further, *Morkinskinna* ascribes an active role to Magnús himself in the long story of Karl's expedition to Novgorod, his return with gifts from Magnús to the magnates, and Sveinn's attempts to capture him, which then leads to Kálfr's defection from Sveinn (*Msk.*: 5–20). Snorri thus plays down the "democratic" and "constitutional" aspect of the conflict, emphasizing the long-term interests of individual magnates. Óláfr's sainthood and the popular opposition against the Danes are used by Einarr and Kálfr to achieve the political positions King Cnut has promised but not given them. Snorri's political interest is probably a more important clue to understanding the difference between him and his predecessors than his aristocratic bias. There is little to indicate that his predecessors were basically more democratic, but they were certainly less explicit in their analyses of the political game.

This comparison between Snorri and other Old Norse historians has confirmed our impression that Snorri is not a unique figure but belongs to a tradition. Most differences between him and his predecessors are differences of degree, not of kind. He describes a game of politics that was there in his sources, but he rearranges his material to make it more explicit and gives a clearer account of people's motives and of social structure. Like his predecessors he keeps the supernatural in the background but tries more energetically to give rational and secular explanations. For this purpose he applies techniques that were already familiar to the saga tradition, relative chronology and speeches and dialogues, but uses them more extensively and successfully than most of his predecessors. Snorri is thus largely a product of a particular social and intellectual environment, and much of his basic assumptions may be regarded as the expression of a common *mentalité*. Thus, in order to compare him with the European historiographical tradition and explain his achievement, we have to distinguish between his basic assumptions, which he had in common with his milieu, and his exceptional ability in using these assumptions to create an intelligent and coherent picture of the past.

The Description and the Reality

The question of the reality behind Snorri's description of society began to be asked—quite logically—by Halvdan Koht, who was the first to fully regard Snorri as a historian in the modern sense with an overall interpretation of history. Koht's answer was that Snorri's description is based on his experience of the last phase of the Norwegian civil wars, the period around 1200 (Koht, 1921: 87 ff.). Later, Gudmund Sandvik, who accepted Koht's main conclusion concerning Snorri as a historian, suggested that his picture of society was derived from contemporary Iceland (1955: 56, 98 f.). Both theories are to some extent based on the belief that the main theme in Snorri's work is the conflict between the king and the aristocracy, which is hardly the case. Still, we cannot exclude the possibility that Snorri was actually describing a contemporary society with which he was himself familiar in the guise of early medieval Norway. We are fortunately on somewhat firmer ground when comparing Snorri's picture to the conditions prevailing in the early thirteenth century than to those of earlier centuries.

Norwegian society of the late twelfth and early thirteenth centuries, as it appears in the contemporary sagas, the laws, *The King's Mirror,* and so forth was probably not fundamentally different from that depicted by Snorri. It differed, however, on two important points. First, the later phase of the civil wars consisted in prolonged struggles between parties, which seem to be fairly constant in their composition, despite different names. Though defections were not infrequent, the total picture of this period is different from Snorri's description of conspicuous victories that led to universal support for the victor.[3] Continuous civil wars of the kind described in *Sverris saga, Bǫglunga sǫgur,* and the early part of *Hákonar saga* do not seem to have occurred before in Norwegian history, and they are also described in the contemporary sagas in a way very different from Snorri's descriptions of conflicts. Second, the members of the aristocracy of the early thirteenth century were apparently royal servants in a much more direct sense than Snorri's magnates. Royal officials play no prominent part in *Heimskringla,* and the magnates there are more popular leaders than royal servants, whereas the opposite seems to be the case in the thirteenth century. This is of course to a considerable extent a consequence of the civil wars. Though scattered references to actual conditions in *The King's Mirror* and other sources indicate that the change should not be exaggerated (Bagge, 1986: 172 f.), it is hardly possible to maintain that Snorri's picture of early medieval Norway was simply based on contemporary Norwegian society.

The case for contemporary Iceland seems stronger, both on a priori and empirical grounds. A priori, Snorri is more likely, consciously or subconsciously, to have derived his description of the political game from his experience of this society, with which he was perfectly familiar, even being one of its most prominent members, than from contemporary or slightly earlier Norwegian society, which he knew more indirectly. Empirically, the political game in Iceland, as it appears in *Sturlunga saga* and the family sagas, is quite similar to Snorri's descriptions in parts of *Heimskringla*. It is hardly to be doubted that Icelandic society of the Sturlung period was important as the intellectual background for Snorri as a "political analyst."

Moreover, some of his peculiarities can be explained from his Icelandic background. As mentioned above, Snorri is not a great military historian. Though he has this in common with most other historians, whether their background was Norwegian or Icelandic, he might be expected to surpass them in this respect as in others, if he really had practical experience. However, even at Snorri's time, the period of the greatest concentration of power and the most embittered conflicts between the chieftains, real battles were few and they were fought with small forces (Byock, 1987: 30 ff.). As implied in *Heimskringla,* political means were probably more important than military ones. Similarly, Snorri's fairly naive treatment of the territorial issues involved in foreign policy as opposed to his acute sense of the game of politics within the country can be explained from the isolated position of Iceland and above all from the fact that the Icelandic chieftains for a long time were primarily political leaders who fought to gain adherents, not to control fixed territorial units.[4] Both his description of the magnates as largely independent popular leaders and his emphasis on their importance in conflicts and decision making conform to contemporary Icelandic conditions. Snorri's insistence on long-term political interests as the real cause of the feuds has its parallel in the description of late twelfth- and early thirteenth-century Iceland in the contemporary *Sturlunga saga,* in contrast to the Icelandic family sagas. His lack of interest in ideological issues fit well in with the power struggle of contemporary Iceland. Finally, his "law" that nothing succeeds like success bears some resemblance to contemporary Icelandic conditions. Admittedly, Iceland was never before Snorri's time united under one ruler. Snorri's lifetime was a period of almost constant struggles between powerful magnates, among others Snorri himself. But significant changes took place during the time when Snorri was probably writing *Heimskringla,* starting in the 1220s. The number of magnates was drastically reduced and those who remained became much more powerful. The "mechanism" of this process was probably the particular magnate's ability to attract adherents, both through generosity and ability to protect clients and through conspicuous victories, which made his adversary's clients desert him to join the victor (Jóhannesson, 1969: 187 ff.; Sigurðsson, 1989: 45 ff., 108 ff.).

Is Snorri then simply describing contemporary Icelandic society in his history of the Norwegian kings? From the point of view of source criticism, there is no reason to be particularly optimistic concerning Snorri's trustworthiness. His view of historical evidence differs radically from ours, and he has no sense of historical change that might prevent him from construing the past in the image of the present as he knew it. Nevertheless, there are reasons to believe that his reconstruction is not totally inadequate. Like our reconstruction of early Norwegian society, Snorri's is based on a number of stories that he did not invent himself, but took from other sources, some written and some oral. Some of these stories are legendary, others have been drastically altered, but it is not unlikely that some of the more spectacular events in the reigns of the kings in the past, such as St. Óláfr, were orally transmitted approximately as they really happened. Though we can rarely be sure of this in any particular case and accordingly have to reject them as evidence of the individual events they describe, it is a little more likely that these stories, whether true or invented, contain some accurate information on society. The stories may certainly be exaggerated and romanticized, but the social conditions that form their background cannot be completely different from the actual ones, at least not if it can be pointed out that they are the same in a large number of stories. To take the kind of stories that are most interesting in the present context: would we have had such a number of feud stories if there were no feuds in Norway in the early Middle Ages?

There is one problem here, however: to what extent are the feud descriptions in the sagas of Icelandic origin? The feud seems to play a more prominent part in the sagas that are undoubtedly of Icelandic origin, *Morkinskinna* and *Heimskringla,* than in the Norwegian ones, such as the works that belong to the milieu around the archdiocese. Of the works of less certain origin, like the *Legendary Saga* and *Fagrskinna,* the former conforms to the Icelandic pattern and the latter to the Norwegian. If this also corresponds to their country of origin, one might suppose that most of the feud stories were derived from an

Icelandic tradition and were not known in Norway—which of course is a strong argument against their truth. But this does not seem very likely. It may well be that events concerning Norwegian history—in particular those involving Icelanders—have been told and embroidered and even to some extent invented in Iceland and that the Icelandic saga writers may have part of their information from their own country. The possible scarcity of such stories in the Norwegian historical works, however, is rather to be explained as deliberate brevity and from ideological grounds, than from their absence in the Norwegian tradition. The ecclesiastical works represent a historiographical genre in which such stories are hardly likely to play a prominent part. To some extent, this also applies to *Fagrskinna,* despite its secular character. This saga is relatively more interested in foreign policy than Snorri, that is: with the heroic deeds of the Norwegian kings leading their people against foreign enemies. Like the ecclesiastical works, it has also much in common with a chronicle, concentrating on the most important events of a reign, without attempting to link them together, and on the portrait of the kings.

Though we cannot trust in this in any particular case, it therefore seems probable that these stories, whether true or not, throw some light on the way politics was conducted in the period. This probability gains in strength through the more trustworthy evidence from the conflicts in the 1150s, which shows the importance of the feud and in the whole indicate political conditions not unlike those described by Snorri.[5] The numerous references to revenge in the laws point in the same direction (Wallén, 1962: 240 f.). Furthermore, *The King's Mirror,* despite its strong propaganda for the social reorganization attempted by the kings of the Sverrir dynasty, indirectly suggests that both the feud and much of the old political structure still existed (Bagge, 1987b: 81 ff., 179 ff.). And finally, the political structure that Snorri attributes to Norway of the tenth to the twelfth century fits fairly well in with what we would expect of a society at this stage of development. Though Snorri cannot be regarded as evidence in the strict sense of social conditions long before his own time, he had the advantage compared to many modern historians that he was able to base his reconstruction on experience from a society that was not fundamentally different.

Snorri and Contemporary Europe: Culture, Society, and Political Analysis

In the preceding pages, Snorri has in several respects emerged as a more "modern" historian than most of his contemporaries. This does not necessarily mean that he was a better historian than, for example, Otto of Freising or William of Malmesbury, only that his interests were different from theirs and to some extent happen to correspond to what modern historians find most interesting. These differences can be summarized under three headings: (1) the importance of the game of politics; (2) the organization of narrative into a coherent story; and (3) explanation in secular terms. The three are closely interrelated in that the game of politics both serves to give Snorri's stories coherence and serves as a principle of explanation instead of morality or supernatural intervention, as in the European clerical tradition.

Then why do we find such a historiography in the outskirts of Europe? Though Snorri is also an exceptional figure in a Nordic context, his originality consists more in refining and systematizing tendencies that were already there in his milieu than in creating something completely novel. The clue to understanding Snorri's originality therefore lies more in comparing societies and intellectual milieus than in focusing on his personal achievement. The difference between the secular historiography of Iceland and Norway and that of feudal Europe is best explained in terms of differences in society. The political game was relatively more and the aristocratic code of honor relatively less important in the North, the aristocracy was not a closed caste of warriors, but functioned as popular leaders, and the ordinary people had far greater political influence. In short: the historians' descriptions were different largely because they described different things. However, literature, including historiography, is not necessarily a direct reflection of actual conditions. There are more or less ideological descriptions of the same reality, different aspects are emphasized, and so forth. Consequently, we need an intellectual and not only a social explanation of the differences, though the intellectual differences may in turn have their social origins. Such an explanation is particularly necessary when we compare Snorri to European clerical historiography, which was different not primarily because it described a different reality but because of the widely different purpose of its description.

As mentioned above, European clerical culture was not favorable to the development of the kind of political historiography that Snorri represents. There were tendencies in this direction in the twelfth century, with greater emphasis on natural explanation, description of individual character, and coherent narrative. But the principal way of giving meaning to history was still by moral and metaphysical interpretation. Then, from the thirteenth century the leading intellectual milieus, connected to the universities, increasingly turned away from history to more abstract and systematic subjects like natural science, law, theology, and political thought.

In European cultural history, the thirteenth century represented both the triumph of scholasticism, abstract thought, and a strictly technical, Latin language and of a secular, narrative, and often romantic literature in the vernacular, which meant a revival of the "literary public" of classical antiquity within the various European language communities (Auerbach, 1958: 177 ff.). This latter was primarily a lay culture, at least in the sense that its public mainly consisted of laymen and—not the least—women, and was primarily attached to courts and other aristocratic milieus and reflected their interests. Whereas Latin was developed into a medium of technical, abstract thought, the triumph of the vernacular generally meant emphasis on aesthetic and emotional qualities. Thus the learned or clerical and the courteous and secular cultures tended to drift apart, leaving important aspects of the humanist inheritance of classical antiquity, including historiography, in the gap between them.

This change took place in the central zone of Europe, with France as the most prominent example. In other parts of Europe, the twelfth-century traditions lingered on, notably in the extreme south, Italy, and the extreme north, Norway and above all Iceland. Scholasticism was not equally prominent at the Italian universities as at the French ones, and from the late thirteenth century a revival of humanistic studies started and reached its full maturity in the Florentine Renaissance from the early fifteenth century (Struever, 1970: 40 ff.; Skinner, 1978 I: 35 ff.). The vernacular held an exceptional importance as a vehicle of literature both in Iceland and Norway, its use being both earlier and more widespread than in most other countries at the time. Latin seems to have had a slight superiority in the rather meager literature of the twelfth century, though the earliest vernacular works date from the first half of this century. From around 1200, the vernacular is virtually the only literary language, Latin being confined to diplomas, and even there mainly to documents concerning the Church or international relations.

Medieval vernacular literature, including that of Norway and Iceland, is often narrative and is evidently far removed from the technical and abstract scholastic treatises. The sagas of kings, bishops, and great men of the past and translations of the Roman historians and the biographies of ancient heroes like Charlemagne and Dideric of Bern, cover a high percentage of extant literature. To this can be added the religious literature, of which the greatest part is narrative in form—characteristically, the parts of the Bible that were translated were the historical books of the Old Testament—and even to some extent the didactic literature, which differed markedly from that of contemporary Europe in having largely a narrative form. Apart from poetry, there are very few exceptions to this. However, neither its use of the vernacular nor its narrative form meant that this literature was without intellectual ambitions. It also included works of learning, such as the grammatical treatises, Snorri's *Edda* and *The King's Mirror,* all written in the vernacular and in a style more resembling the narrative works than that of contemporary scholasticism. Nor is there any doubt of the intellectual ambitions of a narrative work like *Heimskringla,* both in Snorri's attempts to reconstruct the past, including chronology, in a reasonable way and in his explanations of political events.

In a broad sense, this vernacular culture can be regarded as a continuation of the European twelfth-century Renaissance, which was more favorable to the development of historiography. However, the choice between scholastic philosophy and the kind of historiography represented among others by Snorri is also the choice between two different ways of regarding the world. From a purely intellectual point of view the principles of explanation in European clerical historiography may be as satisfactory as those of Snorri and contemporary proponents of "rational" history, presenting a philosophical framework that makes the apparently chaotic events of this world intelligible and even morally acceptable. But they are likely to appeal mainly to the intellectual, who regards the events from a certain distance. To the practical man of action they offer few clues for analyzing the situation and planning his maneuvers, and they may even create serious problems to a participant who believes in the justice of his cause and finds that God favors the unjust.

Galbert de Bruges's *Histoire du meurtre de Charles le Bon,* for the most part written during the dramatic events in Flanders in 1127–1128, may serve as an example of this. Galbert was a cleric and his overall view is clearly religious. Count Charles is described as a hero and a martyr and his murderers as evil men acting on the Devil's instigation (intr., chaps. 1, 3, 12–15). Galbert tries to detect God's finger behind the chaotic events following the murder (e.g., chaps. 11, 25, 26, 57, 84, 116, 119), and he is evidently troubled when God sometimes seems to favor the wrong party.[6] Apart from this, however, his book is not only an unusually vivid account of an eyewitness, but also contains quite good analyses of the political aspects of the conflict and of the actors' motives. The medieval Italian chroniclers, like the Florentines Giovanni Villani and Dino Compagni, share Galbert's and the clerical authors' belief in God's providence and attempt to give a moral interpretation of the events. But they are closer to the events and correspondingly more concerned with their secular and political aspects than the traditional clerical historians. Italian historiography became gradually "secularized" during the fourteenth century, not in the sense that historians ceased to believe in God and the supernatural, but in the sense that this belief did not interfere very much with their interpretation of historical events. Thus, historians turned away from seeking God's finger in history to analyzing its purely human aspect in order to understand and teach others how a politician should behave.

This change corresponds to what Nancy Struever calls the change from logic to rhetoric in the early Italian Renaissance. This meant a change in emphasis from thought in itself to thought as it is expressed in language, and from eternal truth to ideas and opinions of practical, ethical, and political importance. In ethics the virtues should be visible, and it is more important to appear than to be. There is a close connection between form and content; it is of no avail to know the truth if one is unable to present it in such a form that other people may be convinced. Such a culture meant new opportunities for historiography. It is no longer an objection that human action cannot be explained from a priori principles. To understand human action is important from a practical point of view, and it is the duty of the historian to make the apparently chaotic events of the past explicable and relevant to his contemporaries. Consequently, the historian tries to analyze the reasons for and consequences of human actions and present them according to an inner logic of challenge and response (Struever, 1970). To use Aristotle's reasoning on history, the solution to the objection that history merely narrates human events in a haphazard way, is to make history more like literature of fiction: events must be selected and linked together in a coherent story. From a strictly logical and philosophical point of view both the coherence of such a story and its correspondence with reality may be doubted, as it lacks the binding force of the basic principles of Aristotelian logic. From a more practical point of view, however, it may be quite satisfactory, as this is more or less the kind of coherence we expect in daily life when acting together with other men.

To students of European literature of the period, the Icelandic saga literature does not appear particularly rhetorical. Its style is fairly terse and simple, in contrast to the learned or flourishing style of other Old Norse works under stronger influence from Latin literature, and it is notable for its exact and matter-of-fact descriptions of the external world.[7] In a more fundamental sense, however, this culture shares some important qualities with the rhetorical culture of the Italian renaissance. There is no doubt of the importance Snorri and his milieu attach to oratory, both in emphasizing eloquence in the characterization and in Snorri's elaborate speeches, which are often clues to his interpretations of events. The secular outlook and the focus on short-term interests rather than eternal values are also common. Finally, Snorri's way of organizing his material into one, coherent story, of which the saga of St. Óláfr is an excellent example, has its parallel in the Italian Renaissance in the development from the rather chaotic assembling of events in the order they occured in Giovanni Villani's chronicle from the first half of the fourteenth century to the structured narrative of Leonardo Bruni in the early fifteenth century (Phillips, 1986: 48 ff.).

The difference between the two kinds of culture is thus a question of existential, rather than purely intellectual interests. We should expect to find the kind of historiography represented by Snorri and the Italian Renaissance historians in milieus with a close connection between practical politics and intellectual activity and in which government and politics presented serious intellectual and practical problems.

In the central zone of Europe, the contrast between the scholastic and the aristocratic culture corresponds to the one between the highly educated elite of the universities, which to a considerable extent dominated the higher posts within the Church, and the lay aristocracy, whose main training was for war and who had relatively little scholarly education. Admittedly, neither the "ivory-tower" character of medieval clerical culture nor the stability of feudal society should be exaggerated. The Church, including its representatives in the intellectual milieus, was deeply involved in society, being a great landowner and holding extensive judicial and governmental powers. Nevertheless, the scholars at the universities in the central zone of Europe were more of a professional class of intellectuals than any other group of people in the Middle Ages. And even if the individual members of this culture did not lead a life isolated from the events of this world—after all, the aim of most university students was to get an administrative position in the ecclesiastical hierarchy—there is the paradox that the success of the Church in this world largely depended on it not becoming too directly involved in political affairs. Its *raison d'être* was its gospel of salvation in the next life and of eternal principles of right and wrong. Thus, despite its servants' deep involvement in this world, the kind of intellectual life it was most likely to promote was the one associated with abstract and general principles.

Though the similarity between medieval Italy on the one hand and Iceland and Norway on the other should not be exaggerated, both regions differed on some important points from these conditions. In Italy the laity was better educated than in the rest of Europe, a high percentage of the students at the universities were laymen, and the most important subjects taught there were the ones that could be used in practical life, such as medicine and law (Cobban, 1975: 48 ff., 163 ff., 221 f.). Neither the general level of education nor the educational institutions of Iceland and Norway can be compared to the Italian ones. But there was a long tradition for members of the Icelandic aristocracy to receive education of a similar kind as that of the clergy. Until the twelfth century, the Icelandic chieftains, who controlled the churches of the country, often became priests themselves. At least from the thirteenth century, the Norwegian aristocracy, which was then an administrative more than a warrior class, also seems to be fairly well educated (Bagge, 1984: 10 f.; 1987*b*: 222 ff.). As for the clergy, that of Iceland was clearly more subordinated to the lay chieftains than the clergy of most other countries. Though this was not the case in Norway, there was hardly the same possibility of creating a specifically clerical elite culture in such a small country as in the central zone of Europe. In any case, the scholastic culture is markedly less represented in Norway than in Denmark and Sweden. Though for slightly different reasons, the conditions for a unitary, humanistic-rhetorical culture seemed better in Italy on the one hand and Norway and Iceland on the other than in the central zone of Europe.

Thus, in both these regions the intellectual elite and a literary public largely consisted of practical men of action. Whereas in the Italian cities, the social background to these milieus was societies with more economic specialization and a more complex political organization than anywhere else in Europe, Snorri's Icelandic society may be considered fairly primitive and backward. In both societies, however, oratory and political maneuvering held an exceptional importance. One's position in society was more dependent on personal performance than in the more stable and stratified societies of feudal Europe, and the most important aspect of this performance was the ability to gain adherents and outwit one's opponents. By contrast, the members of the European feudal aristocracy regarded themselves as belonging to a closed caste with great needs for separating themselves from the rest of society. Aristocratic historiography performed this function by extolling the code of honor and the specifically aristocratic martial virtues. Though a game of politics of a similar kind as in the North no doubt existed, it was relatively less important and there were less ideological or intellectual reasons for describing it.

On the one hand, Snorri's Icelandic society shared some important characteristics with the more complex and advanced societies of the Italian cities. On the other, it is also possible to point to parallels with rather simple traditional societies, in which there is no very rigid social hierarchy and where it is necessary to make a personal achievement to gain adherents. In such societies, eloquence often has great importance (Sahlins, 1963: 290; Qviller, 1981: 119). This kind of milieu was more likely to produce a humanistic and rhetorical culture than the European clerical milieus. To the men who formed the elites of such societies, short-term aims were more important than eternal truth. To convince was more important than to prove. The main interest of the leaders of society and of the "literary public" in general was in human events and political activity, and it might even be the explicit purpose of literature to teach men how to behave in society. There are traces of this purpose in Snorri.

From a purely social point of view, Snorri's society is probably better compared to this kind of traditional society than to the Italian cities. From an intellectual point of view, however, it had access to a similar kind of culture as the latter, the traditions of the rich and varied humanistic culture of twelfth century Europe. Admittedly, I have been rather reluctant on the preceding pages to point to direct influence from European literature, as there are considerable differences in taste and style, and references to the classics and ancient history are rare among the secular saga writers. However, the intellectual training of the schools, the shift from oral to written culture, and the numerous works translated from Latin and French to Old Norse are clear evidence of European influence. The exact importance of this influence still largely remains to be examined. But the emphasis on writing is evidently a result of foreign influence, and foreign models may well have been an important factor in the development of large, continuous narratives in prose, in composition, the use of speeches, and so forth. The achievement of Snorri and other authors of this milieu may be explained through this combination. The external stimulus made them narrate and analyze past and present political events, whereas the special political conditions of their society inspired them to a kind of historiography that may partly be understood as a continuation of tendencies already present in that of twelfth-century Europe and partly as something completely novel. In short: the combination of the emphasis on rhetoric and narrative in a rather simple traditional society and the tradition of a humanistic culture, going back to antiquity and revived during the twelfth-century Renaissance, may have been extremely fruitful.

We thus return to the social explanation to the originality of Snorri and other Nordic historians. Not only is Snorri's particular way of describing society the result of the particular character of the Icelandic society with which he was familiar and which to some extent is the object of his description. This society also served to create a culture and a literary public that could stimulate the kind of historiography represented by Snorri. Though we cannot state that such a social and cultural milieu must inevitably produce a work of history like Snorri's *Heimskringla,* there is no doubt that it was more likely to stimulate this kind of achievement than either the scholastic or the aristocratic milieus of feudal Europe. Historiography in the North had the prestige and importance that was necessary to attract an extraordinary talent like Snorri, who would most probably have turned to other subjects if he had lived in contemporary feudal Europe.

Conclusion

The preceding examination of Snorri's *Heimskringla* has above all focused on his analysis of politics, which also seems to be a central concern for Snorri himself and a point on which he differs markedly from most other historians of his period. In contrast to European aristocratic chronicles, he does not only describe the events, but seeks to explain them. The politician of *Heimskringla* acts according to his own interests and maneuvers for gain in a way that to some extent resembles the descriptions of politics from the Italian Renaissance and later, but which is very different from the descriptions in contemporary aristocratic chronicles. In the latter, action is not so much spontaneous as determined by the chivalrous code of honor. The question of success or failure is less prominent and descriptions of strategy and tactics are largely absent. In its explanatory, reflective approach, *Heimskringla* rather conforms to contemporary clerical historiography, but differs from it by concentrating on human actions and the short-term perspective and in explaining more in terms of human will and political circumstances than God's providence and morality.

To this difference in the description of politics corresponds a difference in the description of morality, human nature, and society. There are relatively few "rules of the game" and success or failure seem to be the most important criteria of evaluation. The fact that success is essentially a question of winning support, either through an impressive initial victory or by winning popularity through gifts or concessions, indicates that Snorri's society is both relatively loosely structured, without very strong ties of loyalty, and fairly "democratic." Despite some Machiavellian traits in his description of politics, the similarity to the Italian Renaissance and the early modern period should not be exaggerated. First, Snorri's society is a rather primitive society without a state in the real sense, and second, the political maneuvering takes place between persons with certain more or less well-founded legal claims within a rather static system. If Snorri's description of politics corresponds to that of the early modern period, the explanation is rather to be sought in the direction of Bailey's idea of a fairly universal political game than in Snorri anticipating modern development.

Admittedly, similar presentations of the political game are to be found in European historians, but they are less prominent there. By contrast, a comparison with other Icelandic-Norwegian works shows that Snorri's analysis of political history has much in common with the general trend of historiography in this region, though he clearly surpasses most other historians as an analyst of politics. To explain this difference, we therefore have to turn to society and thus to approach the problem stated originally, of the relationship between political behavior and its description in the narrative sources. How far is the difference to be explained in terms of differences in society and how far is it the consequence of different ways of describing similar phenomena? Snorri's emphasis on tactics and the political game as opposed to the code of honor in the European chronicles is to some extent to be explained from the fact that the rules of the game were different, which in its turn is the result of society being different. Though the rules were certainly not always followed in practice, this difference probably also reflects some difference in political behavior. Similarly, the importance of winning universal support, the attention paid to the people, and the relatively "democratic" character of Snorri's society in contrast to the strictly aristocratic society of the contemporary European chronicles can be explained from actual conditions, that is, from Snorri's Icelandic society, though the society described in *Heimskringla* is likely to bear some resemblance to that of Norway in the earlier Middle Ages.

However, it is not sufficient to explain the difference between Snorri and his European contemporaries solely in terms of different realities, as descriptions are rarely exact representations of reality. It is also a question of "realistic" versus "ideological" representation of the same reality. This difference must also be explained in terms of intellectual milieus and genre conventions. Here a significant contrast emerges between Iceland and partly also Norway on the one hand and feudal Europe on the other in the importance and function of history within the intellectual elite. As in Italy, the humanistic culture of the twelfth century survived in the North, whereas thirteenth-century scholasticism was of little importance. This has to do with the composition of the intellectual elite in the North, in which the laity played a prominent part and both the clergy and the lay aristocracy were less exclusive. The intellectual elite consisted primarily of politicians and practical men of action, who had to convince and manipulate to gain influence and be able to govern. This made rhetoric, history, and other humanistic disciplines extraordinarily important and formed the cultural background to an extraordinary achievement such as *Heimskringla*.

Appendix 1
The Rulers of
Heimskringla

Starting with Hálvdan svarti, the following list gives the rulers treated in *Heimskringla*. The dates of their reigns are given according to Snorri's chronology, sometimes with alternatives suggested by modern historians in brackets. For a survey of the modern discussion of the early chronology, see Andersen, 1977: 80 ff.

Hálvdan Guðrøðarson svarti (the Black), 850–860.
Haraldr Hálvdanarson hárfagri (Fairhair), 860–933 (late ninth century to c. 940/945?).
Hákon Haraldsson góði (the Good), 934–960.
Haraldr gráfeldr and his brothers (the Eiríkssons), 960–975 [c. 960–970/974].
Earl Hákon Sigurðarson, 975–995 (c. 970/974–995).
Óláfr Tryggvason, 995–1000 (995–999).
Eiríkr and Sveinn Hákonarsonar, earls, 1000–1015 [1000–1016].
Óláfr Haraldsson (St. Óláfr), 1014–1030 [1015–1030].
Cnut the Great, 1028–1035.
Magnús Óláfsson góði (the Good), 1035–1047 [1035–1046].
Haraldr Sigurðarson harðráði (the Strict), 1046–1066 [1045–1066].
Óláfr Haraldsson kyrri (the Quiet), 1066–1093.
Magnús Óláfsson berfoetr (Bareleg), 1093–1103.
Eysteinn Magnússon, 1103–1122.
Sigurðr Magnússon, 1103–1130.
Óláfr Magnússon, 1103–1115.
Magnús Sigurðarson blindi (the Blind), 1130–1135, 1136–1139.
Haraldr Magnússon gilli (i.e., Gillikristr = the Servant of Christ), 1130–1136.
Ingi Haraldsson, 1136–1161.
Sigurðr Haraldsson munnr (Mouth), 1136–1155.

Eysteinn Haraldsson, 1142–1157.
Sigurðr slembir (i.e., slembidjákn = the Bad Deacon), pretender, 1136–1139.
Hákon Eysteinnsson herðibreiðr (the Broadshouldered), 1157–1162.
Magnús Erlingsson, 1161–1184.

Appendix 2
Summary of Events in
St. Óláfr's Reign
[1015–1028]

Second winter [*1015–1016*]	Ó. in Nidaros; building activities, daily life.	(chaps. 56–58)
Winter [1015–1016]	Messengers from Sweden; conflict.	(chap. 59)
Spring [1016]	Settlement w/Erlingr Skjálgsson.	(chap. 60)
Spring/summer [1016]	Ó. in Viken; conflict with Sweden; Ó.'s allies there.	(chaps. 61–67)
Autumn [1016]	Messengers sent to Sw.	(chaps. 68–72)
Third winter [*1016–1017*]	Ó. at Opplandene; captures the Oppland kings.	(chaps. 73–75)
	Ó. and his brothers.	(chap. 76)
Spring [1017]	Negotiations in Sw.; the king forced to seek peace with Ó.	(chaps. 77–80)
Spring [1017]	Ó. in Tønsberg; Hroerekr's attempts at his life.	(chaps. 81–84)
Summer [1017]– summer [1020]	Hroerekr sent to Iceland; dies there.	(chap. 85)
Summer [1017]	Battle in Úlfreksfjǫrðr (Ireland).	(chap. 86)
Summer [1017]	Ó. to Göta Älv to meet his Swedish bride; the Swedes do not appear.	(chap. 87)
Autumn [1017]	Events in Sw.; pressure on Sw. king.	(chaps. 88–90)

Fourth winter [1017–1018]	Ó. in Borg.	(chap. 90: 167 f.)
Winter–spring [1018]	New embassy to Sw.; Ó. marries the king's daughter; rebellion in Sw.; the king forced to submit, peace.	(chaps. 91–94)
Summer–autumn [1018]	Ó. to Tønsb.; in the autumn to Nidaros. Summary of his successes so far.	(chap. 95)
Fifth winter [1018–1019]	Ó. in Nidaros; Þorkell fóstri from Orkneys visits him.	(chap. 95, cf. 104: 214)
[9. c–1021]	Events in the Orkneys; the earls submit to Ó.	(chaps. 96–103)
Summer [1019]	Ó. in Hálogaland.	(chaps. 104–106)
Sixth winter [1019–1020]	Ó. in Nidaros; Þorkell's second visit, having killed Earl Einarr.	(chap. 106, cf. 99)
Seventh winter [1020–1021]	Ó. in Nidaros.	(chaps. 107–108, 111)
Autumn [1020] Easter [1021]	*Blót* at Mære; Ó. kills Ǫlvi at Egge; promotes Kálfr.	(chaps. 107–110)
Summer [1021]	The Orkn. earls submit to Ó.	(chaps. 100–102, 111)
Summer–autumn [1021]	Ó. converts the regions Møre, Gudbrandsdalen, and Opplandene. The story of Dala-Guðbrandr.	(chaps. 111–114)
Eighth winter [1021–1022]	Ó. at Opplandene.	(chap. 114: 237 f.)
[1022]	Ó. in Eastern Norw.; settlement with Einarr þambarskelfir.	(chaps. 114–115)
Ninth winter [1022–1023]	Ó. in Borg.	(chap. 115)
Spring [1023]	Ó. to W. Norw., settlement with Erlingr Skjálgsson.	(chap. 116)
Summer [1022]	Ásbjǫrn selsbani's expedition.	(chap. 117)
Easter [1023]	Ó. at Avaldsnes; Ásbj. kills Selþórir, is saved by Erlingr.	(chaps. 118–120)

Spring–summer [1023]	Ó. converts inner regions of W. Norw.; via Gudbr.dalen to Nidaros.	(chap. 121)
Summer [1022–1023]	Einarr þ. to England, meets Cnut; then to Rome, home without seeing Ó.	(chap. 121: 265)
Tenth winter [1023–1024]	Ó. in Nidaros.	(chap. 121: 265)
	Ó.'s son Magnús born	(chap. 122)
Spring [1024]	Ó. gives Ásmundr G. *sýsla.*	(chap. 123)
Spring–summer [1024]	Ásm. kills Ásbj. s.	(chap. 123)
Spring–summer [1024]	Ó. southward along the coast to the Sw. border. Summary of Ó.'s reign hitherto.	(chap. 124)
Summer [1024]	Ó.'s embassy to Iceland.	(chaps. 125–126)
Summer [1024]	Messengers from the Faroes to Ó.	(chap. 127)
Autumn [1024]	Ó. to Viken, then to Opplandene.	(chap. 128)
Eleventh winter [1024–1025]	Ó. at Opplandene.	(chap. 128)
Winter–spring [1025]	Marriage arrangements; Ó. to Gudbr.dalen, then to Tønsbg.	(chap. 128)
Summer [1025]	Messages from Iceland and the Faroes.	(chap. 129)
Spring [1025]	King Cnut demands Norw.; presentation of him; embassy to Ó. in Tønsbg.	(chaps. 130–131)
Summer [1025]	Erlingr S.'s sons to Cnut in Engl.	(chap. 131)
Summer–autumn [1025]	Ó. seeks support from *lendmenn;* sends embassy to Sweden.	(chap. 132)
Twelfth winter [1025–1026]	Ó. in Borg.	(chap. 133: 290)
Spring–summer [1026]	Karli and Þórir hundr in Bjarmaland; Þórir kills Karli.	(chap. 133)
Spring [1026]	Ó. meets the king of Sw. in Konghelle, then to W. Norw.; Cnut to Engl.	(chap. 134)

Summer [1026]	Episodes with men from the Faroes and Iceland; Ó. sends Gellir to Icel.; he returns next year.	(chaps. 135–136)
Thirteenth winter [1026–1027]	Ó. in Nidaro.s	(chap. 136: 309)
	Conflict with King of Sw. over Jämtland.	(chap. 137)
Winter [1026–1027]	Stein Skaptason kills Ó.'s *ármaðr;* is protected by Þorbergr Árnason; conflict between Ó. and the Árnasons.	(chap. 138)
Spring [1027]	Finnr Árnason to Hálogaland; Þórir hundr to England; conflict Hárekr–Ásmundr Grankellsson.	(chaps. 139–140)
Winter [1026–1027]	Þóroddr Snorrason in Jämtl.	(chap. 141)
Spring [1027]	Ó. southward with *leiðangr*	(chap. 142)
Spring [1027]–spring [1028]	Ó. sends Moera-Karl to the Faroes; he is killed.	(chap. 143)
Spring–autumn [1027]	Ó.'s expedition against Denmark.	(chaps. 144–159)
Fourteenth winter [1027–1028]	Ó. in Borg.	(chap. 159)
Winter [1027–1028]	On Sigvatr skaldr, Erlingr S., and Þórir hundr.	(chaps. 160–162)
Winter [1028]	Ó. at Opplandene; episode with Bjǫrn *ármaðr* and the sons of Kálfr Á.	(chaps. 162–166)
Spring [1028]	Ó. in Tønsbg.; tries to mobilize against Cnut.	(chaps. 166–168)
Spring [1028]	Hárekr kills Grankell.	(chap. 169)
Spring–autumn [1028]	Cnut takes Norway.	(chaps. 170–173)
Late autumn [1028]	Ó. westward from Tønsbg.; fights Erlingr S., who is killed.	(chaps. 174–176)
Fifteenth winter [1028–1029]	Mobilization against Ó.; Áslákr f. killed. Ó. decides to leave the country; his journey eastward; the length of his reign; the reasons for the rebellion against him.	(chaps. 177–181)

Old Norse Pronunciation

ð   pronounced as *th* in English *though*.

Þ   (capital) and þ   pronounced as *th* in English *think*.

ǫ   open *o*.

á, í, ó, etc.   long vowels.

Abbreviations

Ágr. = *Ágrip.* Ed. and trans. Gustav Indrebø. Oslo, 1936.

Eirsp. = *Eirspennil* (AM 47 fol.). Ed. Finnur Jónsson. Oslo, 1916.

Fsk. = *Fagrskinna.* Ed. Finnur Jónsson. Copenhagen, 1902.

G = "Gulaþingslǫg," in *Norges gamle Love,* vol. 1. Ed. R. Keyser, P. A. Munch, G. Storm, E. Hertzberg. Oslo, 1846: 1–118.

Gesta = *Otto of Freising. Gesta Frederici seu róctius Chronica,* ed. F. J. Schmale. Darmstadt, 1965.

H = "Hirðskrá," in *Norges gamle Love,* vol. 2. Ed. R. Keyser, P. A. Munch, G. Storm, E. Hertzberg. Oslo, 1848: 387–450.

HG = The Saga of Hákon góði, in Snorri Sturluson, *Heimskringla* 1: 165–222.

HGráf. = The Saga of Haraldr gráfeldr, in Snorri Sturluson, *Heimskringla* 1:223–254.

HHarð. = The Saga of Haraldr harðráði, in Snorri Sturluson, *Heimskringla* 3:74–224.

HHárf. = The Saga of Haraldr hárfagri, in Snorri Sturluson, *Heimskringla* 1:98–164.

HHerð. = The Saga of Hákon herðibreiðr, in Snorri Sturluson, *Heimskringla* 3: 398–431.

Hkr. = Snorri Sturluson. *Heimskringla,* vols. 1–4. Ed. F. Jónsson. Copenhagen, 1893–1901.

HN = "Historia Norvegiae," in *Monumenta Historica Norvegiæ.* Ed. Gustav Storm. Oslo, 1880: 69–124.

Holl. = *Heimskringla.* Trans. with intro., etc. by Lee M. Hollander. Auston, 1967.

Hom. = *Gamal norsk homiliebok.* Ed. G. Indrebø, Oslo, 1931.

HS = The Saga of Hálfdan svarti, in Snorri Sturluson, *Heimskringla* 1: 86–97.

HT = *Historisk Tidsskrift* (Norwegian).

Ingi = The Saga of Ingi and His Brothers, in Snorri Sturluson, *Heimskringla* 3: 348–397.

Ísl. = Ari Þorgilsson fróði. "Íslendingabók," ed. J. Benediktsson (Íslenzk fornrit vol. I.1: 1–28). Reykjavík, 1958.

Jóms. = *Jómsvíkinga saga.* Ed. Ó. Halldórsson. Reykjavík, 1969.

Kgs. = [*The King's Mirror*] *Konungs skuggsiá.* Ed. L. Holm-Olsen. Oslo, 1945.

KLNM = *Kulturhistorisk leksikon for nordisk middelalder.* Oslo, 1956–1978.

L = [*The National Law*] *Landslǫg,* in *Norges gamle Love,* vol. 2. Ed. R. Keyser, P. A. Munch, G. Storm, E. Hertzberg. Oslo, 1848: 1–178.

Larson = *The King's Mirror (Speculum regale—Konungs Skuggsjá).* Trans. and intro. Lawrence M. Larson. New York: The American-Scandinavian Foundation, 1917.

Leg. saga. = [*Legendary saga*] *Óláfs saga hins helga. Efter pergamenthaandskrift i Uppsala Universitetsbibliotek, Delagardieske samling nr. 8 ii.* Ed. O. A. Johnsen. Oslo, 1922.

MB = The Saga of Magnús berfoetr, in Snorri Sturluson, *Heimskringla* 3: 233–266.

MB.HG = The Saga of Magnús blindi and Haraldr gilli, in Snorri Sturluson, *Heimskringla* 3: 315–347.

ME = The Saga of Magnús Erlingsson, in Snorri Sturluson, *Heimskringla* 3: 432–492.

MG = The Saga of Magnús góði, in Snorri Sturluson, *Heimskringla* 3: 3–73.

MHN = *Monumenta Historica Norvegiæ.* Ed. Gustav Storm. Oslo, 1880.

Msk. = *Morkinskinna.* Ed. Finnur Jónsson. Copenhagen, 1932.

Msyn. = The Saga of the Magnússynir, in Snorri Sturluson, *Heimskringla* 3: 267–314.

NG = "Nyere Gulathings Christenret," in *Norges gamle Love,* vol. 2. Ed. R. Keyser, P. A. Munch, G. Storm, E. Hertzberg. Oslo, 1848: 306–326.

NGL = *Norge gamle Love.* Ed. R. Keyser, P. A. Munch, G. Storm, E. Hertzberg, vols. 1–5. Oslo, 1846–1895.

OH = The Sage of Óláfr hinn helgi [St. Óláfr], in Snorri Sturluson, *Heimskringla,* vol. 2.

OK = The Saga of Óláfr kyrri, in Snorri Sturluson, *Heimskringla* 3: 225–232.

Oldest Saga = *Otte Brudstykker af den ældste Saga om Olav den hellige.* Ed. G. Storm. Oslo, 1893.

Orkn. = *Orkneyinga Saga.* Ed. Finnbogi Guðmundsson. (Íslenzk fornrit vol. 34). Reykjavík: Hið íslenzka fornritafélag, 1965.

OT = The Saga of Óláfr Tryggvason, in Snorri Sturluson, *Heimskringla* 1: 255–459.

Passio = *Passio et Miracula Beati Olavi.* Ed. F. Metcalfe. Oxford, 1881.

Prol. Hkr. = *Heimskringla. Prologue.* Ed. Finnur Jónsson. Copenhagen, 1893–1901, vol. 1: 1–8.

Prol. OH = *Saga Óláfs konungs hins helpa. Prologue.* Ed. O. A. Johnsen. Oslo, 1941, vol. 1: 1–5.

SagaOT = Oddr Snorrason munkr. *Saga Óláfs Tryggvasonar,* ed. Finnur Jónsson. Copenhagen, 1932.

Separate Saga = *Saga Óláfs konungs hins helga,* vols. 1–2. Ed. O. A. Johnsen. Oslo, 1941.

Sk. = *Det arnamagnæanske Haandskrift 81a Fol. (Skálholtsbók yngsta).* Ed. A. Kjær and L. Holm-Olsen. Oslo, 1947.

Skjalded. = *Den norsk-islandske Skjaldedigtning.* Ed. Finnur Jónsson, A1–B2. Copenhagen, 1908–1914.

SS = *Sverris saga.* Ed. G. Indrebø. Oslo, 1920.

Sturl. = *Sturlunga saga.* Ed. Kr. Kålund, vols. 1–2. Copenhagen, 1906–1911.

Theod. = Theodoricus Monachus. "Historia de antiquitate regum Norwagiensium." In *Monumenta Historica Norvegiæ,* ed. Gustav Storm. Olso, 1889: 1–68.

Vigf. = *Hákonar saga and a Fragment of Magnúss saga.* Ed. Gudbrandur Vigfusson (Rerum Britannicarum medii ævi scriptores 88/2). London, 1887.

Yngl. = The Saga of the Ynglingar, in Snorri Sturluson, *Heimskringla* 1: 9–85.

Notes

Introduction

1. E.g., Bernheim, 1964 [orig. 1918]. For a survey of German research on medieval historiography until the 1930s, see Spörl, 1965: 1 ff. Bernheim's ideas were originally presented in a paper read at the Historical Conference in London in 1913, where Koht was present (Dahl, 1959: 241; Odén, 1975: 227). Though there is no similarity in detail between the two, Koht may well have been inspired by Bernheim in his general attempt to trace the fundamental attitudes implicit in medieval historiography. The influence from Bernheim is more direct in the Swedish historian Curt Weibull's seminal study of Saxo and the hagiographic literature on St. Cnut of Denmark (Weibull, 1964 [orig. 1915]: 168 ff., 178 ff.).

2. See also the survey of scholarship in Ray, 1974: 33 ff.

3. See Duby, 1986, who regards the description of William Marshall in *L'Histoire du Guillaume le Maréchal*, written shortly after the hero's death, as largely an accurate description of chivalrous behavior at the time. For a general, and far more extreme, assertion of this point of view, see Nitschke, 1967: 176 ff.

4. See Clover, 1985: 253 ff. on the problem in general and Jochens, 1986 on the fictional character of the strong, independent woman in the Icelandic family sagas.

5. There is not much in English on Norwegian medieval history. Koht's contribution to the *Cambridge Medieval History,* though somewhat dated, is still worth consulting (Koht, 1964 [orig. 1929]). In Norwegian, there are a number of surveys with different interpretations. Holmsen, 1977 [orig. 1939] and Lunden, 1977 are excellent syntheses of a Marxist inspiration. See also Andersen, 1977 and Helle, 1974, which contain extensive bibliographies and references to the scholarly discussion. For my own interpretation, see Bagge, 1986 and 1989*b*.

6. Weibull, 1948: 245 ff. There was, however, some anticipation of Weibull's position in the nineteenth century. For a discussion of the background and consequences of Weibull's revision, see Dahl, 1959: 196 ff.; Torstendahl, 1964: 335 ff.; Odén, 1975: 148 ff.; and Skovgaard-Petersen, 1987b: 15 ff.

7. For a survey of the sources, see Andersen, 1977: 11 ff. and Helle, 1974: 13 ff. A recent discussion of the sagas as sources, with extensive references to earlier literature is Ólason, 1987: 30 ff.

8. The arguments for this have been stated most recently by Benediktsson, 1955: 118 ff. See also Louis-Jensen 1977: 50, who doubts Benediktsson's assumption that the two references from the sixteenth century are to the same manuscript, and Halldórsson, 1979: 113–138, who points to the evidence from medieval manuscripts. See also Andersson, 1985: 213.

9. On Snorri's life, see Nordal, 1973: 11 ff.; Koht, 1962: 107 ff.; and Karlsson, 1979: 23 ff.

10. On Oddi as a center of learning, see Sveinsson, 1937. The church at Oddi, which the Oddaverjar controlled, was probably the wealthiest in Iceland next to the episcopal sees and the monasteries. As for historical studies, the *Orkneyinga saga* and the now lost *Skjǫldunga saga* were probably written in the milieu around Oddi (see also Guðnason, 1963: 273 ff.). Though there is no direct evidence of this, Snorri must in all probability have had access to several books in Jón's household or at the church.

11. I.e., churches that owned the land on which they were situated. Such churches were often very rich, and control over them was important for the power of the chieftains during the free-state period (Stefánsson, 1975: 86 ff.).

12. For this and the following, see the excellent summary of the scholarly discussion in Andersson, 1985: 197–238.

13. On the difference, see Amory, 1979: 71, quoting Ker, 1925: 141: "These two books [i.e., Theodoricus's and *Historia Norvegiae*] might be picked out of the Middle Ages on purpose to make a contrast of their style with the Icelandic saga."

14. The remains of the *Oldest Saga* are six fragments preserved in the Norwegian National Archive. These were edited by Gustav Storm in 1893, together with two fragments in the Arnamagnæan collection in Copenhagen, which Storm believed stemmed from the same manuscript (*Oldest Saga:* (1) ff.). These latter fragments have a distinctly hagiographic character and one of them can also be dated to the latter half of the twelfth century. But in 1970 Jonna Louis-Jensen reexamined the Copenhagen fragments and argued that they could not belong to the same manuscript as those in Oslo (Louis-Jensen, 1970: 31–60). Jónas Kristjánsson has later supported her conclusion (1972: 156–163, 223, 316 ff.). See also Andersson, 1985: 213.

15. There has been an extensive discussion on the extent of *Grýla* and on the composition of *Sverris saga* in general. By now there seems to be wide agreement that *Grýla* comprises only a small part of the saga, probably ending in 1178 (chap. 31), in the second year of Sverris career. See the most recent treatment of the question by Holm-Olsen, 1972: 551 f., 556 f. with ref.; Blöndal, 1982: 124 ff., 200 ff.; and Andersson, 1985: 225 f.

16. Blöndal, 1982: 170–172 (see Eng. summary: 205 ff.) rejects the idea of

royal patronage by pointing to the objective treatment of Sverrir's adversaries in the middle part of the saga, but this is a doubtful argument in the light of the general character of the sagas (see below).

17. As for authorship, the *Oldest Saga* is commonly assumed to have been written by an Icelander. The latter is only preserved in a Norwegian manuscript, but opinions are divided as to whether it is originally Icelandic or Norwegian (Johnsen, 1922: XVIII ff. with ref.; Nordal, 1953: 206; Holm-Olsen, 1974: 116). The most recent discussion of the matter, by Jónas Kristjánsson (1976: 293), concludes, in my opinion convincingly, that it is hardly a question of the one or the other: the work is a compilation of both Icelandic and Norwegian sources.

18. I.e., the fragments Snorri left out and which have been inserted in some manuscripts of Snorri's *Separate Saga* (*Separate Saga* vol. 2: 683 ff.; see Nordal, 1914: 69 ff.).

19. Alfred Jakobsen (1970: 88 ff.) has argued in favor of a Norwegian author, whereas Bjarni Einarsson (1984: cxxix ff.) defends the traditional opinion, that the author was Icelandic. Whatever his original nationality, there can be no doubt of his close connection with the Norwegian court (see below).

20. The first author to use scaldic poems was apparently the author of *Ágrip*, who did so in a rather awkward way. On the progressively more frequent and efficient use of these sources in the later sagas, see among others Fidjestøl, 1982: 20 ff.

Chapter 1: The Author

1. For a discussion of Steblin-Kamensky's views, see Hallberg, 1974: 102 ff. and 1976: 164 ff.; Steblin-Kamensky, 1975: 187 ff. and 1976: 167 ff.; Weber, 1972: 188 ff., 141 ff.; Clover, 1985: 259 ff.; and Harris, 1986: 187 ff.

2. See Wessén, 1928–1929: 52 ff. with ref. to earlier literature.

3. King Haraldr was killed on 25 September 1066. As there are other sources indicating that Ari was born in 1068, Snorri has probably reckoned the winter 1066–1067 as the one of Haraldr's death and that of 1067–1068 as the one of Ari's birth (Benediktsson, 1968: v).

4. *Prol. Hkr.*: 7 f. Snorri gives the names of ten persons, whom he says Ari refers to as his witnesses. Nine of them are mentioned in Ari's *Íslendingabók*, which is now extant (*Ísl.* chaps. 1, 7, 9), whereas the tenth is probably taken from Ari's *Konunga œvi* (see Ellehøj, 1965: 62).

5. I.e., the right for members of a kindred to buy back land that has been sold by another member to someone outside the kindred. For the law of *óðal* to apply, the land must have belonged to the kindred over a certain period of time, three to six generations or sixty years in the various Norwegian laws. The link to this fairly distant past is established through witnesses who refer to the testimony of their fathers, which is derived from that of their fathers and so on. See Robberstad, 1967: 494 ff. Generally, Norwegian and Icelandic law and European law of the period were based on the evaluation of the witnesses rather than of their testimony, with some exception for canon law. On the parallel between legal and historical evidence, see Guenée, 1980: 132.

6. "en þat er háttr skálda, at lofa þann mest, er þá eru þeir fyrir, en engi

myndi þat þora, at segja sjálfum honum þau verk hans, er allir þeir, er heyrði, vissi, at hégómi væri ok skrǫk, ok svá sjálfr hann; þat væri þá háð, en eigi lof" (*Prol. Hkr.*: 6). Snorri may possibly have had in mind a story from *Morkinskinna* about a French knight, who had behaved cowardly in battle and whom an Icelandic scald ridiculed by reciting a poem, praising his bravery (*Msk.*: 326; see Nordal, 1973: 136).

7. "Þau orð er i qvedscap standa ero en somo sem i fyrstu voro ef rett er kveðit þott hveR maðr hafi siðan numit at auðrom. oc ma þvi ecki breyta. En sogur þer er sagðar ero. þa er þat hett at eigi sciliz aullum a einn veg. en sumir hafa eigi minni þa er fra liðr hvernig þeim var sagt. oc gengz þeim mioc í minni optliga. oc verda frasagnir omerkligar" (*Prol. OH*: 4).

8. Having finished his comments on Ari, Snorri adds: "en kvæðin þykkja mér sízt ór stað foerð, ef þau eru rétt kveðin ok skynsemliga upp tekin" ("As to the poems, I consider them least likely to lead astray, if they are correctly recited and judiciously interpreted") (*Prol. Hkr.*: 8; *my translation*).

9. The alternative explanation, that the prologue was originally written for the *Separate Saga,* which ends in the mid-eleventh century, is unlikely because of the great emphasis on events *before* Óláfr's reign in the prologue (see Wessén, 1928–1929: 55).

10. *Ingi* chap. 11: 365 f.; see chap. 12. The whole passage is found in much the same form in *Msk.*: 433 ff. However, *Morkinskinna* has only a general reference to Eiríkr as an introduction to the story of Sigurðr and the sons of Haraldr (*Msk.*: 419) and does not mention him here. Thus, Snorri seems to have known Eiríkr directly, not via *Morkinskinna;* (cf. Olsen, 1965: 56 f., who has a different opinion).

11. "en þó er mikla fleira óritat hans frægðarverka; kømr til þess ófroeði vár ok þat annat, at vér viljum eigi setja á boekr vitnislausar sǫgur; þótt vér hafim heyrt roeður eða getit fleiri hluta, þá þykkir oss heðan í frá betra, at við sé aukit, en þetta sama þurfi ór at taka. Er saga mikil frá Haraldi konungi sett í kvæði, þau er íslenzkir menn foerðu honum sjálfum eða sonum hans; var hann fyrir þá sǫk vinr þeira mikill" (*HHarð.* chap. 36: 129).

12. At first sight, the prologue to *Sverris saga* seems to give a different picture from the one I have drawn of Snorri, suggesting that even contemporary and recent history presented problems to his contemporaries. Here the author gives a short report of the various sources he has used, the story of Sverrir's early career, which was written under his own supervision, and reports of eyewitnesses, some of which were written down shortly after the events. However, the author is even less interested than Snorri in assessing the relative trustworthiness of these different categories. His main worries are (1) that men who are fully informed about the events—because they have taken part in them?—may find that he has omitted too much, and (2) that his readers may find it difficult to believe that the events he tells actually happened, considering the number of men involved in them, i.e., Sverrir's victories over largely superior enemies. The author thus finds it necessary to point to the *amount* of information at his disposal and to defend himself against charges of telling a story that is too fantastic. As in Snorri's case, there are therefore special reasons for him to account for his sources.

13. Thus, one of the reasons for Storm's positive evaluation of Snorri as a critical historian is that he was himself considerably less critical than became usual after Lauritz Weibull's radical revision in 1911 (above, n. 2).

14. E.g., on Sigurðr slembir (MB.HG chaps. 15–16; *Ingi* chaps. 1–5): he kills Haraldr gilli in Bergen on the night following the feast of Sancta Lucia (13 December 1136), then flees northward. Shortly after Christmas he arrives in Nidaros and takes Magnús blindi out of the monastery. Then the two kings part; Sigurðr goes westward across the sea, whereas Magnús spends the rest of the winter and the whole summer at Opplandene, is defeated by King Ingi's men at Minne, probably in late summer, and retires to Sweden and then to Denmark. The following two invasions, first from Sweden, then from Denmark, which both fail, are left undated, but it appears from the following passage, where Sigurðr is reintroduced, that they took place the same summer (*Ingi* chap. 5). See also *HHerð*. chaps. 2–11: "The next summer" (1158, after Eysteinn's death and Hákon's acclamation as king), Hákon returns to Norway from Western Sweden, captures Konghelle, which Grégóríús leaves. The latter gets reinforcements, returns, and attacks Hákon in Konghelle and defeats him. Hákon then retires to Nidaros and spends the winter there, while Grégóríús and Erlingr remain in Viken. Next spring Hákon moves southward via Bergen to Viken, is defeated once more in Göta Älv, then goes north, arrives in Nidaros before Christmas, and spends the following winter there.

15. E.g., the death of King Sigurðr, 10 June 1155; of Grégóríús Dagsson, 7 January 1161, and King Ingi, 3 February 1161 and the examples above.

16. According to both *Fagrskinna* and *Heimskringla* the battle must have taken place shortly after Christmas. Both sagas tell that Magnus spent Christmas in Tønsberg and then learned that the Birchlegs were staying at Ré, just outside the town (*Fsk.*: 378 f.; ME chap. 42: 488). Similarly, the battle of Göta Älv (1159), which is told in great detail with several speeches, is without exact date (*HHerð*. chaps. 4–11).

17. Erlingr suddenly leaves Bergen in spring (1162) early on a Wednesday morning and goes northward to attack Hákon, who is on his way from Nidaros. The fleets meet on Friday and the battle of Sekken is fought, in which Hákon is killed (ME chaps. 6–7). In 1165 Erlingr leaves Bergen on Tuesday before the Ascension and attacks Nidaros early in the morning on Ascension Day (11 and 13 May, ME chaps. 25–26).

18. See *Ingi* chaps. 13–25, between the story of Sigurðr slembir and the conflicts between the kings. Here Snorri characterizes the kings and introduces the main actors in the following events, such as Erlingr skakki and Grégóríús, tells of Cardinal Nicholas Brekespeare's visit to Norway to establish the archbishopric and of two miracles of St. Óláfr. Some other miracles are inserted between the death of King Ingi and the acclamation of Magnús Erlingsson (*HHerð*. chaps. 20–21).

19. "Óláfr konungr fell miðvikudag iiii. kál. Augusti mánaðar" (OH chap. 235), i.e., Wednesday 29 July. The Roman calendar is mainly to be found in ecclesiastical documents and rarely in sagas or other secular sources. However, if Snorri wanted to indicate the date, he could hardly have used the common method, the saint's day, as the saint in question was Óláfr himself!

20. Koht, 1921: 127 f. Koht's first argument is that according to Theodoricus (chap. 14: 25)—one of the oldest sources—fifteen years passed between the battle of Svolð, which according to the sources took place in 1000 and is one of the cardinal points in the Old Icelandic chronology (Einarsdóttir, 1964: 72 ff.; Ellehøj, 1965: 77 ff.), and Óláfr's return. Secondly, a contemporary English source dates Earl Eiríkr's arrival in England to 1015 (*Gesta Cnutonis* book 2, chap. 7), which means that Óláfr must have returned later than this. Snorri refers to Ari for his information on the length of Óláfr's reign and adds that the fifteen years commonly attributed to him must be reckoned either from the battle of Nesjar till his death or from his return to Norway till his exile (OH chap. 179, vol. 2; Hur: 416 f.). In addition to Ari, Snorri refers to a scaldic stanza by Sigvatr, according to which Óláfr ruled Opplandene for fifteen winters until his death. "Áleifr réð et øfra,/ andprútt høfuð, landi/ fulla vetr, áðr felli,/ fimtán af þvi láni" "Óláfr ruled the upper part of the country for fifteen years until he fell" (OH chap. 246). However, most of Snorri's predecessors, probably including Ari, reckoned the fifteen years from Óláfr's arrival in Norway till his death (see Theodoricus chap. 19: 42 and 20: 44; *Ágr.* chap. 26; *Leg. Saga:* 91; and *Fsk.*: 178 f.).

21. Snorri may have known that King Óláfr of Sweden died in 1020 and dated the negotiations with him accordingly. An independent Russian source, which Snorri has evidently not known, dates Ingigerðr's marriage to King Jarizleifr to 1019 (Storm, 1873: 157), one year later than Snorri (OH chap. 93: 180 f.). Snorri has evidently known from earlier sources that events such as the conflict with Denmark, the battle of Helgå, and the death of Erlingr Skjálgsson took place toward the end of Óláfr's reign. Some of these events are dated in *Leg. Saga:* 59–67 and apparently in *Oldest Saga:* 23 (the fragment only covers Cnut's demand of Norway). Even here, however, Snorri's exact chronology is to some extent a construction and probably contains some errors (see, among others, Koht, 1921: 134 ff.; Schreiner, 1925: 309 ff.; Moberg, 1941: 148 ff.). See also the summaries of the chronology of various sagas in Brynildsen, 1916: 105 ff.

22. This raises the question of the relationship between Snorri and the Icelandic family sagas. There seems to be a similarity between the two both in their general interest in composition, particularly in gradually building up the conflicts and in linking them together by describing how the kinsmen of the parties in the original conflict become involved in new ones. But the sharp contrast between initial success and ultimate failure in Snorri's saga of St. Óláfr is not typical of the Icelandic family sagas, though there are examples, such as the story of Gunnarr in *Njáls saga*. See Andersson, 1967: 3 ff., 291 ff., etc. and Byock, 1982: 47 ff.

23. Snorri mentions the rule only in connection with Opplandene (OH chap. 73: 123 and 162: 384). In the case of Óláfr's last visit there, early in 1028, he makes a curious mistake, telling that the king, because of the difficult situation after Cnut's conquest, had to visit Opplandene despite the fact that less than three years had passed since his last stay there. Actually, according to Snorri's own account, Óláfr had not visited Opplandene for three years and was due to stay there if he had followed the ordinary cyclus. This mistake may be an indication of the chronological errors that Koht attributes to Snorri concerning the years 1026–1028 (Koht, 1921: 135 ff.).

24. Some of these episodes were probably collected in a continuous story before Snorri, in the so-called *Kristnisaga,* which has been partly reconstructed from the *Legendary Saga* (Nordal, 1914: 99 ff.; Berntsen, 1923: 109 ff. See also Andersson, 1988). According to *Kristnisaga,* the conversion of the inner regions which Snorri describes in chapters 111 to 114, including the story of Dala-Guðbrandr, took place toward the end of Óláfr's reign, on his flight after the rebellion against him. This is evident from the *Legendary Saga,* which places the first part of the story of the conversion of Gudbrandsdalen after Óláfr's miraculous escape through Sunnmøre and the rest of the story early in his reign (*Leg. Saga:* 29–35, 67–71). However, the stories of Ǫlvi at Egge and of the conversion of Voss and Valdres are only to be found in Snorri (Berntsen, 1923: 123). For a more detailed discussion of these stories, see chapter 2.

25. These events, Ásbjǫrn's death, Þórir's revenge, and Finnr Árnason's action against him, take place over four years and could hardly have happened over less than three, given the distances. This means that the story could not have been finished before Óláfr's exile.

26. See, e.g., examples from *Sverris saga* in Holm-Olsen, 1953: 71 ff.

27. It is not quite clear to what extent this is Snorri's own achievement. His story is more dramatic and has more shifts of scenes than the one in the *Leg. Saga:* 44–47. The *Oldest Saga,* which has probably been Snorri's source, has also contained it, but only the beginning of the story is preserved there (*Oldest Saga:* 3 f.).

28. The two Latin histories only mention the fact that he conquered Norway (Theodoricus chap. 1, HN: 103 f.), whereas *Ágrip* in addition refers to the battle of Hafrsfjord (chap. 2). *Fagrskinna* is a little more detailed, telling a story of Haraldr's proposal that differs on some points from Snorri's and mentioning his promise not to cut his hair until he had conquered the country and his fight against Earl Atli in Sogn (*Fsk.* chap. 2: 15, 19; see *HHárf.* chap. 12 and Storm, 1873: 114 ff.). Snorri quotes scaldic poetry for some of the events, notably for the battle of Hafrsfjord, but there is nothing in the extant stanzas that could give him information on the chronological order of Haraldr's campaigns.

29. Both regard Hákon's succession largely as the result of Eiríkr's harsh rule and unpopularity, then turn to his attempts at Christianization and finally to the attacks from the Eiríkssons. Both have also a fairly detailed chronology, though not exactly the same as Snorri's (*Ágr.* chaps. 5–6; *Fsk.* chaps. 8–12). Both the strong chronological link and the causal one between Hákon's failure to convert Trøndelag and the Eiríkssons' attack, however, are Snorri's own invention. *Ágrip* links the two events in the opposite way, regarding Hákon's difficulties in the last part of his reign as a punishment for his failure to convert the country (chap. 5: 22 ff.), whereas *Fagrskinna* dates the first event to Hákon's seventeenth year and the second to his twentieth, without commenting on the causal connection (chaps. 8–10: 31 f.). The two Latin histories are both very short, only mentioning Hákon's apostasy and his last battle and death and spending a few words on his performance as a ruler (Theodoricus chap. 4; HN: 106 f.).

30. Both *Ágrip* and *Fagrskinna* list their violent deeds without going into the circumstances or arranging them chronologically (*Ágr.* chap. 9; *Fsk.* chap. 13). The Latin histories are also—as usual—very brief (Theodoricus chap. 4; HN:

107 f.). The author who is closest to Snorri's approach is Oddr munkr, who tells of the meeting between Hákon and the petty kings, the *mannjafnaðr* between Haraldr gráfeldr and his brother Guðrøðr, and their subsequent attack on two of their rivals (*SagaOT* chap. 1), a story that Snorri has taken over, with a few changes.

31. See *Fsk*. chaps. 14–20, on which Snorri relies quite heavily. *Ágr*. gives a short version of Hákon's intrigues and his fall, but omits the battle of Hjǫrungavágr (chaps. 10–14). Oddr munkr gives all three stories, but more briefly than *Fsk*. and *Hkr*. (chaps. 18–21). HN: 111, 115 refers only the barest facts of Hákon's reign in connection with the story of Óláfr Tryggvason, whereas Theodoricus is more detailed, though omitting the battle of Hjǫrungavágr (chaps. 5–7, 10).

32. Harðráði means either "resolute," "having strong character," or "harsh," "strict" (see Fritzner, 1954 with ref.). Both meanings fit in with the descriptions of Haraldr in the sagas. The sobriquet is found in relatively few authors and manuscripts (Aðalbjarnarson, 1951: xxxix, n. 1).

33. Einarsdóttir, 1964: 233 ff. In his review, Knut Helle suggests that this feature may also be the result of European influence and points to the Anglo-Saxon Annals, which also used the kings' reigns for dating (1967: 70 f.). Though this may well be the case, this particular chronological arrangement is better regarded as a deliberate choice than as simply the result of external influence.

34. Both here and below, chapter 5, I have profited greatly from an unpublished manuscript by Anders Johansen, *Historisk tid, mytiske landskap,* which he has kindly allowed me to use. For an abbreviated version, see Johansen, 1988. See also Johansen, 1985.

35. See *HHarð*. chaps. 54–57, OK chap. 6, MB chaps. 20–21, *Msyn*. chaps. 30–31, *Ingi* chaps. 24–25, *HHerð*. chaps. 20–21. The miracles told in the saga of Óláfr kyrri are dated according to the construction of the church of St. Óláfr in Nidaros, and the one in *Ingi* chap. 24 to half a month before Cardinal Nicholas' arrival in Norway. Both these latter events, however, are undated. The miracle of St. Óláfr's sword, which was brought to Constantinople and gave the Greeks victory against their enemies, is placed at the end of the saga of Hákon herðibreiðr, after events told in 1161, though it must have taken place much earlier, as it is mentioned in Einarr Skúlason's *Geisli,* composed in 1152/1153 (strophes 51–56; *Skjalded*. A 1: 440 f., B 1: 468 f.; see *HHerð*. chap. 20: 429).

36. E.g., the birth of Haraldr harðráði, which could easily be dated to 1015, as Haraldr was fifteen when he took part in the battle of Stiklestad and fifty at his death (*HHarð*. chap. 1, 99). Snorri tells a story of him when he was three, which is correctly placed in the internal chronology of Óláfr's reign to the year 1018—though in the wrong season—but is not explicitly dated (OH chap. 76). The birth of Óláfr's son Magnús is told in great detail and placed in the year 1023–1024 according to the internal chronology of his reign, but no date is given. Snorri gives the length of Óláfr kyrri's reign but not his age at death or at his accession (OK chap. 8). His birth is mentioned during his father's reign but is not dated (*HHarð*. chap. 33). For the following reign Snorri's information is fairly detailed (e.g., *Msyn*. chaps. 1, 18, 23, 33), but he says nothing of the age of Magnús blindi and Haraldr gilli. The age of Haraldr's sons can be easily recon-

structed from the letter quoted in *Ingi* chap. 8, but is not explicitly given. Snorri tells the story of Hákon herðibreiðr's conception in detail (*Ingi* chap. 18) but does not give its date, though he mentions Hákon's age at his accession (*HHerð.* chap. 1). When he does date the birth of a king's son, it is probably either because of unusual circumstances, such as the birth of Hákon góði when his father was nearly seventy and the story of him being sent to England for fostering (*HHárf.* chaps. 38–41), the dramatic events of Óláfr Tryggvason's birth and early childhood (OT chaps. 1–4), or the exceptional importance of St. Óláfr (OT chaps. 43–44).

37. An alternative explanation is that Snorri has taken the story from a source that was not a continuous narrative of events relating to the kings. Unfortunately, Snorri's source is unknown. The story is not found in any other extant saga but it may possibly have been contained in a lacuna in *Morkinskinna* in the beginning of the saga of Magnús and Haraldr (Kválen, 1925: 125 ff.). However, it is more likely to have been derived from Snorri's foster father Jón Loptsson, whose foster parents he cites as eyewitnesses (Storm, 1873: 71 f.; Aðalbjarnarson, 1937: 166 ff.). The only feature of the story which does not fit in with an oral source is the exact chronology, but this may have been supplied from some written source.

38. Thus, he seems well informed on the chronology of Cnut the Great's reign, which he uses in connection with St. Óláfr's early career in England (OH chaps. 26–27), but he does not link the chronology of the two kings together when introducing Cnut into Norwegian history with his claim on Norway (OH chap. 130). He tells of Edward the Confessor's accession at Harthacnut's death and gives both the length of his reign and the exact date of his death (*HHarð.* chaps. 75–77), but does not explicitly link it to the reigns of the contemporary Norwegian kings, though he could easily have done so.

39. See *Separate Saga* chap. 11: 20 and chap. 13: 22: Earl Sigurðr was killed two years after the death of King Hákon góði and Tryggvi six years after the death of Sigurðr. The same chronology can be reconstructed from *Hkr.,* HG chaps. 6 and 9.

40. Modern historians usually date the battle to 985 or 986, because of the death of the Danish King Haraldr Gormsson between 985 and 987. According to Saxo, whom most historians trust in this case, it was Haraldr who sent the *jómsvíkingar* against Norway. Even if one accepts Snorri's story that the expedition was the result of their promises during the funeral of King Haraldr, his date is too late. See Munch, 1853: 103 ff.

41. Both in this and other cases, Steblin-Kamensky commits the error of assuming a too close correspondence between language and thought, in accordance with the "Sapir-Whorf hypothesis," which now largely seems to be discredited (Clark and Clark, 1977: 554 ff.; Itkonen, 1989: 111). To take the present example: the lack of distinction between author and scribe in Old Norse only means that one is not forced to make a consistent distinction between the two, not that the distinction is impossible to express and even less that a person who transcribed a manuscript and one who composed a historical work were in the opinion of their contemporaries doing exactly the same thing.

42. One problem in particular, which needs thorough examination, is the

saga style and its relation to oral narrative, which, in its pure form, is incompatible with what we understand by individual authorship. Though the saga style is closer to oral narrative than is modern prose, it cannot be explained simply as oral storytelling. Some features, like the paratactic style and the description of characters from the outside, fit in with Ong's criteria of orality, whereas others do not, such as the terse and exact descriptions, the intricate composition, and the strong links between events that are told in different parts of the work (see Ong, 1982: 36 ff., 139 ff.). See also above on the gradual development of the impersonal saga style.

43. This seems an adequate classification for our present purpose. From a stylistic point of view a two-fold division is more appropriate, i.e., between the "scenes" in which direct speech is an essential element, and the short summaries that serve as introduction and conclusion (Heusler, 1957: 225 f.; Clover, 1974: 57 ff.; see also Harris, 1972: 1 ff.). Though the style is essentially the same in the kings' sagas and the Icelandic family sagas, the former differ on two points: the summaries are often longer, occasionally resembling annals and in addition containing "structural passages" on government and administration, etc. Second, direct speech often takes the form of speeches, which are rare in the family sagas (Knirk, 1981: 214 ff.). Both these additions give additional opportunity to study the author's point of view.

44. It is not quite clear to what extent the saga writers were influenced by the European tradition in this respect. On the one hand, Roman historiography was well known in Norway and Iceland; on the other, the use of speeches is easily explained from the practical importance of oratory in Norwegian and Icelandic society. Nor is the stylistic similarity between Old Norse and Roman oratory particularly strong (Schlauch, 1969: 297 f., 311 f.; Knirk, 1981: 90 ff., 150 ff.). For an interesting attempt to place Old Norse oratory and prose style in general within a common North European, particularly Norman literary tradition, see Amory, 1979: 71 ff.

45. See Koht's formulation of his method: "But just because the sagas normally stick to the narrative form, it is important to examine their expression, to unveil the thought hiding behind it. One has to observe the small, characteristic words that reveal an evaluation, collect and study the scattered generalizations and reflections that are actually to be found in various places. One must probe into the motives that are adduced for the persons' actions" (Koht, 1921: 77 f.). It is clearly necessary to do all these things, but it is not enough.

Chapter 2: The Conflicts

1. "Í þenna tíma var í Noregi fjǫlði lendra manna; óru þeir margir ríkir og svá ættstórir, at þeir váru komnir af konunga ættum eða jarla ok áttu skamt til at telja, váru ok stórauðgir. Var þar alt traust konunganna eða jarlanna, er fyrir landi réðu, er lendir menn váru; þvíát svá var í hverju fylki, sem lendir menn réðu fyrir bónda-liðinu ("At that time there was in Norway a great number of landed-men [lendir menn]. Many of them were powerful and so high-born as to be in direct descent from royal or earls' families, and they were also very rich. Whoever governed the country, whether kings or earls, depended on them,

because in every district it was these landed-men who had the greatest influence with the farmers") (OH chap. 46). See also chaps. 21–23 on the strong position of Erlingr and Einarr and the earls' concessions to them.

2. The oldest example dates from Óláfr's own time, a stanza by Sigvatr, praising him for punishing thieves and robbers and for refusing to accept fines for those who deserve death for their acts (*Skjaldedigtning* A 1: 258, B 1: 240, strophes 5–6; see Schreiner, 1926: 84). Óláfr's justice as a judge—though not necessarily his *strict* justice—is mentioned in the oldest, clerical works, as part of their description of the *rex iustus*. The religious aspect is most pronounced in *Passio Olavi:* 70 f. and Einarr Skulason's poem *Geisli* (*Skjaldedigtning* A 1: 459–473, B 1: 427–445), which have a more or less liturgical function, and in Adam of Bremen, *Gesta* book 2, chap. 61, which may be derived from similar sources. It is also dominant in Theodoricus (chap. 16: 29 ff., 19) and *Ágrip:* 50 ff.—Koht himself does not use the term *rex iustus* and gives only a short sketch of the ecclesiastical ideal of a king. The term was apparently introduced in Scandinavian historiography in 1915 by Curt Weibull, who was inspired by Bernheim and gave a detailed analysis of the hagiography of the Danish King Cnut (Weibull, 1964: 178 ff.). For modern accounts, see chapter 4, n. 12.

3. This is the main reason for the rebellion against Óláfr in Theodoricus (MHN: 29 f.) and *Ágr.:* 54. The author of *Fagrskinna* is the first to change the emphasis, stating that the magnates took the initiative for the rebellion and invited King Cnut to come to Norway to depose Óláfr (*Fsk.:* 166 f.).

4. "sá var einn hlutr til þess, at þeir Knútr ok Hákon hǫfðu kyrru haldit um tilkall í Nóreg, at þá fyrst, er Óláfr Haraldzson kom í land, hljóp upp allr múgr ok margmenni ok vildi ekki heyra annat en Óláfr skyldi vera konungr yfir landi ǫllu; en síðan, er menn þóttusk verða ósjálfráðir fyrir ríki hans, þá leituðu sumir í brot ór landi; hǫfðu farit mjǫk ríkismenn á fund Knúts konungs eða ríkra bónda synir . . ." ("One reason why Knút and Hákon had kept quiet about their claim to Norway was that, at first, when Óláf Haraldsson came to the land, everybody to a man acclaimed him and wanted to have him as king over all the country. But afterward, when men feared losing their independence through his power, some left the country. Very many men of influence, and also sons of powerful yeomen, had joined King Knút under various pretexts") (OH chap. 130: 282 f.).

5. See the story of Eyvindr úrarhorn (OH chaps. 62, 65).

6. The *Legendary Saga* mentions Þórir hundr's killing of Karli, but not the reason for it and does not relate it to the story of Ásbjǫrn selsbani (*Leg. Saga:* 24). The latter is told in great detail, very like Snorri's story, but contains some moralizing concerning Óláfr's enemies (*Leg. Saga:* 44 ff.; see also Sogge, 1976: 31 ff.). The conflict with the Árnasons and Óláfr's killing of Kálfr's stepsons are told briefly (*Leg. Saga:* 58 f., 63). In addition, the author mentions that Óláfr kills four men for Þórir and Þórir three men for Óláfr, which makes Þórir join Óláfr's enemies (*Leg. Saga:* 63). The author is thus interested in explaining the conflict between the king and individual magnates but he is generally more concerned with the *rex iustus*-aspect than Snorri. The story of Ásbjǫrn selsbani follows a passage dealing with Óláfr's strict justice, which brings him into conflict with the magnates, and is apparently intended as an illustration of this statement. The story of Ásbjǫrn is also to be found in the *Oldest Saga:* 2 f.

7. They are not found in any other extant saga. Theoretically, they could have been composed by Styrmir but given Snorri's greater talent as a historian, they are more likely to be his original creation. See Knirk, 1981: 140 ff. and above.

8. Þórir is mentioned as one of the leaders of Earl Hákon's fleet in the battle in Hijrungavǫgr (OT chap. 40: 329) and must then have been a prominent man in his region, Northern Norway. He is one of the leaders of the resistance to Óláfr's Christianization and is killed by him (OT chaps. 59, 78).

9. Though even there, conflicting political interests may be detected. See Miller, 1983 on Njáls saga.

10. He fights against him at Nesjar, leaves the country, is reconciled with Óláfr some years later, though without regaining his veitslur, then leaves the country to join King Cnut in England, according to Snorri's chronology in 1022–1023. He is on Cnut's side during the conflict with Óláfr, but does not take part in the battle of Stiklestad.

11. "þó at ek vilja veizlurnar miðla at sjálfræði mínu, en eigi láta sem lendir menn sé oðalbornir till ættleifðar minnar" (OH chap. 60: 88).

12. Admittedly, there are few examples in Heimskringla to support this conclusion. Generally, chivalry was less important in Snorri's society than in contemporary Europe, though there are examples of defeated adversaries who are pardoned and given a prominent position, mostly when it is politically prudent to do so (see chap. 4). In addition, the institution of sjálfdoemi in contemporary Iceland is a parallel in some respects. This meant that the whole judgment in a case was submitted to one party. This often implied total capitulation and was exploited ruthlessly. But it might also be a way of honoring one's adversary, or the man who received sjálfdoemi sought lasting peace or friendship with his opponent by behaving moderately and generously (see Heusler, 1912: 44 f.).

13. Eiríkr, son of Earl Hákon of Lade, and his foster father Þorleifr spaki have to move their ship to make place in the harbor for Hákon's brother-in-law and favorite Skopti Skagason. Next year Eiríkr fights Skopti and kills him (OT chap. 20). Eiríkr's honor has been offended and he revenges himself. But there are also other circumstances that may explain his behavior. His father is not very fond of him, and Skopti, married to Hákon's favorite daughter Þóra, is clearly a rival. The incident apparently leads to no further conflict, and Eiríkr becomes a great magnate afterward, after a short stay in Denmark, apparently to avoid his father's wrath. Exactly the same matter leads to a conflict between King Magnús góði and his uncle and co-regent Haraldr harðráði. One of Magnús's conditions for sharing his kingdom with his uncle was a certain primacy in rank, expressed among other things in the right of first choice of harbor for his ship (HHarð. chap. 23). Once he finds the harbor occupied by Haraldr's ship, he almost goes to battle with him. Haraldr avoids conflict by ceding to Magnús (HHarð. chap. 27). This story is told as one of numerous incidents that led to enmity between the two kings. A competition (mannjafnaðr) in a drinking party nearly leads to fighting between King Haraldr gráfeldr and his brother King Guðrøðr (HGráf. chap. 9), but their friends manage to part them and preserve the peace. The famous mannjafnaðr between the kings Sigurðr and Eysteinn (Msyn. chap. 21) is mentioned as one of several incidents leading to bad relations between them,

but does not actually result in open conflict. When one of Haraldr harðráði's men is killed by a man in his son Magnús's service, this almost leads to a battle between the two princes but their friends go between and separate them (*HHarð.* chap. 72). A similar conflict occurs between the two great *lendir menn* of King Ingi, Erlingr skakki, and Grégóríús, but is settled through Ingi's intervention (*HHerð.* chap. 12).

14. See the incident between Eiríkr Hákonsson and Skopti, n. 13 above. Another example is the conflict between King Haraldr harðráði and Einarr þambarskelfir. It was probably of little importance to Einarr to save the life of the man whom King Haraldr wanted to hang for theft, or to Haraldr to execute him. Nevertheless, the result was a conflict of life or death, because of the rivalry between them: the execution of the thief would reveal both Erlingr's failure to protect his servants and adherents and his inability to resist the king, whereas liberating the thief would weaken the king's position in a similar way.

15. ". . . kom Einari þat í hug, at ekki myndi undir at hrapa ferðinni meirr, en svá sem hófligast væri, ef þeir skyldi berjask við Óláf konung, en hafa ekki til framflutningar ríkis síns þá heldr en áðr" (OH chap. 194: 442; Holl.: 487 f.).

16. A comparison with *Morkinskinna* and *Fagrskinna* shows that Snorri plays down the moralistic aspect, letting Magnús confine himself to the remark that he ought to be content with the kingdom God has given him, whereas the two earlier sagas are full of pious considerations (MG chaps. 36–37; *Fsk.* chap. 40 f.; *Msk.*: 52 ff.).

17. In addition to the torture of Sigurðr (*Ingi* chap. 12), Þjóstolfr Álason's words to him when he is taken captive may be an indication of this. Taking Sigurðr's white, silken cap off his head, Þjóstolfr says: "hví vartu svá djarfr, þræls-sonrinn, at þú þorðir at kallask sonr Magnús konungs?" ("Why were you so bold, you son of a thrall, as to call yourself the son of King Magnús?") (*Ingi* chap. 11: 365; Holl.: 748).

18. This conforms to the impression the Icelandic sagas give of judicial conflicts, in which resources in the form of kinsmen, wealth, and allies are decisive, but knowledge of the law and some sort of legitimacy is necessary, among other things to get support (see Heusler, 1912: 61 ff.; Byock, 1982: 38 ff.).

19. This applies to Theodoricus chap. 15; *Ágr.* chaps. 23–24, and to some extent to *Leg. Saga:* 19 ff.

20. See, in addition to the earlier stories of Óláfr's accession, the story of Sverrir's rise to power in *Sverris saga* chaps. 16–31 etc. (see Holm-Olsen, 1953: 84 ff.).

21. E.g., King Hákon góði's battles against the Eiríkssons (HG chaps. 19–32), the battle of Hjǫrungavágr against the *jómsvíkingar* (OT chaps. 40–42), the battle of Svǫlð (OT chaps. 100–111), and the battle of Stamford Bridge (*HHarð.* chaps. 87–94).

22. A possible, implicit explanation may be that Óláfr would have had difficulties in mobilizing a large army once more, after his great mobilization the year before. Though there is no explicit rule in the laws forbidding the king to mobilize the *leiðangr* two successive years, it may have been common knowledge in Snorri's milieu that this was a very difficult undertaking. This is a conclusion that suggests itself from a parallel case in *Sverris saga.* In 1197 Sverrir mobilized

the largest *leiðangr*-army mentioned in the sagas, 7200 men, to fight the Croziers in Eastern Norway (SS chap. 133; see Helle, 1974: 191). The following year he was in a desperate situation, probably because he was unable to demand the same sacrifices from the people once more (SS chaps. 142–159).

23. "opt hefi ek heyrt yðr þat mæla, ok þykki mér satt, at lítit lagðisk fyrir Eystein konung, bróður minn, síðan er hann lagðisk á flótta, ok var han vel at sér gǫrr um alla hluti, þá er konung fríða. Nú kan ek þat sjá við vanheilendi mitt, hversu lítit fyrir mik mun leggjask, ef ek tek þat til, er honum skyldi svá mjǫk vefjask, jammikit sem atferð okra skilði ok heilsu ok alt eljan" (*HHerð*. chap. 17).

24. This applies to Haraldr gilli, despite his cruel behavior toward Magnús and some of his friends (MB.HG chap. 8). Most of Magnús's former men are admitted into his *hirð* (MB.HG chap. 12; see also chap. 15). Other examples are the fate of Erlingr Skjálgsson and Einarr þambarskelfir after the battle of Svǫlð and once more after Óláfr's victory over the earls.

25. As usual, Snorri improves and rearranges Oddr munkr's version, whereas *Fagrskinna*'s is shorter than Snorri's (see *SagaOT*: 120, 148, 179–183, 186 ff.; *Fsk.* chap. 22). For the real story of Óláfr's fall, which is one of the most controversial problems in older Norwegian history, see the summary and references in Andersen, 1977: 104 ff.

26. For a modern account of Óláfr's negotiations with Sweden, with references to earlier literature, see Moberg, 1941: 88 ff.

27. The *lǫgmaðr* Emundr compares King Óláfr of Sweden with a man who has accepted to pay indemnity and then cheats with the payment, giving half the value or less. When the king asks for the meaning of this story, one of his councillors points to the fact that King Óláfr of Norway was promised Ingigerðr, who was of royal descent in both lines, but had to be content with Ástríðr, the king's illegitimate daughter, whose mother was a slave (OH chap. 94: 188 f.).

28. Snorri's version is an expansion and rearrangement of the one found in *Leg. Saga:* 35 ff., which, although different in several respects, contains the same infelicities in accounting for Óláfr's marriage to Ástríðr instead of Ingigerðr. By contrast, *Fagrskinna*'s version shows better understanding of the political aspect of the story. Both in *Leg. Saga* and *Fagrskinna* the two kings meet and agree that Óláfr shall marry Ingigerðr. When the Swedish king boasts of his luck in hunting, having captured five birds, and Ingigerðr compares this to the Norwegian Óláfr's capturing the Oppland kings (*Leg. Saga*: 40; *Fsk.*: 155 f.; see also *Hkr.* OH chap. 89), the Swedish king gets furious and breaks the treaty. In contrast to both *Leg. Saga* and *Heimskringla,* the author of *Fagrskinna* lets him offer Óláfr Ástríðr in marriage instead of Ingigerðr. At the advice of his friends, who point to his problems with Denmark, Óláfr accepts this offer (*Fsk.*: 156 f.). For a comparison of the different versions, see Johnsen, 1916: 513–539.

29. See in particular the description of Erlingr's meeting with the people of Viken in Tønsberg, where he declares himself willing to fulfill the treaty with Denmark, if they prefer "to be subject to the king of Denmark, rather than to the king who has been consecrated and crowned to govern this land" ("at þjóna Dana-konungi heldr en þessum konungi, er hér er vígðr ok kórónaðr til landz").

To this leading question he receives the expected answer, the people flatly refusing to serve the Danish king (ME chap. 24).

30. *Fagrskinna* has essentially the same story, with the same patriotic overtones (*Fsk.* chaps. 95–101). Saxo, however, differs markedly but is equally biased in favor of the Danes (*Gesta* XIV. 29.15–18, 34.6–9, 38.1–9, 41.1–3). Nevertheless, his version confirms the suspicion that Erlingr actually had to make greater concessions than Snorri admits. See Helle, 1974: 69 ff. with ref. to the scholarly discussion of these events.

31. ". . . ok oss er ván snarprar orrostu af því liði; þeir eru Norðmenn, sem vér erum" (OH chap. 104). The story is also found in Oddr munkr, *SagaOT:* 210 ff. and *Fsk.*: 125.

32. See MG chaps. 29–35, *HHarð.* chaps. 34–35, 59–64. The Danes are defeated and flee from battle. When King Haraldr twice agrees with King Sveinn to meet and fight a decisive battle, Sveinn fails to appear but attacks when Haraldr has dismissed most of his army. Nevertheless, Haraldr is victorious (*HHarð.* chaps. 34–35, 59, 61).

33. See *Ingi* chaps. 3–4: the Danish king arrives in Norway with 720 ships but achieves nothing. Snorri gives the following comment: "And it was said that there never was a more ill-starred expedition with a great force into another king's land" ("ok er þat mál manna, at eigi hafi verit verri ferð farin í annars konungs veldi með miklu liði") (*Ingi* chap. 4). The story is much the same as in *Morkinskinna* and *Fagrskinna,* which contain the same nationalistic bias (*Msk.*: 416–419; *Fsk.* chap. 83). King Valdimarr's expedition is also unsuccessful, despite his large force, because the people are staunchly against him.

34. Of these stories, that of *Bersǫglisvísur*—including the scaldic stanzas—is the only one Snorri could have taken more or less completely from his predecessors (see *Ágr.* chap. 35; *Msk.*: 24 ff.; *Fsk.*: 197 ff.). The story of the confiscation and return of the *óðal* is also to be found in *Egils saga* chap. 4: 11 f., but in no other source, although *Fagrskinna* has a reference to taxes that were introduced by Haraldr and abolished by Hákon (*Fsk.*: 19, 34). This story may thus be Snorri's invention if he is the author of *Egils saga* (above). For the scholarly discussion of the confiscation of the *óðal,* see Andersen, 1977: 86 ff. and Bagge, 1987b: 34 ff. The resistance to Hákon's Christianization is found in most earlier sagas (*Historia Norvegiæ,* MHN: 106; *Ágr.* chap. 5: 22; *Fsk.*: 31 f.), but Ásbjǫrn is not mentioned and no speech is referred. Þorgnýr lǫgmaðr and his speech seem to be wholly Snorri's invention, possibly under the influence of tradition and political ideas in Sweden, which he may have met during his stay there in 1219 (Sandvik, 1955: 95 ff.; see Weibull, 1964: 241 ff.; Lönnroth, 1964: 16 ff.). For an examination of the constitutional significance of this story, see most recently Lönnroth, 1976.

35. The comparison is at least partly derived from a scaldic stanza, allegedly composed by St. Óláfr, visiting Haraldr in a dream to warn him against his fateful expedition against England: ". . . hlautk, þvít heima sǫtum,/ heilag fall til vallar;/ uggik enn, at tyggi,/ yðr myni feigð of byrjuð,/ . . . / . . . veldra goð slíku" ("A holy death I had, on/ homeland falling, glorious./ Fear that, folk-ruler,/ fey thou wilt be yonder,/ . . . / . . . 'Tis not God's doing" (*HHarð.* chap. 82; see *Msk.*: 267; *Fsk.* chap. 52). This may possibly, though not necessarily,

reflect an ecclesiastical interpretation of Haraldr's failure to conquer England. On the negative evaluation of Haraldr in clerical sources, see Theodoricus's statement that Haraldr was "sui tenax, alieni cupidus" (chap. 28, cf. chap. 25 on his behavior toward his nephew Magnús). The author of *Ágrip,* on the other hand, is more positive (chaps. 39, 41). One of the sources for the negative picture of Haraldr is probably Adam of Bremen, who represents the attitude of the archbishop of Bremen, with whom Haraldr had a long conflict (*Gesta* book 3, chap. 17; see Johnsen, 1968: 12 ff.).

Chapter 3: The Society

1. See Philpotts, 1913: 245 ff.; Sørensen, 1977: 30 ff.; Sawyer, 1982: 43 ff. and 1987; Gaunt, 1983: 186 ff. For the kinship system in Iceland, as it appears in the law code *Grágás,* see Hastrup, 1985: 70 ff. with references to earlier literature. As far as I know, Vestergaard's article (Vestergaard, 1988), which he has kindly allowed me to use in manuscript, is the only anthropological analysis of the Norwegian laws. As for the other sources, Jenny M. Jochens has made some interesting analyses of the Icelandic aristocracy of the thirteenth century (1985: 95 ff.) and the Norwegian royal family (1987a: 327 ff.).

2. Thus Álfr hroði is praised for revenging his father so quickly and reckoned as a much better man than before (*Ingi* chap. 14). Þórir hundr and Kálfr Árnason are blamed by women in their families for their reluctance to risk a conflict with St. Óláfr by taking revenge (OH chaps. 123, 183).

3. Normally, the laws accord less compensation for loss of limbs than for death. But according to the *Gulaþingslǫg,* if a man loses both hand and foot, "he is worse off alive than dead, then compensation shall be given as if he were killed" ("þa er sa verri livande en dauðr. scal giallda sem dauðr se," G 179). See also Grøtvedt, 1965: 111 f.

4. Although the purpose of this act can be explained from the context of Norwegian politics, such treatment of enemies seems fairly unusual there (see chap. 4, n. 43). It was more common in Ireland, where Haraldr had grown up (Simms, 1987: 50).

5. When Óláfr's men urge him to kill Hroerekr after the latter's repeated attempts at his life, Óláfr answers: " . . . I am unwilling to ruin the victory I gained over the kings of the Upplands, the time I captured five in one morning and so managed to gain all their kingdoms without having to deprive any one of them of life, because they all were kinsmen of mine" (". . . en trauðr em ek at týna þeim sigri, er ek fekk á Uplendinga-konungum, er ek tók þá v. á einum morni, ok náða ek svá ǫllu ríki þeira, at ek þurpta einskis þeira banamaðr verða, þvíat þeir váru allir frændr mínir") (OH chap. 84). See also Óláfr's order to Þórarinn Nefjólfsson, who is to take Hroerekr out of the country: he should see to it that Hroerekr never returns to Norway, but not kill him except if absolutely necessary (OH chap. 85: 159).

6. Erlingr was married to a daughter of King Sigurðr jórsalafari and thus did not belong to the royal kindred. His son Magnús was fairly distantly related to the leaders of the opposite faction, as they descended from Haraldr gilli, Sigurðr's half-brother. Erlingr is directly or indirectly made responsible for the

deaths of King Hákon herðibreiðr, son of Sigurðr munnr (ME chap. 7: 444), Níkolás Símunarson, son of Haraldr gilli's daughter Maria (ME chap. 7: 443 f.), Sigurðr Markúsfóstri, son of King Sigurðr munnr (ME chap. 18), and Haraldr Sigurðarson, son of King Sigurðr munnr and Erlingr's wife Kristín and thus Magnús's half-brother (ME chap. 35). One would expect the death of the latter and of Níkolás, whose father was Símun skálpr, one of the leading men in Erlingr's faction, to have led to strong reactions, but technically, Erlingr did not kill his own kinsmen.

7. The story of Þórir hundr, to whom Ásbjǫrn's mother gives her dead son's spear, thus urging him to take revenge (OH chap. 123: 270 f.) suggests something similar. Þórir apparently has not thought of revenging Ásbjǫrn. The gift of the spear, however, which admittedly has not belonged to Ásbjǫrn but which is intimately connected to him by having caused his death, seems to place the moral obligation upon Þórir. However, the special importance of the spear may also be understood against the fact that Snorri seems to imply that Þórir used it to kill St. Óláfr of Stiklestad (Fidjestøl, 1987: 45 f.).

8. See the provision in the *Gulaþingslǫg* (G 37) that one is not entitled to compensation more than three times if one does not revenge oneself in between. For Iceland, Heusler finds numerous examples of revenge being regarded as the highest duty in the Icelandic sagas (Heusler, 1911: 48 ff.), whereas in *Sturlunga saga* political considerations have become more important than honor (1912: 29 f.). Heusler regards this as the result of historical change. An alternative explanation is that the Icelandic sagas take a more romantic attitude to the subject, whereas *Sturlunga saga* reflects actual behavior.

9. Heusler, 1911: 74 f.; Heusler, 1912: 44 f. Characteristically, the magnates who try to save their friends or relatives from St. Óláfr's wrath, such as Erlingr Skjálgsson and the Árnasons, try to placate him by offering him *sjálfdoemi* (OH chaps. 118: 120, 138: 318). In addition, to offer the opposite party *sjálfdoemi* may be a means to show good faith and maintain friendship. This evidently presupposes moderation from the party that is honored in this way (Byock, 1982: 108 f.).

10. According to Snorri's genealogy, Óláfr was the great grandson of Haraldr's son Bjǫrn, whereas Hroerekr was probably the grandson of Hringr, one of Haraldr's sons with another woman. See Munch, 1853: genealogical table 8.

11. Hárekr was the great grandson of Haraldr's daughter Ingibjǫrg, whereas Óláfr was the grandson of Haraldr's son Óláfr (Munch, 1853: tab. 8–9; OH chap. 104).

12. As for Kálfr, Koht points to his marriage to the widow of Ǫlvi at Egge, who was Þórir hundr's sister (1921: 116), but this marriage was the result of Óláfr's initiative. The fact that Finnr married his daughter to Earl Ormr Eilífsson, the grandnephew of Bergljót, daughter of Earl Hákon (OT chap. 19; *HHarð.* chap. 46; see Koht, 1921: 116), is less likely to determine his political adherence than his own marriage to King Haraldr's sister and the king's marriage to his niece (*HHarð.* chap. 45). Rather, Finnr's relations to both sides, through family ties as well as personal friendship (see *HHarð.* chap. 45: 137 f.) explain his role in the negotiations between Haraldr and Hákon Ívarsson.

13. See *Ingi* chap. 10 on the two brothers who fought on opposite sides in the

battle of Holmengrå, the Árnasons in the battle of Stiklestad, and the rivalry between Þórir hundr and his brother and nephew Sigurðr and Ásbjǫrn (OH chap. 117: 242 f.), and between Erlingr Skjálgsson and his second cousin Áslákr.

14. See Clover, 1986, who sees a close connection between women's lament for the dead and their demand for revenge in numerous societies, including medieval Iceland, whereas Jochens, 1987b, is more inclined to explain the figure as a literary construction.

15. The role of women in *Heimskringla* and Snorri's view of them should be subject to a special examination. Despite the secondary role he attributes to them in the political game, he describes a lot of individual women, many of whom play an important part. In contrast to some other historians, such as Saxo Grammaticus, he does not seem to express a negative attitude to them or to demand that they should be strictly subordinated to men (see Strand, 1980: 63 ff. and 1981). On the role of women in the saga literature in general, see also Heller, 1958; Frank, 1973; Heinrichs, 1986; Clover, 1988; and Arnórsdóttir, 1990.

16. The number of kinsmen is clearly an asset for the descendants of Hǫrðakári. When Archbishop Eysteinn manages to make the people of Trøndelag pay their fines in silver instead of ordinary money—i.e., double value— Snorri ascribes it to his prominent kin and great number of relatives in the region (ME chap. 16).

17. According to Jochens (1985: 95 ff.) a kind of de facto transmission of the family's resources to one son was developing within the Icelandic aristocracy at Snorri's time: the father designated one son to succeed him by allowing him to marry and set up his own household. After his father's death, this son received a substantial part of the family property. In Norway sole succession and primogeniture was established for the monarchy during the twelfth century but was hardly extended to the rest of the aristocracy (see Bjørgo, 1970: 1 ff.; Bagge, 1975: 239 ff.; Jochens, 1987a: 332 ff.).

18. Hastrup, 1985: 100 suggests the same pattern for Iceland, though without finding any direct evidence for it in the laws. By contrast, Vestergaard points out that the Norwegian rules of inheritance favor the bride-taking family, whereas the rules of compensation for death or wounds are more balanced. This indicates a system in which it is a financial loss to give away a daughter, but this loss is compensated by the political support one is likely to receive from one's family-in-law, which in turn ought to lead to upward marriage of daughters (Vestergaard: 188 f.). A recent examination of Icelandic sources, particularly *Sturlunga saga,* points in the same direction: within the aristocracy, the partners normally have equal rank, but if there is difference, the man has the higher (Arnórsdóttir, 1990: 103 f.). I have no definite opinion as to how this difference between Snorri and the other sources should be explained, whether through different marriage practices in the royal family and the rest of society or through difference between theory and practice or changes over time.

19. However, these women are not always willing to be used in the game, as Astríðr, Óláfr Tryggvason's sister, and Ragnhildr, Magnús góði's daughter, demonstrate. As described in *Heimskringla* this marriage pattern thus gave women an important position in the political game. The story of the negotiations be-

tween St. Óláfr and the King of Sweden even shows women playing an active role. Ingigerðr wants Óláfr as her husband and tries to influence her father (OH chaps. 72: 121 f., 73: 89, 136), whereas her half-sister Ástríðr marries him against her father's will (OH chap. 91: 176). For a discussion of the reality underlying some of these episodes, see Jochens, 1986.

20. Thus, King Sigurðr jórsalafari takes Borghildr, the daughter of a rich and mighty man, as his mistress and has a son with her, the future Magnús blindi. Borghildr's brother, Hákon faukr, later becomes one of Magnús's closest friends and is taken captive with him and killed (*Msyn.* chap. 19; MB.HG chaps. 7–8). Magnús's foster father, Viðkunn Jónsson at Bjarkøy, supports Sigurðr slembir and Magnús against Haraldr gilli's sons (*Msyn.* chap. 19; *Ingi* chap. 6). King Sigurðr munnr's illegitimate son Hákon herðibreiðr, whose mother is a servant in a mighty family, grows up in this family, whose members later belong to his staunchest supporters (*Ingi* chap. 18; *HHerð.* chaps. 1, 11, 16; ME chap. 3, etc.). Markús at Skog fosters another illegitimate son of Sigurðr, also called Sigurðr, and becomes the leader of his faction (ME chap. 9). As is indicated in the famous story of Haraldr hárfagri sending his son Hákon for fostering to King Athalstan in England (*HHárf.* chap. 39) and confirmed by the examples above, the foster parents were normally socially inferior to the real parents, in contrast to custom in feudal Europe (Miller, 1983: 326; Hastrup, 1985: 99 f.; see Duby, 1985: 221 f.).

21. Evidently, this is quite different from making one's adversary *útlagr,* which was a normal sanction during the internal struggles in thirteenth century Iceland (Heusler, 1912: 74 ff.). Though *útlegð* was a serious punishment in contemporary Norway, it was far removed from Erlingr's drastic measure.

22. See the genealogies in Munch, 1853–1857, Tjersland, 1937–1940: 112 ff., and Koht, 1921: 115 ff. and 1936: 92 ff.

23. Hárekr comments on this in the following way: "en þó gerðu ekki svá inir fyrri hǫfðingjar, at minka várn rétt, er ættbornir erum til ríkis at hafa af konungum, en fá í hendr bóanda-sonum þeim, er slíkt hafa fyrr ekki með hǫndum haft" ("but the former rulers did not diminish our dominion to which we are entitled from the king by reason of our birth, and assign them to farmers' sons who never before had such power in their hands") (OH chap. 123: 268; Holl.: 391).

24. "þvíat mér er lítils ván, at frændum þínum sé soemð at þér, þvíat móðurætt þín ǫll er þrælborin" (*HHárf.* chap. 26). For the same idea, see the story of the queen who bears two hideous sons and exchanges them with the son of a slave woman, who is beautiful. As the children become older, however, their true nature is shown, the two boys are accepted as the queen's sons, and in turn become great kings (*Sturl.* I: 1–3).

25. *Yngl.* chap. 26. The slave, Tunni, has been *féhirðir* (treasurer) with the former king and has gathered a large fortune, which he uses to gain support from other slaves, robbers, and the like. He defeats the lawful king, Egill, eight times, until Egill finally manages to overcome him with help from Denmark.

26. See the remark in *Bǫglunga sǫgur* that the younger and less-established members of the factions in the civil war opposed the peace settlement of 1208 because they had not yet had the opportunity to enrich themselves (*Eirsp.*: 468).

See also Sverrir's speech to his men before the battle of Kalvskinnet in 1179, promising them promotion to the rank of the men they kill in the battle (SS chap. 35). There is no direct statement of this kind in Snorri's account of the civil wars, but the importance of winning goods and honor through war and plundering is frequently implied, e.g., in the early careers of men like Earl Eiríkr Hákonarson (OT chaps. 20, 89–90), St. Óláfr, and Haraldr harðráði.

27. Hárekr buys a farm on the island of Tjøtta, where there are many small farmers, and in a short time succeeds in expelling them all and making the whole island into one, large farm (OH chap. 104).

28. On Hárekr, see OT chap. 77 and above. As for Þórir, he was held in greater esteem than his brother Sigurðr because he was the king's *lendr maðr* (OH chap. 117: 242).

29. Tobiassen, 1964: 191 ff.; Gunnes, 1971: 62 ff.; Bagge, 1987b: 22 ff., 208 ff., etc. For the historians of the twelfth century, see Koht, 1921: 168 ff.; Johnsen, 1939: 64 ff.; Tobiassen, 1956: 60 f.

30. For an attempt to trace this and to connect Sveinn to his supporters among the Norwegian aristocracy, see Tjersland, 1937–1940: 115 ff.

31. As Haraldr's father was a petty king, Sigurðr sýr, who admittedly descended from Haraldr hárfagri, and had only the same mother as St. Óláfr, his right to the throne could hardly be considered equal to that of Magnús by thirteenth century standards. Snorri therefore clearly implies that his wealth, ability as a warrior, and the danger represented by the alliance between him and King Sveinn of Denmark were decisive for Magnús's decision to share the kingdom with him (*HHarð.* chaps. 18, 21).

32. The attitude to royal descent in the early Middle Ages, as reflected above all in the scaldic poetry, has recently been analyzed by Claus Krag (1989), who concludes that there is very little to suggest that kings like Óláfr Tryggvason, St. Óláfr, and Haraldr harðráði actually claimed descent from Haraldr hárfagri. I thank Mr. Krag for having allowed me to use his article in manuscript.

33. Despite the fact that King Sverrir clearly had the ambition to become a strong ruler and the idea of the king as God's representative on earth was prominent in his milieu (see Gunnes, 1971: 357 ff.), he appears mainly as the warrior hero in his saga, both in the narrative and the characterizations (Bagge, 1987b: 110 ff.). *Hákonar saga* attributes greater importance to the king's performance as a ruler both in its characterization of him and a long summary of his deeds towards the end, which includes his legislation and efforts in maintaining justice, but does not include such activities in the narrative (Bagge, ibid.; see also *Vigf.*: 357 ff.).

34. Examples of this are the conflict between St. Óláfr and Erlingr Skjálgsson over royal government and administration of Western Norway (OH chap. 116), Óláfr's sentence in the case between Ásmundr Grankellsson and Hárekr at Tjøtta (OH chap. 140), King Magnús góði's action against Kálfr Árnason, which arises out of a court case, in which the one party tries to attract the king's attention by accusing Kálfr (MG chap. 13), and the conflict between King Haraldr harðráði and Einarr þambarskelfir, which is brought to a head when a former servant of Einarr's is tried for theft (*HHarð.* chap. 44).

35. Another *ármaðr*, Bjǫrn, is distantly related to Queen Ástríðr (OH chap.

163), although this does not necessarily mean that he had a prominent family background, as she was the daughter of a slave.

36. On the development of the local administration from the eleventh until the thirteenth century, see Andersen, 1977: 278 ff.; Helle, 1974: 206 ff.; Krag, 1982: 105 ff.; and Bagge, 1986: 169 ff.

37. "Ek geri þat lostigr, at beygja hálsinn fyrir þér, Óláfr konungr, en hitt mun mér ǫrðigt þykkja, at lúta til Selþóris, er þrælborinn er í allar ættir" ("I gladly submit to you, King Óláf, but that I find it hard to bow my head to Seal-Thórir, who is thrall-born on all sides") (OH chap. 116: 241).

38. Óláfr's reasons for this strictness are that Þórir has been killed during Easter, in the king's hostel and even before his very eyes, and "that he used my feet as the chopping block" ("er hann hafði foetr mína fyrir hǫggstokkinn") (OH chap. 118: 252 f.). Two of the three reasons thus concern the king's honor.

39. He marries his half-sister Gunnhildr to Ketill kálfr at Ringnes, a great man and Óláfr's staunch ally but hardly of the same rank as, e.g., Erlingr Skjálgsson; and he marries his mother's sister to Þórðr Guthormsson at Steig, "the mightiest man in Northern Gudbrandsdalen" (OH chap. 128).

40. See the discussion between the leaders of King Ingi's faction after his death, during which four men, who were all related to the royal family through kinship or marriage, were brought forward as the possible leader of the faction (ME chap. 1). The one who was elected, Erlingr skakki, was married to the daughter of King Sigurðr jórsalafari. For other examples, see Koht, 1921: 117 ff. An exception to the rule is Grégóríús Dagsson, who owed his position as the virtual leaders of Ingi's faction to his wealth, personal ability, and close friendship to the king. This would no doubt have resulted in his marriage into the royal family but for the fact that the crippled King Ingi apparently did not have offspring and his female relatives were already married off by his elder brothers.

41. See above. There is no explicit reference to this analogy in the sources but both the duty of revenge and the close relationship between members of the *hirð* which is often mentioned in *Heimskringla*, e.g., between Bjǫrn stallari and Hjalti Skjeggjason (OH chaps. 68–69), Skjálgr Erlingsson and Þórarinn Nefjólfsson (OH chap. 118: 253), and Ásmundr Grankellsson and Karli (OH chap. 123: 269), seem to suggest it. The community between the *hirðmenn* is also emphasized in the *Hirðskrá* (e.g., chaps. 31, 41). The ceremonial for admission to the *hirð* (see Hamre, 1961: 57 ff.) bears some resemblance to that of vassalage, an institution that has also been interpreted according to the model of kinship (le Goff, 1980: 256 ff.).

42. In some cases, however, this arrangement resembles that of taking hostages, which was a common way of guaranteeing contracts and settlements (Gundersen, 1960: 331 ff.) and which is frequently mentioned in *Heimskringla* (e.g., OT chap. 67: 383; OH chaps. 111, 121: 264). Thus, Erlingr Skjálgsson's son joins St. Óláfr's household after their settlement at Avaldsnes before the episode of Ásbjǫrn sélsbani. When St. Óláfr asks the leading Icelanders to join him in Norway after their rejection of his demand for Grímsey, they are in a dilemma: if they go, the king has all the leading men of the country under his control. If they refuse, they risk to lose his friendship (OH chap. 126).

43. This attitude is not really surprising against a thirteenth-century Norwe-

gian background, notwithstanding the exaltation of monarchy in the official ideology. In *The King's Mirror* the Son has considerable difficulties in understanding why people who receive no reward from the king are nevertheless obliged to serve him (*Kgs.*: 42, lines 32–34; see Bagge, 1987*b*: 30 f., 183 ff.), and even the Father admits that the death of a king means that his men are left without a lord (*Kgs.*: 49, lines 25–28; see Bagge, 1987*b*: 204).

44. See the negotiations between Magnús góði and Harthacnut (MG chap. 6), Magnús and his uncle Haraldr harðráði (*HHarð.* chap. 21), and Haraldr harðráði and Sveinn and the example of St. Óláfr and the negotiations with Sweden mentioned above. See also Sandvik, 1955: 47 f.

45. See the statement attributed to Cardinal William of Sabina that it was inappropriate that the Icelanders were not subject to a king like all other men (*Sk.*: 603).

46. "Nos quoque hujus schedulæ hic finem facimus, indignum valde judicantes memoriæ posterorum tradere scelera, homicidia, perjuria, parricidia, sanctorum locorum contaminationes, Dei contemptum, non minus religiosorum deprædationes quam totius plebis, mulierum captivationes et ceteras abominationes, quas longum est enumerare" (chap. 34: 67).

47. Both Theodoricus's clerical attitude in general and his dedication of his work to Archbishop Eysteinn, who actively supported Erlingr skakki and Magnús, clearly indicate that his sympathy was also on this side. This does not necessarily mean that his work was directly intended as propaganda for this faction, as has often been assumed (Koht, 1921: 168 ff.; Johnsen, 1939: 71 ff.; Hanssen, 1949: 96 f.). See Bagge, 1989*a*.

48. *Fagrskinna* gives mainly an "ideological" explanation of the conflict between Haraldr and Einarr. Einarr is a dangerous man, and he breaks the law in saving a thief from execution. This interpretation is further emphasized by the author's omission of most examples of actual conflicts between Haraldr and Einarr, found in the earlier *Morkinskinna*, which is less favorable to Haraldr (*Fsk.*: 264 f.; *Msk.*: 171–180; see Indrebø, 1917: 198 ff.). Characteristically, the author ends the story of Haraldr and Einarr with a remark that the *lendir menn* in those days were unruly (ofkátir) and went away to Denmark whenever they had something against the king (*Fsk.*: 265 f.). Finnr Árnason serves as an example of this. This generalization is also found in *Morkinskinna*, but does not serve as an overall interpretation in the same way (*Msk.*: 180; see Indrebø, 1917: 209). By contrast, Snorri plays down the ideological aspect of the conflict and presents it more in terms of a power struggle between individual actors.

49. See his negative characterization of the Eiríkssons (Indrebø, 1917: 140 ff.). His description of the "constitutional crisis" that resulted in Sigvatr's *Bersǫglisvísur* does not differ substantially from *Morkinskinna* and *Heimskringla*, though it has been abbreviated. See Indrebø, 1917: 193 f.

Chapter 4: Morality and Human Character

1. The dialogue is derived, partly verbatim, from *Morkinskinna* (*Msk.*: 382 ff.), but Snorri differs from his source both in presenting the *mannjafnaðr* as a

deliberate confrontation and in making it into a more elaborate discussion of royal virtues. For a comparison between the two versions and the descriptions of the two kings in general, see Kalinke, 1984: 152 ff., particularly 162 ff.

2. See Lönnroth, 1965: 85 ff. for a comparison with the characterizations in the medieval tradition influenced by Suetonius, which contain the same mixture of idealization and apparently realistic description, though the former element is more prominent there. See also Teuffel, 1914 for characterizations in German chronicles of the earlier Middle Ages.

3. Further, there is the amusing story of Þórarinn Nefjólfsson, whose feet were incredibly ugly (OH chap. 85). When King Óláfr sees one of them, he declares that another, equally ugly is not to be found. Þórarinn bets that there is one and shows him his other foot, which lacks one toe. Óláfr, however, declares that the first one was the uglier, since it had five ugly toes, whereas the last one had only four. It would be far-fetched, however, to draw conclusions concerning aesthetic opinions from this example, as the story is intended as an example of Óláfr's smartness.

4. Haraldr hárfagri's hair, which has given him his sobriquet, is of course long and exceptionally beautiful when it has been cut and combed after the ten years it took the king to conquer Norway (*HHárf.* chap. 23). Sigurðr Búason with the long, golden hair is taken captive and given *grið* after the battle of Hj;7rungágr (OT chap. 41: 334 f.). Óláfr kyrri's hair is yellow like silk and falls beautifully (OK chap. 1). Sigurðr slembir's hair is thin but beautiful (MB chap. 13).

5. Óláfr kyrri, who is in one sense a good king but who achieves nothing remarkable, is described as an exceptionally handsome man and very tall. He was mild and cheerful at the drinking table, but rather quiet and no great speaker at the assemblies (OK chap. 1). In other words: except for his looks not a very impressive personality. Hákon herðibreiðr, who was too young when he died to have achieved very much, is described as tall, good-looking, and cheerful (ME chap. 8). The Eiríkssons and Magnús blindi, who receive the most negative characterizations of all kings in *Heimskringla,* are praised for their beauty and athletic abilities (*HGráf.* chap. 2). Sigurðr and Eysteinn Haraldssynir, whom Snorri also dislikes, are not without good qualities. Sigurðr is strong and handsome and an excellent speaker, whereas Eysteinn is intelligent (chaps. 21–22).

6. Thus Haraldr hárfagri (*HHárf.* chap. 42), Earl Sigurðr (*HHárf.* chap. 37), Hákon góði (*HHárf.* chap. 40), Earl Hákon (*HGráf.* chap. 8), St. Óláfr (below), Haraldr harðráði (*HHarð.* chaps. 36, 99–100), Eysteinn Magnússon (*Msyn.* chap. 16), Eysteinn Haraldsson (*Ingi* chap. 22), and Erlingr skakki (*Ingi* chap. 17, ME chap. 37).

7. E.g., St. Óláfr (OH chaps. 7, 12–13, 30, 112–114, 121, 149–150, 175–176) and Haraldr harðráði (*HHarð.* chaps. 6–10, 35, 58). See also the examples of political ability above.

8. OT chap. 50, OH chap. 181: 422, though the latter is said to be fond of wealth (fégjarn), despite his generosity (OH chap. 58). As for the former, Snorri apparently does not consider the vice that did lead him to his fall, his love of women, equally shameful, though he evidently regards his way of satisfying his sexual appetite as highly imprudent (OT chap. 45; see below, chap. 3).

9. In this case, however, Snorri is fairly sober compared to some other

288 Notes to Pages 149–152

historians. *Morkinskinna* contains some rather fantastic stories of the way Sigurðr impresses his Byzantine hosts (*Msk.*: 348 ff.; see Kalinke, 1984: 156 ff.). A later version of *Heimskringla* contains the well-known story of Sigurðr shoeing his horse with golden shoes and then arranging for one of them to drop off and forbidding his men to notice (*Codex Frisianus, Msyn.* chap. 11—an early fourteenth-century manuscript).

10. E.g., Hákon góði's and Grégóríús Dagsson's golden helmets (HG chaps. 28, 30, *Ingi* chap. 26) and Hákon's sword Kvernbítr (*HHárf.* chap. 40), Óláfr Tryggvason's ship Ormr inn langi (OT chap. 88), Sigurðr munnr's and Níkolás Sigurðarson's shields (*Ingi* chap. 28, ME chap. 40), St. Óláfr's men's equipment in the battle of Nesjar (OH chap. 49), and the swords he intended for Christmas presents, of which Sigvatr skáld received one (OH chap. 162). See also the descriptions of the wealth and spending of men like Erlingr Skjálgsson and Grégóríús Dagsson.

11. See the description of Ásbjǫrn's dress and the house at Avaldsnes when he kills Selþórir (OH chap. 118: 251) and of the pagan cult place in Bjarmaland with the statue of the Jómali (OH chap. 133: 293 f.).

12. OH chaps. 32–34, 35: 50. Sigurðr's entertainment of Óláfr and his men is also mentioned in *Leg. Saga:* 23 and *Fsk.*: 147, but the descriptions there are much shorter.

13. For the ideal of the *rex iustus* in Norwegian sources, in its ecclesiastical and monarchical version, see, e.g., Tobiassen, 1964: 196 ff.; Gunnes, 1969: 154 ff.; and Bagge, 1987*b*: 97 ff.

14. For this ideal, see among others Ehrismann, 1970; West, 1938; Painter, 1940: 30 ff.; de Boor, 1970: 386 ff.; Keen, 1984: 3 f., 21 ff., 30 ff., 34 ff.; Duby, 1986: 86 ff. Not all aspects of this ideal are equally prominent in feudal Europe, however. Romantic love plays a subordinate part in the early thirteenth-century *L'Histoire du Guillaume le Maréchal*, which may serve as a mirror of aristocratic virtues (Keen, 1984: 22; Duby, 1986: 87). The importance of the polished courtier as a general aristocratic ideal may also be doubted (Jaeger, 1985: 101 ff., 196 ff.). The essential virtues, which were prominent even before the twelfth century, were generosity, magnificence, and a strong sense of honor (Bosl, 1977: 32 f.; see also below).

15. "hagr ok sjónhannarr um smíðir allar, hvárt er hann gerði eða aðrir menn" (OH chap. 3; *my trans.*).

16. OH chap. 133: 290 f. The same attitude occurs in other Norwegian and Icelandic works, such as *The King's Mirror* (*Kgs.*: 3–7, 38, lines 26–31; see Bagge; 1987*b*: 223).

17. Thus, Snorri uses a fairly long passage to introduce Sigvatr skáld, referring both to his father and to his life before he entered King Óláfr's service, but does not describe him (OH chap. 43). Nor are there characterizations of most of Óláfr's other men, not even prominent ones like Bjǫrn stallari (see OH chap. 57) and the Árnasons, though the latter are formally introduced in the story with mention of their father (OH chap. 110). See also the numerous references to Óláfr's local supporters, above. Exceptions to this are Ásmundr Grankelsson, who is mentioned as one of the best sportsmen in Norway (OH chap. 106) and Karli, who excels in a similar way, and who is described as a very handsome man

(OH chap. 123). Among Óláfr's adversaries, Þórir hundr is not characterized, though most of the other leaders are.

18. E.g., Snæfríðr (*HHárf.* chap. 24: 133), with whom Haraldr hárfagri falls passionately in love, Þóra, the mother of Hákon góði (*HHárf.* chap. 37), Gunnhildr (*HHárf.* chap. 32: 145), married to Eiríkr blóðøx and mother of the Eiríkssons, Ástríðr (OH chap. 88: 163), married to St. Óláfr, Álfhildr, his mistress and mother of Magnús góði (OH chap. 122), and Borghildr, Sigurðr jórsalafari's mistress and Magnús blindi's mother (*Msyn.* chap. 19).

19. In addition to the examples referred to above, n. 17, there are Ragnhildr, mother of Haraldr hárfagri (HS chap. 6), and Sigríðr stórráða (OT chap. 43: 339).

20. This applies to Haraldr hárfagri (*HHárf.* chaps. 1, 42), Hákon góði (HG chaps. 1, 32—with a long quotation of a scaldic poem), St. Óláfr (OH chaps. 1, 3, 58, 181), Haraldr harðráði (*HHarð.* chaps. 36, 99–100), Magnús berfoetr (MB chaps. 7, 16, 26), and Sigurðr and Eysteinn (*Msyn.* chaps. 16–17, 23, 33). Óláfr Tryggvason does not receive an *elogium* in the strict sense, but the description of his last battle is unusually detailed, with numerous quotations from scaldic poetry, and Snorri ends his story by discussing the rumors that he escaped from the battle (OT chap. 112). St Óláfr's *elogium*, which has more in common with the classical model than most others in *Heimskringla*, giving a summary of the king's deeds and an assessment of his reign, comes after his exile and not after his death. This is quite appropriate, since the former event marks the transition between Óláfr the king of Norway in the ordinary sense and Óláfr the saint and eternal ruler of the country.

21. Similar examples of minor characters showing loyalty to their masters or particular bravery in fighting for their cause are the anonymous workman who saved the four-year-old son of Einarr Laxapálsson from Sigurðr slembir's men by telling them that the boy was his own son (*Ingi* chap. 7), Hreiðarr Grjótgarðzson, King Magnús blindi's *hirðmaðr*, who is killed, carrying his master in the battle of Holmengrå, and is praised for his loyalty (*Ingi* chap. 10), and finally an anonymous Birchleg after the battle of Ré. When seeing the body of his master, he tries to kill King Magnús, and is killed himself. When it turns out that he was heavily wounded, dragging his intestines after him, he is praised for his bravery by all (ME chap. 42).

22. See *The King's Mirror* on the social reality behind this: the king often prefers men of low status in his service, because they are completely dependent on him and therefore more trustworthy (*Kgs.* 40, lines 28–31; see Bagge, 1987b: 178).

23. After his victory, he blinds and castrates Magnús and cuts off one of his feet, kills one of his men and blinds another, and hangs a bishop (MB.HG chap. 8). See also the story of the two *lendir menn* taken captive by Haraldr, of whom one is to be hanged and the other to be thrown into a waterfall (MB.HG chap. 4).

24. In this case, however, it does not appear directly from the narrative whether Óláfr is himself responsible for this course of action. In his instruction to Finnr when sending him to Northern Norway, Óláfr does not mention Þórir at all (OH chap. 139: 320 f.). However, he does not blame Finnr at his return,

implying in his comment that he would not have been able to trust Þórir in any case: "I believe Thórir is our enemy, and the farther [he is] from us, the better" ("trúi ek því, at Þórir mun vera oss óvinr, ok þykki mér hann ávalt betri firr mér en nærr") (OH chap. 139: 326, Holl.: 422). This way of telling the story may be partly intended to relieve Óláfr of responsibility, although it is difficult to think that Snorri imagines Finnr to have acted completely on his own.

25. The main source for his description of cruelty and aggressiveness is Luchaire, 1967: 249 ff., who has been accused of generalizing too much from reports on chaos and internal strife (see Baldwin's introduction p. x).

26. For these rules and examples of such behavior, see Painter, 1940: 28 ff.; Keen, 1984: 162 ff.; and Duby, 1986: 78 ff. But see also Gillingham, 1988, who criticizes Duby for having misinterpreted his source and exaggerated the chivalrous behavior there.

27. For instance, according to William of Malmesbury, Earl Robert of Gloucester was taken captive because of this (*Historia Novella* chap. 500). See also the examples in Huizinga, 1955: 98 f. of strategic interests being sacrificed to honor.

28. See, in addition to the references in nn. 25, 26, the example of King Stephen, who, according to William of Malmesbury, gave his enemy, Empress Mathilda, an escort when she came to fight him, that she might safely join her ally, Earl Robert of Gloucester (*Historia Novella* chap. 478). William adds that an honorable knight does not refuse this even to his deadliest enemy.

29. The hundred years war is of course an excellent example of this. On the one hand, the chivalrous warfare between the aristocrats reached its highest peak and was celebrated by Froissart and other authors, on the other, the strategy mainly consisted in enriching oneself and providing one's army by plundering and forcing the enemy to submission through massive terror. The Black Prince, for instance, who was famous for his chivalrous treatment of his noble adversaries, was quite merciless toward ordinary people. The chronicles refer casually to such terror and massacres (Brandt, 1966: 132 ff.). Even members of the aristocracy might be cruelly treated, particularly when they were considered guilty of treason or breach of fealty. Edward I had the Scot rebel William Wallace dragged by a horse to the scaffold, where he was hanged and quartered (Powicke, 1953: 712). An aristocrat who behaved dishonorably might suffer a humiliating and painful punishment (cf. Keen, 1984: 174 f.).

30. E.g., chaps. 50, 54, 58–63, 91–96. On Villehardouin as a politician and a historian, see Archambault, 1974: 25 ff., according to whom he was "intelligent enough to be a scoundrel," but who has no definite opinion on the sincerity of his pious phrases. On honor and the heroic ideal in Villehardouin, see Beer, 1968: 46 ff. Even in Froissart, who is mainly concerned with chivalry and shows little understanding of strategy (Contamine, 1981: 132, 137 f.), some kind of political game is discernible. His heroes are largely opportunistic, seeking their own advantage and shifting sides accordingly (Archambault, 1974: 71).

31. For an interesting application of Elias's theories to the evolution of bourgeois culture in Sweden in the late nineteenth and early twentieth centuries, see Frykman and Löfgren, 1979.

32. For a counter-example to the one referred to here, see the story of Egill

Skalla-Grímsson, who complains about the goods he has lost in Norway and gets his friend Arinbjǫrn to go to the king to claim them. When the king refuses to do anything in the case, Arinbjǫrn compensates Egill's loss out of his own property, and Egill is completely satisfied, apparently forgetting the question of honor (*Egils saga* chap. 68).

33. Earl Eiríkr is famous because of his victory in the two greatest battles in the Northern countries (OH chap. 24). Princess Ingigerðr praises St. Óláfr for his great victory, when he captures five kings in one day, and thus provokes her father to cancel their marriage (OH chap. 89), Ásbjǫrn selsbani earns shame because of the failure of his two expeditions to Southern Norway (OH chaps. 117, 120). King Magnús góði is so famous after his victory at Hlýrskógsheiðr that many men think that it will be impossible to fight against him (MG chap. 28). Both Sigurðr jórsalafari and Erlingr skakki receive much honor because of their successful expeditions to the Holy Land (*Msyn.* chap. 13; *Ingi* chap. 17). During the conflict between Erlingr and Grégóríús in Bergen, Erlingr regards it as shameful to be defeated by people from Viken in a region where he has numerous kinsmen (*HHerð.* chap. 12). See also Snorri's comments on the shameful defeats the Danish kings suffered in Norway, above.

34. For the traditional idea of honor as the fundamental value of Germanic or Nordic society, see Grønbech, 1955 I: 57 ff.; Gehl, 1937: 18 ff.; Bandle, 1969: 12 ff. Andersson, 1970: 575 ff. criticizes this view, pointing to numerous examples of moderation being highly regarded, which he explains as the replacement of a warrior ideal with a social ideal. Though I shall not attempt a general analysis of the Old Norse idea of honor in this context, it seems to me that some of the more extreme examples of "pure" honor in the Icelandic sagas have a literary ring and may represent ideas of heroic behavior in the past more than actual norms at the time the sagas were written down. Nor can we exclude the possibility that some such examples may be influenced by European chivalrous literature. Generally, modern anthropological research suggests that the rules of honor in traditional societies are more nuanced and subtle than particularly Gehl's picture of the Germanic warrior hero implies. One is not expected to take revenge against someone far more powerful than oneself. Conversely, a mighty man is expected to show moderation in dealing with his inferiors; it is dishonorable to exploit one's superiority too much (Bourdieu, 1977: 12 ff., based on examples from Kabylia). Such considerations may explain some of Andersson's examples of honor apparently being disregarded, such as Blund-Ketill's toleration of Hœnsa-Þórir's provocations (1970: 578) and Hallr of Síðu abstaining from demanding compensation for his dead sons to avoid a conflict that would split Icelandic society (1970: 587; see Grønbech, 1955 I: 63 f.): a man can afford to be moderate when there is no doubt of his superiority and ability to protect his honor, and may even promote his honor in this way.

35. St. Óláfr and King Ǫnundr of Sweden's victory at Helgå, where they inundate a large part of King Cnut's fleet and army, is actually an escape from an overwhelmingly superior enemy, who has surrounded them. Characteristically, the two kings find it best to withdraw afterward (OH chaps. 150–51). In his last battle against Erlingr Skjálgsson, Óláfr also intends to escape. When he discovers that this is impossible, he lays an ambush for Erlingr instead (Oh chap. 175).

Nor does Snorri point to any objection against his leaving the country when the enemy becomes too numerous. Other examples of this are Haraldr harðráði's retreat from King Sveinn, when he throws overboard valuable goods to uphold the enemy (*HHarð.* chap. 35), Magnús berfoetr's retreat when surprised by an Irish army (MB chap. 25), and Sigurðr Sigurðsson's advice to King Magnús blindi to withdraw to Trøndelag instead of fighting in Bergen, an advice of which Snorri clearly approves (MB.HG chap. 5).

36. An example is Ívarr skrauthanki, who was ransomed—with difficulties—after the battle of Holmengrå by his brother Jón, who was in the victorious army (*Ingi* chap. 10). In the contemporary sagas we frequently hear of people who save the lives of their relatives who have fought with the opposite party (n. 37). It is not unreasonable to assume that this often happened against payment to those who had most reason for revenge, in analogy with the normal custom of accepting payment instead of taking revenge. But the circumstances clearly indicate that there was no strong custom in favor of this, and that relatives who were absent or still belonged to the opposite party were hardly able to achieve anything.

37. When in 1201 the garrison of Slottsfjellet outside Tønsberg surrendered to King Sverrir, the king, after some discussion with his men, gave them *grið* and included them in his own army (SS chap. 179). See also the episode of Jón kuflungr, who gave *grið* to the Birchlegs who asked for it and included them in his army but did not demand an oath of submission from them, with the result that they all defected to Sverrir. This provoked Sverrir to the comment that Jón's behavior showed that he was not fit to be a chieftain (SS chap. 105). The difficulties involved in giving *grið* is demonstrated in the battle of Strindsjøen (1199), when some Birchlegs complain to King Sverrir that their relatives, whom they have given *grið,* have been killed by men in the army. Sverrir's advice is that they should kill these men's relatives in return (SS chap. 159: 169). Before the battle, Sverrir, contrary to the normal practice the saga attributes to him, had asked his men not to give *grið* (SS chap. 159: 168). His reason for this illustrates the logic of the system: many of the Croziers are perjurers and traitors to the king. The enemy can therefore only be defeated by arms. This means that the *grið* had failed in its purpose, to bring the enemy over to Sverrir's side.

38. Eiríkr's decision might possibly be regarded in the context of his bad relations with his father, who is actually very angry at his pardoning Vagn, and his need to build up a *clientela* independently of his father (*HGráf.* chap. 8; OT chap. 20). However, although Eiríkr's good relations with Denmark are essential to his later successes (OT chaps. 90, 98), Snorri does not imply that the pardoned *jómsvíkingar* had any importance in this respect.

39. "nú hjóttu Nóreg ór hendi mér" (OH chap. 176: 406).

40. Snorri frequently mentions kings' and magnates' illegitimate children but rarely their love affairs. One such reference occurs in the story of the birth of St. Óláfr's son Magnús (OH chap. 122). See also the story of King Sigurðr munnr, who, when passing a farm, hears the beautiful song of a woman. He sleeps with her and she gives birth to a son, the later King Hákon herðibreiðr (*Ingi* chap. 18). By contrast, Snorri omits Styrmir's story of St. Óláfr's affair with Steinvǫr (cf. *Separate Saga:* 683, 685 f., 695 f.), which was without political relevance.

References to women, including their love affairs, are rarer, but Snorri tells without further comment that Erlingr skakki's wife, Kristín, went to Constanti-nople with a lover and that she had illegitimate children (ME chaps. 30, 35). Snorri apparently does not consider such illegitimate connections shameful. They may even be politically useful. But it can be dangerous to take other mens' women. King Sigurðr Eiríksson slefa rapes the wife of Klyppr hersir and is killed by him (HG chap. 14: 249 f.). Earl Hákon, who is very fond of women, is killed by the people of Trøndelag because of his offenses to their wives and daughters.

41. A rare example of this is the story of King Sveinn of Denmark, who, having been defeated by Haraldr harðráði in the battle of Nisså, seeks refuge with a farmer. He is given water to wash. But when he dries his hands on the middle of the towel, the farmer's wife snatches it from him and says: "You have no manners. It is boorish to wet all the towel." Sveinn answered: "I shall yet come to a place where I can dry my hands on the middle of a towel" ("fátt gott kantu þér; þat er þorpkarlegt at væta allan dúkinn senn . . . þar køm ek þá enn, er ek þerri mér meirr á miðri þerru") (HHarð. chap. 64; see Msk.: 214 f.). Though this is a unique example, it is characteristic of Snorri to find the contrast between the life of the aristocracy and that of the people in such a small detail from everyday life! See also Bagge, 1987b: 106 ff. on The King's Mirror, which, though more concerned with courteous manners than Snorri, differs in a similar way from European courtly literature.

42. See Steblin-Kamensky, 1973: 106 f. on the attitude in the Icelandic sagas. For a Norwegian example, see Kgs.: 6, where the Father urges the Son to show prudence and circumspection when taking revenge. In Snorri's own examples of revenge (e.g., OH chaps. 123, 133, 169, 178; HHarð. chap. 72; Ingi chap. 14) little is said about feelings. An exception is Ásbjǫrn selsbani, who behaves imprudently when rushing forward to kill Selþórir (OH chap. 118). But Ásbjǫrn is subject to an extreme provocation, being ridiculed before a large audience. Besides, Snorri hardly regards him as a great chieftain or a very intelligent man.

43. As has been noted by several scholars (e.g., Heusler, 1912: 41 f.; Steblin-Kamensky, 1973: 113 ff.), Norway and Iceland compare favorably to most other countries of medieval Europe in this respect. Torture and especially painful means of execution are rarely mentioned in the sources and were not institution-alized in the laws as in many other countries. But it is probably going too far to suggest that the examples that did occur were inspired from Europe. The fact that these examples date from after the introduction of Christianity may simply be the result of the sources being more detailed after this time. Moreover, there is a possibility that people belonging to the lower levels of society were more exposed to cruel treatment, either from the aristocracy or from people of their own rank. The miracle accounts, in Snorri and elsewhere, give some quite nasty examples of cruelty, e.g., the story of the poor young man who had his tongue cut off by King Sigurðr jórsalafari's mother for a trivial offense (Msyn. chap. 30) or of the young priest, who was tortured and maimed by some great men because of rumors of an affair between him and their sister (Ingi chap. 25). On the one hand, such stories give glimpses of milieus other than the top aristocracy, with which the main narrative of the sagas deal. On the other hand, miracle

accounts are hardly the most trustworthy sources and may easily give an exaggerated picture of cruelty.

44. "en þar váru á krókar ok lágu þar á tágar af hjartanu, sumar rauðar, sumar hvítar; ok er hann sá þat, mælti hann: [vel hefir konungrinn alit oss] feitt er mér enn om hjartaroetr. Siðan hné hann aptr ok var þá dauðr" (OH chap. 234). The words in brackets are only found in one of the manuscripts of *Heimskringla* but occur in the *Separate Saga* chap. 234. See also the words of Magnús berfoetr, who is wounded by a spear passing through both his thighs and breaks its shaft: "Thus break we every leg-spar, men!" ("svá brjótu vér hvern sperrilegginn, sveinar") (MB chap. 25). A quarrel between two housecarls, of whom the one has let himself be bled and the other accuses him of being too pale and thus not behaving sufficiently manly almost leads to a full battle between Erlingr skakki and Grégóríús (*HHerð.* chap. 12).

45. *Ingi* chap. 12. Although the description of Sigurðr's sufferings is truly exceptional and bears considerable resemblance to the story of a martyr (Guðnason, 1978: 96 ff., 171), it may be worth considering how far it can be explained in terms of the heroic ideal. There is little in Sigurðr's life as a whole that resembles a saint's *vita*. The only direct reference to religion in the story of his torture is the statement that he recited one-third of the psalter before his death. Though this is clearly evidence of both learning and piety, it also serves as an indication of the length of time the torture lasted and above all of his self-control: he was able to talk and his voice did not change from normal. This is in fact Snorri's explicit comment: "Hall [the eye-witness] thought that betokened endurance and strength beyond that of other men" ("ok lézk honum [Hallr] þat þykkja umfram eljan ok styrk annarra manna"). The story of Sigurðr's torture is found in a slightly different version in *Morkinskinna,* in which some scaldic stanzas, mentioning the recitation of the psalter, are quoted (*Msk.*: 436 f.).

46. E.g., the dialogues between the captive *jómsvikingar* and their victors after the battle of Hjǫrungavágr (OT chap. 41), between St. Óláfr and Earl Hákon when the latter is taken captive (OH chap. 30), between St. Óláfr and Erlingr Skjálgsson during their last battle (OH chap. 176), and between King Eysteinn Haraldsson and Símun skálpr, who takes him captive and kills him (*Ingi* chap. 32).

47. For the concepts, see Benedict, 1946, who used them to characterize the difference between Japanese and Western mentality. Though some of her conclusions may be doubtful and her dichotomy too sharply drawn (see, e.g., Doi, 1976: 48 ff. and Benton, 1982: 271), the concepts seem useful in contrasting medieval and modern attitudes.

48. On Haraldr, see above. On Erlingr, see Snorri's remark that he was silent and spoke quietly to those of his enemies whom he had decided to kill, whereas he scolded those whom he intended to pardon (ME chap. 35). Other examples are Hárekr at Tjøtta and Kálfr Árnason. When Ásmundr Grankellsson and his men beat Hárekr's housecarls, Hárekr makes the following comment: "It is always interesting to hear news. That has never occurred before that my men were beaten" ("tíðendi þykkja nýnæmi ǫll þetta hefir eigi fyrr gǫrt verit, at berja menn mína") (OH chap. 140; *my trans.*). He confines himself to this, is calm and cheerful, and apparently accepts the king's verdict in favor of Ásmundr a little

later. But he bides his time and revenges himself by killing Ásmundr's father (OH chap. 169). Before the battle of Stiklestad, Finnr Árnason comments on his brother Kálfr's conciliatory words to St. Óláfr that he always speaks fair when he intends to do evil (OH chap. 224).

49. "Halldórr var manna mestr ok sterkastr ok inn fríðasti; þat vitni bar Haraldr konungr honum, at hann hafi verit þeira manna með honum, er sízt brygði við váveilifliga hluti, hvárt er þat var mannháski eða fagnaðartíðendi eða hvat sem at hendi kom í háska, þá var hann eigi glaðari ok eigi óglaðari; eigi svaf hann meira né minna eða drakk eða neytti matar, en svá sem vanði hans var til. Halldórr var maðr fámæltr ok stirðorðr, bermæltr ok stríðlundaðr ok ómjúkr, . . ." (HHarð. chap. 36).

50. However, there are various opinions on how dangerous warfare was to the members of the military aristocracy. Duby, 1986: 91 f., 149 f. probably minimizes its dangers; cf. Gillingham, 1988. See also Keen, 1984: 220 ff., and demographic data for the English aristocracy of the later Middle Ages, which show considerably higher mortality for men than for women, because of men's participation in warfare (Hollingsworth, 1965). Though reliable statistics are scarce, other sources give a similar impression (see Leyser, 1979: 56 f. and Shahar, 1983: 129 with ref.).

51. The general point behind this explanation is not to state that people only act according to norms if such action serves their own interests, but that there is some connection between the self-imposed norms of a given group and the interests of its members.

52. See Shorter, 1979 and Stone, 1982, who suggest that people in the early modern period, and by implication also in the Middle Ages, were more cold, cynical, and calculating in their relations to other men, particularly relatives. Though these theories have been criticized, it seems reasonable to assume that less distinction between public and private also meant that the private sphere was less emotional than in our society. See also Bagge, 1989c.

53. "Vita Prima" book 1, chaps. 1–5. By contrast, the later "Vita Secunda" (book 1, chaps. 1–7) is more conventional. On the various biographies of St. Francis, see Brooke, 1967: 177 ff.

54. Lönnroth, 1963–1964: 24 ff. This doctrine, which was current throughout the Middle Ages, was known also in the Nordic countries, as appears from several manuscripts examined by Lönnroth (op. cit.: 34 ff.).

55. There is almost verbatim correspondence between Snorri's story of the conflicts at the Orkneys during these years and the Orkneyinga saga (OH chaps. 96–103 = Orkn. chaps. 13–19). The common explanation to this is that these chapters were copied from Snorri's Separate Saga during a revision of the Orkneyinga saga (Guðmundsson, 1965: xxvii ff. and 1967: 700). However, we cannot exclude the possibility that Snorri has been influenced by the original version of the Orkneyinga saga, which is now lost.

56. E.g., his fight against the Vikings near Sotaskjær (OH chap. 6), his escape from Lake Mälaren by leading the water away (OH chap. 7), and his destruction of London Bridge by covering his ships with shields of tree roots, branches, etc., sailing under the bridge and dragging it down by ropes (OH chaps. 12–13).

57. *siðlátr,* i.e., a man who lived according to the commands of Christianity; see Fritzner.

58. "Svá er sagt, at Óláfr konungr var siðlátr ok boenroekinn til guðs alla stund ævi sinnar, en síðan er hann fann, at ríki hans þvarr, en mótstǫðumenn eflðusk, þá lagði hann allan hug á þat, at gera guðs þjónostu; dvalði hann þá ekki frá aðrar áhyggjur eða þat starf, sem hann hafði áðr með hǫndum haft, þvíat hann hafði þá stund, er hann sat í konungdóminum, starfat þat, er honum þótti mest nytsemð at vera, fyrst at friða ok frelsa landit . . . en síðan at snúa landz-fólkinu á rétta trú . . ." (OH chap. 181).

59. In addition to the dream that makes him decide to return to Norway, he sees the whole country in a vision (OH chap. 202) and dreams that he is climbing a high ladder that leads to heaven (OH chap. 214).

60. Thus, Suetonius's picture of Augustus bears some resemblance to Snorri's of St. Óláfr in that both the brutal and ruthless general of the civil wars and the mild and moderate statesman of the following period are described without any attempt to bridge the gap between them (e.g., *De vita Caesarum* chaps. 13 ff., 27 for the former and chaps. 21, 28 ff., 41 ff., 51 ff., 54 ff., 67 for the latter). See also Suetonius's different judgment on his private morality, especially concerning sexuality, where he had a reputation for being dissolute, particularly in his early period, and his self-control and moderation in most other respects (chaps. 68–78).

61. Lönnroth, 1965: 79 ff. In particular, Lönnroth refers to Dares Phrygius's *Historia de excidio Troiae,* which is preserved in an Old Norse translation, *Trójumanna saga,* most probably from the late twelfth century (Lönnroth, 1965: 82 f., 100 ff.).

62. See above and Kirn, 1955: 152 ff. and 179 ff., who points to Gerald of Wales as a master, not the least in indirect characterization.

Chapter 5: The Historian

1. E.g., his reference to the change in the royal title from *dróttr* to *konungr* (*Yngl.* chap. 17), the introduction of the *leiðangr* by Hákon góði (HG chap. 20), the administrative system of Haraldr hárfagri (*HHárf.* chap. 6), the changes in customs in the reign of Óláfr kyrri (OK chaps. 2–3), etc.

2. See Dahl, 1959: 46 ff., 60 ff., 168 ff., with reference to Rudolf Keyser, P. A. Munch, and above all Ernst Sars, one of Koht's teachers, who produced one of the most brilliant syntheses of Norwegian history (Sars, 1874–1891).

3. Queen Ragnhildr, married to King Hálfdan svarti and later mother of King Haraldr hárfagri, dreams that she draws a thorn out of her dress, which then grows into a large tree. The lowest part of its stem was red like blood, higher up it was beautiful and green, and its top was white like snow. It had large branches which spread over the whole country and even longer (HS chap. 6). Later, Hálfdan dreams that his hair grows long and spreads out in a large number of locks, one of which is longer and far more beautiful than the rest (HS chap. 7). Both dreams are interpreted as referring to Haraldr and his descendants: the stem of Ragnhildr's tree is Haraldr, its colors symbolizing the different phases of his life: the long wars of conquest with much shedding of blood, the growth of his *ríki* (probably = power, see Bagge, 1987*b*: 187 ff.), and finally his

old age. The branches, like the locks of Hálfdan's hair, are his descendants, who have ruled Norway since then. And the longest and most beautiful lock in Hálfdan's hair is St. Óláfr (*HHárf.* chap. 42; HS chap. 7).

4. See *Yngl.* chap. 5, where Óðinn establishes himself in Sigtuna as the ruler of Sweden, dividing the other countries of the north between his sons. Most of *Ynglinga saga* then deals with the dynasty's rule of Sweden, until the Swedish invasion of Eastern Norway as the result of hunger in Sweden (chaps. 43–44).

5. For a review of the various interpretations of this process, see Andersen, 1977: 40 ff. The focus on internal, Norwegian factors is characteristic both of nineteenth-century historiography, with its nationalistic approach, and of more recent analyses, stressing social and economic aspects. There thus seems to be a strong tendency to regard Norway as a kind of unity that existed already before the political unification. A more adequate interpretation in my opinion is to regard the unification of the three Nordic kingdoms as one process and explain the division of territory between them in terms of resources and distance to the respective centres of power, see Bagge, 1989*b*.

6. "Bar þá Óláfr einn konungsnafn í Nóregi" (OH chap. 75).

7. Erlingr and Einarr almost act as independent rulers of large regions of the country, Erlingr in Western Norway, Einarr in Trøndelag. Snorri refers to Erlingr as the "best" and "noblest" ("gǫfgastr") of all the *lendir menn* that have been in Norway, which probably both refers to his personal qualities and his status and resources. He held a *hirð* like a king, having at least ninety men around him and two hundred if the earls were around. He had a ship which was manned by two hundred men when he went on expeditions (OH chap. 22). In the twelfth century Grégóríús Dagsson had ninety men, fully armed and with helmets, whom he held at his own cost, and two ships. He wore a golden helmet and he never drank in public houses (í skytningum) without his housecarls drinking with him (*Ingi* chap. 26). Though Grégóríús is not quite the equal of Erlingr, this hardly indicates a great gap between the members of the aristocracy of the twelfth century and that of the early eleventh.

8. See Bjørgo, 1970: 2 ff. and Bagge, 1975: 239 ff. with reference to earlier literature.

9. For the successions, see *Msyn.* chap. 33, MB.HG chap. 1. Peace was kept well in the first part of the reign of the Haraldssons, i.e., c. 1139–1155 (*Ingi* chap. 21). During the conflict between Hákon herðibreiðr and Ingi, Snorri notes that it now (1159) happened for the first time as long as men could remember that the district between the towns had been ravaged by an army ("milli kaupanganna," *HHerð.* chap. 4). As this took place at Møre, Snorri most probably refers to the district between Nidaros and Bergen, not the country as a whole. Nevertheless, Snorri hardly regards the period c. 1130–1160 as particularly violent.

10. "þá var sú tíð komin, at fyrir doemask skyldi blótskaprinn ok blótmenninir, en í stað kom heilog trúa ok réttir siðir" (OT chap. 50; *my trans.*).

11. See particularly the prologue, where Snorri gives a euhemeristic explanation of the Old Norse religion, while at the same time stressing man's natural cognition of God (Lönnroth, 1969: 5 ff.; Baetke, 1973: 206 ff.; Dronke and

Dronke, 1977: 153 ff.; Clunies Ross, 1987: 13 ff.; Weber, 1987: 102 ff.; von See, 1988: 69 ff.).

12. Thus Weber, 1987: 111 ff. An example is Haraldr hárfagri's oath by "God . . . who created me and governs all" ("Til guðs, þes er mik skóp ok ǫllu ræðr," *HHárf.* chap. 4) not to cut his hair until he has conquered all Norway. See also Lönnroth, 1969: 1 ff., 12 ff. on this belief in the sagas.

13. *Edda* chap. 53: 135 f.; see Weber, 1987: 102. In the prologue to *Edda* Snorri traces the genealogy of Óðinn back to the Trojans, like Geoffrey of Monmouth did with the dynasty of the Britons (Hanning, 1966: 106, 140, 156 ff.), and makes him leave Troy, i.e., contemporary Turkey, to acquire fame by conquering the northern half of the world (*Edda:* 3 ff.). Though Snorri is a little more explicit here, the connection with classical and Christian history is not particularly strong.

14. "Í þann tíma fóru Rúmverja-hǫfðingjar víða um heiminn ok brutu undir sik allar þjóðir (. . .) en fyrir því, at Óðinn var forspár ok fjǫlkunnigr, þá vissi hann, at hans afkvæmi myndi um norðrhálfu heimsins byggva" ("At that time the generals of the Romans moved about far and wide, subjugating all peoples (. . .) And because Óthin had the gift of prophecy and was skilled in magic, he knew that his offspring would inhabit the northern part of the world") (*Yngl.* chap. 5: 14).

15. For the European parallels in the former, see Johnsen, 1939: 29 ff. and Hanssen, 1949: 78 ff. Theodoricus links Norwegian history to universal history through typological parallels, such as the one between the peace between Magnús góði and Harthacnut and the history of Charlemagne (chaps. 22–23). See Bagge 1989*a*. For the latter, see Storm's introduction (*Islandske Annaler:* i ff.).

16. *Prol.Hkr.* I: 5. This periodization also occurs in Ásbjǫrn of Meðalhús' speech against King Hákon's attempt at Christianization (HG chap. 15).

17. He refers to Óðinn's law that dead men should be buried (*Yngl.* chap. 8), then to the mound built over Freyr (chap. 10), then to some burnings, and finally, from Álfr and Yngvi (chap. 21), he seems to assume that the kings were buried in mounds.

18. See Lie's criticism of Brekke, 1958, who goes very far in classifying *Sverris saga* as a piece of propaganda (Lie, 1960–1961: 26 ff.).

19. "Ek hugsa þat . . . hvé ilt mér þykkir, ef engi skal saga ganga frá mér, áðr en þrýtr líf mitt" (*Sturl.* vol. 2: 162; see Paasche, 1967: 73 and Foote, 1984: 52).

20. Finley, 1962: 144 ff. The political importance of such drinking parties in Homeric Greece and early medieval Norway is discussed by Bjørn Qviller in a forthcoming article, which he has kindly allowed me to use.

21. "bæði er . . . at mikill er virðinga-munr vár frænda Ásbjarnar, enda gerir hann svá, slíkt starf sem hann lagði á í sumar, at soekja kynnit til Erlings á Jaðar, en hann vill eigi hér fara í næsta hús til mín; veit ek eigi, hvárt hann hyggr, at Selþórir myni í hverjum hólma fyrir vera" (OH chap. 117: 249).

22. This may be an alternative explanation to the one offered by Blöndal, 1982, that the "objective" attitude to Magnús Erlingsson in large parts of *Sverris saga* is evidence that the author has incorporated parts of a saga of King Magnús, which is now lost. See Bagge, "Propaganda."

23. "ok hafa þeir verit miklu gǫfgari en vér, ok hefir oss þó dugat þessi átrúnaðr" (HG chap. 15).

24. *SagaOT:* 131 ff. The only important difference is that Snorri—characteristically—has omitted Oddr's introduction that the Devil had become jealous when seeing Óláfr's many good works in God's cause and now attempted to seduce him.

25. As this story is derived from a—more or less—clerical source, another interpretation might suggest itself, namely, the past as a temptation to distract Óláfr from his real task, to establish the new, Christian epoch in Norway, thus implying a fundamental difference between two historical epochs. Though such a view is less unlikely in a clerical source than in Snorri, there is nothing in the story that has to be explained this way. There may be some opposition between pagan and Christian wisdom but the bishop's reaction seems rather to be the result of suspicion against the person Óláfr is talking to than against the contents of their talk. The Devil may use things that are in themselves good or at least morally neutral to seduce men. Knowledge of the past is thus used in the same way as the excellent food Óðinn procures and which Óláfr orders to be destroyed when he has discovered the identity of the stranger.

26. "at heldr vildu menn hafa útlenda konunga yfir sér ok vera sjálfráðari, þvíat útlendir hǫfðingjar váru þeim jafnan fjarri ok vǫnduðu lítt um siðu manna" (OH chap. 36: 51 f.).

27. Haraldr gráfeldr died fifteen winters after Hákon góði (OT chap. 14). Although Snorri is not quite explicit at this point, he seems to imply that this happened in 975 (OT chaps. 1, 9), which means that Hákon must have died in 960 (see Koht, 1921: 37) or fifty-five years before Hroerekr's speech. As Hroerekr is an old man, he may have some recollection of Hákon from his youth, but not of his predecessors, Haraldr hárfagri and Eiríkr blóðøx.

28. "Sva er nu mykel fyrnd at heiminum at varla munu nu þæir luter kunna til at værða er æigi munu doemi til finnaz at fyrri hava orðit oc munu þvi varla þeir luter kunna til hannda bæra er æigi mann froðr maðr doemi til finna" (*Kgs.*: 78, l. 21–23; Larson: 259).

29. E.g., their different treatment of the tyrant and the doctrine of tyrannicide, *Polycraticus* book 4, chap. 1 and book 8, chaps. 17–22 and *De regimine principum* book 1, chaps. 4–6. See Bagge, 1987*b*: 171 ff.

30. "furðu seint fúna menn í sandinum; ekki myndi svá vera, ef hann hefði í moldu legit" (OH chap. 244; see Bull, 1912: 209 f.; 1967: 426).

31. See Paasche, 1967: 429. It is clear from the context that Snorri disagrees with Álfífa, as she is proved wrong in the next two tests. The fact that Snorri omits to quote Einarr þambarskelfir's harsh words in *Leg. Saga,* that Álfífa ought to burn instead of St. Óláfr's hair (*Leg. Saga:* 91), cannot be evidence of his approval of her attitude, but must be intended to play down the enmity between her and Einarr or may be an indication that he finds it disrespectful to address such words to a queen.

32. *Fagrskinna* is the saga that resembles *Heimskringla* most at this point, containing even fewer miracles (Indrebø, 1917: 245 f.). Considering that *Heimskringla* is far longer than *Fagrskinna,* however, the former is the more restrictive (Nordal, 1973: 156).

33. *SagaOT:* 141; OT chap. 78. Snorri thus explains the reference to a fight between the dog and the hart from Þórir's nickname. This is both expressed in

his statement that Þórir was an extremely fast runner and in the words Óláfr adresses to the dog: "Vígi, tak hjǫrtinn" ("Vigi, get the hart").

34. Theodoricus (chap. 14) and the authors of *Historia Norvegiae* (MHN: 118 f.) and *Ágrip* (chap. 20) express doubts on the point, whereas the author of *Fagrskinna* is most inclined to reject the story, taking it as evidence of the great love his men felt for him, which made them refuse to believe that he was dead (*Fsk.*: 131 f.).

35. In addition to the stories mentioned above, this includes the story of Óláfr's conversion through his meeting with a hermit (OT chap. 31) and of Rauðr, who creates a gale by magical means to prevent Óláfr from attacking him, but is defeated with the help of the Christian ritual, taken captive, and killed by a snake put into his mouth (OT chaps. 78–80).

36. Each of the subsequent sagas except those of Magnús blindi and Haraldr gilli and Magnús Erlingsson contains between two and four, normally three miracles. See *HHarð.* chaps. 54–57, OK chap. 6, *Msyn.* chaps. 30–31, *Ingi* chaps. 24–25, *HHerð.* chap. 20–21.

37. Storm, 1873: 170 ff. Their authenticity has apparently not been doubted by later scholars. Lie points out, however, that their style often differs from the rest of the work in being more emotional and subjective (Lie, 1937: 47 f.). This is no argument against their authenticity, but confirms the impression that they are fairly isolated within *Heimskringla* as a whole.

38. E.g., the story of Kolbeinn, who had his tongue cut off by Sigurðr jórsalafari's mother. Here Snorri quotes Einar Skúlason, who had himself seen the man (*Msyn.* chap. 30). In the case of the priest Ríkarðr, who was blinded and maimed, Snorri gives names and details and finally mentions that a white scar appeared on both his eyelids after his healing (*Ingi* chap. 25).

39. Admittedly, most of the miracles told in *Passio Olavi* contain few references to place, time, and other circumstances. But Snorri does not include the one that happened to a king when the church at Stiklestad was consecrated (*Passio:* 94 f.; see *Hom.*: 128 f.), nor the one Archbishop Eysteinn told happened to himself (*Passio:* 104 f.). However, it is possible that Snorri did not know the latter miracle, as it is not found in the Old Norse translation of *Passio* (*Hom.*: 108 ff.), which seems to be the one current in Iceland (Storm, 1873: 170 ff. and MHN: xxxvi f.; see also Gunnes, 1973: 1 ff. on the relationship between the two versions of *Passio*).

40. These are the following: Óláfr's miraculous victory during a raid in Shetland, when he was separated from his men, but appeared to the enemy as a great army, so that they submitted to him (*Separate Saga* vol. 2: 749 ff.), and his fight against two monsters (ibid.: 751 ff.). Of supernatural events in addition to the miracles worked by Óláfr himself may be mentioned his meeting with the hermit (ibid.: 760), who prophecies his future, a story resembling the one told of Óláfr Tryggvason (OT chap. 31). For the reconstruction of Styrmir's saga of St. Óláfr, see Nordal, 1914: 69 ff. with a summary of the fragments: 89 ff.

41. Snorri refers to the following miracles in this part of his work: on his journey from Norway Óláfr leads his men through a scree that is impossible to pass and provides them with food although there is nothing left of their provisions. He spends the night in a chalet, where an evil spirit is burned by his

prayers. A spring in which the king has washed his hands is later able to heal sick animals, and he promises the owner of the farm in which he has stayed that he will always have enough to support him, for the grain will never be damaged by frost (OH chap. 179). In Russia, he miraculously heals a boy with a boil in his throat (OH chap. 189). The fragments from Styrmir contain the following additions: Óláfr leads his men over a lake that is impossible to pass, heals his horse, and changes water into wine (*Separate Saga* vol. 2: 815 f., 819 f.). Finally, the story of Óláfr punishing himself for working on a Sunday is presented as a miracle in some of the earlier sagas: Óláfr burns the slivers in his hand, but is not hurt (*Leg. Saga:* 97 f.; *Passio:* 82). In this case, Snorri's omission improves the story from a Christian point of view, in stressing Óláfr's will to punish himself (see, e.g., Paasche, 1916: 377 f.).

42. An exception to this is the battle of Hlýrskogsheiðr against the Wends, which is won because of St. Óláfr's intervention (MG chaps. 27–28): he visits his son Magnús in a dream, and on the day of the battle people hear the sound of bells in the air. Magnús and his men rush forward and win a great victory. During the Wends' attack against Konghelle the holy relics almost cause their king's ship to burn (MB.HG chap. 11: 338).

43. OH chap. 18; see *Fsk.*: 143. According to Theodoricus (chap. 15), Óláfr's return is the result of his visit to a pious hermit, whereas *Ágrip* vaguely refers to God's intervention in bringing him home (*Ágr.* chap. 23).

44. *Leg. Saga,* which is generally more inclined toward the supernatural than Snorri, merely refers to Óláfr's decision, giving the death of Earl Hákon as the event that finally led Óláfr to carry out his plan (*Leg. Saga:* 74). *Ágrip* only mentions the fact that Óláfr returns to Norway (chap. 31), whereas *Fagrskinna* tells that he returned having received a message from Norway that the country was without a ruler after Earl Hákon's death (*Fsk.*: 180, chap. 28).

45. ". . . fylgir svá mikil ergi, at eigi þótti karlmǫnnum skammlaust við at fara, ok var gyðjunum kend sú íþrótt" (*Yngl.* chap. 7: 19; *my trans.*). The basic meaning of *ergi* is that of sexual perversion, of a man who accepts being used sexually by another man. Generally it is used of everything that is shameful for a man, e.g., cowardice, unmanliness (Sørensen, 1983: 18 ff.).

46. E.g., by Holmsen, 1977: 201. The only statement in Snorri's text to indicate that he regarded them as such, is a reference in a speech by Erlingr skakki to their plundering (*HHerð.* chap. 9). Apart from this, his reference to their large number of men, including many magnates, rather indicates that he considered them a perfectly normal faction in the civil wars (*HHerð.* chaps. 2–3, 11).

47. On Christian versus pagan or traditional attitudes to dreams, see Glendinning, 1974: 25 ff., who, in my opinion convincingly, regards the Icelandic examples he analyzes as a mixture of both. See also Turville-Petre, 1966: 343 ff. and 1972: 30 ff. and Miller, 1986: 105 ff.

48. Glendinning, 1974: 37. Examples of this in Snorri are Óláfr's words to Haraldr, which suggest moral disapproval of his expedition against England, though Snorri himself appears to take a relaxed attitude toward the matter, and possibly Karkr's dream when hiding with Earl Hákon for Óláfr Tryggvason (OT chap. 49). Karkr dreams that Óláfr lays a golden necklace around his neck.

Hákon, who fears that he will betray him, warns him that this means that he will receive a blood-red ring around his neck, and is proved right, when Karkr is hanged for having killed his master. Karkr behaves despicably and misinterprets the warning in the dream.

49. Thus, the reports on such phenomena in Snorri and other saga writers are in a general way evidence of contemporary beliefs, although many particular stories and descriptions of pagan cult, etc. may of course be inventions or influenced by contemporary Christian practice (see Schomerus, 1936; Baetke, 1951, particularly: 36 ff. on magic).

50. "Svá segja menn (. . .) en eigi veit ek sann á því" (*HHerð* chap. 16).

51. By contrast, Oddr munkr and the author of *Jómsvíkinga saga*, who were Snorri's sources, accept the sacrifice as a fact and describe it in some detail (*SagaOT:* 61 f.; *Jóms.* chap. 34).

52. Baetke, 1973: 212; Lönnroth, 1969: 4; Dronke and Dronke, 1977: 155. Von See (1988: 79 ff.) is no doubt right that this is not Snorri's consistent view of the pagan gods, but at least the story of Óláfr Tryggvason and Óðinn is best interpreted in this way.

53. See Green, 1972: 20 ff., 116 ff. on the gradual substitution of God's providence by *fortuna* in Italian historiography from the late thirteenth until the late fourteenth century.

54. *Chronica* I.26: 92, VI.9; see Koch, 1961: 321 ff.; Lammers, 1961: li ff.; and Goetz, 1984: 86 ff., 122 ff. on *mutatio rerum* in Otto's philosophy of history. To Pickering, 1977: 1 ff., there is a sharp contrast between a "Boethian" interpretation of history, based on *fortuna*, and an "Augustinian" one, based on God's providence, in Otto and other medieval historians, a contrast that seems to me a little exaggerated.

55. See Otto of Freising's story of how Frederick Barbarossa was saved from a flood, which is told expressly to show that *fortuna* had consistently favored him from his early youth until the present day (*Gesta* book 2, chaps. 47–48: 218 ff.; see Bagge, 1990: 6 ff.).

56. Commenting on the death of Earl Einarr of the Orkneys at the hands of Þorkell fóstri, Snorri gives as one of the reasons for his men's failure to revenge him that Fate so willed it that Þorkell should survive Einarr: "bar þat til með auðnu þeiri, er Þorkatli var auðit lengra lífs" (OH chap. 99; *Hkr.* vol. 2: 206). But he also gives other explanations, that Einarr's men were mostly unarmed and that his killing was totally unexpected. The passage is almost identical with *Orkn.*: chap. 16: 34 (see above).

57. Other terms are *goefa, gipta,* and *auðna.* See Baetke, 1973: 347 and Hallberg, 1973: 147 ff. *Hamingja,* which is the most common term in *Heimskringla,* is derived from *hamr* = "outer clothing," "guardian spirit." It is partly synonymous with *fylgja,* which, however, often has the more concrete meaning of "guardian spirit" (Turville-Petre, 1972: 52 ff.).

58. "ok þurfum vér nú þess mjǫk, konungr, at leggir hamingju þína á þessa ferð" (OH chap. 69: 106; see Hallberg, 1973: 158 f.).

59. E.g., Gunnes, 1971: 31 f.; Ström, 1967: 62 f.; Hallberg, 1966: 271 ff.; and—most fully—1973: 143 ff. For a summary and evaluation of the discussion, see McTurk, 1974–1977: 139, who tends to favor the traditional opinion. Fugle-

stad, 1979: 47 ff. gives an interesting comparison between the ideas on this matter in the written sources and sacred kingship in Western Africa.

60. At this point, Baetke's criticism of the traditional view, at least in the form propounded by Grønbech, is based on a misunderstanding. Grønbech does not maintain that luck is inherent in the king's "office" or anything like that, but that the king is supposed to surpass other people in this respect as in others (1955 vol. 2: 108 f., 120 f. etc.; see Baetke, 1964: 22 ff.). Nor is Baetke's objection that kings were not always victorious and even not expected to be so, particularly relevant (1964: 24 f.). Evidently, there are ups and downs in life, and one can hardly always be favored by the *hamingja.* This sentiment is well expressed by the young Earl Hákon when taken captive by St. Óláfr: "It is not that luck has deserted us. It has long been the case that now the one, now the other of the two parties have lost out. . . . It may be that we are more successful another time" ("ekki er þetta óhamingja, er oss hefir hent; hefir þat lengi verit, at ýmsir hafa sigraðir verit . . . kann vera at oss takisk annat sinn betr til en nú") (OH chap. 30). Though the earl is proved wrong in this particular case—Óláfr suggesting the possibility that he may not have another chance—his opinion is probably in accordance with common sense, as expressed among other things in the shifting defeats and victories described in Snorri's narrative. A king who consistently fails, however, is not likely to last long.

61. On Snorri's version of this story compared to earlier ones, see Bagge, 1989*a*: 127 f. The story contains a number of inconsistencies and improbable events, which Snorri has attempted to iron out, though not entirely successfully.

62. For the same idea in the Icelandic sagas, see the statement on Gísli Súrsson that he was a brave man although no man of luck: "Lykr þar nu æfe Gisla, ok er þat alsagt, at hann hefir hinn mesta hreystemadr verit, þo at han være eigi i ǫllum hlutum gæfumadr" (*Gísla saga* chap. 36: 71).

63. "gæfumaðr ertu mikill, Sigvatr; er þat eigi undarligt, at gæfa fylgi vizku; hitt er kynligt, sem stundum kann verða, at sú gæfa fylgir óvizkum mǫnnum, at óvitrlig ráð snúazk til hamingju" (OH chap. 122: 267; *my trans.*).

64. For an explicit reference to the connection between the two, see Snorri's comment to Óláfr Guðbrandsson's attack against Erlingr skakki, which failed despite the fact that Óláfr had a largely superior force and took Erlingr by surprise: "It was said that Óláf and his men had the worst kind of ill luck in this encounter, seeing how Erling and his men were delivered into their hands, if only he had proceeded with more sense. Thereafter, people called him Óláf Ill-Luck" ("Þat var kallat, at þeir Óláfr hefði ina mestu óhamingju borit til fundarins [*lit.:* had brought the worst ill-luck to the encounter], svá sem þeir Erlingr váru fram seldir, ef þeir Óláfr hefði meirum ráðum fram farit. Síðan kǫlluðu menn hann Óláf ógæfu" (ME chap. 33). The story, including the explanation of Óláfr's nickname, is also told in *Fagrskinna,* though without the blame directed at his unwise behavior (*Fsk.* chap. 105).

65. OT chap. 16, quoting a scaldic stanza, and 45.

66. In *Yngl.* chap. 43 Snorri tells that the Swedes killed their king and sacrificed him to Óðinn because of bad harvests. He adds, however, that the wiser among them later understood that the reason for the bad harvests was that the country was overpopulated.

67. See Baetke, 1951 and 1964 and particularly Lönnroth, 1986: 73 ff., who attributes to Snorri the idea of a development from Óðinn and his successors who manipulated the people to sacrifice to them, via the founders of the Norwegian kingdom, who believed in one God or their own strength (mátt ok megin), to the true charismatic kings, the Óláfrs, who introduced Christianity.

68. There are references to Christian kings' power to heal apart from the miracle stories. St. Óláfr calls himself a *læknir* (physician) when Þórir Ǫlvisson tries to hide the fact that he wears King Cnut's ring on his arm by saying that he has a boil there (OH chap. 165: 388). This may equally well be a reference to Óláfr's ordinary skill as to supernatural powers. There is a more explicit reference to the supernatural in the story of Magnús góði, who after the battle of Hlýrskógsheiðr appointed twelve men as physicians by touching their hands. These men later became excellent physicians, despite the fact that they had never practiced the art before (MG chap. 28: 50). The story, which is not found in any other extant source, is one of several examples of supernatural events happening around this great battle against the pagans. Neither this story nor the one above on St. Óláfr indicate any general belief in the supernatural powers of the Christian king.

69. I do not deny that Christian ideology in the Middle Ages included the idea of God giving the king supernatural support. Christian ideas, particularly associated with royal unction, may have influenced belief in the healing powers of the French and English kings, though they are hardly its only source (Bloch, 1924: 79 ff.; Schramm, 1960: 151 ff.). Though the idea of the good king promoting fertility does occur, however, it apparently does not belong to the standard picture of the Christian king in the mirrors of princes (Bagge, 1987b: 97 ff. with ref.).

70. Bull, 1912: 208 ff. This idea is derived from Bull's basic assumption, which he almost takes for granted, that the Norwegians and Icelanders were little influenced by Christianity in the Middle Ages (1912: 11 ff.). Bull's conclusions are discussed by Kolsrud, 1967: 398 ff. and Paasche, 1967: 413 ff.; see Bull's comments, 1967: 422 ff. See also Bagge, 1979: 211 ff.

71. Douglas, 1970: viii ff., 99 ff., 140 ff., etc. According to Douglas the human body universally serves as a symbol of society, and taboos, ideas of pollution, etc. thus in one way or another serve to emphasize group solidarity. See also Douglas, 1966: 23 ff.

72. See William of Malmesbury's interpretation of the eclipse at Henry I's last crossing from England to France, prophesying his death three and a half years later (*Historia Novella* chap. 457). See also Brandt's numerous examples of astrological phenomena, which were interpreted, apparently completely at random, to signify human events (1966: 52 ff.).

73. Allegory was mainly derived from ancient philosophy, notably from the school of Plato, whereas typology is a Judeo-Christian phenomenon. In the former the phenomena in the external world are regarded as symbols of the real, immaterial world. In the latter the two phenomena that are linked are of the same kind, usually historical events, as when the crossing of the Red Sea signifies baptism. Typological thought is therefore dynamic and concerned with history, whereas allegorical thought is static. Both, however, differ in the same way

from modern thought in focusing on inner meaning, regardless of time or space, rather than causal connections (Daniélou, 1950; Auerbach, 1967: 65 ff. and 111; Ohly, 1977: 1 ff.; Frye, 1982: 78 ff.). There is some discussion as to what extent typology was applied to profane history in the Middle Ages (Schröder, 1977: 64 ff.; see Ray, 1985: 259 f.; Weber, 1987: 97 ff.), but this is less important in our context, since this kind of thought is not confined to theological and philosophical milieus but is current in popular culture in many societies, including that of the middle ages (Auerbach, 1967: 79 f.; see Leach, 1976: 29 ff.).

74. Wolters, 1959: 52; Southern, 1971: 173 f.; Smalley, 1974: 180 f.; Guenée, 1980: 32 f.; Ray, 1985: 264. More recently, it has been pointed out that although history was removed from the *artes* curriculum, it was still important in the higher faculties of law and above all theology (Schmale, 1985: 76 f.; Goetz, 1985: 165 ff.; Werner, 1986: 39 f.), and further, that the prestige of historiography depended less on its position within the universities than nowadays (Werner, ibid.). Nevertheless, the historical studies at the higher faculties do not seem to have stimulated the numerous chronicles of the thirteenth century. Despite their possible prestige and political importance, these works were hardly superior to those of, e.g., Otto of Freising or William of Malmesbury in literary achievement, interpretation of history, or description of character.

75. See Ehlers, 1981: 433, who refers to Aquinas's statement, echoing that of Aristotle (above), that men's thoughts, actions, etc. are fortuitous and thus cannot be the object of scientific study.

76. See the official attitudes to astrology, which were concerned with protecting the doctrine of free will, though allowing some influence by the stars on human life (Flint, 1982: 211 ff.; Tester, 1987: 147, 176 ff.; North, 1987: 5 ff.).

77. Recently, R. Vaughan has attempted to show that the references to God or morality in medieval historians are merely pious phrases (1986: 1 ff.). Though he can point to numerous examples of medieval historians' interest in the past for its own sake, this does not alter the fact that God and morality were of crucial importance for historians who wanted to give an intellectually satisfying picture of the past and that such considerations accordingly very much influenced their selection and arrangement of material. See, e.g., Ray, 1974: 42 ff.; Weber, 1987: 97 f. with reference and Bagge, 1989*a*.

78. See the detailed description of Robert's motives for accepting Stephen's rule in the first place and then to renouncing his homage and supporting his sister Mathilda against him (*Historia Novella* chaps. 463, 467) and his noble behavior in general (e.g., chaps. 500, 503, 508). See also the long references of meetings and discussions (chaps. 469–477 on the arrest of the bishops, chaps. 491–499 after the capture of the king) in contrast to the short descriptions of the war (e.g., chap. 483: general description of the miseries of war and chap. 489: the battle of Trent, in which the king was taken captive). When telling of Earl Robert's capture, William gives no description of the event itself, but concentrates on his hero's chivalrous behavior: he finds it dishonorable to flee, and his spirit is not broken because of his mischance (chap. 500). In addition, William refers to the supernatural, commenting on the coincidence that both the king and the earl were taken captive on the day of a great feast, which was also a Sunday.

79. See his blame of Duke Henry of Bavaria, who fled without battle and who later tried to capture his enemy Duke Frederick by treason and Otto's discussion whether or not this treason could be defended because of "higher reasons" (*Gesta* book 1, chaps. 19–20), and his description of his hero King Frederick in book II, in which his virtues are emphasized much more than his successes (see above).

80. Evidently, he was a Christian in the conventional sense, like other Icelandic aristocrats. References to Christianity or religion in general are fairly rare in the Icelandic sagas, nor should one exaggerate its importance in the daily life of this class (see Foote, 1984: 31 ff., 50 ff.)—nor for that matter in the life of the contemporary European aristocracy (Duby, 1985: 12 ff.).

Chapter 6: The Context

1. See above, chapter 2. Having murdered Einarr þambarskelfir and his son Eindriði, Haraldr sends Finnr Árnason to negotiate a settlement with their relative and heir Hákon Ívarsson (*HHarð.* chaps. 45–48). Finnr succeeds in this by offering Hákon Ragnhildr, the daughter of the late King Magnús, in marriage. But Ragnhildr refuses to marry a man who is not of princely rank (útiginn maðr) and Haraldr refuses to make Hákon earl. The settlement then breaks down, and Hákon leaves the country to join Haraldr's adversary, King Sveinn of Denmark. The ensuing conflict between Haraldr and Hákon, interrupted by occasional settlements, becomes one of the dominating motives of the saga and serves both to link together the two most important conflicts between Haraldr and the magnates and this latter conflict and the one with Denmark. This, however, may not be Snorri's original achievement, but borrowed from the saga of Hákon Ivarsson, which is preserved in fragments and in a Latin summary (Storm, 1873: 236 ff.; Helgason and Benediktsson, 1952: 1 ff. [the fragments], 38 ff. [the Lat. summary]). See also Storm, 1873: 182 f. and Aðalbjarnarson, 1937: 153. The infelicities in this story—from a political point of view—may also possibly be a result of Snorri borrowing from the Hákon Ivarsson saga: Haraldr's refusal to make Hákon earl seems difficult to understand, given his desperate situation. A possible explanation is his fear of the consequences of including Hákon in the royal house. But then it becomes difficult to understand why he allows Hákon to marry Ragnhildr when he returns from Denmark, having been expelled by Sveinn, and accordingly not in a position to demand great concessions (*HHarð.* chap. 50).

2. It is possible that the author of *Fagrskinna* and Snorri did not know the story, as it belongs to the number of episodes that are probably interpolated in *Morkinskinna* from *Ágrip* (Nordal, 1914: 39 f.; Jónsson, *Msk.*: xxxv; Aðalbjarnarson, 1937: 137 ff.). In discussing Snorri's criteria for selecting his material, however, Nordal regards it as a deliberate omission (1973: 209). This receives some support from the text of *Heimskringla:* "A great many things happened which led to disagreement between the brothers, but I shall mention only this one thing which, it seems to me, led to the most important consequences" ("Nú gerðisk mart þess í með þeim broeðrum, er til sundrþykkis var, en ek mun þó

hins eins geta, er mér þykkir mestum tíðendum sætt hafa") (*Ingi* chap. 22; see a similar statement in *Fsk.*: 351).

3. See, for the following, Lunden, 1977: 32 ff. and Bagge, 1986: 156 ff.

4. Formally, the Icelandic chieftains based their power on holding office as *goðar*, i.e., as local leaders, above all in legal matters. The concentration of political power in the thirteenth century took the form of increasing concentration of *goðorð* (offices as *goði*) in the hands of a few chieftains, such as Snorri. A *goðorð* was not a territorial unit, however, but implied leadership over a certain number of *þingmenn*, who were free to defect to another *goði* if not satisfied with the one they had (Jóhannesson, 1969: 46 ff.; Sigurðsson, 1987: 24 ff., 47 ff.). For the economic foundation of the power of the Icelandic chieftains, see Byock, 1988: 77 ff., 103 ff., who lays particular emphasis on the incomes from judicial conflicts and advocacy. However, with the increasing concentration of power more clearly defined territorial units (ríki) did emerge (Sigurdsson, 1987: 70 ff.).

5. It would of course have been easier if we could be sure that these stories were derived from the almost contemporary *Hryggjarstykki*. There are fairly good arguments for thinking that this saga ended in 1139, however, so there is no evidence that they were written down before the earliest extant texts. The story of Geirsteinn, which Snorri omits, is first found in *Ágrip*, probably written about 1190, thirty-five to forty years after the event (*Ágr.* chap. 60). It is precise regarding time and places and has generally an authentic ring. This also applies to the stories dealing with the outbreak of the civil war. These are first found in *Morkinskinna* (c. 1220) but may well have been derived from *Ágrip*, which is probably incompletely preserved (Ellehøj, 1965: 197).

6. See chaps. 105 and 108, where he tells of one of the traitors to the count who is acquitted in an ordeal. Galbert's explanation is that he must have repented, so that God has given him another chance. When he is killed in battle shortly afterward, Galbert's explanation is that he has not proved himself worthy of God's grace and is punished for his original offense. In chaps. 119–121 Galbert tells how God made an end to the civil war by letting one of the pretenders die, but is worried because it immediately seems that this was the one who was most worthy.

7. See above. By contrast, Saxo Grammaticus's *Gesta Danorum*, which also deals with Nordic history, is closer to European historiography of the twelfth-century Renaissance; see most recently Skovgaard-Petersen, 1987.

Bibliography

Abélard, Pierre. *Historia calamitatum.* Ed. J. T. Muckle. *Mediaeval Studies* 7, 1950: 163–213.

Adam of Bremen. *Gesta Hammaburgensis ecclesiæ pontificum.* Ed. Bernhard Schmeidler (Monumenta Germaniae historica. Scriptores rerum Germanicarum in usum scholarum). Hannover, 1917.

Aðalbjarnarson, Bjarni *Om de norske kongers sagaer* (Skrifter utgitt av Det norske vitenskapsakademi i Oslo, II. Historisk-filosofisk klasse no. 4, 1936). Oslo, 1937.

Aðalbjarnarson, Bjarni, ed. *Heimskringla* (with notes, intro., etc., Íslenzk fornrit vols. 26–28). Reykjavík, 1941–1951.

Ágrip. Ed. and trans. Gustav Indrebø (Norrøne bokverk 36). Oslo, 1936.

Amory, Frederic. "Saga Style in Some Kings' Sagas," *Acta Philologica Scandinavica* 32, 1979: 67–86.

Andersen, Per Sveaas. *Samlingen av Norge og kristningen av landet 800–1130* (Handbok i Norges historie vol. 2). Oslo: Universitetsforlaget, 1977.

Andersson, Theodore. *The Icelandic Family Saga.* Cambridge, Mass.: Harvard University Press, 1967.

Andersson, Theodore. "The Displacement of the Heroic Ideal in the Family Sagas," *Speculum* 45, 1970: 575–593.

Andersson, Theodore. "The Conversion of Norway According to Oddr Snorrason and Snorri Sturluson," *Medieval Scandinavia* 10, 1977: 83–95.

Andersson, Theodore. "Kings' Sagas." In *Old Norse—Icelandic Literature: A Critical Guide,* ed. C. Clover and J. Lindow. Ithaca: Cornell University Press, 1985: 197–238.

Andersson, Theodore. "Lore and Literature in a Scandinavian Conversion Episode." In *Idee, Gestalt, Geschichte. Festschrift Klaus von See,* ed. Gerd W. Weber. Odense: Odense University Press, 1988: 261–284.

Aquinas Thomas. "De regimine principum ad regem Cypri." In *Opuscula philosophica*, ed. R. M. Spiazzi. Rome 1954: 257–358.

Archambault, Paul. *Seven French Historians*. Syracuse: Syracuse University Press, 1974.

Ari Þorgilsson fróði. "Íslendingabók," ed. J. Benediktsson (*Íslenzk fornrit* vol. I.1: 1–28). Reykjavík: Hið íslenzka fornritafélag, 1958.

Ariès, Philippe. *L'enfant et la vie familiale sous l'Ancien régime*. Paris: Seuil, 1973 (orig. 1960).

Aristotle. *Poetics,* ed. and trans. W. H. Fyfe (*The Loeb Classical Library* 199: 1–118). London: Heinemann, 1953.

Armstrong, A. H. *The Greek Philosophical Background of the Psychology of St. Thomas* (The Aquinas Papers 19). London: Blackfriars, 1952.

Arnórsdóttir, Agnes S. *Kvinner og "krigsmenn." Om kjønnenes stilling i det islandske samfunnet på 1100- og 1200-tallet*. Master's thesis, Bergen, 1990.

Auerbach, Erich. *Literatursprache und Publikum in der lateinische Spätantike und Mittelalter*. Bern: Francke, 1958.

Auerbach, Erich. "Figura," *Gesammelte Aufsätze zur romanischen Philologie*. Bern: Francke, 1967a: 55–92.

Auerbach, Erich. "Typological Symbolism in Medieval Literature," *Gesammelte Aufsätze zur romanischen Philologie*. Bern, Francke, 1967b: 109–115.

Baetke, Walter. "Christliches Lehngut in der Sagareligion," *Berichte über die Verhandlungen der sächsischen Akademie der Wissenschaften zu Leipzig*. *Phil-hist. Kl.* 98.6. Berlin: Akademie-Verlag, 1951: 7–55.

Baetke, Walter. "Yngvi und die Ynglingar. Eine Quellenkritische Untersuchung über das nordische 'Sakralkönigtum'," *Sitzungsberichte der sächsischen Akademie der Wissenschaften zu Leipzig*. *Phil-hist. Kl.* 109.3. Berlin: Akademie-Verlag, 1964.

Baetke, Walter. "Zur Frage des altnordischen Sakralkönigtums," *Kleine Schriften. Geschichte, Recht und Religion in germanischem Schrifttum*. Weimar: Böhlau, 1973: 143–194.

Bagge, Sverre. "Samkongedømme og enekongedømme," HT 1975: 239–274.

Bagge, Sverre. "Kirken og folket," *Norges kulturhistorie*, vol. 2. Oslo: Aschehoug, 1979: 211–248.

Bagge, Sverre. "Nordic Students at Foreign Universities Until 1660," *Scandinavian Journal of History* 9, 1984: 1–29.

Bagge, Sverre. "Borgerkrig og statsutvikling i Norge i middelalderen," HT 1986: 145–197.

Bagge, Sverre. "The Formation of the State and Concepts of Society in 13th Century Norway," *Continuity and Change*, Proceedings of the Tenth International Symposium Organized by the Centre for the Study of Vernacular Literature in the Middle Ages (Odense 1985). Odense: Odense University Press, 1987a.

Bagge, Sverre. *The Political Thought of The King's Mirror* (Medieval Scandinavia Supplements 3). Odense: Odense University Press, 1987b.

Bagge, Sverre. "Theodoricus Monachus—Clerical Historiography in Twelfth Century Norway," *Scandinavian Journal of History* 14, 1989a: 113–133.

Bagge, Sverre. "State Building in Medieval Norway," *Forum for utviklingsstudier* 1989b: 129–147.

Bagge, Sverre. "Det politiske menneske og det førstatlige samfunn," HT 1989c: 227–247.

Bagge, Sverre. "Snorri Sturluson und die europäische Geschichtsschreibung," *Skandinavistik* 20, 1990: 1–19.

Bagge, Sverre. "Science and Political Thought in The King's Mirror," unpublished article.

Bagge, Sverre. "Propaganda, Ideology and Political Power in Old Norse and European Historiography: A Comparative View," *Conference, Medieval Historiography,* Paris, 1989 (to be published).

Bailey, F. G. *Stratagems and Spoils.* Oxford: Basil Blackwell, 1980.

Bandle, Oscar. "Isländersaga und Heldendichtung," *Afmælisrit Jóns Helgasonar.* Reykjavík: Heimskringla, 1969: 1–25.

Barth, Fredrik. *Features of Person and Society in Swat.* London: Routledge & Kegan Paul, 1981.

Beeler, John. *Warfare in Feudal Europe 700–1200.* Ithaca, N.Y.: Cornell University Press, 1971.

Beer, Jeanette. *Villehardouin. Epic Historian.* Geneva: Droz, 1968.

Benedict, Ruth F. *The Chrysanthemum and the Sword.* Boston: Houghton Mifflin, 1946.

Benediktsson, Jakob. "Hvar var Snorri nefndur höfundur Heimskringlu?," *Skírnir* 129, 1955: 118–127.

Benediktsson, Jakob. "Formáli." In Ari Þorgilsson fróði, *Íslendingabók,* ed. J. Benediktsson (Íslenzk fornrit vol. 1.1): v–xlix. Reykjavík: Hið íslenzka fornritafélag, 1968.

Benton, John E. "Consciousness of Self and Perceptions of Individuality." In *Renaissance and Renewal in the Twelfth Century,* ed. Robert L. Benson and Giles Constable. Oxford: Clerendon, 1982: 263–295.

Bernheim, Ernst. *Mittelalterliche Zeitanschauungen in ihrem Einfluss auf Politik und Geschichtsschreibung.* Aalen: Scientia, 1964 (orig. 1918).

Berntsen, Toralf. *Fra sagn til saga.* Oslo, 1923.

Beumann, Helmut. "Widukind von Korvei als Geschichtsscreiber und seine politische Gedankenwelt," *Geschichtsdenken und Geschichtsbild im Mittelalter,* ed. W. Lammers. Darmstadt: Wissenschaftliche Buchgesellschaft, 1965: 135–164.

Beumann, Helmut. *Ideengeschichtliche Studien zu Einhard und anderen Geschichtsschreibern des früheren Mittelalters.* Darmstadt: Wissenschaftliche Buchgesellschaft, 1969.

Beyschlag, Siegfried. "Snorris Bild des 12. Jahrhunderts in Norwegen," *Festschrift W. Baetke.* Weimar: Böhlau, 1966: 59–67.

Bjørgo, Narve. "Samkongedøme kontra einekongedøme." HT 49, 1970: 1–33.

Bloch, Marc. *Les rois thaumaturges.* Strasbourg, 1924.

Bloch, Marc. *Feudal Society* vols. 1–2. London: Routledge & Kegan Paul, 1967.

Blom, Grethe Authén. "St. Olavs lov." In *Olav. Konge og helgen—myte og symbol,* ed. J. Bruce. Oslo: St. Olavs forlag, 1981: 61–84.

Blöndal, Lárus H. *Um uppruna Sverrissögu.* Reykjavík: Stofnun Árna Magnússonar, 1982.

Bøe, Arne. "Jarl," KLNM 7, 1962: 559–564.

Bøe, Arne. "Lendmann," KLNM 10, 1965: 498–505.

Børtnes, Jostein. *Visions of Glory. Studies in Early Russian Hagiography.* Oslo: Solum, 1988.

Bosl, Karl. "Leitbilder und Wertforstellungen des Adels." In *The Epic in Medieval Society,* ed. H. Scholler. Tübingen: Niemeyer, 1977: 18–36.

Bourdieu, Pierre. *Outline of a Theory of Practice.* Cambridge: Cambridge University Press, 1977.

Brandt, William J. *The Shape of Medieval History.* New Haven: Yale University Press, 1966.

Brekke, Egil Nygaard. *Sverresagaens opphav. Tiden og forfatteren* (Skrifter utgitt av Det norske vitenskapsakademi i Oslo, II. Historisk-filosofisk klasse 1958 no. 1). Oslo, 1958.

Brooke, Rosalind. "The Lives of St. Francis of Assisi," *Latin Biography,* ed. T. Dorey. New York: Basic Books, 1967: 177–198.

Brunner, Otto. *Land und Herrschaft.* Vienna: Rohrer, 1959.

Brynildsen, R. K. *Om tidsregningen i Olav den helliges historie.* Oslo, 1916.

Bull, Edvard. *Folk og kirke i middelalderen.* Oslo, 1912.

Bull, Edvard. "Borgerkrigene i Norge og Haakon Haakonssons kongstanke," HT 5 series, vol. 4, 1917–1920: 177–194.

Bull, Edvard. "Kristendom og kvad," *Norske historikere i utvalg,* vol. 1, ed. A. Holmsen and J. Simensen. Oslo: Universitetsforlaget, 1967: 422–426 (orig. in *Norsk teologisk tidsskrift,* 1915).

Bynum, Caroline Walker. "Did the Twelfth Century Discover the Individual?," *Journal of Ecclesiastical History* 31.1, 1980: 1–17.

Byock, Jesse. *Feud in the Icelandic Saga.* Berkeley, Los Angeles, London: University of California Press, 1982.

Byock, Jesse. "Dispute Resolution in the Sagas," *Gripla* 6, 1984: 86–100.

Byock, Jesse. "The Age of the Sturlungs," *Continuity and Change,* Proceedings of the Tenth International Symposium Organized by the Centre for the Study of Vernacular Literature in the Middle Ages (Odense 1985). Odense: Odense University Press, 1987: 27–42.

Byock, Jesse. *Medieval Iceland: History and Sagas.* Berkeley, Los Angeles, London: University of California Press, 1988.

Chenu, Marie-Dominic. "Conscience de l'histoire et theologie au XIIe siècle," *Archives d'histoire doctrinale et literaire du Moyen Age* 21, 1954: 107–133.

Chrétien de Troyes. "Erec et Enide." In Chrétien de Troyes, *Sämmtliche Werke,* vol. 3, ed. Wendelin Foerster. Amsterdam: Rodopi, 1965 (orig. 1890).

Christophersen, Heidi. *Gunnhild kongemor—Eirikssønnenes rådgiver: En studie av Gunnhildskikkelsen i Heimskringla med utgangspunkt i rådsmøtet mellom kongemoren og hennes sønner.* Master's thesis, University of Oslo, 1987.

Ciklamini, Marlene. *Snorri Sturluson.* Boston: Twayne, 1978.

Clark, Herbert, and Eve Clark. *Psychology and Language.* New York: Harcourt, Brace, Jovanovich, 1977.

Clover, Carol. "Scene in Saga Composition," *Arkiv for nordisk filologi* 89, 1974: 57–83.

Clover, Carol. *The Medieval Saga.* Ithaca, N.Y.: Cornell University Press, 1982.

Clover, Carol. "Icelandic Family Sagas." In *Old Norse-Icelandic Literature: A*

Critical Guide, ed. C. Clover and J. Lindow. Ithaca, N.Y.: Cornell University Press, 1985: 239–317.

Clover, Carol. "Hildigunnr's Lament," *Structure and Meaning in Old Norse Literature,* ed. J. Lindow, L. Lönnroth and G. W. Weber. Odense: Odense University Press, 1986: 141–183.

Clover, Carol. "The Politics of Scarcity: Notes on the Sex Ratio in Early Scandinavia," *Scandinavian Studies* 60, 1988: 147–188.

Clunies Ross, Margaret. *Skáldskaparmál.* Odense: Odense University Press, 1987.

Cobban, Alan B. *The Medieval Universities.* London: Methuen, 1975.

Collingwood, R. G. *The Idea of History.* Oxford: Oxford University Press, 1966.

Contamine, Philippe. "Froissart: Art militaire, pratique et conception de la guerre." In *Froissart: Historian,* ed. J. J. N. Palmer. Woodbridge: Boydell Press, 1981: 132–144.

Dahl, Ottar. *Norsk historieforskning i det 19. og 20. århundre.* Oslo: Universitetsforlaget, 1959.

Daniélou, Jean. *Sacramentum futuri. Études sur les origines de la typologie biblique.* Paris: Beauchesne, 1950.

de Boor, Helmut. "Hövescheit." In *Ritterliches Tugendsystem,* ed. G. Eifler. Darmstadt: Wissenschaftliche Buchgesellschaft, 1970: 377–400.

Doi, Takeo. *The Anatomy of Dependence.* Tokyo, 1976.

Douglas Mary. *Purity and Danger.* London: Routledge & Kegan Paul, 1966.

Douglas, Mary. *Natural Symbols.* New York: Pantheon Books, 1970.

Dronke, Ursula. "Classical Influence on Early Norse Literature." In *Classical Influences on European Culture A.D 500–1500,* ed. R. R. Bolgar (Proceedings of an International Conference held at King's College, Cambridge, April 1969). Cambridge: Cambridge University Press, 1971: 143–150.

Dronke, Ursula and Peter Dronke. "The Prologue of the Prose Edda," *Sjötíu ritgerðir helgaðar Jakobi Benediktssyni,* vol. 1. Reykjavík: Stofnun Árna Magnússonar, 1977: 153–176.

Duby, Georges. *Le dimanche de Bouvines.* Paris: Gallimard, 1973.

Duby, Georges. *The Chivalrous Society.* London: Edward Arnold, 1977.

Duby, Georges. *The Knight, the Lady and the Priest.* Harmondsworth: Penguin Books, 1985.

Duby, Georges. *William Marshall: The Flower of Chivalry.* London: Faber and Faber, 1986.

Earle, J., and Ch. Plummer. *Two of the Saxon Chronicles: Parallel I–II.* Oxford, 1892–1899.

Edda Snorra Sturlusonar, see Snorri Sturluson.

Egils saga Skalla-Grímssonar. Ed. S. Nordal (Íslenzk fornrit, vols. 1–2). Reykjavík: Hið íslenzka fornritafélag, 1933.

Ehlers, Joachim. *Hugo von St. Victor* (Frankfurter historische Abhandlungen, vol. 7). Wiesbaden: F. Steiner, 1973.

Ehlers, Joachim. "Historiographische Literatur." In *Neues Handbuch der Literaturwissenschaft,* vol. 7, ed. H. Krauss. Wiesbaden: Athenaion, 1981: 425–460.

Ehrismann, Gustav, "Die Grundlagen des ritterlichen Tugendsystems." In *Rit-*

terliches Tugendsystem, ed. G. Eifler. Darmstadt: Wissenschaftliche Buchgesellschaft, 1970 (orig. 1919): 1–84.

Einarsdóttir, Ólafia. *Studier i kronologisk metode i tidlig islandsk historieskrivning* (Bibliotheca historica Lundensis, vol. 13). Stockholm: Natur och kultur, 1964.

Einarsson, Bjarni. "Formáli," *Ágrip—Fagrskinna*, ed. Bjarni Einarsson (Íslenzk fornrit, vol. 29). Reykjavík: Hið íslenzka fornritafélag, 1984: v–cxxxi.

Einhard. *Vita Karoli Magni*, ed. O. Holder-Egger (Monumenta Germaniae Historica. Scriptores rerum Germanicarum). Hannover, 1911.

Elias, Norbert. *Die höfische Gesellschaft*. Darmstadt: Luchterhand, 1975.

Elias, Norbert. *Über den Prozess der Zivilisation*, vols. 1–2. Frankfurt: Suhrkamp, 1977 (orig. 1939).

Ellehøj, Svend. *Den ældste norrøne historieskrivning*. Copenhagen: Munksgaard, 1965.

Fagrskinna (Noregs kononga tal). Ed. Finnur Jónsson. Copenhagen, 1902.

Fidjestøl, Bjarne. *Det norrøne fyrstediktet*. Bergen: Alvheim og Eide, 1982.

Fidjestøl, Bjarne. "Legenda om Tore Hund," *Festskrift til Alfred Jakobsen*. Trondheim: Tapir, 1987: 38–51.

Finley, Moses I. *The World of Odysseus*. London: Penguin Books, 1962.

Flint, Valerie. "World History in the Early Twelfth Century; the 'Imago Mundi'." In *The Writing of History in the Middle Ages: Essays Presented to Richard William Southern*, ed. R. H. C. Davis and J. M. Wallace-Hadrill. Oxford: Clarendon, 1982: 211–238.

Foote, Peter. "Secular Attitudes in Early Iceland." In *Aurvandilstá: Norse Studies*. Odense: Odense University Press, 1984: 31–46.

Foote, Peter. "The Audience and the Vogue of the Sagas of Icelanders—Some Talking Points." In *Aurvandilstá: Norse Studies*. Odense: Odense University Press, 1984: 47–55.

Fourquin, Guy. *The Anatomy of Popular Rebellion in the Middle Ages*. Amsterdam: North-Holland, 1978.

Frank, Roberta. "Marriage in Twelfth- and Thirteenth-Century Iceland," *Viator* 4, 1973: 473–484.

Freed, John B. "Reflections on the German Nobility," *The American Historical Review* 91.3, 1986: 553–575.

Fritzner, Johan. *Ordbog over Det gamle norske Sprog*, vols. 1–3. Oslo: Juul Møller, 1954 (orig. 1883–1896).

Fritzner, Johan. *Ordbog over Det gamle norske Sprog*, vol. 4: *Rettelser og tillegg*, ed. F. Hødnebø. Oslo: Universitetsforlaget, 1972.

Frye, Northrop. *The Great Code*. New York: Harcourt, Brace, Jovanovich, 1982.

Frykman, Jonas, and Orvar Löfgren. *Den kultiverade människan*. Lund: Liber, 1979.

Fuglestad, Finn. "Earth-Priests, 'Priest-Chiefs' and Sacred Kings in Ancient Norway, Iceland and West Africa," *Scandinavian Journal of History* 4, 1979: 47–74.

Funkenstein, Amos. *Heilsplan und natürliche Entwicklung*. Munich: Nymphenburger Verlagshandlung, 1965.

Funkenstein, Amos. "Periodization and Self-Understanding in the Middle Ages and Early Modern Times," *Medievalia et Humanistica*. *New Series* 5, 1974: 3–24.

Gagnér, Sten. *Studien zur Ideengeschichte der Gesetzgebung*, Uppsala: Almquist och Wiksell, 1960.

Galbert de Bruges. *Histoire du meurtre de Charles le Bon, comte de Flandre* (*1127–28*), ed. H. Pirenne. Paris, 1891.

Gamal norsk homiliebok. Ed. G. Indrebø. Oslo, 1931.

Gathorne-Hardy, G. M. *A Royal Impostor.* Oslo: Aschehoug, 1956.

Gaunt, David. *Familjeliv i Norden.* Malmö: Gidlund, 1983.

Gehl, Walter. *Ruhm und Ehre bei den Nordgermanen.* Berlin: Junker und Dünnhaupt, 1937.

"Gesta Cnutonis regis." In *Scriptores minores historiae Daniae*, vol. 2, ed. M. Cl. Gertz. Copenhagen, 1922, repr. 1970: 375–426.

Gillingham, John. "War and Chivalry in the *History of William the Marshall*," *Thirteenth Century England*, vol. 2, Proceedings of the Newcastle upon Tyne Conference 1987. Woodbridge: Boydell Press, 1988.

Gísla saga Súrssonar. Ed. Finnur Jónsson. Copenhagen, 1929.

Glendinning, Robert James. *Träume und Vorbedeutung in der Islendinga Saga Sturla Thordarsons.* Bern, 1974.

Gluckman, Max. *Politics, Law and Ritual in Tribal Society.* Oxford: Blackwell, 1965.

Goetz, Hans-Werner. *Das Geschichtsbild Ottos von Freising.* Cologne: Böhlau, 1984.

Goetz, Hans-Werner. "Die 'Geschichte' im Wissenschaftssystem des Mittelalters." In Franz-Josef Schmale, *Funktion und Formen mittelalterlicher Geschichtsschreibung.* Darmstadt: Wissenschaftliche Buchgesellschaft, 1985: 165–213.

Gransden, Antonia. *Historical Writing in England c. 550 to c. 1307.* London: Routledge & Kegan Paul, 1974.

Green, Louis. *Chronicle into History.* Cambridge: Cambridge University Press, 1972.

Grønbech, Vilhelm. *Vor Folkeæt i Oldtiden*, vols. 1–2. Copenhagen: Gyldendal, 1955.

Grøtvedt, Per N. "Sårbøter og drapsbøter i brev fra norsk senmiddelalder," HT 44, 1965: 105–140.

Guðmundsson, Finnbogi, ed. *Orkneyinga Saga* (Íslenzk fornrit vol. 34). Reykjavík: Hið íslenzka fornritafélag, 1965.

Guðmundsson, Finnbogi. "Orkneyinga saga," KLNM 12, 1967: 699–702.

Guðnason, Bjarni. *Um Skjöldungasögu.* Reykjavík: Bókaútgafa Menningarsjóðs, 1963.

Guðnason, Bjarni. *Fyrsta sagan* (Studia Islandica 37). Reykjavík: Bókaútgafa Menningarsjóðs, 1978.

Guenée, Bernard. *Histoire et culture historique dans l'Occident médiéval.* Paris: Aubier, 1980.

Gundersen, Dag. "Gisslan" (Norway), KLNM 5, 1969: 331–333.

Gunnes, Erik. "Rex iustus et iniustus," KLNM 14, 1969: 154–156.

316   Bibliography

Gunnes, Erik. *Kongens ære*. Oslo: Gyldendal, 1971.
Gunnes, Erik. "Om hvordan Passio Olavi ble til," *Maal og minne*. 1973: 1–11.
Gurevich, Aron Ya. "Space and Time in the *Weltmodell* of the Scandinavian Peoples," *Medieval Scandinavia* 2, 1969: 42–53.
Gurevich, Aron Ya. "Saga and History. The 'Historical Conception' of Snorri Sturluson," *Medieval Scandinavia* 4, 1971: 42–53.
Gurevich, Aron Ya. *Les catégories de la culture médiévale*. Paris: Gallimard, 1983.
Gusdorf, Georges. "Conditions and Limits of Autobiography." In *Autobiography: Essays Theoretical and Critical*, ed. J. Olney. Princeton: Princeton University Press, 1980: 28–48.
Hallberg, Peter. "Medeltidslatin och sagaprosa," *Arkiv for nordisk filologi* 81, 1966: 258–276.
Hallberg, Peter. "The Concept of *gipta—gæfa—hamingja* in Old Norse Literature," *First International Saga Conference, Edinburg 1971*. London, 1973.
Hallberg, Peter. "The Syncretic Saga Mind: A Discussion of a New Approach to the Icelandic Sagas," *Medieval Scandinavia* 7, 1974: 102–117.
Hallberg, Peter. " 'Medieval Man'—and Saga Studies," *Medieval Scandinavia* 9, 1976: 164–166.
Hallberg, Peter. "Direct Speech and Dialogue in Three Versions of Ólǎfs Saga Helga," *Arkiv for nordisk filologi* 93, 1978: 116–137.
Halldórsson, Ólafur. "Sagnarítun Snorra Sturlusonar." In *Snorri: Átta alda minning*. Reykjavík: Sögufélag, 1979.
Halvorsen, Eyvind Fjeld. "Lærd og folkelig stil (Norway, Iceland)," KLNM 11, 1966: 119–123.
Hamre, Lars. "Gåve," KLNM 5, 1960: 653–661.
Hamre, Lars. "Hird," KLNM 6, 1961: 568–577.
Hanning, Robert W. *The Vision of History in Early Britain*. New York: Columbia University Press, 1966.
Hanning, Robert W. *The Individual in Twelfth-Century Romance*. New Haven: Yale University Press, 1977.
Hanssen, Jens S. Th. "Theodoricus Monachus," *Symbolae Osloenses* 27, 1949: 70–127.
Harris, Joseph. "Genre and Narrative Structure in Some *Íslendinga þættir*," *Scandinavian Studies* 44, 1972: 1–27.
Harris, Joseph. "Saga as Historical Novel," *Structure and Meaning in Old Norse Literature*, ed. J. Lindow, L. Lönnroth, and G. W. Weber. Odense: Odense University Press, 1986: 187–219.
Hastrup, Kirsten. *Culture and History in Medieval Iceland*. Oxford: Oxford University Press, 1985.
Hávamál. Ed. Finnur Jónsson. Copenhagen, 1924.
Hay, Denys. *Annalists and Historians*. London: Methuen, 1977.
Heers, Jacques. *Family Clans in the Middle Ages*. Amsterdam: North-Holland, 1977*a*.
Heers, Jacques. *Parties and Political Life in the Medieval West*. Amsterdam: North-Holland, 1977*b*.
Heinrichs, Anne. "*Annat er várt eðli:* The type of the prepatriarchal woman in

Old Norse literature," *Structure and Meaning in Old Norse Literature,* ed. J. Lindow, L. Lönnroth, and G. W. Weber. Odense: Odense University Press, 1986: 110–140.

Helgason, Jón, and Jakob Benediktsson, ed. *Hákonar saga Ívarssonar,* with intro. etc. Copenhagen, 1952.

Helle, Knut. "Tendenser i nyere norsk høymiddelalderforskning," HT 40, 1960–1961: 337–370.

Helle, Knut. [Rev. of] Olafia Einarsdóttir, *Studier i kronologisk metode i tidlig islandsk historieskrivning,* and Svend Ellehøj, *Den ældste norrøne historieskrivning,* HT 46, 1967: 68–78.

Helle, Knut. *Norge blir en stat.* Oslo: Universitetsforlaget, 1974.

Helle, Knut. "Norway in the High Middle Ages," *Scandinavian Journal of History* 6, 1981: 161–189.

Heller, Rolf. *Die literarische Darstellung der Frau in den Isländersagas.* Halle: Niemeyer, 1958.

Hertzberg, Ebbe. "Lén og veizla i Norges sagatid." In *Germanistische Abhandlungen zum LXX. Geburtstag Konrad von Maurers.* Göttingen, 1893.

Heusler, Andreas. *Das Strafrecht der Isländersagas.* Leipzig, 1911.

Heusler, Andreas. *Zum isländischen Fehdewesen in der Sturlungenzeit* (Abhandlungen der königlichen preussischen Akademie der Wissenschaften). Berlin, 1912.

Heusler, Andreas. *Die altgermanische Dichtung* (Handbuch der Literaturwissenschaft, ed. O. Walzel). Darmstadt: Hermann Gentner, 1957.

"Historia Norvegiae." In *Monumenta Historica Norvegiæ,* Ed. Gustav Storm. Oslo, 1880: 69–124.

Historia Novella, see William of Malmesbury.

Hollingsworth, T. H. "A Demographic Study of the British Ducal Families." In *Population in History,* ed. D. V. Glass and D. E. C. Eversley. London: Edward Arnold, 1965: 354–378.

Holm-Olsen, Ludvig. *Studier i Sverres saga* (Skrifter utgitt av Det norske vitenskapsakademi i Oslo, II. Historisk-filosofisk klasse, 1952, no. 3). Oslo, 1953.

Holm-Olsen, Ludvig. "Konungs skuggsjá og norrøn poesi," *Studier over Konungs skuggsiá,* ed. M. Tveitane. Oslo: Universitetsforlaget, 1970: 104–109.

Holm-Olsen, Ludvig. "Sverris saga," KLNM 17, 1972: 551–558.

Holm-Olsen, Ludvig. "Middelalderens litteratur i Norge," *Norges litteraturhistorie,* vol. 1, ed. E. Beyer. Oslo: Cappelen, 1974: 19–342.

Holm-Olsen, Ludvig. "Til diskusjonen om Sverres sagas tilblivelse." In *Opuscula septentrionalia. Festskrift til Ole Widding.* Copenhagen: Reitzel, 1977: 55–67.

Holm-Olsen, Ludvig. "Forfatterinnslag i Odd Munks saga om Olav Tryggvason." In *Festskrift til Alfred Jakobsen.* Trondheim: Tapir, 1987: 79–90.

Holmsen, Andreas. *Norges historie. Fra de eldste tider til 1660.* Oslo: Universitetsforlaget, 1977 (orig. 1939).

Holtsmark, Anne. *En tale mot biskopene* [*A Speech Against the Bishops*]. *En sproglig-historisk undersøkelse.* [Text and intro.] (Skrifter utgitt av Det norske vitenskapsakademi i Oslo, II. Historisk-filosofisk klasse, 1930 no. 9). Oslo, 1931.

Hovstad, Johan. *Heim, hov og kyrkje.* Oslo: Det norske samlaget, 1948.
Huizinga, Johan. *The Waning of the Middle Ages.* London: Penguin, 1955 (orig. 1924).
Iggers, Georg G. *New Directions in European Historiography.* Middleton, Conn.: Wesleyan University Press, 1975.
Indrebø, Gustav. *Fagrskinna.* Oslo, 1917.
Indrebø, Gustav. "Den gamle norske fylkesskipnaden," *Norsk middelalder,* ed. A. Holmsen. Oslo: Universitetsforlaget, 1966: 9–32.
Islandske Annaler indtil 1578. Ed. G. Storm. Oslo 1888 (repr. 1977).
Itkonen, Esa. "Language, Thought and Culture in 'Post-Modernism': Some Implications for General Historiography," *Historisk Kundskab og fremstilling. Den 20. nordiske fagkonferanse i historisk Metodelære (Studier i historisk metode* vol. 20). Århus: Aarhus Universitetsforlag, 1989: 109–118.
Jaeger, C. Stephen. *The Origins of Courtliness.* Philadelphia: University of Philadelphia Press, 1985.
Jakobsen, Alfred. "Om Fagrskinna-forfatteren," *Arkiv for nordisk filologi* 85, 1970: 88–124.
Jochens, Jenny M. "En Islande médiévale: A la recherche de la famille nucléaire," *Annales ESC,* 1985: 95–112.
Jochens, Jenny M. "The Medieval Icelandic Heroine: Fact or Fiction?," *Viator* 17, 1986: 35–50.
Jochens, Jenny M. "The Politics of Reproduction: Medieval Norwegian Kingship," *The American Historical Review* 92, 1987: 327–349.
Jochens, Jenny M. "The Female Inciter in the Kings' Sagas," *Arkiv för nordisk filologi* 102, 1987: 100–119.
Jóhannesson, Jón. *Islands historie,* vol. 1. Oslo: Universitetsforlaget, 1969.
Johansen, Anders. *Historisk tid, mytiske landskap.* Unpublished manuscript, Bergen, 1984.
Johansen, Anders. "Tid, tvang, teknologi—teori. Om tid som 'handlingsskjema' og 'realabstraksjon'," *Tidsoppfattelse og historiebevissthed. Oplæg fra den 18. Nordiske fagkonferanse i historisk metodelære i Ølken, 26.–29. August 1983 (Studier i historisk metode* vol. 18). Århus, 1985: 108–150.
Johansen, Anders. "Mytiske landskap," *Profil* 1988: 12–27.
John of Salisbury. *Policraticus,* vols. 1–2, ed. C. C. I. Webb. Oxford, 1909.
Johnsen, Arne Odd. *Om Theodoricus og hans Historia de antiquitate regum Norwagiensium* (Skrifter utgitt av Det norske vitenskapsakademi i Oslo, II. Historisk-filosofisk klasse 1939 no. 3). Oslo, 1939.
Johnsen, Arne Odd. *Fra ættesamfunn til statssamfunn.* Oslo: Aschehoug, 1948.
Johnsen, Arne Odd. "Biskop Bjarnhard og kirkeforholdene i Norge under Harald Hardråde og Olav Kyrre." In *Bjørgvin bispestol. Frå Selja til Bjørgvin,* ed. P. Juvkam. Bergen: Universitetsforlaget, 1968: 11–26.
Johnsen, Oscar Albert. *Olav Haraldssons ungdom indtil slaget ved Nesjar 25. mars 1016* (Skrifter utgitt av Det norske vitenskapsakademi i Oslo, II. Historisk-filosofisk klasse 1916, no. 2). Oslo, 1916*a.*
Johnsen, Oscar Albert. "Friðgerðar-saga. En kildekritisk undersøkelse," *HT* 5 series, vol. 3, 1916*b*: 513–539.
Jónsson. Finnur. *Den oldnorske og oldislandske literaturs historie,* vol. 2. Copenhagen: Gad, 1923.

Kalinke, Marianne E. "*Sigurðar saga jórsalafara:* The Fictionalization of Fact in *Morkinskinna,*" *Scandinavian Studies* 56, 1982: 152–167.

Karlsson, Gunnar. "Stjórnmálamaðurinn Snorri." In *Snorri átta alda minning.* Reykjavík: Sögufélag, 1979: 23–51.

Keen, Maurice. *Chivalry.* New Haven: Yale University Press, 1984.

Kelley, Donald. *Foundations of Modern Historical Scholarship.* New York: Columbia University Press, 1970.

Ker, W. P. "The Early Historians of Norway." In *Collected Essays* vol. 2, ed. C. Wibley. London, 1925: 131–151.

[*The King's Mirror*] *Konungs skuggsiá.* Ed. L. Holm-Olsen. Oslo 1945.

Kirn, Paul. *Das Bild des Menschen in der Geschichtsschreibung von Polybios bis Ranke.* Göttingen: Vandenhoek und Ruprecht, 1955.

Klinkenberg, Hans-Martin. "Die Theorie der Veränderbarkeit des Rechtes im frühen und hohen Mittelalter," *Lex und Sacramentum im Mittelalter, Miscellanea Medievalia* 6, Berlin, 1969: 157–188.

Knirk, James. *Oratory in the Kings' Sagas.* Oslo: Universitetsforlaget, 1981.

Koch, Josef. "Die Grundlagen der Geschichtsphilosophie Ottos von Freising." In *Geschichtsdenken und Geschichtsbild im Mittelalter,* ed. W. Lammers. Darmstadt: Wissenschaftliche Buchgesellschaft, 1965: 321–349.

Koht, Halvdan. "Sagaenes opfatning av vår gamle historie." In *Innhogg og utsyn.* Oslo, 1921: 76–91.

Koht, Halvdan. "Kampen om makten i Noreg i sagatiden." In *Innhogg og utsyn.* Oslo, 1921: 92–123.

Koht, Halvdan. "Norsk historieskriving under kong Sverre, serskilt Sverresoga." In *Innhogg og utsyn.* Oslo, 1921: 156–196.

Koht, Halvdan. "Norsk historie i lys frå ættehistoria," *Norsk slektsshistorisk tidsskrift* 5, 1936: 89–104.

Koht, Halvdan. "Snorre Sturlason," *Norsk biografisk leksikon* 14, Oslo, 1962: 107–120.

Koht, Halvdan. "The Scandinavian Kingdoms until the End of the Thirteenth Century," *The Cambridge Medieval History,* vol. 6. Cambridge: Cambridge University Press, 1964 (orig. 1929).

Kolsrud, Oluf. "Kirke og folk i middelalderen." In *Norske historikere i utvalg,* vol. 1, ed. A. Holmsen and J. Simensen. Oslo: Universitetsforlaget, 1967: 398–412 (orig. in *Norsk teologisk tidsskrift,* 1913).

Koselleck, Reinhart. "Modernity and the Planes of Historicity," *Economy and Society* 10, 1981: 166–183 (also in Koselleck, *Futures Past,* Cambridge, Mass.: MIT Press, 1985: 3–20).

Koselleck, Reinhart. "Chance as a Motivational Trace in Historical Writing." In *Futures Past.* Cambridge, Mass.: MIT Press, 1985: 116–129.

Krag, Claus. "Ármannen," HT 61, 1982: 105–127.

Krag, Claus. "Norge som odel i Harald Hårfagres ætt. Et møte med en gjenganger," HT 1989: 288–302.

Kristjánsson, Jónas. *Um Fóstbrœðrasögu.* Reykjavík: Stofnun Árna Magnússonar, 1972.

Kristjánsson, Jónas. "The Legendary Saga." In *Minnjar og menntir. Afmælisrit helgað Kristjáni Eldjárn.* Reykjavík: Bókaútgafa Menningarsjóðs, 1976: 281–293.

Kristjánsson, Jónas. "Egilssaga og konungasögur." In *Sjötíu ritgerðir helgaðar Jakobi Benediktssyni 20. júli 1977*, vol. 2. Reykjavík: Stofnun Árna Magnússonar, 1977: 449–472.

Kválen, Eivind. *Den eldste norske kongesoga*. Oslo, 1925.

Lammers, Walter, 1961, see Otto of Freising, *Chronica*.

Larson, Lawrence M. (trans. and intro.). *The King's Mirror (Speculum regale— Konungs Skuggsjá)*. New York: The American-Scandinavian Foundation, 1917.

Leach, Edmund. *Culture and Communication*. Cambridge: Cambridge University Press, 1976.

Leff, Gordon. *Paris and Oxford Universities in the 13th and 14th Centuries*. New York: Wiley, 1968.

[*Legendary Saga*] *Óláfs saga hins helga. Efter pergamenthaandskrift i Uppsala Universitetsbibliotek, Delagardieske samling nr. 8 ii.* Ed. O. A. Johnsen. Oslo, 1922.

Le Goff, Jacques. "The Symbolic Ritual of Vasallage." In *Time, Work and Culture in the Middle Ages*. Chicago: The University of Chicago Press, 1980: 237–287.

Lehmann, Paul. "Autobiographies of the Middle Ages," *Transactions of the Royal Historical Society* 5.3, 1953: 41–53.

Leyser, Karl. *Rule and Conflict in an Early Medieval Society*. London: Edward Arnold, 1979.

Lie, Hallvard. *Studier i Heimskringlas stil* (Skrifter utgitt av Det norske vitenskapsakademi i Oslo, II. Historisk-filosofisk klasse 1936 no. 5). Oslo, 1937.

Lie, Hallvard. [Rev. of.] E. N. Brekke, *Sverre-sagaens opphav*, HT 40, 1960–1961: 26–40.

Lie, Hallvard. "Heimskringla," KLNM 6, 1961: 299–302.

Lie, Mikael H. *Lensprincipet i Norden*, Oslo, 1907.

Lönnroth, Erik. "De äkta folkungarnas program," *Från svensk medeltid*. Stockholm: Aldus/Bonnier, 1964 (orig. in: *Kungl. Humanistiska Vetenskaps-Samfundet i Uppsala. Årsbok, 1944*).

Lönnroth, Lars. "Studier i Olaf Tryggvasons saga," *Samlaren* 1963: 54–94.

Lönnroth, Lars. "Kroppen som själens spegel," *Lychnos* 1963–1964: 24–61.

Lönnroth, Lars. "Tesen om de två kulturerna," *Scripta Islandica* 15, 1964: 1–97.

Lönnroth, Lars. "Det litterära porträttet i latinsk historiografi och isländsk sagaskrivning—en komparativ studie," *Acta Philologica Scandinavica* 27, 1965: 68–117.

Lönnroth, Lars. "The Noble Heathen: A Theme in the Sagas," *Scandinavian Studies* 41, 1969: 1–29.

Lönnroth, Lars. "Rhetorical Persuasion in the Sagas," *Scandinavian Studies* 42, 1970: 157–189.

Lönnroth, Lars. "Ideology and Structure in *Heimskringla*," *Parergon* 15, 1976: 16–29.

Lönnroth, Lars. "Dómaldi's death and the Myth of Sacral Kingship." In *Structure and Meaning in Old Norse Literature*, ed. J. Lindow, L. Lönnroth, and G. Weber. Odense: Odense University Press, 1986: 73–93.

Lottin, Odon. *Psychologie et morale aux XIIe et XIIIe siècles* vol. 1. Louvain, 1942.

Louis-Jensen, Jonna. " 'Syvende og ottende brudstykke': Fragmentet AM 325 IV," *Opuscula* 4 (*Bibliotheca Arnamagnæana* 30). Copenhagen, 1970: 31–60.

Louis-Jensen, Jonna. *Kongesagastudier: Kompilationen Hulda—Hrokkinskinna* (Bibliotheca Arnamagnaeana 32). Copenhagen: Munksgaard, 1977.

Luchaire, Achille. *Social France at the Time of Philip Augustus.* New York: Harper and Row, 1967 (orig. 1909).

Lunden, Kåre. *Norge under Sverreætten* (Norges historie 3). Oslo: Cappelen, 1977.

Machiavelli, Nicolò. *The Prince,* ed. and trans. Q. Skinner and R. Price. Cambridge: Cambridge University Press, 1988.

McLaughlin, Mary. "Abélard as Autobiographer: The Motives and Meaning of his 'Story of Calamities'," *Speculum* 42, 1967: 463–488.

McTurk, Rory W. "Sacral Kingship in Ancient Scandinavia: A Review of Some Recent Writings," *Saga-Book of the Viking Society,* 19, 1974–1977: 139–169.

Matthew Paris. *Chronica majora,* ed. H. Luard (Rerum Britannicarum medii ævi scriptores [Rolls Series] 57.1–7). London, 1872–1884, repr. 1964.

Maurer, Konrad. *Über die Ausdrücke altnordische, altnorwegische und isländische Sprache.* Munich, 1867.

Maurer, Konrad. *Die Bekehrung des Norwegischen Stammes,* vols. 1–2. Osnabrück, 1965 (orig. 1855–1856).

Miller, William Ian. "Justifying Skarpheðinn: Of Pretext and Politics in the Icelandic Bloodfeud," *Scandinavian Studies* 55, 1983: 316–344.

Miller, William Ian. "Dreams, Prophecy and Sorcery: Blaming the Secret Offender in Medieval Iceland," *Scandinavian Studies* 58, 1986: 101–123.

Misch, Georg. *Geschichte der Autobiographie,* vols. 3.1–3.2. Frankfurt: Schulte-Bulmke, 1959–1962.

Moberg, Ove. *Olav Haraldsson, Knut den store och Sverige.* Lund, 1941.

Morkinskinna. Ed. Finnur Jónsson. Copenhagen, 1932.

Morris, Colin. "Individualism in Twelfth-Century Religion. Some Further Reflections," *Journal of Ecclesiastical History* 31.2, 1980: 195–206.

Morris, Colin. *The Discovery of the Individual.* Toronto: University of Toronto Press, 1987 (orig. 1972).

Müller, P. E., *Om Kilderne til Snorres Heimskringla og disses Troværdighed.* Copenhagen, 1823.

Munch, Peter Andreas. *Det norske Folks Historie* vols. 1–4. Oslo, 1852–1859.

Nisbet, Robert A. *Social Change and History.* New York: Oxford University Press, 1969.

Nitschke, August. *Naturerkenntnis und politisches Handeln im Mittelalter.* Stuttgart: Klett, 1967.

Nordal, Sigurður. *Om Olaf den helliges saga.* Copenhagen, 1914.

Nordal, Sigurður. "Sagalitteraturen." In *Literaturhistorie. Norge og Island,* (Nordisk Kultur 8b). Oslo, 1953: 180–273.

Nordal, Sigurður. *Snorri Sturluson.* Reykjavík, 1973 (orig. 1920).

Den norsk-islandske Skjaldedigtning. Ed. Finnur Jónsson, A1–B2. Copenhagen, 1908–1914.

North, J. D. "Medieval Concepts of Celestial Influence: A Survey." In *Astrology, Science and Society. Historical Essays,* ed. Patrick Curry. Woodbridge: Boydell Press, 1987.

Oddr Snorrason munkr. *Saga Óláfs Tryggvasonar,* ed. Finnur Jónsson. Copenhagen, 1932.

Odén, Birgitta. *Lauritz Weibull och forskarsamhället* (Bibliotheca historica Lundensis 39). Lund: Gleerup, 1975.

Ohly, Friedrich. *Schriften zur mittelalterlichen Bedeutungsforschung.* Darmstadt: Wissenschaftliche Buchgesellschaft, 1977.

Ólason, Vesteinn. "Norrøn litteratur som historisk kildemateriale." In *Kilderne til den tidlige middelalders historie. Rapporter til den XX nordiske historikerkongres, Reykjavík 1987,* vol. 1 (*Ritsafn Sagnfrædistofnunar* vol. 18). Reykjavík: Sögufélag, 1987: 30–47.

Olney, James. "Autobiography and Cultural Moment: A Thematic, Historical and Bibliographical Introduction." In *Autobiography: Essays Theoretical and Critical,* ed. J. Olney. Princeton: Princeton University Press, 1980: 3–27.

Olsen, Thorkil Damsgaard. "Kongekrøniker og kongesagaer." In *Norrøn Fortællekunst,* ed. H. Bekker-Nielsen, T. Damsgaard Olsen, and O. Widding. Copenhagen: Akademisk Forlag, 1965: 42–71.

Ong, Walter. *Orality and Literacy.* London: Methuen, 1982.

Otte Brudstykker af den ældste Saga am Olav den hellige. Ed. G. Storm. Oslo, 1893.

Otto of Freising. *Chronica sive de duabus civitatibus,* ed. W. Lammers (with trans.). Darmstadt: Wissenschaftliche Buchgesellschaft, 1961.

Otto of Freising. *Gesta Frederici seu rectius Chronica,* ed. F. J. Schmale (with trans. by A. Schmidt). Darmstadt: Wissenschaftliche Buchgesellschaft, 1965.

Paasche, Fredrik. "Heimskringlas Olavssaga," *Edda* 6, 1916: 365–383.

Paasche, Fredrik. "Tendens og syn i kongesagaen." In *Norske historikere i utvalg,* vol. 1, ed. A. Holmsen and J. Simensen. Oslo: Universitetsforlaget, 1967: 56–75 (orig. in *Edda* 12, 1922).

Paasche, Fredrik. "Kristendom og kvad." In *Norske historikere i utvalg,* vol. 1, ed. A. Holmsen and J. Simensen. Oslo: Universitetsforlaget, 1967: 426–429 (orig. in: *Norsk teologisk Tidsskrift* 1915).

Painter, Sidney. *French Chivalry.* Baltimore: Johns Hopkins University Press, 1940.

Pálsson, Hermann. *Art and Ethics in Hrafnkel's Saga.* Copenhagen: Munksgaard, 1971.

Pálsson, Hermann. *Uppruní Njálu og hugmyndír.* Reykjavík, 1984.

Pálsson, Hermann. *Leyndarmál Laxdælu.* Reykjavík, 1986.

Partner, Nancy. *Serious Entertainments: The Writing of History in Twelfth Century England.* Chicago: University of Chicago Press, 1977.

Passio et Miracula Beati Olavi. Ed. F. Metcalfe. Oxford, 1881.

Petersen, Niels M. *Bidrag til den oldnordiske Literaturs Historie.* Copenhagen 1866.

Phillips, Mark. "Representation and Argument in Florentine Historiography," *Storia della storiografia* 10, 1986: 48–63.

Philpotts, Bertha. *Kindred and Clan in the Middle Ages and After.* Cambridge, 1913.

Pickering, Frederick P. "Historical Thought and Moral Codes in Medieval

Epic." In *The Epic in Medieval Society,* ed. H. Scholler. Tübingen: Niemeyer, 1977: 1–17.

Pospisil, Leopold. "Feud," *International Encyclopedia of the Social Sciences,* vol. 5: 389–393.

Powicke, Maurice. *The Thirteenth Century 1216–1307* (Oxford History of England). Oxford: Oxford University Press, 1953.

Qviller, Bjørn. "The Dynamics of the Homeric Society," *Symbolae Osloenses* 56, 1981: 109–155.

Qviller, Bjørn. "The King in Dark Age Greece and Medieval Norway: The Evolutionary Significance of Sympotic Kingship," unpublished article.

Radding, Charles M. "The Evolution of Medieval Mentalities," *The American Historical Review* 83.3, 1978: 577–597.

Radding, Charles M. *A World Made by Men.* Chapel Hill: University of Carolina Press, 1985.

Ray, Roger D. "Medieval Historiography Through the Twelfth Century: Problems and Progress of Research," *Viator* 5, 1974: 33–60.

Ray, Roger D. "Historiography, Western European," *Dictionary of the Middle Ages,* vol. 6, ed. J. L. Strayer. New York, 1985: 258–265.

Reeves, Marjorie. *The Influence of Prophecy in the Later Middle Ages.* Oxford: Clarendon, 1969.

Robberstad, Knut. "Odelsrett. Norge, etc.," KLNM 12, 1967: 494–499.

Saga Óláfs konungs hins helga, vols. 1–2. Ed. O. A. Johnsen. Oslo, 1941.

Sahlins, Marshall. "Poor Man, Rich Man, Big-Man, Chief," *Comparative Studies in Society and History* 5, 1963: 285–303.

Sandvik, Gudmund. *Hovding og konge i Heimskringla.* Oslo: Akademisk forlag, 1955.

Sars, Ernst. *Udsigt over den norske Historie,* vols. 1–4. Oslo, 1874–1891.

Sawyer, Peter. *Kings and Vikings.* London: Methuen, 1982.

Sawyer, Peter. "The Blood-Feud in Fact and Fiction." In *Tradition og historieskrivning. Kilderne til Nordens ældste historie,* ed. K. Hastrup and P. Meulengracht Sørensen (*Acta Jutlandica* 63:2). Aarhus, 1987: 27–38.

Saxo Grammaticus, *Gesta Danorum,* vols. 1–2, ed. J. Olrik and H. Ræder. Copenhagen, 1931.

Schlauch, Margaret. "The Rhetoric of Public Speeches in Old Scandinavian (chiefly Icelandic)," *Scandinavian Studies* 41, 1969: 297–314.

Schmale, Franz-Josef. "Mentalität und Berichtshorizont, Absicht und Situation hochmittelalterlicher Geschichtsschreiber," *Historische Zeitschrift* 226, 1978: 1–16.

Schmale, Franz-Josef. *Funktion und Formen mittelalterlicher Geschichtsschreibung.* Darmstadt: Wissenschaftliche Buchgesellschaft, 1985.

Schoebe, Gerhard. "Was gilt im frühen Mittelalter als geschichtliche Wirklichkeit?" In *Festschrift Hermann Aubin zum 80. Geburtstag,* ed. O. Brunner et al. Wiesbaden: F. Steiner, 1965: 625–651.

Scholes, Robert, and Robert Kellogg, *The Nature of Narrative.* New York: Oxford University Press, 1966.

Schomerus, Rudolf. *Die Religion der Nordgermanen im Spiegel Christlicher Darstellung.* Leipzig, 1936.

Schramm, Percy Ernst. *Der König von Frankreich.* Weimar: Böhlau, 1960.

Schreiner, Johan. "Olav Haraldssons siste regjeringsår," HT 5 series, vol. 6, 1925: 309–328.

Schreiner, Johan. *Tradisjon og saga om Olav den hellige* (Skrifter utgitt av Det norske vitenskapsakademi i Oslo, II. Historisk-filosofisk klasse 1926 no. 1). Oslo, 1926.

Schröder, Werner. "Typologie-Begriff und Typologie-Verständnis in der mediävistischen Literaturwissenschaft." In *The Epic in Medieval Society,* ed. H. Scholler. Tübingen: Niemeyer, 1977: 64–85.

See, Klaus von. *Mythos und Theologie im skandinavischen Hochmittelalter* (Skandinavistische Arbeiten 8). Heidelberg: Carl Winter, 1988.

Shahar, Shulamith. *The Fourth Estate: A History of Women in the Middle Ages.* London: Methuen, 1983.

Shorter, Edward. *The Making of the Modern Family.* London: Fontana/Collins, 1979.

Sigurðsson, Jón Viðar. *Frá goðorðum til ríkja: þróun goðavalds á 12. og 13. öld.* Reykjarvík: Bókaútgafa Menningarsjóðs, 1989.

Simms, Katherine. *From Kings to Warlords: The Changing Structure of Gaelic Ireland in the Later Middle Ages.* Woodbridge: Boydell, 1987.

Skinner, Quentin. *The Foundations of Modern Political Thought* vols. 1–2. Cambridge: Cambridge University Press, 1978.

Skovgaard-Petersen, Inge. *Da Tidernes Herre var nær. Studier i Saxos historiesyn.* Copenhagen: Den danske historiske forening, 1987*a.*

Skovgaard-Petersen, Inge. "Studiet av kilderne til den ældste nordiske historie. En historiografisk oversigt." In *Kilderne til den tidlige middelalders historie. Rapporter til den XX nordiske historikerkongres, Reykjavík 1987,* vol. 1 (*Ritsafn Sagnfrædistofnunar* vol. 18). Reykjavík: Sögufélag, 1987*b*: 7–29.

Smail, R. C. *Crusading Warfare.* Cambridge: Cambridge University Press, 1956.

Smalley, Beryl. *Historians in the Middle Ages.* London: Thames and Hudson, 1974.

Snorri Sturluson. *Heimskringla,* ed. F. Jónsson, vols. 1–4, Copenhagen, 1893–1901 (references are to chapters of the different sagas in this edition, see Abbreviations.)

Snorri Sturluson. *Edda,* ed. F. Jónsson. Copenhagen, 1931.

Snorri Sturluson. *Heimskringla: History of the Kings of Norway,* trans. with intro., etc. by Lee M. Hollander. Austin: University of Texas Press, 1967 (quotations in English from *Heimskringla* are from this edition, unless otherwise stated).

Sørensen, Preben Meulengracht. *Saga og samfund.* Copenhagen: Berlingske, 1977.

Sørensen, Preben Meulengracht. *The Unmanly Man.* Odense: Odense University Press, 1983.

Sogge, Ingebjørg. *Vegar til eit bilete. Snorre Sturlason og Tore Hund.* Trondheim: Tapir, 1976.

Sommerfeldt, Axel. "Comment" [to K. Odner, *Economic Structures in the Early Iron Age*], *Norwegian Archeological Review* 7, 1974: 138–147.

Southern, Richard W. *Saint Anselm and His Biographer.* Cambridge: Cambridge University Press, 1966.

Southern, Richard W. *Medieval Humanism and Other Studies*. Oxford: Basil Blackwell, 1970.

Southern, Richard W. "Aspects of the European Tradition of Historical Writing, 1–4," *Transactions of the Royal Historical Society* 20, 1970: 173–201; 21, 1971: 159–179; 22, 1972: 159–181; 23, 1973: 243–265.

Spörl, Johannes. "Das mittelalterliche Geschichtsdenken als Forschungsaufgabe." In *Geschichtsdenken und Geschichtsbild im Mittelalter*, ed. W. Lammers. Darmstadt: Wissenschaftliche Buchgesellschaft, 1965: 1–29.

Spörl, Johannes. "Wandel des Welt- und Geschichtsbildes im 12. Jahrhundert? Zur Kennzeichnung der hochmittelalterlichen Historiographie." In *Geschichtsdenken und Geschichtsbild im Mittelalter*, ed. W. Lammers. Darmstadt: Wissenschaftliche Buchgesellschaft, 1965: 278–297.

Spörl, Johannes. "Die 'Civitas Dei' im Geschichtsdenken Ottos von Freising." In *Geschichtsdenken und Geschichtsbild im Mittelalter*, ed. W. Lammers. Darmstadt: Wissenschaftliche Buchgesellschaft, 1965: 298–320.

Steblin-Kamensky, Michail. *The Saga Mind*. Odense: Odense University Press, 1973.

Steblin-Kamensky, Michail. "Some Considerations on Approaches to Medieval Literature," *Medieval Scandinavia* 8, 1975: 187–191.

Steblin-Kamensky, Michail. "Further Considerations on Approaches to Medieval Literature," *Medieval Scandinavia* 9, 1976: 167–172.

Stefánsson, Magnús. "Kirkjuvald eflist," *Saga Íslands* vol. 2, ed. S. Lindal. Reykjavík: Hið íslenzku bókmenntufélag/Sögufélagið, 1975: 57–146.

Stone, Lawrence. *The Family, Sex and Marriage in England 1500–1800*. London: Penguin Books, 1982.

Storm, Gustav. *Snorre Sturlassons Historieskrivning*. Copenhagen, 1873.

Strand, Birgit (now: Sawyer). *Kvinnor och män i Gesta Danorum*. Gothenburg: University of Gothenburg, Department of History, 1980.

Strand, Birgit (now: Sawyer). "Women in Gesta Danorum." In *Saxo Grammaticus: A Medieval Author between Norse and Latin Culture*, ed. K. Friis-Jensen. Copenhagen: Museum Tusculanum Press, 1981: 135–167.

Ström, Folke. "Kung Domalde i Svitjod och 'kungalyckan'," *Saga och sed* 1967: 52–66.

Struever, Nancy. *The Language of History in the Renaissance*. Princeton: Princeton University Press, 1970.

Struve, Tilman. *Die Entwicklung der organologischen Staatsauffassung im Mittelalter*. Stuttgart: Klett, 1978.

Sturlunga saga. Ed. Kr. Kålund, vols. 1–2. Copenhagen, 1906–1911.

Suetonius Tranquillus, Gaius. *De vita Caesarum*, vol. 1, ed. J. C. Rolfe, (The Loeb Classical Library 31). Cambridge, Mass.: Harvard University Press, 1951.

Sveinsson, Einar Ólafur. *Sagnaritun Oddaverja*. Reykjavík, 1937.

Sverris saga. Ed. G. Indrebø. Oslo, 1920.

Tester, S. J. *A History of Western Astrology*. Woodbridge: Boydell, 1987.

Teuffel, Rudolf. *Individuelle Persönlichkeitsschilderung in den deutschen Geschichtswerken des 10. und 11. Jahrhunderts* (Beiträge zur Kulturgeschichte des Mittelalters und der Renaissance, Heft 12). Leipzig, 1914.

Theodoricus Monachus. "Historia de antiquitate regum Norwagiensium." In *Monumenta Historica Norvegiæ,* ed. Gustav Storm. Oslo, 1880: 1–68.

Thomas of Celano. "Vita prima S. Francisci," *Legendae S. Francisci Assisiensis saeculis XIII et XIV conscriptae* (Analecta Franciscana, vol. 10). Quaracchi, 1926–1941: 1–126.

Thomas of Celano. "Vita secunda S. Francisci," *Legendae S. Francisci Assisiensis saeculis XIII et XIV conscriptae* (Analecta Franciscana, vol. 10). Quaracchi, 1926–1941: 127–268.

Tjersland, Leif. "Studier i saga-ætter," HT 31, 1937–1940: 103–138.

Tobiassen, Torfinn. "Ágrip," KLNM 1, 1956: 60 f.

Tobiassen, Torfinn. "Tronfølgelov og privilegiebrev," HT 43, 1964: 181–273.

Torstendahl, Rolf. *Källkritik och vetenskapssyn i svensk historisk forskning 1820–1920.* Uppsala: Svenska Bokförlaget, 1964.

Townend, G. B., "Suetonius." In *Latin Biography,* ed. T. Dorey. New York: Basic Books, 1967: 82–107.

Turville-Petre, Gabriel. "Dream Symbols in Old Icelandic Literature," *Festschrift Walter Baetke.* Weimar: Böhlau, 1966: 343–354.

Turville-Petre, Gabriel. "Dreams in Icelandic Tradition," *Nine Norse Studies.* London, 1972.

Vaughan, Richard. "The Past in the Middle Ages," *Journal of Medieval History* 12, 1986: 1–14.

Verdery, Katherine. "A Comment on Goody's *Development of the Family and Marriage in Europe,*" *Journal of Family History* 13, 1988: 265–270.

Vestergaard, Torben. "The System of Kinship in Early Norwegian Law," *Medieval Scandinavia* 12, 1988: 160–193.

Villehardouin, Geoffroy de. *La conquête de Constantinople,* vols. 1–2, ed. and trans. E. Faral (Les classiques de l'histoire de France au moyen âge 18–19). Paris: Les belles lettres, 1961.

Vinaver, Eugène. *The Rise of Romance.* Oxford: Oxford University Press, 1971.

Wallace-Hadrill, J. M. "The Bloodfeud of the Franks." In *The Long-Haired Kings,* London: Methuen, 1962: 121–147.

Wallén, Per-Edwin. "Hämnd," KLNM 7, 1962: 239–246.

Ward, Benedicta. *Miracles and the Medieval Mind.* Aldershot: Scholar Press, 1987.

Webb, G. *An Introduction to the Cistercian De Anima.* London: Aquin Press, 1962.

Weber, Gerd W. " 'Fact' and 'Fiction' als Mass-Stäbe literarischer Wertung in der Saga," *Zeitschrift für deutsches Altertum und deutsche Literatur* 101, 1972: 188–200.

Weber, Gerd W. "Irreligiosität und Heldenzeitalter. Zum Mythencharakter der altisländischen Literatur." In *Speculum Noroenum: Norse Studies in Memory of G. Turville-Petre.* Odense: Odense University Press, 1981: 474–505.

Weber, Gerd W. "Intellegere historiam. Typological perspectives of Nordic prehistory." In *Tradition og historieskrivning,* ed. K. Hastrup (*Acta Jutlandica* 63:2). Århus: Aarhus Universitetsforlag, 1987: 95–141.

Weber, Max. *Wirtschaft und Gesellschaft* vols. 1–2. Cologne: Kiepenhauer und Witsch, 1964.

Weibull, Curt. "Saxo 'Grammaticus'." In *Källkritik och historia*. Lund: Aldus/ Bonnier, 1964 (orig. 1915): 153–240.

Weibull, Curt. "Snorres skildring av Sveriges samhälls- och författningsförhållanden. Torgny lagmann." In *Källkritik och historia*. Lund: Aldus/Bonnier, 1964 (orig. 1915): 241–247.

Weibull, Lauritz. "Kritiska undersøkningar i Nordens historia omkring år 1000." In *Nordisk historia. Forskningar och undersøkningar,* vol. 1. Stockholm: Natur och Kultur, 1948: 245–360.

Weintraub, Karl J., "Autobiography and Historical Consciousness," *Critical Inquiry* 1, 1975: 821–848.

Werner, Karl Ferdinand. "Les structures de l'histoire à l'âge du christianisme," *Storia della storiografia* 10, 1986: 36–47.

Wessén, Elias. "Om Snorres prologus till Heimskringla och till den särskillda Olovssagan," *Acta Philologica Scandinavica* 3, 1928–1929: 52–62.

West, Constance Birt. *Courteoisie in Anglo-Norman Literature.* Oxford: Blackwell, 1938.

White, Hayden. *Metahistory.* Baltimore: Johns Hopkins University Press, 1974.

Whorf, Benjamin Lee. *Language, Thought and Reality: Selected Writings.* Cambridge, Mass.: MIT Press, 1956.

William of Malmesbury. *Historia Novella.* Ed. and trans. K. R. Potter. London: Thomas Nelson, 1955.

Wolf, E. R. *Europe and the People without History.* Berkeley and Los Angeles: University of California Press, 1982.

Wolter, Hans. "Geschichtliche Bildung in Rahmen der Artes Liberales," *Artes Liberales. Von der antiken Bildung zur Wissenschaft des Mittelalters,* ed. Josef Koch. Leiden, 1959: 50–83.

Wormald, Jenny. "Bloodfeud, Kindred and Government in Early Modern Scotland," *Past and Present* 87, 1980: 54–97.

Index

Designer: UC Press Staff
Compositor: Huron Valley Graphics
Text: 10/12 Times Roman
Display: Helvetica
Printer: Thomson-Shore, Inc.
Binder: Thomson-Shore, Inc.